THE TRUTH ABOUT LOVE AND FEAR

Love controls our lives,
Fear determines how we will live.

RUDOLF ECKHARDT

BALBOA®
PRESS

A DIVISION OF HAY HOUSE

Balboa Press books may be ordered through booksellers or by contacting:

Balboa Press
A Division of Hay House
1663 Liberty Drive
Bloomington, IN 47403
www.balboapress.com.au
1 (877) 407-4847

Print information available on the last page.

ISBN: 978-1-5043-1011-6 (sc)
ISBN: 978-1-5043-1010-9 (e)

Balboa Press rev. date: 02/26/2018

INTRODUCTION

The book, 'The Truth about Love and Fear' was written to bring knowledge and awareness to your life by allowing you to see the illusions by which you live to recognise the truth of who you really are.

The truth, you will come to realise, is very simple compared to the illusions or lie by which you live. In the absence of our awareness of the truth, our experience of reality appears to be very complicated, causing us to be deceived by our perception of reality.

The answers, we arrive at when we begin to question reality can initially be confusing. Should we accept our inner experience of reality or the one we share with others, as the truth of what is real? Or, should we accept the reality created by our intellect and logic or that by our emotions and feelings as true? If you are confused, you are not alone.

The intention of the book is to give answers to questions about consciousness; life and living you may have never thought to ask. Answers that relate to concepts that right now control every aspect of your life experience.

Life and the way you live it is actually about 'Being' and not of 'Doing'. This book will show you how you can be a powerful person rather than just engage in acts of power. You will see that genuine change is very different from only changing your feelings, behaviours or attitude. Imagine, changing the thinker instead of the thought or changing the doer instead of what he or she does.

It will educate you about love, fear and guilt and how it influences your mind and controls your behaviour. It will lead you to a new understanding of the nature of unconditional love, acceptance and trust and explain the potential of your personal power and the lack of it in your life. It will challenge your present way of thinking and cause you to question your perception. Be warned because it will change how you see yourself and the way you see your life as you have lived it so far. It will alter your perception of your past, present and future.

It will expose you to concepts that are both spiritual and psychological because our mind and spirit are one. You have the opportunity to get a perspective of yourself and your life, presently hidden from your awareness. This information will reveal insights into the process of living life that will give you a new perception of yourself, others and the world.

We live every day without being aware that fear controls many of our choices and decisions. The consequences our fear based behaviour has on our life and relationships, also contribute to the collective of fear and distrust in the world. If we were to recognise fear for our emotional survival for what it really is, we might initiate an effort to deal with it. Taking individual responsibility for our issues by addressing our fears and insecurities does not only transform our lives but also affects all of those around you. Dealing with your issues makes a significant contribution to changing the collective. All change in the world has to start with us, and therefore taking responsibility for how you live our life is of much greater importance than it may seem. As long as the emotion we call fear is in control of why and how we make the choices that create our life experiences the future will be a continuation of our past. The absence of love, acceptance and trust that is unconditional and all the negative emotions that are a consequence, are such strong influence in our emotional lives that they determine our human destiny.

A LITTLE ABOUT ME

Even though I have not been one to hide from truth or to avoid confrontation with my issues, it has taken me time to understand their origin and their impact on me. My effort to find resolution has led me to a deeper understanding of the meaning of existence and the process by which I and others live our lives. My introduction to a series of books written by Jane Roberts — beginning with Seth Speaks — in my early thirties was the beginning of insight into the nature of my consciousness. These insights caused me to experience life ever greater awareness. Ten years later, I learned an alternative therapy called 'kinesiology' in my early forties and began to work with clients. I was not completely satisfied with the results of the method I had learned and began to focus on solutions for emotional issues within the context of spirit, mind and body. Combining spiritual concepts with psychology, I developed a methodology and therapy — Core Belief Therapy.

The feedback from clients showed the healing process to be very effective in resolving psychological issues. 'Core Belief Therapy' allows us to alter the nature of who we believe ourselves to be — our sense-of-ourselves. We can create genuine change by releasing the fears and insecurities that control our feelings, thoughts and behaviour, in fact, our lives. This book is an explanation of the philosophy that evolved from this therapy and how you can explore true change for yourself.

Resolving the emotional issues of my clients from about 1990 until now has given me enormous scope to learn and understand human consciousness. My desire to achieve positive outcomes for my clients prompted me to apply myself without fear or preconceived limitations. This approach has allowed me to explore and discover new aspects of human consciousness and the process by which it experiences reality.

My learning has been facilitated by my clients who trusted me to work with them. The contribution they made to my knowledge and understanding has been a primary reason for the writing of this book.

Besides my clients, there are others to whom I want to express my gratitude. I also thank those who have provided emotional support through the years: The loving and unfailing support from my partner Andrea, my daughter Nikola and my friend Nagui, who designed the book cover. My close friend and retired chef Roger, Emma, Glenn, Frank, Duane, Henry, Carlos and all of my clients, many of whom I count as friends. Special thanks go to my friend Saxon for his support and faith in my work and for inspiring me to rewrite the much longer, initial version of this book.

THE MASTERPIECE

Spirit is carved from the wastelands of my mind.
It takes its form while gathering my woes,
my tears my hopes and wishes.
With tools in hand, it shapes for me my dream.
It smoothes away the sadness to reveal the soft edges.
It grinds away the despair
to expose the velvet texture of my bliss.
Spirit's mallet pounds away at the indentations
left by the footprints of my fears.
Standing back, Spirit inspects
what has come forth from this chaos
Changes are made allowing my hidden emotions
to be shown the way out of their abyss.
Now the carved sculpture stands for all to see
in the splendour that is SPIRIT
and the Grace that is me.

By Andrea Eckhardt
07-07-13

CONTENTS

Chapter 3

—

The Beginning of Everything **27**

Chapter 4

—

The Power and Influence of Parenting **41**

Chapter 5

—

The Power of Belief Systems **53**

Chapter 6

—

The Origin of Your Feelings **61**

Chapter 7
—

The Power of Intent **69**

Chapter 8
—

Relentless Needs **79**

Chapter 9
—

The Illusion of Being Free **91**

Chapter 10
—

Our Greatest Fear **107**

Chapter 11
—
Your Emotional Body 116

Chapter 12
—
Creators of Our Own Reality..................................123

Chapter 13
—
Responsibility Without Blame 134

Chapter 14
—
Conditional Relationships 154

Chapter 15
—

The Quest for Happiness 187

Chapter 16
—

Power Without Fear 196

Chapter 17
—

Transcending Fear 213

Chapter 18

—

Fantasy and Imagination 223

Chapter 19

—

Living Your Unconditional Potential 230

Chapter 20

—

Our Conditional Mind 254

Chapter 25
—

Living Unconditional Love 353

Chapter I

FEAR, ILLUSIONS AND THE
TRUE NATURE OF LOVE

Love Rules Our Lives
but
Fear Controls How We Will Live It

What would it be like to be the person you were always meant to be, living the life of which you always dreamed? How would it feel, if you were to live your life without fear, confident in yourself, trusting your direction in life and clear of what you want to achieve, to have the capacity to determine your destiny and create a life that is representative of the potential with which you were born?

The reality is that for many, life is not what they thought it would be. It can feel that life is nothing but a series of problems, difficulties and obstacles for us. That we are unhappy in our relationship because our partner is not the person we thought they were. At work, we feel we are struggling to be noticed and rewarded for our contributions. Or, we and hope that our shortcomings and failures go unseen. We may move from one relationship to another to find the person we hope will make us happy. We often spend our lives chasing dreams and fulfilling expectations that are not even of our choosing. We try to achieve an idea of happiness and success that ultimately does not give us a sense of completion and wholeness we expected. More than often, life becomes a struggle between our desire to fulfil a fictional idea of what our lives should be and the emotional issues that stop us from making it a reality. In the meantime, the stress created negative emotional experience can be persistently painful and debilitating. To escape feeling stressed and unable to cope, we may choose to medicate ourselves with alcohol, drugs, sex or whatever else we can find so that we can still have "a good time".

To feel better about our lives, we deal with our issues by engaging in different forms of mental distraction and thereby conveniently avoid confronting our problems. Many choose to self-medicate to create an illusionary world of love, significance or power to escape the person they fear they we are. Even though we would like to find solutions to deal with our problems, we do not know where to start looking for a solution. Instead, we resort to a variety of behaviours to avoid having to confront our fears and negative feelings. The fundamental problem is that we do not know ourselves well enough to be aware of what we need to do to find a resolution. Our belief and understanding of 'who we are' is a mixture of our habitual behaviours and feelings coupled to likes and dislikes the origin of which we do not even know. We tend to assume that our insecurities and fears are an intrinsic part of our personality. We certainly do not realise that all of this and more forms the foundation of why and how we create the life we experience. While we recognise the effect that life experiences have on us through what we feel, we are involved in creating them in the first place.

How different would your life be, if you were in charge of every aspect of your life experience? You might think that this would only be possible if you were in control of everything and everyone around you. You may ask how else is it possible to have your life the way you want it to be?

The truth is that you were born with the capacity to have control over the experiences you manifest in life through the expression of your authentic self and innate potentials. The real problem is that the only one that stands in the way of achieving this is you because of the fears you hold. Without your fears and insecurities, you would become the creator of your life experiences. Your relationships, aspirations and happiness would be under your control if you were to release the program of fear that presently runs your life.

TRAPPED BY YOUR HISTORY

We believe that we are powerless to be in control of our life because our life experiences reaffirm what we have learned from our parents. At the same time, we adhere stubbornly to the same type of resolution we learned in childhood to escape our negative experiences of life. We set about to try and control our behaviour and modify our thoughts and feelings, convinced that we could only avoid our emotional and life issues if we change how we behave. Unfortunately, it is highly unlikely that we can maintain our new behaviours and so forth and thereby our experiencing our issues and problems. Consciously replacing our behaviour, feelings or thoughts with positive ones requires a constant state of awareness of the very aspects of your emotional self with which you are trying to deal. Before you can replace a good behaviour with one that is bad you have to feel or experience the negative first and therein lies the problem. Somehow no matter how hard we try, your fears will always come to the surface, and your response will be automatic. Our issues and the negative emotions that go with them are always likely to return. Once they return we quickly fall back into old emotional habits and behaviours that take us back to the same emotions and thoughts, we sought to escape.

It becomes easy to justify your issues when most of the people you know share your experience of life. We are easily distracted by the pressure of having to provide to have a roof over our heads, to meet the financial responsibilities of our family and deal with the problems of everyday life. Living can then feel like a struggle with sparse moments of joy or space for one's needs and self-fulfilment.

Our issues can make the task of having to take responsibility for our existence and for those who depend on us stressful and overwhelming. Become successful can be daunting expectations for many and emotionally challenging. Fame, money, wealth, happiness and abundance can appear to be one decision or one step away or be the preserve of those who seem to be more fortunate than we are. The examples of those who reach these pinnacles of success appear all around us but somehow achieving the same for ourselves eludes us. When we try to understand why and how we did not succeed, we blame our mistakes, others or circumstances, but we rarely do look at ourselves. The conclusion we come to is that we somehow should have done it differently or that we were disadvantaged or deceived by others. When we fail, our perception of the outcome of our choices can convince us that we must be failures, inadequate or plain unlucky. Often, we have no choice but to accept our failures and perceived shortcomings because the answers we arrive at do not lead us to solutions. Frequently, limited by our perspective, with our dreams still in our eyes, we may try again in the hope that this time we will succeed, by doing it differently. The problem is that we do not recognise that we are changing what we do but not the person who is doing it.

DECEIVED BY THE OBVIOUS

Your traditional approach to resolving your emotional issues will cause you to miss what is most important. The reason you missed it is that it is almost too obvious for you to recognise and understand its significance. It is truly a case of not seeing the wood for the trees. First of all, you have not realised that without exception, YOU are the common factor in every event — negative or positive — in your life. The intensity with which you are involved with everyone and everything around you distract you from the awareness that you are the central force in everything that has happened to you in every moment of your life.

You have been and will always be the core figure in every one of your life's failures or achievements whether they are social with friends, at work or play. If each negative emotional event in your life were a crime, they would arrest you as the prime suspect. Even though, you may not understand how and why, but your presence at every event points to you being the instigator of your life experiences.

It should also be obvious however that you and many others are not aware how and why you manifest these negative experiences in your lives. It seems illogical that you would consciously choose to create a painful or negative life. The likelihood is that you make a conscious effort to do exactly the opposite to avoid drama and negative experiences. However, your attempts to avoid creating negative emotional experiences is likely also to be unsuccessful even though you try and use strategies or behaviours to negate undesirable outcomes. Characteristically, life will keep returning you to the same old behavioural patterns you have relied on for so long.

One of the primary limitations to our self-understanding is that the person we believe we are does not represent who we were born to be. You may be aware that you are very reactive and easily upset or angry with others. You may constantly be concerned about the judgment of others and what they think of you. You may feel insecure about making decisions that others for fear that others may judge and criticise you. You may be in fear of losing control over your life or relationships and resort to aggressive and dominating behaviour. Confrontation with authority or the opposite sex may terrify you, and so you avoid any form of conflict, argument or challenge. The way others speak to you or treat you may easily offend you, or you may take a confronting and aggressive approach to avoid being invalidated, criticised or negated. You may be a pleaser and fear that you can cope if you do not know who others expect you to be for them and how you are supposed to behave and respond. Your fear of being unwanted and unloved make you afraid of being alone, and therefore you constantly need to have people around you. You feel powerless or insignificant in the presence of dominating, aggressive or confrontational personalities or have the need to be controlled to feel significant. Does it seem to you that others are always better off, more successful, have fewer problems than you do? Do you think that you exist to serve those around you and your turn to receive never seems to come? Are you angry and resentful with others over the slightest thing? Even though you may have all or any of these issues, none of these fears is representative of who you truly meant to be.

You may feel that all the people in your life have an enormous control and influence over you and how you can live. Somehow, external emotional forces — the attitudes, behaviours, needs and negative emotions expressed by others control how you will behave, feel and think and consequently your decisions and choices. If this is how you live much of your life, it is logical that you think and believe that others and your environment cause your life issues and problems. The belief that others must be responsible for difficulties in life and relationships makes it understandably difficult to know where to begin to look for solutions.

If this is the case, you may well ask: Why is my life not my choice?

WHAT IS LIFE AND WHO CONTROLS IT?

The more precise question is: What is the nature of life and who and what determines how you will live it? You may wonder why your life is so different from that of others. Why do others not feel the same way in the same circumstances and with the same people as I do? How come I attract certain personalities and situations in my life? Why can I not achieve my goals and why do my life experiences always fall short of my expectations? Why do negative things happen to me when I try so hard to do what is right? Why am I not treated as being exceptional and significant the way others are? Why is what I say not heard and taken seriously by others? Why do I feel that I do not matter to anyone? Why do I fear how others judge me? Why do I believe that I am not good enough?

These questions and many others may have crossed your mind at one time or another. How did you explain the reasons for your negative life experiences? What answers did you come up with for the presence of these negative beliefs, feelings and thoughts? Did you blame yourself because of guilt or did you hold others, circumstances or the world in general responsible?

Finding fault with yourself by labelling yourself with your perceived shortcomings is not just self-destructive. It is a way to give yourself a seemingly irrevocable excuse for what is wrong in your life. By blaming everything on yourself, you have made yourself into a victim of who you think you are. Your conviction that you cannot help being who you are and therefore unchangeable might allow you to absolve yourself from any responsibility for your life experiences. Of course, if everyone else is responsible and you see yourself as the victim, you can to excuse yourself from being responsible for your life's miseries.

Once you believe that others are in control and have power over you; what can you possibly do? How can you be in control of your life when you are subject to forces created by others such as their rules and expectations, control and needs? When confronted with an issue, we are usually quick to make a judgement of what the cause is. Our understanding and interpretation of events appear to make it clear who or what is responsible for creating our negative emotional experiences. By coincidence, we are known to go to great lengths to prove that others or the world are to blame and conveniently exclude ourselves.

We do not realise how deeply we have been affected by our parent's behaviour, emotional responses, fears and insecurities. The way they communicated their needs, expectations, control and emotions, convinced you that you are the person you believe yourself to be. Their concept and understanding of themselves, of others and their view of life shaped who we perceive we are to ourselves. They were not aware that they taught us to believe that the quality and experience of life is subject to others and the world. As a result, we do not understand why we feel, think and behave the way we do, just how it was for them when we were just children. We are not sure why we engage in behaviours and make choices that ultimately do not benefit us and are unaware of the motivations and the reasons for many of our choices and attractions. Then we wonder why negative events happen in our lives and relationships. Our conditioning is so all-encompassing that most of the time it does not even occur to us to question the way we think, what we feel and how we act and behave. We ignore the elephant in the room that is our life experience by not questioning the nature of our consciousness.

We are, nevertheless, frustrated by our attempts to change our life: To turn our failures into successes, to find a relationship that will bring us joy and happiness instead of argument and conflict, to feel and think positively about ourselves and the world instead of being burdened by pessimism and doom. We feel trapped in the fear-based negativity of our mind, and by life situations, we feel powerless to change. We feel resentful of being victimised by failure and disasters but have no choice but to live with them. We try to find what we need to do to change our lives but usually, no matter how hard we try to implement these changes, in the long term we still falter and fail. It can take a long time before we return to old patterns of thoughts, feelings and behaviours, but when we do, we find ourselves back having the same unwanted experiences.

There are four fundamental questions we need to answer:

Are we in control over our lives or are others?

Do we have the capacity to change who we believe we are or are we stuck with our issues?

Are we responsible for creating our personal life experiences or are we the victims of others?

Instead of using strategic behaviours, can we change who we believe we are and thereby transform our lives?

Most people think that they are in control of their lives only some of the time and at other times subject to others and circumstances. There is the tendency to believe that the amount of influence and control is dependent on circumstances and with whom they are. By accepting that we do not have the power to be responsible for our life experiences, we have unwittingly given away our power and control to others. We do not realise that we have chosen to become a victim of others and circumstances. We made ourselves subject to the whims and will of others. The decision to be in control of your life or be the victim of others is the choice between accepting total responsibility for your life or making others responsible for your life experiences. We have been guilty of choosing explanations that were emotionally convenient for us because they absolved us from some level of blame. They provided us with proof of our innocence and secondly because they justified for the actions and choices that brought about undesirable consequences from which we try to redeem ourselves.

Alternatively, we can choose to accept that we are the creators of our life experiences and that we are the active instigators of every event and encounter in our lives. If we accept this, then we must also be responsible for the consequences of everything that we manifest through our behaviour, choices and attitude. One cannot exist without the other.

Assuming that we being the creators and instigators of our life experiences is a natural part of the expression of our consciousness we were also born with the power to influence and control it. However naturally possessing the capacity to be in charge of your mind does not mean that you were born with the awareness of how it functions. However, as long as you hold the belief that outside influences define who you are and limit your power and control in life. Your mindset will exclude you from the innate capacity to be in charge of your life.

In other words, by accepting your role as the creator of the experiences of our existence, you automatically give yourself access to your capacity to change who you believe you are. Should you be determined to accept that you are the victim of others and life, your choices will render you powerless in life.

The key question is whether each of us can change the inner-nature of who we are and thereby change our lives or are we destined to spend our lives battling external forces that appear to control our existence? Do we have no choice but to accept a life in which we cannot avoid failure, disappointment, pain and suffering and so on? Or, could it be that we need a brand-new understanding of the nature of who we are as an individual consciousness? What do we need to learn and understand to be able to change 'who we are' so that we can create positive life experiences?

THE BATTLE FOR PERSONAL CHANGE

Considering the rows of self-help books lined up on the bookshelves of just about any bookstore in the world, we are not short on advice on how to change our lives. These approaches divide broadly into three areas.

The most common principle we apply when we need a solution to your problems is to do things differently. The message is that there are the specific behaviours on, thinking you have to engage in and a correct attitude you need to develop to have the life you want or to have what you want out of life. The second strategy is achieving change in life through disciplined practice: meditation, some styles of martial arts and yoga. The third is change through exercising control over your thinking, emotions or attitude, which can involve mantras or other directed sayings.

Without question, all of these methods have the potential to have some level of success in getting positive personal results, depending on the commitment of the practitioner. These outcomes are not necessarily enduring particularly in respect to emotional issues. Changing what you do through consciously and strategically altered behaviour and choices, changes your behaviour and choices but not the person making them. None of this activity addresses the core of your issues. It can in the short-term change exactly what it intends to change — how you behave and how and what you choose— but you as an individual remain the same. While this can create good and positive results at the time, it is also very likely to apply to one circumstance and be temporary. You will only maintain a level of success if, in every situation where there are issues, and this behaviour is appropriate, you remember to diligently and consciously apply it in every detail. Should there be any changes in the emotional situation for which your strategy is to act as a solution, they are very likely to fail you.

Change through discipline and practice can be powerful but requires consistent commitment and dedication by the practitioner to be effective. The intent of practice is to develop a disciplined mind with the capacity to surrender to a neutral state of being to achieve personal change through self-realisation and expanded consciousness. The most immediate result practice provides a sense of emotional release, inner-balance, peace and harmony, which for many can only be maintained by persistent practice.

Even though many make references to self-change, it is also the least understood. Meditation and yoga have developed now ancient philosophies to lead practitioners to find the essence of their being. There are different understandings of what represents a transformation or change in a person. Most modern practices of personal transformation promote strategies which are new ways of what to do and how to do it, what to think as the means to deal with personal issues. The emphasis is on understanding and knowing what to do and how to do it. The assumption is that our actions, thoughts, behaviours and feelings are responsible for our negative state of mind and our experiences. The general concept is that we have to engage in a new set of emotional and mental strategies or use coping behaviours to overcome our issues with ourselves or in life. In reality, that still does not represent a change in 'who you are' as a person.

Changing the beliefs that define who you are to yourself — changing your inner-identity — requires an understanding of the nature of your consciousness. Learning how your consciousness creates and manifests its own experiences in life is essential to changing who you believe you are. Expanding your awareness also requires you to look at the nature of your mind and the beliefs that make up your sense-of-self. So that instead of changing what we do and how we do it, you will let go the beliefs that define who you are — your sense-of-self. So far, your perception of yourself has been contracted by your fears and insecurities.

Your distorted view of yourself has stopped you from recognising who or what is responsible for your fears. Because of this, you cannot fathom the reasons for your negative experiences.

If potentially to get you the same result you may wonder why it is more important to change "who you are" rather than "what you do". First of all, your 'strategic doing' is usually a response to the negative event that has already happened. Or, a strategy that pre-empts your fear becoming a reality. In other words, you have already become the victim, or you are about to become one. You do not realise that by using your strategic behaviours as a solution, you are not addressing the reason why these events are happening to you in the first place. By only being concerned about the result of your actions and choices, and not the person who is behind them, you do not recognise that you are dealing with the symptoms of your problems and not the reasons for them. Consequently, similar negative events are likely to repeat themselves in your life again and again.

Just imagine that you not only understood the causative factors for your issues but also released them so that they are no longer a part of you. Without these negative elements present in your sense-of-self you would no longer manifest these negative events in your life. Your strategic behaviours will then be redundant. By changing the fear-based beliefs that you held about yourself and formed your inner-identity, you released the origin of your negative life experiences. The transformation of who you are, also has the effect of changing your thoughts, perception and feelings, choices and decisions, thereby altering your relationships and life. We should expect genuine personal change to deliver this outcome.

However, you need to know who you believe you are and why you should change your perception of who you are. Understanding why and what to deal with, requires you to have a new insight into the negative and positive qualities of your sense-of-self or ego. You will need to know how you acquired this negative inner-identity and why you so committed to it. You will also need to develop a clearer insight into your feelings and emotions, to understand what drives them and why you respond to them beyond reason and common sense.

Before you can incorporate these new concepts and alter your perception of yourself, others and life you will need to change many of the commonly held beliefs about the way our consciousness and psychology functions. Your perception of the way life works as a process will change and create a deeper understanding of the emotional dynamics in relationships. You will come to realise new truths about yourself and the world in which you exist but let us take it one step at a time.

Chapter 2

LOVE

With the whole world in pursuit of feeling and experiencing love and find happiness, it seems strange to think that most of us are actually in fear of love that is unconditional. To even suggest that there might be something in us, that actively avoids this kind of love would seem a paradox. However, it is common to have emotional problems with committing to, receiving, giving love or trusting love unconditionally. The question is: "Why do we have issues with love if we strive to be loved, to feel loved and to have someone to love"?

To understand this, we need first of all to ask what the nature of love is and why it is the most significant aspect of our lives. Society depicts love in a myriad of different ways that are in some respects a result of the limits imposed by linguistic expression. Love can present itself as romantic love, sexual love, family love, religious love, love for your country, love for the objects we own or wish to own and so on. Amongst all these interpretations, we have lost the perspective of what genuine love is because the love in all of these descriptions is clearly not the same. Finding a definition of what love is at its core value and that we can share universally has become almost impossible. Individual differences in perception only add more confusion to something that is already difficult to explain. But, the power and significance of love are undeniable and present in everyone's life, without exception. And so, regardless of what definition we arrive at, there is no doubt that love is a central force in our lives and part of every relationship.

No doubt, state of absolute love state of love, acceptance and trust are unconditional and the core values of human consciousness. If clearly understood, will be the basis by which we can determine the authentic nature of who we are and also who we are not. Our awareness and understanding of unconditional love will also clarify what part of who believe we are is conditional in its expression of love, acceptance and trust. Our insight of what love is, will reveal the underlying nature, motivation and intent of our consciousness and potentially that of others. From this, we will be able to develop a new appreciation of what the meaning and significance love has in our personal lives and our relationships or how it is conditional and absent. Evolving a harmonious relationship with unconditional love will not only serve our sense of being but will also have a profound effect on the way we impact others and the environment. Our perception of love is reflected in the language we speak, as each language is a manifestation of the mind-set of the population using it. Some languages lack definitive labels for love in its various forms while others have developed separate words for different kinds of love. In the absence of such clarity, we frequently have to resort to metaphors and stories to try and explain the nature and value of love.

The fact that almost all religious and spiritual belief systems have love as their core value in one form or another is a testament to its significance to us. On a personal level, love is the foundation for nearly every intimate human relationship and its derivatives unconditional acceptance and trust more so in all others. Ultimately, you will find that it is the link that binds all human consciousness together, regardless of nationality, race or religion or any ideas or concepts and beliefs created by society.

Unconditional love is the most influential emotional force in existence and thereby represents an immense and irresistible power that gives us the capacity to transcend our greatest fears.

If you doubt this, then consider the effect and consequences on the human consciousness when love is in control or when love is absent. There is proof on all levels that human consciousness cannot exist for long and without pain and suffering in the absence of unconditional love acceptance and trust. If we cannot find love that is unconditional, we will settle for love, acceptance and trust that is conditional but we cannot live without it. Through personal transformation, we have the opportunity to realise that 'Unconditional Love' is the essence of who we are and central to our existence.

WHAT TRUE LOVE IS NOT

Amidst the many definitions we give of love, one would imagine there that there would be one that approaches its true nature. But, there is no consensus of what love is. Our understanding of what love is will be clearer if we begin by excluding everything that love is not.

- True Love is Never Conditional (it becomes something entirely different if conditional).
- True love is not represented by our neediness or attachment to others, objects, power and control.
- True love does not need, demand or expect reciprocation.
- True love does not expect nor require you to sacrifice in any way.
- True love cannot be acquired by force, coercion or manipulation.
- True love does not set out to fulfil the needs and expectations of others.
- True love is not conditional to self-sacrifice or by putting others before yourself.
- True love is not acquired or created through lies, deceit and misrepresentation.
- True love does not exploit the weaknesses in others.
- True love does not need to dominate or control through aggression or power.
- True love does not require you to surrender your voice, power or control.
- True love will be lost by being a victim, self-deprecation, self-abuse or self-harm.
- True love does not manifest in response to being over-responsible and misplaced guilt.
- True love does not demand servitude, submission or subjugation.
- True love does not require you to be inferior, worthless or insignificant in respect to others.
- True love is not given or acquired through judgment, criticism and blame.
- True love does not demand your sacrifice, suffering, and pain.
- True love is not a part of you if you live in fear of abandonment, rejection, exclusion and loneliness.
- True love is not present in embarrassment and shame.
- True love is not a part of you if you believe you do not belong and are not wanted.

After reading this list, ask yourself if any of these conditions are a part of the way you live your life. If so, why and how did you come to accept them as the person you believe you are.

THE TRUE NATURE OF UNCONDITIONAL LOVE

- True love is always unconditional
- True love is fearless, without any angst.
- True love accepts and trusts unconditionally.
- True love gives and receives unconditionally.
- True love always takes responsibility for the state of its being and the consequences of its manifestations.
- True love will always seek to exist in harmony within you and with others.
- True love is always spontaneous, open and free in its self-expression.
- True love is aware and recognises when love is conditional and appears as lies, deceit or falseness.
- True love gives freedom to the expression of your authentic self and your unique potentials, talents and abilities.
- True love gives you the freedom to choose.
- True love respects the nature of others and does not impose itself.
- True love is self-confident, aware and conscious of itself.
- True love is self-empowered and empowers others.
- True love does not need to have power over others.
- True love is and will always be truthful.
- True love seeks to evolve its potential and supports others to fulfil theirs.
- True love is without criticism or judgement.
- True love ensures that others accept responsibility for the nature of their being and the outcomes this creates in their lives.
- True love has the intent to support others in evolving their spirit without denying them the experiences they manifest in their life.
- True love recognises emotional disharmony in self and others.
- True love has the innate intent for harmony and balance for oneself and with others and the environment.
- True love teaches and allows others to learn for themselves without criticism or judgment.
- True love is optimistic, creative and expansive in its intent.

There are likely to be some statements in this list you might find challenging to accept, but you will learn that the reasons for your resistance lie within the nature of your ego or sense-of-self.

FEAR AND LOVE

Love and fear are at the opposite ends of the scale of our emotional range. When our physical survival is threatened, the fear we feel is very different to the fear that our thoughts or beliefs trigger. This fear is in respect to our emotional survival and is brought about by beliefs we hold and which inhibit us from being who we were born to be and authentically are. The fear of speaking our mind, expressing our truth, needs, expectations, desires, being spontaneous and so on. Emotional issues of this kind are a product of fears held by our mind. Even though in the real sense, they cannot physically hurt or kill us, our response to the feelings they create is characterised by worry and concern, stress and anxiety, submissiveness and avoidance, aggression and anger, powerlessness and helplessness and so on. Try and remember those moments when you reacted aggressively or defensively to an emotional confrontation, criticism or someone's imposition on you. The embarrassment or guilt we feel when asking for things we are should be entitled to receive or have. The emotions that make us feel shy and withdrawn when put in a position where we are expected to speak our truth or express our needs. Others may act differently and for fear of never getting what they want, engage behaviour that is aggressive and demanding. Of course, we always have a million excuses and justifications for our responses and reactions or what we express, but the question we should ask is: "Why do we behave in this way at all and what drives it"? What is there to fear about saying to someone what your real emotions, needs and desires are and what you want? Are they going to abuse you, be critical of you or angry or is it you who fears that you cannot cope with the potential consequences? Or, perhaps you need to ask yourself why you have to be aggressive, demanding and confronting whenever expressing your needs and expectations and are afraid that you will miss out.

Ask yourself: "How real and valid are the fears that dominate my perception and determine my behaviour'?

The reality is that they are not a threat to our physical survival although many may feel as if this is the case when in the moment of the experience. Although our senses, in response to our emotions, create the sensation that makes our fears feel real, they are a product of illusions held by our minds. You will learn that all of our negative emotions, thoughts, feelings, perceptions and behaviours are a product of our fears. We identify with them as if they represent who we are and act as if we cannot exist without them. We do not realise that we have learned to depend on these same fears to keep us emotionally safe and secure from threats which are only real to us.

Fear as an emotion which is manifested by our sense-of-self and presents itself through a state of hyper awareness, alertness and vigilance to keep us safe from perceived threats. The reality of any fear depends on the actual reality of the threat and therein lies our problem. Your perception of a person or an emotional situation will determine whether they are a threat of not and therefore if you are safe or should be afraid. We then trust what we feel to inform us to go into fear or are safe We do not question the process by which our feelings manifest and tend to react to them as if they are real and dangerous. However, our mind has difficulty discerning illusions from reality and therefore an illusionary threat from one that can endanger us. Once feelings of fear are triggered, they cause us to experience a mild or high degree of stress and anxiety, frequently accompanied by physical discomfort, and this reinforces the perception that our fears are real. We do not realise that once fear dominates our minds, our emotional response puts us in contradiction with unconditional love, acceptance and trust. Our attachment to fear is reinforced by our emotional and physical response to them, and this increases our belief that they are real and not illusions. Our negative emotions also drive our attachment to these illusions. Repeated experiences of fearful situations or encounters only serve to make us more dependent on our fears for our emotional survival. Once fear controls our feelings, thoughts and behaviour, we are unaware that we have lost the trust that unconditional love will always support us.

Living your life in response to your fears will cause you to feel that love is conditional just like acceptance and trust. When you believe that love acceptance and trust are conditional, it requires you to meet conditions set by others to be loved or accepted. The fear that you may not be able to meet these requirements to the other person's satisfaction will control your feelings and behaviour. As long as you manage to meet the conditions you believe exist, you will avoid the realisation of your fears. The conviction that love is conditional will ensure that you will hold on to your fears. The problem is that once conditional love is the only love you know, you will begin to accept it as being real and trust and depend on it as if it is normal. Normalising your fears and insecurities will cause you to live a life in which you constantly have to prove to others that you are worthy of their love, acceptance or trust. The neediness for love, acceptance and trust, which are a part of closeness and intimacy in relationships, will become the emotional forces that control your behaviour and choices. Your emotional neediness makes you compromise your standards and values to be loved and wanted, or become controlling and manipulative to make yourself attractive and desirable. You will employ learned strategic behaviours to satisfy your need for attention, love, acceptance and feeling wanted by your opposite gender. Their response to you will be proof that you are either lovable, acceptable and wanted or that you are not. If they reject or ignore you, your fear of being unlovable will have become a reality because you are completely dependent on their response to fulfil your needs. Their rejection of you will confirm that you must be unlovable and unacceptable, even though this is an illusion held by your mind. Rejection raises the fear that if you cannot meet the conditions that you believe exist you will never be loved, accepted and wanted, as childish as that may appear. Your fears can become a source for manifesting stressful, negative encounters with others, no matter what behaviour you display.

Once the fear of not being loved and unaccepted dominate your sense-of-self, they are in control of your senses and interactions. The negative beliefs at the source of your issues can translate into fear of abandonment, rejection, judgment, criticism, exclusion, shame, ridicule, powerlessness, insignificance and more. Your fears will reaffirm the necessity to be in a state of constant psychological vigilance and hyper-alertness to be ready engage in strategic behavioural games that you believe are essential for your emotional survival. Your fears have specific, negative belief systems to support them, each of which warns of the potential negative consequences should you ignore them. Ironically, once you believe your fears to be real and you rely on fear to protect you from the consequences they imply, your dependence on your them will be complete, and you will feel that you cannot live without them. Because of this, in the first 8 to 10 years of your life, you will lose the innate trust in your expectation that you will be unconditionally loved, wanted, accepted and trusted. In the absence of this, your belief that unconditional love will support you and keep you safe and support you in the expression of your authentic self will also leave you.

UNCONDITIONAL LOVE

Even though unconditional love is central to our sense of being and therefore our life, its presence reaches much further into our consciousness. Above all, unconditional love is the essence of our spiritual nature and acts as an eternal reference point for the positive or negative state of our mind. Its presence allows us to be aware whether our state of being is in harmony or out of harmony with unconditional love and acceptance. The spiritual nature of each of us is unique and different from another. Each of us becomes conscious with the capacity, power and resources to manifest all of our potentials, talents and abilities by using our innate intent to express, learn and evolve our minds. Our consciousness releases its life force with creative intent supported by fantasy and imagination to fulfil the potentials, unique talents and abilities with which we arrived in life. Each one of us is born with the capacity to create and manifest our lives and to learn and evolve our consciousness to ever greater levels of awareness and insight. Each of us is endowed with emotional senses that allow us to experience who we believe we are, through the life experiences we create and manifest in material reality. Together with our intellect and other facilities of our minds, we create the intent that is executed by our decisions and choices to generate our life experiences. Beyond this, there are faculties and capacities yet undeveloped, suppressed or unused of which we get occasional glimpses through flashes we call intuition, predictions, awareness's or psychic insights. The potentials of many of these innate qualities are yet to reveal themselves to us but provides our consciousness with an infinite variety of pathways through which to channel the potential of its being.

Our present level of psychological and spiritual development still limits our capacity to understand the true nature and power of unconditional love in respect to our consciousness. Therefore, we do not understand the process by which we manifest and create the events that make up our life, at work and in relationships. Consequently, we do not know when or how we should be accepting responsibility for arguments, failure, disappointment, unhappiness, anger, aggression and so on, that are a result of our choices in life. Our distorted interpretation of who we believe we are, due to our childhood experiences, has so convincingly displaced our authentic sense-of-self. We reject our authentic self for reasons that will be explained further on and embrace a version of ourselves that is a product of our parent's issues. Right now, we can no longer distinguish who we were born to be from the person we believe we are, as a result of having meet emotional conditions accepted in childhood.

You identify yourself with your behaviour, thoughts feelings and perception. Convinced that these represent who you are, you never question it. Your self-perception controls how you see yourself and your value and significance. You interact with others without being necessarily aware of the deeper motivations within you or for that matter what theirs are. Your parents taught you to believe that how they react and respond to you represents who you are. If they criticised you, it convinced you were a disappointment, a failure, incompetent, not good enough or inadequate. If they were angry with you, it made you believe that you were the cause of it and to blame and therefore unwanted, a nuisance or a burden but also powerless. If they continually ignored you and showed no interest in you, then you felt that you were insignificant, worthless of no value, uninteresting or unlovable.

By defining who we are in respect to the way others treat us or deal with us, we cannot differentiate who we truly are from our emotional encounters. We are so used to being in relationships with others in which we apply our conditions and meet those of others, that we do not even see that our lives are shrouded in fear. Just about everyone in the world lives life in fear and is a stranger to the power of unconditional love, acceptance and trust.

Our tendency to use the word love indiscriminately for our partners, objects or activities distorts its true meaning and capacity. The manner in which we use the word love often implies that a person or even an object has the power to create the kind of love we feel for it. Without realising, we put the reason and therefore the responsibility for what we feel outside of us. We can confuse the attraction for someone to be true love or acceptance when what we feel is essentially a product of our neediness to be loved, wanted or accepted or to be sexually desirable. Over time, we have structured our perception to convince us that others are responsible for the way we perceive them and our response to them. By accepting this to be the case, we unconsciously give others emotional control over us. Our fear based issues cause us to endow others or objects with non-existing powers and qualities. As a consequence, we live life depending on others to feel loved, accepted, wanted and trusted. We remain in constant fear that by failing to meet the conditions we believe exist to qualify for love, we risk being rejected, abandoned, blamed or judged.

Unconsciously, by surrendering to our fears, we give others control over our emotional life but still feel responsible for the success or failure of our relationship. In doing so, we have allowed ourselves to become subject to the whims, issues and insecurities of our partner or others. We live in constant fear that anything we do or say, will attract criticism or judgement and lead to argument and perhaps to judgment or rejection. We are sensitive to conflict and argument because we may already feel that we are unacceptable and unlovable and so on. Since we do not recognise our complicity in this situation, we are likely to be in avoidance or hold our partner responsible.

CONDITIONAL LOVE IS FEAR

Why is "being unconditional" is so significant and why is it so important to strive to live your life in an emotionally unconditional state? Is it something that anyone can achieve and live by in all situations at all times?

We are all born with the expectation that the essence of our spirit — unconditional love acceptance and trust — will continue when we begin our experience of life through our interaction with our parents. Although our parents may have the conscious intent to love us unconditionally, their fears and insecurities prevent them from expressing it. Their child interprets their behaviour to mean that it must not be lovable and acceptable because it has to meet conditions to receive its parent's love, affection or acceptance. Constant repetition of similar experiences will eventually determine who it believes it is and dictates the way it will live its life. It is naïve acceptance of the parent's conditional behaviour, and attitude becomes the source for emotional issues that will affect many aspects of a child's life and becomes a source of unhappiness, inferiority and potentially a host of other problems.

Consider this: If we were to be suddenly in the presence of absolute unconditional love, we may expect that we would feel wonderful. We would also automatically feel the expectation to respond in kind by being unconditional ourselves. Being unconditional would demand we let go of all of the defensive mechanisms developed over a lifetime to protect us from our fears. These are the same fears we have learned to depend on to avoid consequences we believe we cannot cope with or overcome. While transcending one's issues is always a possibility, most will feel overwhelmed by the prospect of giving up the fear-based strategic tools on which they depend. They believe they cannot exist without them for the sake of their emotional survival. We identify so intensely with the conditions for love, acceptance and trust that letting go of these beliefs and supporting strategies will feel like giving up who we are. Our surrender to love will require us to accept that unconditional love is the only legitimate emotional force that we can trust to support us in our existence. Choosing to live life in the complete absence of fear, without any defensive or coping strategies and fear based needs is too challenging for many. The prospect can be so confronting that it is very likely that their fears will win the day. However, the influence of unconditional love is such that even though fear may triumph in a situation or circumstance, the pervasive power of love will always win out in the long term but not necessarily in the way you might think.

We experience unconditional and conditional love as a paradox at the beginning of our life:

- Exposure to parents who are controlled by their issues teaches us to distrust and reject our authentic and unconditional essence. Our physical dependence on them gives us no choice but to accept the conditional relationship our parents offer us unconsciously.

- We accept the conditions they place on love, and these become our we believe we are, which then determines our perception and strategic behaviour. They also become the source of our negative feelings, needs and thoughts.
- As we mature, our conditional state of mind manifests the negative life experiences which act as emotional triggers for our pessimistic and self-judgemental feelings and thoughts.
- We are left with the innate yearning for the lost oneness with the essence of our being through unconditional love, acceptance and trust that existed at birth.
- Unaware of the reasons for our negative life experiences, and dependent on our fear-based strategies, needs and feelings to get love, acceptance and trust, we now fear letting go of them.
- As long as we are afraid of releasing the mind-set that causes us to maintain fear and insecurities based on the idea the love, acceptance and trust are conditional, we trap ourselves in a world of limitations. Fear will prevent us from accepting unconditional love into our lives.

Unconditional love is to our consciousness what thread is to a tapestry — it is its core and foundation but also forms the patterns that define it. Just like the tapestry could not exist without thread, our spirit would not be without unconditional love at its core. From the beginning of our existence, even before we breathed the air of our new physical experience, it is already our most compelling inner frame of reference. From birth, we are already innately aware when we are unconditionally loved and accepted, wanted and trusted and also immediately sense when we are not. Physical survival is not enough for a human consciousness to be in existence. Our emotional survival will ultimately supersede our physical needs, if love is a part of our life experience, even if it is compromised and conditional

OUR HISTORY OF FEAR

Conditional love is a learned aspect of our emotional mind because we are born with the expectation to exist in a state of unconditional love and the innate entitlement to experience, give and receive unconditional love. Our mind forms its sense of itself i.e. its ego in the first 8 to 10 years of our life at which time our parents and family are our most profound influence. Our mother and father grew up subject to the influence of their parents and culture, which defined their state of mind. You have become the recipient of this generational legacy of emotional distortions, which you — just like your parents — have accepted as the truth of who you are. It evolved in you to become your definition of who you are to yourself and who you believe you are to others. Without realising, you have formed behaviours as a strategic means to deal with the fear-based conditions your mind has accepted as reality. From here on in, you are more who you believe yourself to be, rather than who you are authentically meant to be.

Our learned fears are not static states in our mind but are active propositions that have the intent to manifest the reality they represent for you. They will actively steer our behaviour and attract events, people and conditions that reflect fear's intended nature. If for example, you fear confrontation, you will do your best not to upset anyone even if it means that you have to suppress what you want or your truth. Your fear will control how you communicate by altering the manner and tone of your speech to avoid creating any negative reaction in others. Unconsciously sensing your fears, they will feel safe to confront you with their demands or criticism for example because they feel that you will not stand up for yourself. Unconsciously your passive, fearful state of mind attracts the very confrontation you seek to avoid. Your fear sets you up to be an easy victim. Even though our passive strategic behaviour has the intent to avoid confrontation, in reality, it acts as an attraction for those who are only brave enough to be aggressive with someone who is passive and fearful as you. Your state of mind will lead you to compromise how you are in the world and how much of your emotional self you are prepared to express and expose to others.

The sense-of-self we form by internalising the fears and insecurities of our parents separates us from who we are truly meant to be — our authentic self. If we do not change who we are, we will in many ways become our parents, have similar relationships by choosing similar partners and become the same parents to our children as they were to us. We will perpetuate an emotional generational cycle that already existed before we were born. Our choice to change who we are will also become a decisive act of breaking a generational cycle of emotional issues.

There is a lot more to this than you might think. You are likely to be unconscious of much of what is negative in your sense-of-self even though it controls how you see the world and how you make your choices. Without the awareness of what the negative aspects of your sense-of-self you cannot know what drives your decisions and choices, why you are attracted to certain personalities and the reasons for your negative emotions and feelings. Without recognising how you are the creator of your life experiences, you live with the idea that in most circumstances, you are powerless. You often feel that others, and not you, are in control.

It is crucial to our understanding of ourselves that we recognise that once love or any other state like acceptance or trust is conditional, we enter a state of emotional powerlessness, distrust and neediness and become fear-driven.

Without the innate security that unconditional love, acceptance and trust provide, we live in fear that we are not able to meet the conditions that we now believe exist before we are deserving and entitled to love, acceptance and trust.

Conditional love creates internal conflict because it contradicts our innate expectation to be unconditionally loved, wanted, accepted and trusted.

Inner-harmony depends on being in a state of unconditional love, acceptance and trust with ourselves — our spiritual essence.

This contradiction in our emotional dialogue can only be resolved if we accept that, to begin with, we are at the core of our very nature, unconditionally lovable and acceptable, wanted and trustworthy. Finding personal resolution for this inner conflict and thereby transcending our limited mind-set makes the process of living life our greatest human and spiritual challenge.

Our conversation about conditional love also covers every other emotional aspect of human relationships such as conditional self-expression, acceptance and trust and so on. Conditional love causes everyone to look for love and acceptance from others in an attempt to find the harmony and fulfilment they lack within. When we eventually do find love in relationships, we often discover it is not what we expected it to be. Most live with the naive assumption that the love from a partner will resolve their inability to love themselves.

Reality paints a very different story. In most relationships — instead of finding love and harmony — partners experience emotional difficulties and conflict with each other. When two people are attracted to each other, there is obviously a lot more going on than what meets the eye.

If they are not aware that they bring their fears and insecurities into the partnership, the love, acceptance and trust between them will usually be conditional in its very nature. Fear forces them into particular behavioural strategies, designed to protect them from realising them.

The person who is exposed to the strategies of their partner is expected to respond in a way that satisfies the fears held by them because if they do not, they will be made responsible for how the strategic partner feels. If for instance, one partner has a strategy to avoid criticism and judgement than the other cannot hold them responsible without risking conflict. To feel safe, they have to change their behaviour to accommodate the partner's insecurities and avoid arguments. They fear that if they do not, the strategic partner will blame them and hold them responsible for what they feel.

OUR HIGHER PURPOSE

Feelings are like the alarm system of your mind. They are the communication your spirit-mind uses to make you aware that there are conflict and disharmony between its essence — unconditional love — and who you believe yourself to be. Or, it will show that both are in harmony with each other.

Your negative feelings and thoughts indicate that you are in a state of inner-disharmony which has the potential to create negative life experiences.

When they are positive, it is a reflection of inner-harmony which has the potential to manifest positive life experiences. (With the exception, when these positive emotions are a product of strategic behaviours which will be explained further on).

All feelings have the capacity to dominate your senses and thereby your mind. Your current state of perception and understanding is biased to believe that the event or the people that trigger your negative feelings are also responsible for them. Your most likely initial response will be to find fault with them and prove yourself innocent. At that moment, it will not occur to you that you must have had a significant part to play in the creation of the event just like all the other participants. Your behaviour may be temporarily effective in influencing others to believe in your innocence, but this will not stop it from happening again. The power that you may exercise by persuading another does nothing to release the causes within your mind which are responsible for your creation of the event.

The nature of spiritual reality is that you are responsible for creating and manifesting your experience of life — every relationship and event in your life. Nothing happens by accident or misfortune. Accepting that you are the creator of your experience of reality makes you responsible for the consequences of what you manifest. Being responsible also gives you the power to change your life, by changing who you believe yourself to be. The control you want to have over your life but do not know how to acquire is in part present in your capacity for self-change. Your life will change in every way, once you have chosen to confront and understand the reasons for the negative aspects of your sense-of-self, and then release them.

Your feelings and emotions, perception and awareness, behaviour and responses will change the moment fears have left your mind. Consequently, so will your decisions and choices. You will not lose your sense of identity but who you believe yourself to be will be different in the absence of fear. The nature of who you are meant to be will emerge layer by layer as you dispose of more of the negative belief systems that support your fears. You will become aware that you think, feel and react differently in situations that would otherwise have bothered or upset you. Your inner-transformation changes your experience of others and how they relate to you. Releasing self-limiting beliefs is a decisive step, which will require you to discard your old fear based beliefs and ultimately demands your faith in the innate integrity of the essence of your spirit — unconditional love. Each change brings in new elements of your authentic self to your awareness causing it to become more representative of the original nature of your being. This process is a natural response of your consciousness as it aligns itself progressively with unconditional love, trust and acceptance. Each cycle of self-change will bring you closer to your original self and provide greater freedom to fulfil your potentials, talents and abilities.

The power of intent plays a central part in your process of change. Intentions are a core element of the beliefs that create your experience of life because it controls your expression in life. By understanding the source of your intention in life through understanding the beliefs by which you identify who you are, you can begin to take charge of your life. Changes will not come by just wanting or wishing for them, but you can make the first decisive step by consciously choosing to change by accepting responsibility for every situation in your life whatever they may be. Your conscious effort will create the intent that will support your confrontation with your issues and the changes you need to make. Commitment gives power to your intention to manifest a path along which your process of change can find reality.

Although it may seem we are no longer talking about love, we are.

We can only create harmony in ourselves by releasing the negative beliefs rooted in a fear that separates us from being in a state of unconditional love. The capacity and the propensity to achieve this inner state of harmony is innate in our being, but once it gets lost, its recovery becomes a life quest.

The life journey we all take has the profound intent that we evolve into conscious creators in harmony with our essence.

Our search for Unconditional Love to experience the oneness with our Origin is the Core Inspiration for All Consciousness.

It is the fire that fuels our creative expression and the fulfilment of our potential being.

Chapter 3

THE BEGINNING OF EVERYTHING

Our embryonic consciousness first experiences being present and alive through the activation of its awareness and senses; our first breath, emotional sensation and physical contact. We are at the very centre of experiencing being conscious and alive, and only we, through all of our senses, can know what it is like for us. No one can say what being 'us' is like because without exception, we are unique from one another and therefore our experience of conscious existence is individual and exclusive.

We create our experience of life from the way our consciousness translates the input from our mental, emotional, physical and meta-senses. Each contributes to a unique mosaic of emotional, intellectual and physical sensations that we come to call life. Living in physical reality, we are most of our awareness is built on the sensations of our physical senses, visual, auditory and tactile. It is a significant part of our learning process, and command our greatest attention, but that does not indicate that they necessarily are the most pervasive influence. Even though they feel furthest removed from our daily awareness, the honour goes to our meta-senses, which are sensory aspects of our spirit-consciousness. The ultimate intent of its consistent influence is to provide us with the capacity to know the difference between unconditional love and fear. Its presence gives our consciousness an emotional reference point distinguishes harmony from disharmony, peace from conflict, truth from deception, illusions from reality and so forth. Living in harmony with this spiritual quality has the intent to lead us to exist in harmony and oneness with all consciousness, within the framework represented by unconditional love, acceptance and trust. This part of our inner being is the key to our emotional, physical health and well-being and to evolving our consciousness to its greatest potential. It plays a leading role in how and why we create the kind of life we live and experience.

The connection our physical senses have with material reality is experienced differently from person to person. The interpretation of the information that comes through our eyes and hearing, touch and taste and so on, will depend on the emotions they trigger in us — how it makes us feel. Significantly, this can make us believe that external forces are responsible for our perceptions and feelings.

Therefore, it can appear as if others and the environment are the most immediate, powerful influences over life. The emotions and thoughts they activate seem to act as an irresistible force, driving our actions, reactions and choices. When our intellect and reasoning leave our response to fear-based emotions unchecked, the outcomes are often not what we want them to be. Our emotional behaviour creates an identity by which we know ourselves and others know us. It provides us with so-called personality traits such as being shy or aggressive, withdrawn or extroverted, which in turn allows others to pigeonhole us as a distinct personality type. There are many reasons why we adopt behaviours and attitudes and why our emotional mind has such a defining influence over us. Labelling our style of self-expression does not in itself establish the causes for them within us.

CONTROLLED BY ILLUSIONS

You could say that our emotions rule our life and this even applies to the most logical and intelligent of individuals. Often science-focused intellectuals tend to reject anything emotional, intuitive or instinctive. They tend to hold the belief that only logical reasoning and physical or statistical proof can be trusted, as a sound basis for understanding themselves, people and life. The exclusion of anything that cannot be scientifically quantified by their standards of objectivity restricts access to other vital and natural elements of their consciousness. The dismissal of higher creative forces persists in spite of the fact that intuition, fantasy, imaginations, dreams and inspirations instigate many discoveries and developments. Frequently, the distrust they have of their emotions, intuition, creativity and feelings, underlies the need for logic and supposed objectivity. That does not mean, that our intellect with its capacity for reasoning and logic is not an important part of our mind. Each aspect of our consciousness has meaning and purpose for us, and we need to use it in balance with all others to which we have access. There is no aspect of our consciousness is redundant whether it is our intellect, emotions, psychic, intuition, inspirations, creativity or senses that are still perhaps dormant in us. Trusting some and excluding others is indicative of an imbalance in self-expression and this will ultimately manifest as issues in our lives.

We can divide feelings and emotions into two extremes: on one side we have unconditional love, the key elements of which are trust, acceptance and belonging and being wanted. On the other, there are all kinds of fears such as rejection, abandonment, exclusion, powerlessness, worthlessness, being insignificant and of no consequence and so on. The fundamental nature of emotional fears is the result of the belief that you will be excluded or separated from unconditional love, acceptance and trust. Once this conviction becomes a part of you, it will also represent your sense of who you are, and cause you to be conditional in how you relate to others. You will subconsciously place conditions on giving and receiving love, acceptance and trust. In other words, you cannot be critical of someone and then say that you are accepting of them or only want them in your life if they are will to behave and act in a manner that suits you. Fears of every kind prevent us from being unconditional in our relationships. If for example, you fear of being rejected or abandoned, you are in fear that there are conditions to being accepted and acceptable that you fear you cannot meet. Under these circumstances, you may believe that you are unlovable, inferior, not good enough, not smart enough, inadequate, the disappointment, a failure, not wanted and so on.

Your feelings and emotions play an inescapable part in every aspect of life — relationships, work, friendships and leisure. The capacity to deal with life becomes restricted when negative emotions dominate your senses. If you were to express to them freely, you are liable to run into trouble because they may trigger anger, shame, criticism, aggression, blame by others. Their response to you may, in turn, cause you to be rejected or being made to feel guilty. For example, if a situation or person in your environment causes you react with anger or frustration, it is because your experience of them has activated the reasons for them within you. These triggers are already pre-existing in your mind, and the emotional reaction they create in you are not the responsibility of those with whom you had the experience. Once your angry feelings overtake your senses, you are likely to be unaware of what is happening within you. Your attention will be entirely consumed by the external forces, that you believe to be responsible for your feelings. In these moments, your intellect and reasoning do not help you to understand the reasons for your behaviour and responses.

Not knowing the source of our feelings, we tend to accept that they are a dependable and justifiable reason for our actions and choices. In the belief that our emotions, thoughts and perceptions tell us the truth, we find it easy to blame outside influences as the reason for our negative or positive feelings and the behaviour that follows them. As a consequence, we do not even consider the idea that we may be the originators of our own life experiences. A beautiful sunset can make us breathless with awe, or we can ignore it. A musical score can be deeply moving for some, but others can be irritated by it. How is it we are all not equally affected by the same experience? There is a lot more to this than the fact that we are unique from one another.

If we feel powerless and diminished because someone is abusing us and putting us down, then it seems logical that they must be responsible for what we feel and how we react. We similarly believe, that if one partner rejects another and leaves, they are judged as being aggressive and therefore responsible for the suffering of the partner who they abandoned. The one who is left behind is commonly seen as the victim because we believe that proactive partner is the aggressor.

Our understanding of who is responsible for what we feel seems to indicate that our interactions with others generate our feelings. Should that be true, we should also have the power to make others feel the way we want, but we all know that this is not possible. We cannot deliberately make someone love, want or trust us when they have no intention to do so. However, if we were to manipulate their perception of us by convincing them that we are the opposite of who they believe us to be, we might persuade them to be attracted to us. However, emotional manipulation is not the same as directly creating feelings within someone. The outcome would not constitute a genuine and sincere relationship. We are rooted in the habit of blaming others for our pain, suffering, anger and resentment and so on, and consequently do not bother to look for other explanations for our negative emotional experiences. You do not realise that you are living an illusion if you believe that others control your emotions and your perception of yourself.

If others do not create our feelings and emotions, then how and why do feelings become a part of us? What is the source of our feelings and why do they become such an intense experience when we go through conflictual situations involving others?

OUR RELATIONSHIP WITH EVERYONE AND EVERYTHING

Whether we are aware of it or not, we are in a constant relationship with everyone and everything in the world —through our mental, physical, emotional and meta-senses. The emotional experience of this intensifies, when we become involved in intimate relationships. All of our relationships whether with the world in general or with people specifically are always subjective. The nature of our consciousness does not allow us to have purely objective relationships because we do not function in the absence of our unique and authentic self and emotional self, even if we like to believe that we can.

Our relationships range from the connection with our partner or child to that with a flower or a sunset, from friends and business colleagues to our pets. Our most significant relationship, however, is the one we have with ourselves. It is not possible to connect with something without your unique perception and emotions colouring the sensations of experience. It is not a conscious choice but a reflection of how human consciousness relates to itself and consequently to everyone and everything.

Regardless of whether we are attracted to or repulsed by something, or even indifferent to it there is always a deeper emotional reason for how and why we relate to it the way we do. On the whole, we are not aware of the emotional filters that shape our perception and colour the way we see ourselves and others. Understanding what they are and why and how they are a part of us, would allow us to become aware how they affect and potentially distort our perception. These filters are a result of the belief systems that form our sense of ourselves and determine our perception of who we are and how we see others. Our belief of who and what we are is at the core of why and how we create and experience our lives in our particular way.

Our judgment, responses, reactions and choices are not necessarily spontaneous or even a conscious choice. Much of what drives us in life is a product of what we have learned in childhood through our parents, our culture and other environmental influences. The lack of a reference point for testing the reality and truth of your feelings, thoughts, responses and choices causes you to accept them without question. You are unable to remember what it felt like for you in the first three years of life and compare it with your who you believe yourself to be right now.

The awareness of who you truly are — the authentic and original nature of your being — left your conscious memory a long time ago.

How is it that we no longer know who we authentically are, and how and when did it get lost? How can we know who we should be?

In the absence of being our authentic self, we are left to live life as aggressive or passive victims of the beliefs we hold about ourselves. The emotional environment that we face every day is a manifestation of the beliefs that form our mind. As a result, we struggle to find truth, meaning and happiness in our existence. It is not like that all the time, but to a greater or lesser extent, we do not live life to the fullness of our potential. To discover the answers that can lead us out of this predicament, we need to look at the first eight to ten years of our existence, without judgment or guilt.

YOUR INNOCENT ARRIVAL

We come into this world as unique spirits. Our innate and unique potentials, talents, abilities and capacities endow our consciousness with the resources to manifest a life that fulfils our aspirations. We arrive with a natural drive to evolve and grow physically and emotionally driven by our incessant curiosity and desire to learn. We want to mature and be independent and self-sufficient to survive — not only physically but also emotionally and mentally. Our attractions, fascinations and interests motivate our curiosity and stimulate our desire to learn and gain awareness and knowledge. We want to solve problems and know, understand and explore the world around us. Our impetus to achieve and succeed is a natural part of us but in its essence, it does not necessarily correspond to the values and standards of the culture and the society in which you live.

An attraction to rhythmic or ordered patterns and structure might lead to music or mathematics. A creative desire to build things may point to architecture, design or organisational talents. For a child, the possibilities are endless, but whether they will be realised commonly depend on the environment, in which it grows up. The negative or positive nature of family influences from the beginning of life can stimulate our growing mind or act as a damper on our mental capacities, potentials, talents and abilities.

Born as an individual consciousness with innately unique characteristics, you have no awareness of how the behaviours and attitude of your parents will impact you. You exist without knowing who or what you are and of what you are capable. You have an identity, but at this time you have no sense or realisation of what and who that is. In the absence of this awareness and without a history of life experiences to reflect on, you lack a proven sense of ourselves in which you can have confidence and trust. The need to come to the inner realisation of what your identity represents, to know who you are, is in itself a motivating force that drives us towards engaging others and life. In the absence having the security of knowing the characteristics that define our consciousness, we become vulnerable to external influences, such as the fears and insecurities of our parents and family members.

For example, if we have never seen our body, we will not know our physical appearance until we see a reflection of ourselves in a mirror. Similarly, we do not know who we are as a person until we see ourselves in a 'psychological mirror'. The behaviour and attitude of our parents represent the mirror by which we determine who we are and our worth, value and significance. The absence of an emotional reference point by which to measure our interaction with others leaves us in a position where we have no choice but to accept that their behaviour or judgement is justified and right and ours is wrong. Their behaviour and attitude can leave us with the belief that we are a disappointment, a failure or that there is something wrong with us.

However, we arrive in life with the innate need, entitlement and expectation for unconditional love and attention, support and approval, validation and guidance to learn and understand who we are to ourselves, others and the world.

The sense of who we are needs to be experienced in a framework of unconditional love and acceptance, trust and belonging to express our authentic self spontaneously.

We are born with the primal emotional expectation that we will be unconditionally loved, accepted, wanted and trusted by those responsible for raising us — our mother and father. Whether this is fulfilled or denied will be a determining influence on how we will form our sense of self. First of all, it will build the relationship we have with ourselves. We depend on the unconditionally loving and caring interaction between our parents and us to have the sense that we are lovable, wanted and acceptable validated. The influence of unconditional love is so powerful that it rules everyone's life without exception.

Our spirit is at one with the emotional quality that is unconditional love. When we are born, we expect to be in the experience of it. It is the core vibration of our conscious and individual being. It describes the nature of the source from which we came, and it is an intrinsic part of our human spirit. Regardless of what we may do in life or what our goals are, subconsciously, we will always strive to exist in a state of unconditional love acceptance and trust. Should we be denied, we will feel forced to accept the conditional version of love which will typically become fear. In the first eight to ten years of your life, you lack the awareness to make reasoned conscious choices about this even though you do feel its incessant influence on you. Its presence will always make itself known and felt in your life. No matter how you develop as an individual, you will find yourself ultimately existing in harmony with unconditional love or living your life in contradiction with it. Living in disharmony with unconditional love and acceptance will cause you to live a life of fear, anxiety and stress.

We spend our lives in pursuit finding relationships and other emotional connections in which love, acceptance and trust are unconditional and are unhappy, frustrated, depressed and so on when we cannot. The emotions we are then subject to show the destructive effect that the absence of unconditional love has on us. The feelings, thoughts and behaviour generated by our fear of rejection, exclusion, shame, guilt, embarrassment, inferiority, powerlessness, helplessness, being denied and so on are all derivatives of the absence of unconditional love and acceptance. The circumstances and conditions in childhood that create the emotional experiences by which we come to believe that love and acceptance are conditional will be critical to the kind of life we will live as adults. They will determine the nature of the fears that generate the negative state of mind which then become an unavoidable part of many of our interactions in life.

Unconditional love is not just confined to the kind of love we associate with intimate relationships or romance. This love is much more than the love for another individual because it encompasses everyone and everything that exists and you can only experience the reality of its nature through your inner-self. This love is by its very nature unconditional in all respects to everyone and everything and can only be a part you, by loving and accepting yourself unconditionally. Your fears separate you from being in a state of unconditional love, acceptance and trust with yourself. Releasing them will reveal that you are lovable and acceptable and allow you to engage your innate capacity to give and receive love unconditionally. You are then free to extend the core values of love to others and the world. Fear is the foundation for everyone's issues, and by releasing the reasons or causes for them, we would create ever-greater harmony within us. Each release will be a new step towards self-love and self-acceptance.

We can only realise the nature of our issues if we recognise what they are and how they affect us. An emotional issue is much more than just a bad feeling, a negative thought, disappointment, feeling lonely or having a horrible experience. On deeper levels of our sub-consciousness, every emotional issue is a product of fear. At this stage of your awareness, it may be difficult to make these connections within yourself, but that will change. Just keep in mind that whatever your fears may be, they are a result of believing that you are separated and excluded from unconditional love. Using this idea as a central premise will help you to understand your issues and discover their origin.

The simple truth is that every human being innately seeks to feel and experience unconditional love, acceptance and trust. When you become an adult, the child that felt the pain of conditional love is still active in you. The fearful, hurt and damaged child you once were, is running your life by pulling the strings of our feelings, thoughts, perception and behaviour. We tend to believe however that what we feel represents who we are as if it is a justified explanation for our behaviour and attitude. Not knowing, why we are the way we are, there appears to be no other choice but to cope and deal with it, the best way we know how. You may think that your childhood was not bad, but the conclusion is that if you have issues or difficulties in life, it could not have been as perfect as you think it was.

"How and why does this happen to us?"

To understand how we have come to have issues or fears, we need to go back into our personal history — our childhood. The external influences on the first eight to ten years of life shaped the foundation that determined the way we came to perceive ourselves and the world today.

The nature of our ego or sense-of-self is crucial to how we will live and experience our lives. To take it one step further, the way our sense-of-self evolved in childhood is central to the daily reality we create. What follows will explain exactly how that works, what the consequences of living by our fears are and how we can change it.

THE BEGINNING OF FEAR

At birth, we have the innate expectation that unconditional love, acceptance and trust continues just as it is a part of our spiritual state and then physically experienced inside our mother's womb. For that sensory, emotional experience to become a part of our sense-of-self, it is necessary for our parents to receive us, and behave and interact with us, unconditionally in every aspect of their being and self-expression. They can only meet this requirement if they live their life and relationship by and large in the absence of fear.

What would the actual capacity of the nature of unconditional love be if it were the natural emotional and mental state of our consciousness?

The quality of unconditional love is 'god-like' in its magnitude and, at this stage of our being, probably beyond our capacity to conceive what it represents. It is hard to imagine what it would be like for everyone to be in a state of unconditional love and acceptance of everything that is and to live in the absolute absence of all fear. Nothing, not even death, pain or any loss would generate fear, anxiety or revulsion. Once you achieve that state of mind, your capacity to love, accept, trust, give and receive could become infinite.

The underlying intent of your life journey is to fulfil the potential of your unique being. Each of us is different, and so the manner in which we achieve your goal of personal transformation from fear to love is not in itself important. Holding the expansive destiny of your spirit in your awareness will help you to appreciate where your journey will take you. Even though you may not be aware of it, but no matter where you are it in life, you are on this journey right now. The process by which every person creates and manifests their lives does not allow anyone to opt out. Every unhappy, disappointing, upsetting, angry or powerless experience in life is a sign that you are creating life situations from a fear based perspective.

The origin for your fear-based conditions starts at home with your mother and father. The fears and insecurities they inherited are unintentionally passed on to you. If they were truly unconditional in every aspect of their behaviour and attitude, you would have learned to be just like them. Should their behaviour, responses and attitudes be a product of their fears, you will take them on as if they are your truth. You will form the nature of who you believe yourself to be — your sense-of-self dues to being exposed to their fears and emotional issues.

The expression sense-of-self will be used throughout this book to make a distinction from the word ego, which has taken on a different meaning for many. (Someone with an ego is often deemed to be superior to others)

Your sense-of-self is who you believe yourself you are — the inner-picture you have of yourself, consciously or subconsciously.

From the moment of birth, the actions and reactions of a child are spontaneous and mostly driven by their physical needs. Even though helpless and powerless to fend for itself, it has no direct fears for its emotional or physical survival as long as it senses that its connection with its mother is secure. Before birth, a baby is unconditionally taken care of by the mother's body. It is a period where the mother's body gives priority to the physical needs of her unborn child, putting her physical needs second. From the time of birth, a child still has the innate expectation for this physical experience as well as in the form of unconditional love, acceptance, trust and support, to continue. With these expectations as it's only emotional reference points, a child begins to develop its sense-of-self through the exposure to the emotional experiences with its parents and family environment.

There are mental and emotional forces within its spirit-consciousness that it must respond to because they are an inseparable part of the nature of its being. Besides the underlying drive to exist in harmony with unconditional love, it also seeks to create from its innate qualities and manifest its unique and different potential in life. It is naturally driven to learn, to express itself in physical reality coupled to our natural drive to survive on both an emotional and physical level. By engaging others and the world with all of its emotional and physical senses, a child seeks to learn, grow and evolve. It uses experimentation, exploration and discovery as the means to expand its awareness, knowledge and skills. A child's mental, physical and emotionally curiosity and an irrepressible desire to learn is also motivated by its need to develop its capacity to survive and exist independently.

You might say that the only condition a small child has for its relationship with its parents is that it expects to be raised, nurtured and guided with unconditional love, acceptance and trust. Were this to be the case the child's authentic self would feel validated and find free expression. The expectation of being unconditionally loved is there by default because can only communicate basic feelings and emotions such as hunger, pain, and fear. Beyond that, there are no expectations as it spontaneously and fearlessly launches itself into life. In a sense, the absence of fear is the often very reason why young children get themselves into so much trouble with their parents. Initially, they behave and express themselves without fear of judgment, rejection, abandonment and so on. Should they transgress the fear-based conditions the parents have set in their relationship with them, this spontaneous behaviour may get a negative response. Its dependence on its parents for its emotional and physical survival puts it in a vulnerable position over which it has little or no control. Still without life experience and physically and emotionally dependent it is too naive to be in a position to make reasoned choices and decisions. At this stage of life, a child is a vessel that can only receive emotional and other information to learn how to respond to the parent. Any experience that emotionally challenges the expectation for unconditional love and acceptance creates confusion that becomes insecurity and then develops into fear. The emotions this creates and lacking the ability to respond, can add a deep sense of powerlessness which only serves to increase the intensity of the fear.

Our consciousness has the innate sense, that we are only whole and complete by existing in the state of unconditional love and only then at one with the origin of our being. Therefore, the absence of unconditional love is the core reason for our fear of emotional survival.,

It is the reason why children need unconditional and unbiased guidance and support so that they do not come to believe that they are unlovable, unacceptable, unwanted, judged, made wrong, failures and so on. Unfortunately, this is rarely the experience a child has. Most people are not aware enough or prepared to accept responsibility for their emotional issues and to deal with them before they become parents. In fact, most do not like to admit that they have any emotional issues at all, let alone accept that they have affected their children negatively.

THE LOSS OF OUR AUTHENTIC SELF

A child naively expects that unconditional love; acceptance and trust will be a consistent part of its new emotional environment. Parents who have issues will unconsciously set specific conditions in their relationship with their child. Suddenly love acceptance and trust have become conditional, and it cannot understand the reasons and motivations for this. It senses the absence of unconditional love like you would a missing step on a staircase in the dark.

The child does not have experience, awareness or insight to draw on. It feels that its spontaneous, authentic-self has been disapproved of by its parents and has failed to meet the conditions that it has to fulfil if it is to be loved and accepted. Unable to determine who or what is responsible for this feeling, it concludes that it must be to blame. Believing that the fault must somehow lie with whom it is it searches for the reasons within itself. Lacking the awareness of itself that would give it the ability to separate its natural self from the negative emotional experience, it assumes that something must be wrong with who it is. The conditions the parents set are taken to be a sign of disapproval, rejection and judgment of who it is. It is blind to the fact that their conditional behaviour is a product of their fears and insecurities.

Exclusion from unconditional love through rejection and judgment may seem to be insignificant, but it will create deep and fundamental trauma and fears in child and adult alike. Born with the innate trust that it can entirely depend on the emotional and physical support of its parents, the child now plunges into a new and unknown emotional state — fear.

Unconditional love and acceptance are an intrinsic part of your being without which your consciousness has no reference point, core intent or focus for its sense of emotional being. Disapproval by your parents causes you to feel separated from it because it feels that you can no longer trust them to be your emotional support anymore. This disconnect creates the emotion we call fear, that unconditional love has become unattainable and conditional. The emotional sensations can be the fear of rejection, abandonment, failure, being wrong, embarrassment, shame and so on. Your fears communicate that unless you can meet certain expectations, standards or values your parents expect you meet, you will no longer be loved, wanted, accepted or trusted. Born with the belief that love will always be there, you are now in fear that you cannot survive in its absence. You begin to accept that you will only be loved wanted and accepted if you can get the approval from your mother or father. For that to be the case, you meet the conditions implied by their expectations, standards and values they placed on you through their behaviour or attitude. The belief that you can only acquire love and acceptance from others takes deeper root in you. As a result of the manner in which your parents responded to your naive and spontaneous self-expression causes you to start editing your behaviour and your authentic-self. You begin to doubt that your intrinsic entitlement to receive love and be accepted and wanted unconditionally can be depended on or trusted. As you experience the repetition of these conditions and new ones are introduced your distrust and rejection of your authentic self will grow, and over time you will forget who that was. These changes will reconfirm for you that love is conditional and that you have to change who you are to experience it. The kind of conditional love, acceptance and trust you ultimately settle depends on the nature of the standards, values and expectations to which your parents expect you to conform.

As adults, we can easily relate to our fear for our physical survival, but our emotional survival fears are more difficult understand. The most likely explanation for this is that we live and express ourselves with different levels of emotional fear most of the time. Many of these fears are in a general sense shared with others allowing us to normalise them as an acceptable part of the human psyche. We often use this as a way to justify our feelings and thereby our issues. It is not uncommon for someone to say; "But no one likes to be alone" or "Everyone fears rejection" or "Everyone has troubles in their relationships" and so on. Though there may be truth in these statements, it does nothing to solve our emotional issues.

Each time a child feels that its spontaneous actions, intentions, responses and emotional expression are dismissed, ignored, overruled, invalidated, judged or rejected, it believes there are more conditions to be met. Every emotional experience causes it to internalise more fears. Before long it becomes convinced that giving expression to who it was born to be, is unacceptable. The fear of being who it was born to be, grows every time a child experiences some form of admonishment or disapproval that it interprets as rejection, judgement, criticism and so on. The negative emotional pressure forces a child to meet the conditions it has learned to believe exist, by becoming who it is expected to be. There is no alternative for this choice because it senses that it is dependent on its parents for its survival. In the absence of its authentic self, it will not have the same chance to unfold its potentials, talents and abilities and the capacities of its mind. A fear based conditional-self has gradually is replacing it and taking control over its perception, thoughts, awareness, feelings and behaviours. The authentic-self and its spontaneous self-expression have now become something to fear and suppress to avoid the repercussions the child has learned to expect as a consequence of its expression.

Something dramatic has happened to the child psyche, but it went completely unnoticed by its parents. No one seems to be able to see the destruction of the unconditional and authentic self of the child and the appearance of fear. How can this happen and why?

Chapter 4

THE POWER AND INFLUENCE OF PARENTING

When you are a child,
the emotional environment created by your parents
shapes your sense-of-yourself
When you become a parent
your sense-of-yourself will determine the environment
that will shape the minds of your children.

There is no escaping the fact that parents are a significant influence on the psychological and emotional development of their children. Their role is not just in being guides, mentors, caretakers and providers for them but also to instil values, standards and principles by which their children will live. Self-discipline and responsibility, accountability and an awareness of consequence are essential qualities for a productive and positive experience of life. The personality of the parents represented by their behaviour and attitude is the most immediate and critical influence on their offspring. Other elements such as the values and beliefs set by religion, culture and nationality or the absence of them can all play a role. What they appear to be in the eyes of the child are dependent on the personalities and the manner in which they convey these elements.

Parents have a much greater influence on their children than most would be willing to accept and many are resistant to the idea that they may have a significant responsibility for the way their child turns out. Their good intentions are usually confused with the actuality of the emotional paradigm they created in the family with their fears and insecurities. When parents play out their relationship dynamic between each other and their children, they commonly do not realise the influence their insecurities have on them.

Most parents would not recognise what part of their child's behaviour is representative of its authentic self and what part is a result of their negative influence. The lack of awareness of their issues is a result of their childhood experiences. At this time of their life, when fears and insecurities dominate their minds they are unlikely to know who they were originally born to be. Consequently, they will not recognise it in their children. Parents are unaware that their perception is distorted by their fears and are not conscious of the origin of their issues. Once fear controls your mind, it is impossible to be objective and have clarity of vision.

It is not unusual for couples to become parents when they are still in the infancy of their relationship. Not only do they have little or no awareness of the personality of their partner, but each also has not as yet developed a clear understanding of themselves. The problems begin when we commit ourselves to someone without knowing what drives us to want to be with them. We convince ourselves that our attraction for another is love, while we do not know how to love and accept ourselves. The cold reality is that we cannot see what someone else is like if we do not even have an understanding of who we are—our sense of ourselves. Unfortunately, logic and intellect offer no help if we have not developed the awareness of who we are to ourselves and others.

When the extended family structure is absent, it is unlikely that a young woman will be aware of the demands motherhood will place on her. She will not be prepared for the changes this will bring into her life. Similarly, the young man who is to become the father is often not ready for the responsibilities of fatherhood, not to mention the emotional changes that will occur in his partner as a result of becoming a mother.

The problem is not about the lack of good intentions or our desire to raise a child. The difficulties already start in childhood before the notion of having a relationship and a family are even conscious in us. The way we identify with who we are, as a result of the way we were raised, is at the origin of our problems in life and relationships. The issues we bring into a relationship in life began in childhood, and it will be the same for our potential partner. Without recognising what creates the distortions in our perception, we cannot see what issues they bring with them.

Parents raising their first child will discover that it is as much an emotional challenge and learning curve for them as it is a testing time for their child. For example, should a mother feel powerlessness in life, feel insecure and fearful, it is likely that she will tend to worry and be anxious. As a consequence, her behaviour with her baby may appear to be very protective and caring, but she is subconsciously creating a fear driven environment. Driven by her anxiety and stress, her emotional behaviour and expression become a part of an over-zealous and over-protective attitude. A child, exposed to this environment, would feel that there is something to fear and worry about, even if it is not tangible. Its senses will go to a high level of alertness in anticipation of a threat for which there is no real evidence. It may start to develop a fear of the unknown and unexpected changes and feel to need to hold itself in constant anticipation of any threat, just to be safe. The child will subconsciously follow its mother's emotional lead because is dependent on her and lacks the capacity to discriminate illusionary fears from reality.

The changes a newborn child brings into a relationship can bring up issues in each partner, and these can become the source of conflict between them. A first-time father, who resents losing the attention of his partner because of the time she gives to her child, is unconsciously competing and his child will sense this. There may even be a resentment towards the child. The adversary state that this will cause in each of them will shape the emotional environment of the family and become part of the child's experience. Many have the assumption the arguments should not affect their child if it is not directly involved in the conflict. They do not recognise that their child will conclude regarding its own vulnerabilities from witnessing any emotional or physical conflict or abuse to seek to protect itself. Even if parents do not target it directly, exposure aggression and conflict will create fear and potentially have a life-changing impact on the formation of a child's mind.

TRAPPED BY CONDITIONAL LOVE

Our thoughts and feelings dominate and control nearly all of our actions, responses and choices to ensure our emotional survival. As emotional beings, people do not change because they become parents. Parenting makes demands on them, which because of the issues, challenges their state of mind. In too many instances, they unwittingly replicate the family dynamic with which they grew up, even though it may not have been their original intent. Avoiding this becomes even harder to accomplish when you consider that the partner they chose is likely to be a psychological representation of the characteristics of one or both of their parents. When these cause us behave and act to our children with the same negative behaviours and attitudes our parents did with us, the consequences will be unavoidable.

Initially, a child does not know how to be anything other than its self, and therefore, it expresses itself without an emotional agenda — spontaneously and unconditionally. The parent, however, cannot make the same claim. They have already made the same journey with their parents that their child is about to make with them. When they grew up, they were exposed and influenced by the fears, issues and problems of their parents. And, just like their child, they did not have a frame of reference to understand whether their behaviour was a product of unfounded fears or beneficial and positive for them. Unable to determine one from the other, they accepted the fear-driven behaviour or attitude as being relevant and real. Now they can all but act and react to their emotional fears and insecurities because they feel as if they are a natural and unchangeable part of their personality. The negative thoughts and feelings this brings up for them are accepted without question, as being representative of what is happening in their lives. The experience also reinforces the belief that others are responsible for causing their negative thoughts, feelings, reactions and behaviour. By accepting this as the truth, they do not realise that they are avoiding being responsible for life experiences they created. They also do not understand how the expression of their fears affects the way their children are growing up. They cannot see that through their behaviour they are teaching their children to believe that they are also the victims of others and their environment.

The sense-of-self of an individual can be seen to have two aspects as a product of their childhood experiences:

First is the original and authentic self of which the parents disapproved.

Second is the mind that holds the programmed beliefs that it has to meet the conditions set by the parent's fears and insecurities.

Each parent, just like every child, did not only come into the world with the full capacity of their spontaneous life-force, potentials, talents and abilities but also with the innate expectation of unconditional love, acceptance and trust intact. Between birth and adulthood, they learned to suppress it, and now they are no longer who they were originally meant to be. Without parents undertaking personal change, the emotional family history they create for their children will determine their destiny.

UNSEEN INFLUENCES

We have an incredible list of descriptions for our fears, issues and insecurities depending on their nature and origin.

The fear of being: unlovable, unacceptable, unwanted, mistrusted, distrusted, not good enough, inferior, inadequate, incompetent, worthless, insignificant, blamed, accused, not being of any consequence, undesirable, unattractive, ugly, repulsive, powerless, helpless, weak, etc.

Our fears create feelings of anger, resentment, rejection, exclusion, abandoned, judged, criticised, guilty, responsible, powerlessness, helplessness, being a victim, jealousy, envy, embarrassment, shame, impatience, self-doubt, inferiority, worthlessness, insignificance, self-doubt insecurity, betrayed lied to, taken advantage of, being deceived, suspicion, etc.

Fears motivate strategic behaviours such as being: self-critical or being critical of others, being dominating, being controlling, pleasing, compromising, suppression, aggression, accommodation, being confrontational, argumentative, conflictual, withdrawal, refusal, blaming, accusing, avoiding responsibility, avoiding being held accountable, lying, deceiving, manipulating, etc.

All are negative emotional states that can become a part of who we believe we are because of the absence of unconditional love. The common base for all of these negative states is always fear. Even though we may only feel our issues in specific situations or with certain people, they have never-the-less become a typical emotional part of our mind and consequently our sense-of-self.

The question is: How have these negative emotional states become such a persistent and intrinsic part of us and why do we keep experiencing them in the same situations and with the same people usually in the same way?

A child's sense-of-self is formed by the endorsement or disapproval of its authentic self within the framework of its expectation to be unconditionally loved, accepted, trusted and wanted. A child will perceive blame, neglect, unwanted or criticism of these needs as a rejection of its innate expectations and potentially a dismissal of who it is. At that moment, it feels rejected or abandoned and believes that it can no longer expect to be unconditionally loved and accepted. Instead, it begins to feel disconnected from its core emotional values with which it felt safe and at one with at birth. Unable to discern who is responsible for the fear it assumes that it must somehow be guilty of the reason for love is withdrawn. Repeated exposure to judgement, rejection, criticism, a child will come to the inevitable conclusion it is the failure and not good enough. Fear and insecurity now challenge its initial trust that it would be unconditionally loved and accepted.

The child's dilemma lies in its innate need to be able to trust in unconditional love, acceptance to emotionally survive and the dependence on its parents to physically survive. It will only be allowed back into its parent's grace if it complies with their expectations. Instinctively it will choose to accept the conditions it now believes it has to meet to survive. Fear becomes the emotion that will begin to control many of its behaviours and choices. Even though the emotional exchange between parent and child is conditional and therefore distorted, it still has the potential of providing support for a child's emotional needs. The child's immature state assures it is dependent on the emotional, psychological and energetic bonds that exist with mother and father. Its need for love affection attention and acknowledgement give it no choice but to accept the terms and conditions determined by the behaviour and attitude of its parents. Unfortunately, this choice is not without deep emotional consequences for the child over its lifetime.

We need to dispel the idea that only gross acts of verbal abuse, physical violence, aggression, exclusion and manipulation will have a definitive, negative impact on a child. This conclusion creates the misconception that our childhood was 'normal' because of there was an absence of violence and abuse. Based on this assumption we should not have any issues if we had a 'normal' family with 'normal' parents who gave us a 'normal' upbringing. The implication is that if you do have issues, you must have been born with them. That means that who you are, is intrinsically flawed and therefore cannot change.

So, what happens to a person who is convinced that others are to blame for their emotional problems and believe that there is nothing wrong with them? For one, they will continue to re-experience and repeat whatever is wrong in their life. If you accept that you were born with your fears, it follows that they must be an indivisible part of you. Consequently, there will be little you can do to your issues. But, if you can recognise that you acquired them in childhood, they cannot represent your authentic self, because you were born without fear. Having learned to accept them as if they are the truth about you, you can also 'unlearn' them by releasing them. Your capacity to let go of fear opens up the possibility for real and permanent resolutions.

Take a family where both mother and father have an issue with expressing their emotions. The parents taught their children that showing emotions and feelings is embarrassing, shameful, inappropriate and confronting for others. Now, they still feel too ashamed to openly show positive or negative emotions and feel embarrassed when exposed to a display of emotions by others. They even place the same restrictions on each other and their children. As a result, each parent does not only avoid showing any feelings of anger, or resentment but also love and affection. Their fearful behaviour actively suppresses the emotional voice of their children who know better but to comply. They learn very early to hide any spontaneous feelings, such as love and affection, issues and problems, pain and suffering and so on. In some families, members are only allowed to show 'happy and positive' emotions so that the parents will not feel offended or upset. Now they are parents; they are not aware that they are repeating the same behaviour for the same reasons with their child. They do not realise that the childhood experience they had with their parents will have the same effect on their offspring as it did on them. Their internalised fears make them blind to consequences of their behaviour has on others. Their issues are the reason for their inability or unwillingness to recognise the consequences of their actions and responses; not just the suppression of undesirable feelings. The child will feel that their attitude is a judgement of its spontaneous emotional-self, which it then interprets as a rejection of who it is as a person and consciousness. No matter in which form the issues of the parents take, and what conditions they create, the child will always feel that it has no choice but to accept them and be responsible for them.

A child learns to believe that the expression of emotions — negative or positive — is an imposition on others. Convinced that it will only be worthy of its parent's acceptance and love if it does not confront and burden them with its emotions a child will begin to suppress itself. Controlled by the fear instilled by its parents, it feels no longer free to give a voice to its true feelings and its fear and insecurities. Unconsciously, the child will develop a critical distrust of its own emotions and of others, inclusive of love and affection for fear that they make him or her unacceptable. Living in constant fear provoking criticism and blame for being an embarrassment it is not difficult to imagine that it will become an emotionally closed and inaccessible adult. Its sense of guilt and shame will continue to prevent it from being emotionally present and expressive.

This child grew up in a family dynamic where the parents did not yell or scream. No one raised their voice, used abuse or physical violence. In fact, it was quite the opposite: both parents never made a display of their emotions, so it what hard to know what their real feelings were. On the surface, they appeared to get on well. And so, without any display of conflict or argument to point at, it may seem that there is no reason for their children to have issues in adulthood.

The reality is that there was an intense emotional conflict fought by the child's unformed consciousness. Without a voice, power and influence its innate entitlement to be free to be its authentic self and unconditionally loved, accepted and trusted is squashed by the conditions set by the parents. As a result, it struggles with negative, fear-based feelings of powerlessness, guilt and shame and so on. From the outset, it fought a losing battle, but its defeat will become a lifelong quest for the rediscovery of unconditional love, acceptance and feeling wanted. Once it has made the transit from childhood through teenage-hood into adulthood, it will unconsciously seek to return to a state of inner-harmony with itself through unconditional love. This unceasing intent will underpin all of its self-expression, actions and choices in the future and become an overwhelming force in its life. By its very nature and influence, this intent to reunite its conscious being with the state of unconditional love will create a life of emotional challenges, which it needs to transcend to live its life to its fullest potential.

THE NATURE OF YOUR SENSE-OF-SELF

Our sense-of-self or ego is central to the function of our mind and therefore appears in many explanations. We cannot claim to know ourselves until we question our sense of who we are. Much of what we believe represents who we are is in reality just a collection of assumptions and beliefs by which we define ourselves. Some of these may be authentic to who you are but will not. In the current perception of how we should change or reach our goals, you may wonder whether it is enough to believe it to be true if it appears to give you positive results. You will discover that the difference between knowing who you are not versus who you are is life changing. If your beliefs do not reflect the authentic nature of your spiritual, emotional and physical reality, then the perception it creates will distort your experience of life and relationships. The way you will see yourself and the world, behaviour, judgement, choices, emotions and so on will be a distortion of the reality of what they are. The negative beliefs that are the basis of your distorted perspectives will delude you into living life under the spell of the illusions they create. Questioning the nature of your belief systems that form your sense-of-yourself is like asking: 'Who is the real me?'

Let us go back to the family where the parents cannot cope with emotional expression and therefore passively suppress this faculty in their children. These children are made to believe that showing negative emotions such as discontent, disagreement, unhappy feelings and that even exuberant joy and happiness can be undesirable and inappropriate. They have become the victims of their own emotions and feelings as well as those of others. Lacking the capacity to make their own judgement, they have no choice but to accept the reasons for their parent's behaviour as being justified. Even though, when they were children, these distorted values only operated within their family, consistent exposure to this acted to cement it as an emotional reality.

Living by these negative beliefs will have severe consequences for their future. It will alter their sense of who they are, their perception, the nature of their awareness, behaviour, their emotional self-expression, decisions, choices and intent in life. Our indoctrination into fear and insecurity is so surreptitious that most will not be conscious that they are playing out their childhood history. It will nevertheless affect their relationships because of the type of partner they will be attracted to as a consequence. Subconsciously they will choose someone, who is a psychological match for their issues. They will experience their fear and guilt for openly expressing their emotions also in the workplace and friendships. The people they attract and are attracted to in relationships and friendships are also likely to have complementary issues.

The influence and power that emotional fears have over us are the primary reasons for our readiness to accept the conditions placed on us at an early age. Unable to understand what the underlying intent behind the behaviour of our parent is, we assume the guilt and responsibility for them. Not conforming to the conditions implied by our parents causes us to feel vulnerable to rejection or abandonment. Our most fundamental fear is the separation from the unconditional love on which we innately depend for emotional balance and stability and feel entitled to receive. Our passive or aggressive strategic behaviours evolve a result of the realisation our parents can withdraw love, acceptance and trust, whenever they are displeased, upset or disappointed in us. They become the instruments by which we seek to retain their acceptance of us even if it is conditional.

Our unique nature as a consciousness causes our interpretation of the conditional behaviour of a parent to be particular to us. The structure of the negative beliefs we take on reflects this. The intent, context, circumstances and implied consequences under which we experienced our fears, shaped the belief systems from which we draw our sense-of-our self. Once we continue to feel the disapproval of our authentic self, we stop trusting it and suppress its presence. The conditions we accept, are the foundation for the negative or fear-based belief systems that become our identity. Not only does this distort our sense of who we are but also sets us up for what will become a lifelong inner-conflict. In our effort to be, act and behave according to a set of expectations we have been taught to subscribe to we lose everything that is real, authentic and sincere in us. We feel this through the sense of being unlovable, unwanted, worthless, powerless, unfulfilled, unhappy, feeling denied, anger and frustration with ourselves. Our lack of self-understanding will then lead us to find relationships we believe will be a solution for everything we feel. We go from relationship to relationship, convinced that a partner would fix what feels broken inside of us. When our partner fails us, we tend to believe that he or she is the problem, even though we are the only consistent presence in all of our relationships. The actual conflict we are fighting is within us; our fears versus our need and desire to exist in a state of unconditional love and acceptance.

The particular standards and values, concepts and convictions in a family dynamic depend on the unique characteristics each parent brings with them. These qualities include their fears and insecurities and expose their children to a wide variety of ideas, concepts and belief systems. The expression of many of these will be conditional when fear plays a part of their relationship dynamic. They are unlikely to remember how they came to think, feel and behave the way they do now in the first place. Most will accept that if they feel worthless, it proves they have no value, or if feeling dumb, it must be due to a lack intelligence, or if being powerless that they have no power and influence. They will never question what they feel in their relationship with each other and believe that their emotions represent the truth.

If for instance, our parents are disappointed in us for not meeting their expectations, we will accept that we are responsible for being a disappointment to them. If our parents only love us if we are who they want us to be, we will not feel loved by them. If love requires us to meet conditions, then we will also not feel loved and accepted. If they cannot show love and affection without making us feel indebted to them, we will believe that we have to give love to be loved by them. In all these relationship dynamics, we will come to believe that we are unlovable, unacceptable and undesirable.

The emotional family environment your parents created for us, is likely to be very similar to what they experienced in their childhood. Should our parents resent taking care of us and are more concerned with themselves, each other or work, we are likely to take on the belief that we are insignificant, uninteresting and that we do not matter. A parent who makes a child wrong so that they can prove themselves right initiates all manner of fears in them. The fear of failure, being wrong, not being able to trust in its mind. In childhood, our feelings and thoughts convince us to believe that an emotional experience represents a truth that we accept as being representative of who we are. These beliefs collectively form our opinion of who we are, our inner identity. The strategic behaviours we adopt to deal with our fears are an extension of our negative beliefs that define who we believe we are.

Once fears control our minds, we express the feelings, thoughts and behaviours they generate without question or thought. We find this often hard to acknowledge because it means that our fears control us, not our intelligence or conscious will.

TRUSTING FEAR

Ideally, we evolve who we are from the natural and unique elements of our authentic self, under an umbrella of unconditional love, acceptance and trust from our parents. This kind of family environment would provide the freedom to express our original nature, our unique potential. Without the restrictions created by fear, we would be allowed to evolve the full capacity and power of our consciousness. However, this is commonly not the case.

Raised by parents with insecurities, you cannot help but create a sense-of-yourself that has its roots in fear. The emotional sensation created by fear will make them feel very real cause you to believe that the reasons you experience them are also real. When you manifest your fears as events in your life the experience they create will convince you that they are a product of external influences. What you manifest, as a negative experience will feel very real but is ultimately illusionary because the beliefs that underpin it, have no foundation in truth. Fear is a highly influential emotion that implies that we must be in danger, and therefore it will consistently demand our attention, making itself central to our focus in life. It urges us to respond to its call by implying we will risk our emotional survival if we were to ignore it.

For convenience, we can divide our sense-of-self into two different areas. The original and unique nature of who we are born to be and the belief systems it attains through negative experiences with our parents, family and the world. The convictions we accept as our identity will either harmonise with the core nature of our authentic self or prove to be in contradiction with it. When these beliefs are in contradiction with our original self, we are no longer the individuals we were meant to be, and living becomes a distorted process.

This state of mind will create inner conflict because your initial expectations — to be unconditionally loved, accepted and trusted — were not met. You are pushed into a state of inner disharmony and conflict because your parents invalidated your primary expectations with their fear-based and conditional behaviour. Your need to survive has left you with little or no choice but to accept their fear based reality they presented you with, as your truth. This newly realised negative part of your sense-of-self will become the source for fearful, negative and painful experiences and feelings. You must resolve the disharmony within you, in order dissolve your fear and pain, and thereby become who you were meant to be. Subconsciously you will always try and seek out unconditional love and acceptance in life or relationships to find the inner harmony you lost because of your fears. How you go about this will be decisive in achieving change.

The reasons that your parents are not perfect are the same reasons why you are not. It is therefore pointless to blame your parents and hold them responsible for your issues. If you feel the victim of their behaviour and attitude, then realise that they were victims of their parent's fears and insecurities. Since you are responsible for holding the beliefs that determine who you are to yourself, you are also the only one that has the power to change. That leaves you no choice but to accept responsibility for the events your fears and insecurities will create in your life. It is the only way you will have the power to release the fear-based beliefs that control your experience of life and relationships.

Do not think that your negative beliefs attached themselves to you; you have attached yourself to them. Together with strategic behaviours, they have become your means to overcome your fear of rejection, exclusion, being unacceptable, not good enough, unlovable, suspicious, distrusted and so on. Subconsciously you have made them into your life support system and a part of your sense-of-self. You can only transcend your issues by accepting them and acknowledging that your beliefs are your responsibility.

Trying to change others will not change you and blame and accusation will only serve to keep you locked in your illusionary fears and an issue filled existence.

Chapter 5

THE POWER OF BELIEF SYSTEMS

The power that our beliefs have over our minds is quite incredible and mostly not well understood. Like the wind, the emotional kind of fear we carry with us in life is not visible to us. Just like we can see the wind because it moves the leaves on a tree, we recognise the way fear affects us emotionally through our feelings. Unfortunately, seeing the effect that fear has on us or others does not necessarily explain its origin. The influence of fear is so seamless that it is not easy to appreciate and accept the extent to which it controls our lives. As our fears grow in number in the first eight years of our life, so will the consequences they create. By the time, we reach our teenage years; we have already learned to depend on fear for security and suppress and dismiss our authentic self.

In this phase of our lives, we have no idea that many of our likes and dislikes, attractions, behaviours and responses are a product of our negative belief systems. None of this would be of any concern if it were not for the fact that on balance, too many of our beliefs have fear at their basis. Therefore, we tend to respond more out of fear than self-trust and self-confidence, and our behaviours tend to be more strategic than spontaneous. If you believe you can only work well under stress, then you will be motivated by fear; the fear of failure, disappointing others, criticism or committing yourself to the needs and expectations of others, not being able to meet specific standards or values or deal with new concepts or choices. Being needy of a relationship is driven by the fear of being alone, unlovable, or in some way not good enough, attractive enough and so on. The list of fears that can cause us some form of stress and act as a limiting factor on our capacity to manifest a fulfilling life are pretty well endless. The reason they are such a powerful influence on us lies in their capability to convince us that we cannot survive without depending on our fears. Believing that we cannot cope with the consequences should our fear become a reality we feel we have no choice to respond to it.

Once we accept our fears as a reflection of our inner-identity, they will determine who we believe we are. Without being aware that they are not a natural part of us, their presence in us effects how we think, feel and behave. Fear as an emotion creates anxiety and stress, but as a part of a belief system, it comforts us. In this form, it portrays itself as an early warning system that will protect us from the potential of damaging outcomes. Beliefs that are fear based create the illusion that they will keep us safe from the disastrous consequences they imply. If for example, you have the fear that others will not like you, you will anticipate rejection and exclusion. You might engage in strategic behaviour such as pleasing to make them like and accept you. By changing your behaviour to accommodate their needs and expectations, you cannot be the person you were born to be. Fear now controls your relationships with others, causing you to think and feel that pleasing is the only way you can make yourself acceptable.

An emotional fear, as distinct from fear of a physical threat is supported by a unique belief structure. When a child experiences some form reprimand because of Its behaviour or what it says, it will tend to take it personally. The negative comment or criticism will be taken as a judgement of who it is and not to its response or behaviour.

The interpretation in a child's mind is something like this:

Anytime I have the spontaneous impulse and desire to play with that particular thing, my mother or father yells at me and is angry with me.

And, therefore, I have to suppress my spontaneous impulses and desires because if I do not, they will cause me to be rejected and feel unwanted because it is always my fault that my mother or father is angry with me. And, so because of that I have to be fearful of being spontaneous and respond to my desires because I am not entitled, and I do not have the right to do what I want.

The previous is an example of one kind of situation, but you will find that a very similar inner-dialogue underwrites all of our fears.

The question is: How much does it matter whether they accept you or not, like you or not? Is it worth the stress and anxiety this creates in you and will it make a real difference in your life? When fear is the driving force in the belief-systems that form our sense-of-self, it does not only change how you think, feel and behave in the world. First of all, it alters your perception of who we are to yourself and your belief of who you are to others. Once your negative emotions are in control, it is nearly impossible to differentiate your original self from your fear-based self. Secondly, it alters the reality of every experience where one of your fears plays a role. You may think that your understanding of an event you experienced represents the truth, but fear will warp your interpretation. The level of distortion that fear creates in our thinking and reasoning only confirms the power of its influence over our minds.

We have all woken up from an upsetting or terrifying dream. Even though we were safe in our beds, we find ourselves in a sweat, with our hearts racing. We know that they are manifested by our minds and are thus of our creation even if we do not understand why and how. Nevertheless, in the dream, everything feels very real and emotionally intense. They affect us emotionally and physically as if we are in the living experience of a real threat or drama. The physical response to some dreams proves how realistic they can appear to us. At the time our minds cannot differentiate reality from the illusion. We may on reflection casually dismiss our dream episode as an illusion, but we cannot ignore our physical and emotional response to it. Fears, which do not come from a physical threat have a very similar effect on us but are in fact also an illusion. Rejection, judgment, criticism, failure and so on, will never cause us any real harm but our emotional response to them causes us to believe that we cannot survive their consequences.

We do not realise that the fear-based beliefs that we have learned to rely on to save us from our fears are also responsible for producing our negative life experiences. Negative emotions founded in illusion stop us from recognising that the distorted reality that we create with our fears. The powerful influence that fear has over our perception and emotions convinces us that what we hear, see and feel must represent the truth and therefore reality. Our fear of the potential consequences portrayed by our negative beliefs, ensure that we will never ignore them. As a result, we lose the capacity to distinguish emotional illusions from reality.

The persuasive influence of negative beliefs has on the perception of our minds cause us to be submissive to the fear it holds for us. The emotional potency of fear dictates a response that demands we invalidate any other option for dealing with our feelings, thoughts and perception. The beliefs that make up our sense-of-self and determine who we think we are and thereby shape the nature and value of our being. Fear alters our inner-identity so that our self-expression, perception and emotional priorities no longer support the authentic nature of our sense-of-self. Instead, it will conflict with the core values of our consciousness — unconditional love, acceptance and trust.

For example, you will believe that others think you do not matter if hold the belief that you do not matter to yourself. Self-criticism can be evidence that you believe that you are not good enough and therefore do not matter. Once you accept this as your truth, you will try and convince others that you do matter, have something to offer and are significant, through your behaviour and attitude. Alternatively, you may accept your insignificance and worthlessness being representative of who you are and live your life accordingly. The same applies if you believe you are powerless, unlovable, unwanted and so on. Each of these negative beliefs forms your sense of yourself and control of how you live your life, conduct relationships and deal with difficulties and obstacles. These belief systems will determine how you are present in the world — in the positive or negative sense.

We acquire our negative sense-of-self generally in the first eight to ten years of our childhood. We will begin to define who we are by what we are told about ourselves as early as the first 4 or 5 years of life. If criticism at home has made us believe that we are a disappointment, dumb or inadequate, our self-confidence will be affected as soon as we start school. Our lack of self-trust will convince us that we will not be able to understand the lessons we are expected to learn. What we have learned from our family about who we are will cause us to anticipate rejection, failure and so on at a very early age. Take a girl, who is criticised for her appearance and has never been appreciated or praised by her parents for her unique presence and what she brings into the world. She will believe she has no value and nothing to contribute. As soon as she encounters her peer group, she will feel and experience her low self-esteem. Lacking self-confidence as she matures, she is likely to suffer the consequences created by her negative self-beliefs on a daily basis in her friendships, work and intimate relationships.

HOW FEAR CONDITIONS THE MIND

In a perfect world, all qualities and potentials that represent our authentic and unique self as a part our conscious spirit will be unconditionally welcomed, loved, accepted and trusted. In the very first part of its existence, a child expresses its original self without fear or self-judgement. Unconditionally and spontaneously revealing its truth, it infuses every aspect of self-expression with its unique nature.

It fearlessly shows that although our origin is central that we are at the same time different from one another in many subtle, yet significant ways. Throughout our existence, our unique authentic-self represents all of the core characteristics of our being, and the very nature of its intent to evolve, demands fulfilment. Fear will stop this from happening and keeps us recycling the same life experiences over and again without making progress.

We are engaged in the process by which we create our reality as soon as we open our eyes. The naivety, lack of emotional development and experiences make it impossible for babies and young children to know the consequences of their behaviour, judgement and choices. Learning about themselves for the first time, through their interactions with people and the material world, they should not be expected to know. The opportunity to deal with our issues usually only presents itself later in life, when we have reached a level of emotional maturity and self-realisation. Logically, no child consciously chooses to grow up in the absence of love, conditional acceptance and trust. But, when this is the case, the negative belief-systems they acquired will subconsciously manifest the consequences of this throughout their lives.

A belief that forms a part of your sense-of-self can be negative or positive in respect to your concept of who you are. We are born with the expectation and need to express our authentic self in harmony with unconditional love, acceptance and trust. This congruency is crucial to the fulfilment of our innate potential and growth as a conscious spirit. When fear is the foundation of the beliefs that form our sense-of-self, we unconsciously choose to live our life conditionally — in fear. The result is that we will put the conditions we have learned to accept on the way we express our emotions and needs, choices and decisions and so on. We unwittingly restrict our field of creative expression thereby suppress our authentic self and limit the fulfilment of our potential. Our conditional sense-of-self will live in conflict with our authentic nature until we release the fear-based negative belief systems that control us.

You can only live in harmony with unconditional love if the beliefs that form your sense-of-self are in congruence with it. Once your sense-of-yourself is in congruence with the unconditional, love acceptance and trust, your ego will cease to exist because your consciousness will be at one with your spirit. It will feel as if you have no ego because they will be the same. Your sense of who you are and your spiritual essence will essentially have the same core values and intent. In the absence of fear, your self-expression, creativity, behaviour and choices are free to be spontaneous and without ulterior motives, intent. Your truth, feelings and emotions will have a voice free from fear of judgement and rejection, and you can live your life as a self-responsibility and not feel restricted. Each act of releasing fear-based beliefs will increase the harmony you will feel within yourself, and progressively allow you to reach this state of mind.

A significant aspect of a parent and child relationship is the manner with which parents judge and then react to a child's innocent and spontaneous behaviour. The intent that motivates their response to an event involving the child will determine the experience the child will have of itself. What this experience will depend on the issues and fears played out by the parents. The difficulty lies in the fact that if parents do not deal with their fears and insecurities before they have children, it is inevitable, that these will contaminate their parenting. Their issues will become an intrinsic part of the relationship dynamic they develop with their children. It is an illusion to think that becoming a parent will somehow automatically release you from your emotional issues because you have the intent to love and accept your child unconditionally. Once your issues have become part of your sense of self, the conditional relationship you have with yourself will dictate who you feel and how you behave. You cannot help but play out your fears and insecurities in every part of your life, in particular as a parent and partner.

The dynamic between our parents and us teaches us to believe that we are not unconditionally lovable, acceptable and wanted. The sense that we cannot exist without unconditional love causes us to accept the conditions our parents impose on us because of fear. Their fears as they become ours. We cannot imagine our existence without love and acceptance, being wanted and trusted and so we feel we have no choice but to accept the conditions presented to us. Whenever we express our spontaneous life-force and authentic self, our parents display behaviour which invalidates its expression in some way. Their critical response convinces us that we cannot depend on it to keep us safe and secure. We learn to believe and expect that if we were to give our authentic-self free expression, it will provoke a negative reaction from our parents and later from others. The resulting fear of rejection and judgement causes us to suppress our unique and authentic nature. We become fearful of who we truly are and adopt who we are expected to be, to avoid attracting criticism and abandonment. At the time, it feels as though we have no choice. Instead, we learn to depend on fear, as a part of our negative beliefs, to tell us who we have to be for our parents. Fear will control how to behave and express ourselves so that we can meet the expectations according to the conditions set by values and standards distorted by our parent's insecurities. We created these behavioural strategies subconsciously in response to the negative emotional experiences in childhood. Our strategies hold the promise of keeping us safe from rejection and judgment and lead us to be loved and accepted. Unfortunately, the actual effect on us is the opposite to what we expect to achieve.

These are some examples: A parent who angrily reprimands his or her child because they are irritated by the noise they make while playing does not realise that they are holding the child responsible for their feelings of annoyance. Instead of owning that they are annoyed and irritated for reasons within themselves, they blame the child and thereby convince it that it is guilty of being 'the annoyance and irritation'.

A parent who blames their child for embarrassing them is not aware that they are not taking responsibility for their own shame and make their child responsible for being the cause of being embarrassed. Naively accepting their parent's judgment, it believes itself to be 'the shame and embarrassment' it is accused of being.

A father who criticises his child for not meeting his expectations does not see that he the creator of them but is making his child responsible for fulfilling them. If his child should not do this to his satisfaction, he can only blame himself for being disappointed. Instead, he blames his child for what he feels, thereby convincing it that it is the disappointment.

A mother or father who has difficulty coping with life and just looking after themselves will be even more stressed having to care for their offspring. Their fears cause them to prioritise their need for fulfilment and security over that of their children. Their children will sense and conclude that their existence, and the expression of their innate needs and expectations, are the cause of this stress and anxiety. By accepting responsibility for their parent's fears and insecurities, they also subconsciously accept that their innate needs and expectations, as well as the expression their unique being, is responsible for causing their parents stress and worry.

Children will begin to suppress what are ultimately natural desires, needs and expectations to avoid being guilty of being a burden to their parents. Instead, they try and be what they believe their parents expect them to be by behaving in a compliant and submissive fashion. The intent is to show that their parents will not have to meet their needs and expectations. Not even their innate need for love and acceptance is allowed to find a voice in this environment, and so this too needs to be suppressed. In fear of being too demanding for their parents, they subconsciously make themselves emotionally and physically independent and self-sufficient as they can. Reducing their needs and expectations to the bare minimum; they avoid being an imposition. In adulthood, they are often unable to express their needs and expectations or to ask others for help, support or advice. Not showing issues or anything that might potentially upset their parents or others are strategies to avoid the guilt of being a burden and being the cause for stress, anxiety or worry. This self-imposed restriction includes the fear of expressing love and affection and the desire to receive it. As a result, they will inherit many of the same fears and insecurities held by their parents. Later in life, these issues will become a negative influence in their relationships and parenting. This state of mind will deny them the freedom to live life to the fullest potential of their unique and authentic self.

Regardless of whether a child comes from a place of inner-harmony or inner-conflict, it will usually accept its parents' emotional expression and behaviour unconditionally as "truth and reality". A child lacks the experience and capacity to be discriminating of its parents' behaviour and attitudes. When parents cause their child feel wrong or judge it to be a failure it naively believes and accepts that it is responsible. It will come to the conclusion that it is to blame for not meeting the conditions its parents set in their relationship. Most parents do not realise that their behaviour and attitude are a psychological mirror in which their children try to recognise who they are and evolve their consciousness. The erroneous self-perception parents create in their children with their fears and insecurities, will become a source of emotional conflict, issues and problems for the rest of their life.

Chapter 6

THE ORIGIN OF YOUR FEELINGS

Our feelings are not just a product of random sensations generated by our mind, thoughts or behaviour. They have a definitive origin and reason for being a significant part of the emotional experience we call life. It is hard to imagine living life without feelings, particularly when it often seems as if our emotions control every action and choice we make.

The influence our feelings and emotions have over our choices and behaviour is much greater than most of us would like to admit. No matter how objective we believe we are when it comes down to the line, absolute objectivity is difficult to maintain. It is safer to accept that objectivity does not exist for a human being than to assume that you can be objective. This way you are not deluding yourself, and you have a chance to measure the level of your objectivity with clarity.

The truth is that at the core of our being we are biased because of our innate expectation to be unconditionally loved, wanted, accepted and trusted. Our spirit is constant in its search for harmony between this intent and the state of our subconscious and conscious mind. Our core values are a persistent bias in our minds which seeks to be harmony with our spirit. As a result, all of our self-expression, actions and choices, revolve around creating harmony between our mind and our spirit in our life. In spite of all of the fears that define our sense-of-self, the intent of our spiritual essence is the over-riding force that controls our consciousness and creates the bias that directs us to exist in a state of inner-harmony. The effect of fear-based emotions causes us to search for this harmony outside of us, with others and the world, rather than within our self.

Over time our involvement with the others grows and so does our belief and expectation that we can fulfil the needs created by our fears through our relationships. If you come out of your childhood feeling unlovable, unacceptable, inferior or inadequate, etc., you are likely to be attracted to a person who will have the appearance that they can fulfil this need in you. The same would be the case if you were feeling invalidated, worthless, powerless or helpless and so on. The idea that we can satisfy our needs and expectations through another person will in the long term not work. It does not matter whether we are passive and waiting to be loved or aggressive and dominate and control our partner. Making your partner responsible for needs which are a representation of your fears and insecurities, and will never be an effective solution. The type of relationship is likely to culminate in argument and conflict.

THE INCEPTION OF FEELING

Fundamentally there are only three types of feelings — those generated by unconditional love, those rooted in fear or a product of conditional love. We can also have feelings by being exposed to experiences to which we have no attachment. Every feeling will be a derivative of these. Given that our sense-of-self has a biased expectation to exist in harmony with unconditional love and our fears are in contradiction with that, we have all the elements for inner-conflict. The belief systems that make up our sense-of-self divide themselves in the same way —positive beliefs are in alignment with unconditional love, and negative, fear-based beliefs set the stage for conditional love and acceptance.

Self-beliefs that resonate in harmony with unconditional love, acceptance and trust create positive events, generate positive feelings and reflect your innate intent and expectation to exist and be at one with the core values of your spirit-consciousness.

Fear based belief systems manifest negative events and therefore generate negative feelings because they contradict the fundamental values of your spirit. What you feel on the surface as anger, powerlessness, loss or loneliness and so on, is a result of your alienation from unconditional love, acceptance and trust within yourself. Your feelings and thoughts create the perception that unconditional love and acceptance are unattainable for you. The internal alienation from love reflects the disconnection you feel from others and the world.

NOT BEING YOUR FEELINGS

Our feelings play a dominating role in all of our life experiences and no more so than in our intimate relationships. The way we interpret and then react to an emotional situation, argument or conflict shows that we tend to give our feelings an enormous validity. Our feelings are so closely connected to us that we believe that we are what we feel. If we feel ashamed, we become embarrassed as well as the embarrassment. Should we feel judged, criticised, excluded or rejected, we become unacceptable, undesirable, unwanted, worthless, or insignificant. Should the words or actions from someone else cause us to feel unloved, we become unlovable. The problem is that the emotion you feel is real but is it a realistic description of who you are?

By comparing the emotional sensation of feeling with the way your body processes sensory information, you will notice some significant differences in the way perception works. Put you put your hand in warm water or ice, and you will feel the distinct differences between them. However, there is not a thought in your mind to suggest that by touching the water or the ice that you will become water or ice. Touching rough wood or smooth silk, each will create a unique sensation you will recognise for what they are, but you will never think that you will become what you feel. The main reason for this is that you are acutely aware of your physical body as a separate entity to everything else material. Because you take this for granted, you do not question any other feeling sensation you experience.

Why is it, that we do not view what we feel emotionally in the same way? It should be obvious, that most people struggle to detach ourselves from negative feelings and emotions. Our response to our emotional feelings shows the impact, influence and control they have on us, our relationships and life. Many people see themselves at the mercy of their emotions if not the victims of what they feel. Clear we do not understand the relationship we have with ourselves. Our consciousness has an emotional feeling experience of itself in response to events and interactions with others. We erroneously accept that this sensation characterises 'who we are' in relation an experience we had. Our change in emotions and the awareness of what we feel becomes statement within us that delineates the relationship we have with ourselves. Without knowing the origin and reasons for these emotional feeling sensations, you cannot be sure that they are representative of the real and authentic self. Your emotions may be real, but they do not necessarily define who and what you are. Even though the mind can sense and interpret your emotional environment, fear sabotages its capacity to discriminate between what is real and what is an illusion.

Our body does not have this problem, and therefore it does not transform in what it feels but fear can make us afraid of touching certain things. Our body physically tangible and we can see what we do, and touch and that makes separating our body from its environment simple. Our minds only give us the luxury of a similar physical confirmation when going through a negative emotional experience when we feel sick in the stomach or have a choking sensation. Beyond any physical sensation, who believe we are as a person is a product of the beliefs by which we identify ourselves; positive or negative. When these beliefs are fear-based, they will generate the negative feelings. The emotion of fear will coerce us into enacting strategic behaviours to avoid the negative consequences becoming a reality in our relationship or life. If it does, the result may be self-defining for us. Should we be for disappointing someone's expectations, we may feel and believe that we are the disappointment. But, how can we be a disappointment when we were not responsible for creating the expectation in the first place? The reality is that we — our consciousness — experiences feelings which together with matching thoughts come to conclusions and make a judgment about who we are. If the feelings and thoughts are averse to unconditional love and acceptance, our consciousness is giving a signal that they are a product of fear. Our emotions reveal that the motivation for our behaviour, feelings and thoughts is fear and that we are not our authentic selves.

WHEN FEAR IS IN CONTROL

Once negative beliefs systems are a part of our sense-of-self they take tend to control. We internalise our belief systems as a result of experiencing negative emotional interactions with our parents in the first eight to ten years of life. Later in life, these are retriggered by situations and people which recreate the emotional context of the original childhood experience. You will respond to this as if you are still the child as though you have no choice in the matter. Take for example; that you have unresolved issues feeling powerless and fearful of confrontation because an abusive dominating father and a passive mother raised you. It will be likely that you recreate the same experience with the partner you choose, or perhaps your boss or co-worker. They will in all probability be dominating and controlling in behaviour, causing you to react and respond as if you are still the powerless fearful child. The truth is that we relive our childhood every time our fears take control regardless of what form our response takes.

Feelings are the first active emotional ingredient in any relationship. Your belief systems are similar to a pre-set program that determines every aspect of your potential behaviour, including your feelings, thoughts and perception. Depending on how your fear-based sense-of-self has altered your feeling, perception and thoughts, they will determine whether you will be angry or laugh, feel offended or indifferent, uninterested or motivated and so on. Your reactions and responses to negative feelings and thoughts are mostly beyond your conscious control because you are unaware of the programs or belief systems that prompt them. Feelings based in fear refuse to be suppressed, and will always demand your immediate attention.

Once we become adults, the relationships with our parents are in many ways unresolved because we never received the unconditional love, acceptance and trust we expected. We will subconsciously seek out the same conditional relationships, to find a resolution for our damaged emotional selves with others who have similar characteristics. Without realising we recreate the same emotional relationship, we had with our parent with our new partner. This response to our emotional issues has created the understanding that girls will marry their father and boys their mothers. However, negative traits of our parents are the controlling influence that draws us to certain people, and so it is also possible to choose someone who carries the combined negative qualities of both parents.

The truth is that it will only be the case as long as your mind holds on to a sense-of-self that is controlled by the negative beliefs from childhood. Once you release them, your choice of relationships will change, because your attraction to personalities that reflect your issues will be absent. Changing who you will cause you to be attracted to and to attract a different kind of partner. Permanently breaking your connections with a negative past requires you to change your sense-of-self, your inner-identity. Consciously changing your behaviour or strategies, feelings and thoughts will never be enough to bring about real and lasting change.

We animate our mind with the best of intentions to do good and create positive outcomes, but regardless of our focus, the resulting experiences will ultimately define who we are and re-affirm the nature of our sense-of-self.

It is inevitable that the process of expressing our sense-of-self to fulfil our aspirations will cause us to be attracted to and to attract those people and situations that fit the nature of our intent. To counteract the purpose and consequences of our negative belief systems, we evolve behavioural strategies that allow us to avoid them. As long as our fears are still a part of us we have to rely on our strategic behaviours to keep us safe. The negative life circumstances we bring into relationships, friendships, work or at home are evidence of the disharmonious part of our sense-of-self. In absolute terms, there is there is no escape from this, but at the moment these issues appear it always seems as if learned behavioural strategies can save us. Relying on strategic behaviour only postpones inevitable re-occurrence of the same confrontation conflict, argument or disagreement.

If for instance guilt were an issue, we will attract or create through our behaviour or attitude circumstances in which we will feel responsible for upsetting someone or making them feel disappointed. The guilt we will feel is an expression of an issue that makes us believe we are responsible for the feelings and emotions of others. Our issues, in the form of negative belief systems, are individual to us. Besides being unique from inception, the parents that raised us were also born as unique individuals. Each child will interpret an emotional event involving their parents through their primary individuality — their authentic and unique self. Each will translate their experience according to their original sense of being, with which they will draw deep personal conclusions. If these determinations cause a child to feel separated from unconditional love and acceptance, it will feel a level of rejection or abandonment by its parent. As a result, a child will sense the emotion that we call fear.

Any emotional experience will influence the way a child will shape its sense-of-self — which it believes itself to be. Exposure to experiences harmonious with unconditional love and acceptance reinforces the child's natural inner-concept that it is unconditionally lovable, acceptable, trustworthy, wanted, included, significant and so on. Disharmonious experiences will do the opposite, causing it to feel unwanted, unacceptable, unlovable and so on, and result in fear and stress.

LIVING LIFE CONDITIONALLY

How we will experience our fears later in life depends on the negative beliefs we hold and the nature of the event that triggers them. For example, feelings of shame are a different fear than worthlessness, rejection or being a burden. Each of our negative belief systems contains specific intentions. The situations that trigger our fears can vary markedly from person to person. The intensity of a negative emotional experience usually does not only depend on the severity of your issues but also on the insecurities of those that are the trigger for you.

We usually respond with resentment and fear to feeling unlovable and unacceptable, insignificant or rejected, or being of no consequence and so on. Believing that our feelings are the issue distracts us from searching for the real causes. Instead, we respond with strategic behaviours to resolve our issue because we think that they will save us from emotional disaster. Our goal is to prevent a situation from happening that will make us feel bad or upset. You could compare the effectiveness of this to getting rid of the smoke without extinguishing the fire. In other words, the origin of your issue will still be there. You can be intermittently successful in dealing with your emotional issues by finding a way to make yourself feel better, but it will never be a permanent solution. In fact, it only makes understanding ourselves all the more confusing. We avoid the exploration of our issues with our tendency to seek immediate solutions by using our strategic behaviour to deal with what we feel.

Our feelings are not just a sense to experience life. The significance of our capacity to feel is more than this. Our feelings serve a higher purpose in evolution our spirit consciousness that we need to understand to know why it is a part of us. Without feelings, our experience of living in physical reality would not be what it is right now, regardless whether your feelings are positive or negative. The senses of our consciousness act like an alarm system when the sensation of fear threatens our emotional survival. What we then feel is the alert that our sense-of-self is not in harmony with our spiritual essence — unconditional love.

In that way, our feelings serve the mind by bringing conditions to our attention that are either of a harmonious and positive nature or a disharmonious and negative nature. Positive or negative feelings tell us whether our sense-of-self is in harmony with unconditional love — the core nature of our spirit — or in conflict with it. Without feelings, we would be completely unaware of the negative disharmonious state we hold in our subconscious mind. In the absence of this awareness, we would ignorantly play out our fears without the possibility for resolution. We would not know that our fear-based beliefs control us and therefore never recognise the need to take responsibility for the consequences of their expression. We would be repeating the same choices or behaviour with the same disastrous results without a care in the world because it would not matter to us.

Negative thoughts and feelings and the beliefs that create them do not define the authentic nature of who we are, even though it may feel like that. We rely completely on our emotional and physical senses for the experience of being alive. We sabotage our capacity to discriminate positive from negative feelings with our lack of self-awareness and self-knowledge. Most people identify themselves with the feelings generated by their sense-of-self without questioning why they feel what they feel. Consequently, we are left ignorant that we are responding to emotions which only have a basis of truth within us and with no one else because they are a product of our fears.

Take for example someone who experienced abandonment or rejection in childhood; He or she lives in constant fear of rejection, judgment and criticism, with the belief of being unwanted, undesirable and not good enough. Every relationship will be approached with trepidation and caution to avoid a repetition of past experiences. They will subconsciously look for a partner who would not do this to them — potentially that will be someone who is also fearful of being rejected or abandoned themselves. The security that each provides for the other lies in their dependence on each other's fear of rejection. In reality, their mutual assurance is founded in illusions because neither can save the other from their fear of rejection. Their fear ensures that they have no choice but to hold on to their fear for emotional safety. Their fear limits their capacity to give themselves wholly to the relationship by expressing love, acceptance and trust unconditionally. Initially, though, their behaviour towards each other will create the mutual impression that they are a perfect match for one another.

Our rejected friend may become emotionally cautious and withdrawn to avoid confrontation for fear of conflict and ultimately rejection. His partner of choice may present herself in apparent contradiction to his fears. She may give a lot of attention and affection, seemingly without fear and the more time he spends with her, the safer he feels from his fears. He does not have to make any initial effort and thereby avoids exposure to potential rejection. She is not conscious that her behaviour is a strategy learned in childhood. Being the pleaser and compliant is the only way she knows how to get him to want, love and trust her — just like her mother did with her father. The deeper intent of their strategic behaviours is to avoid rejection and often guilt. He does it by being cautious, distrusting and non-confrontational and she does everything she can to prove that she loves him by pleasing him and meeting his needs to ensure he will not reject her. Their behaviours make them think they are very different from each other, but in reality, their issues are very much the same.

There are other emotional elements at play, such as intent, needs and expectations. On the surface, the reason this couple chose each other was on the surface motivated by their need for love and their mutual sexual attraction. However, their desire to be together is also determined by their fears. Initially, they depend on each other's behaviours to fulfil the needs and expectations that each has created with their issues. In that sense, their fears and insecurities and behaviour are complementary

Chapter 7

THE POWER OF INTENT

Undertaking an action or making a choice with a calculated outcome in mind shows intent and it exists literally within everything conscious. Being alive and conscious, your body and practically every belief, concept, thought, idea, desire and wish, action and choice you give expression to have intent. It is usually easier to see the intent in an action or a choice than it is to recognise it in our thoughts and beliefs and so on. We are aware when we consciously determine a purpose, such as wanting to be the best at something, getting a positive result or just being on time somewhere. The power of intent, however, goes much deeper and further than you might think.

Our consciousness relies on the power and influence of its creative intent to manifest lives that present us with emotional and intellectual experiences from which we can evolve. Understanding the nature of intent and the context in which we express it, is important because it reveals our responsibility for consequences.

We are the creators of our intents but do not realise that many are subconscious. Innate qualities that are inherent in consciousness underpin the very nature of our expression of life. Knowledge and experience of the past combine with our creative inventiveness in the present, to form the basis for intent to manifest the emotional experience that we call life. Our strongest intentions are to learn and evolve our consciousness, to create and manifest life experiences, to survive emotionally and physically, to develop independence and to procreate. The positive intent of unconditional love etc. competes with that generated by fear-based belief systems.

Our conscious intentions can be in contradiction with intentions that are subconscious. Often, we cannot fathom how planned strategies can fail us when we formulated a well thought out path towards a preconceived goal. In these situations, we do not consider that other forces in our mind may be active that are in contradiction with our conscious intentions. Usually, we are only aware of creating a purpose for our actions and choices when we have decided on a result we want. In most situations, we need to physically experience and emotionally feel an outcome or consequence, before we become conscious that we acted with intent. Intentions are a part of everything we express or do in life. We do not think about them or consider the consequences of their power and influence. We are in most situations unaware whether the intents we express through our behaviour, dialogue, conversation, attitude, choices and decisions are founded on unconditional love, trust and acceptance, or in fear.

There is little that goes on in our minds that do not contain some form of intent: it is part of nearly every belief and thought, every idea and concept that we express. Intent gives our consciousness immense power and influence over the experiences we manifest in life. Even though it may seem subtle, it has not only the capacity to control our perception of others and the world but also every experience of reality itself. In our relationships, intents will cause us to attract and be attracted to people, circumstances and events that reflect the purpose of our intent. Fear-based intent causes us to be involved in situations, and with people where these fears are being played out, realised and experienced. The idea that we create what we fear is true but the manner in which we do this is not understood. Our fears need to have form, context and consequence to formulate an intent. That is the reason why they hold so much power over us when they are a part of beliefs with which we identify ourselves. When a set of circumstances activate all these elements, fear becomes a negative experience for us. The negative events we subconsciously create will not necessarily go to their most extreme potential when manifested the first or second time. But, if we do not deal with the emotional causes within us, they will gradually get worse and emotionally more intense with every repeated experience. Every negative belief you hold can become equally present in your relationships and life. Sometimes it depends on your relationship choices and the circumstances you attract.

The nature of our sense-of-self is a determining factor for the life experiences we create.

Ultimately, we manifest positive or negative life experiences to show ourselves the harmonious or disharmonious state of our sense-of-self. Only then can we recognise what we need to change in our minds to create harmony with our spirit, with the intention to evolve and become conscious creators.

Once we are adults, we are responsible for our beliefs and the intent they hold regardless of whether we are aware of them or not. It follows that we then are also responsible for the expression of these beliefs in life, and the consequences of their manifestation in the world. It is the intent within our belief-systems that make us the originators of our life experiences, not only as individuals but also as a collective.

When a group of people share a particular intent, its capacity to manifest increases exponentially. When it becomes a part of a collective, the likelihood of it being realised increases dramatically. This effect is not only true for the positive concepts, but also for collective fears and insecurities. When the collective power of intent becomes a choice that culminates into action, it can unleash powerful forces that are greater than the numbers would have you believe. By the same token, when shared negative ideas, concepts or issues in society are not resolved, we unwittingly create the psychological space that allows them to thrive. However, the ultimate power of a collective force always remains with the intent held by each participant.

In the East, where the power collective of intent is well understood, prayer and meditation have shown to change disharmonious situations. By using our mind to focus our intent, we can influence and change a negative state. There are many accounts of the power of meditation over negative situations or environments. Astonishing outcomes are possible, whenever people unite their intent to achieve a shared purpose. We may not have the capability to focus our minds like monks, but this does not reduce our capacity to manifest our intent individually or collectively.

There are specific practices such as self-discipline, meditation and positive affirmations to create the outcomes we desire in life. Meditation requires practice and commitment to focus the mind with the intent to achieve a harmonious state of mind. Moving your mind into a state where there is an absence of distraction or random thoughts is part of the process. Controlled self-discipline requires the consistent suppression of undesirable impulses and desires to create a 'strong' mind. Positive affirmations are a constant reminder of who you should or want to be, but also by implication, who you are presently not.

Asking why you are so affected by your fears and insecurities is the most constructive way to deal with your emotional issues. Instead of asking yourself what you have to do, not to have these negative feelings, will make more progress by questioning yourself why you have these feelings in the first place. Understanding the origin for the fears responsible for your current emotional state of mind, allows you take measures to resolve them. Your negative beliefs about who and what you are will be the source of your problems and releasing them the solution. The intent inherent in negative beliefs will find expression through your behaviour, choices or attitude. We have the natural tendency for our fear-based beliefs to engage with others with complementary fears to take advantage of each other by capitalising on one another's weaknesses and vulnerabilities. This dynamic results in shared experiences where each person lives through their fears in response to the other.

Every belief that makes up your sense of self, whether positive or negative, whether conscious or subconscious, holds intent.

The influences that our belief-systems have on us and our lives come from in the intent they contain. The convincing quality intent adds to a belief is highly significant if you want to overcome your issues. By understanding the nature of the intentions encapsulated in your choices, behaviour or self-expression, it becomes possible to recognise whether your beliefs are positive or negative. It is important to keep in mind that your intent is an indivisible part of your sense-of-self when dealing with your issues.

The intent of unconditional love and acceptance is to give and receive love and acceptance without placing any expectations or conditions on others. Being in a state of unconditional love and acceptance is to know and accept that you are unconditionally lovable, acceptable and trustworthy.

The intent of the essence of your spirit — is to love and be loved, accept and be accepted, trust and be trusted, unconditionally.

This intention acts, like an inner motivation and as a reference point for your mind. It represents the natural positive value and standard that consistently informs us when our sense-of-self manifests our life in harmony with our spirit and when it does not.

Our life experiences, strategies and feelings provide the evidence of whether we are acting out of unconditional love or fear. This most profound of intents influences the expression of who we believe we are, whether we know it or not, think about it or not and believe it or not. The intent within unconditional love cannot be turned on or off — it is an indelible part of who we are. Any attempt to consciously control it through suppression or denial is futile because the force of its presence defines every other emotional state we experience. All you would be doing is to create a new intent in conflict with unconditional love, the consequences of which will be negative for both mind and body.

The spell the innate intent of unconditional love holds over our being is like an encompassing force that steers our consciousness unfailingly towards harmony with the essence of our spirit — within ourselves, with others and the world. The essence of our spirit is by far the most powerful and positive force in us, and we cannot extinguish it. Its intent will ultimately override all fears and insecurities, and in time, even our innate drive for emotional and physical survival.

Releasing negative beliefs will not automatically cause the mind to fall into a state of unconditional love and acceptance. There are layers of issues to work through, and your transformation will be consistent and gradual. Generally, within those who can already imagine a positive sense of being, the change to a positive state of mind can occur almost seamlessly.

THE INTENT OF FEAR

We will experience fear if loved, accepted and trusted become conditional because it is our innate response to being separated from unconditional love and acceptance. The belief systems we form in response to our fears depend on our interpretations of the conditions we perceive we have to meet. These conditions are defined by our mind and then become a negative influential part of our sense-of-self.

The intent of all of our fears is to make us trust that they will protect and save us from rejection and abandonment, powerlessness and helplessness, doubt, deceit and betrayal, and so on. The reality is that fear will keep us from finding and realising unconditional love, acceptance and trust and with it, our authentic self.

You are unconsciously taught to respond to your negative beliefs in a very particular way. Your parent's belief that you are responsible for their negative emotions convinces you that others are responsible for how you feel. Just like they expected you to change to accommodate their fears and insecurities, you learn to expect that others should change for you. Just as your parents held you responsible for being irritated, disappointed, resentful, burdened and more, you learn to blame others in the same way. You become convinced that others need to change their behaviour or attitude towards you for you to feel safe from your fears and insecurities. Once this becomes your view of life and yourself, you subconsciously act and behave as if the world should change to accommodate your fears and insecurities.

CONTROLLED BY GUILT

Instead of blaming others, you may have learned to accept responsibility for the negative experiences of others. As a result, your fear of being guilty compels you to suppress yourself emotionally to avoid being held accountable for what they feel. You do not realise that you unconsciously give others power over how you exist and express yourself and that their fear and insecurities now dictate your behaviour and self-expression. Your guilt has the intent to avoid blame and being held accountable, for any negative experiences or feelings others may have. The suppression of your authentic self and true emotions will come at significant cost to your mind and is harmful in the long term.

On the other side of the equation is the intent of the person about whom you feel guilty. Your issue concerning guilt would have begun in childhood. One or perhaps both parents would have believed themselves to be powerless, fearful, insecure and vulnerable. Their fears would cause them feel as though they could not cope with responsibilities, expectations, difficulties and potentially, being held accountable or blamed. Their behaviour with you would have made you feel that your needs and expectations as a young child are a part of the reason your parent cannot cope. Exposure to their insecure behaviour and emotions from a very young age creates the belief that you are responsible for how they feel. This belief causes you feel guilty for the stress and worries they show in dealing with you. Even though your need and expectations are natural at your age because you do not have the maturity to be independent and take care of yourself. Accepting responsibility for the fears and insecurities of your parent(s) forms the beliefs that become a part of your sense-of-self. When your mother or father cannot cope with their parenting role, you may come to believe that your life is a burden to them and an unwanted responsibility. To avoid feeling guilty, you may suppress your needs and expectations. I, therefore, have to hide my needs to avoid being the cause for what they feel, because without realising you have made their inability to cope with life your responsibility and adopted behaviour to avoid being the cause that they get upset or angry, disappointed or stressed.

Parents who fear responsibility will act out whatever they have learned in their childhood to avoid being held accountable. When fear of being powerless causes them to feel vulnerable, they will act as though they are the victims of the needs and expectations of their children. Their sense of powerlessness provides them with justifications and excuses for not being there for you the way they should as a parent. When confronted and held accountable, their pattern of behaviour often takes them from aggressive denial or blame to being unfairly victimised and powerless. Their final escape can be to physically and emotionally withdraw as if the victim of their parental responsibilities. By not taking responsibility a child will automatically accept the guilt because it does not know any better. A child cannot find a resolution for their feelings of guilt because they do not have the means to confront their parents. Trying to deal with parents over this kind of issue is still difficult when you are an adult.

AGGRESSIVE CONTROL

Parents who force a strict set of personal standards and values, rules and expectations on their family are dominating and controlling. They often need to be right, do not listen to others and avoid being challenged on their point of view. When others do not comply, they tend to get angry and can be abusive with their partner and offspring. This behaviour has the intent to avoid being exposed as being inadequate, dumb, inadequate powerless, inferior and so on. The fear of being powerless and losing control is the driving force behind their aggression. To avoid this, they need absolute control over their environment, which in this case their family. Making everyone conform to their expectations, values and standards disguises their deep-seated fears of powerlessness, inferiority and shame. They would have grown up with a parent who treated them in a very similar manner. Their behaviour convinced them that they were powerless and had no control, causing them to feel insecure with themselves. In a family such as this, one or more children will adopt the same aggressive dominating attitude and behaviour and the others may become passive and powerless.

In this kind of family dynamic, one parent is usually dominating, and the other passive but both can act as though victims when held accountable. When confronted by their child, they will commonly justify their behaviour by blaming them for being the problem.

DESTRUCTIVE CRITICISM

You are likely to be critical of yourself and others if the parents that raised you were consistently critical of you. In their perception, you did not meet their expectations, or they found fault with you because they wanted to prove they knew more than you.

By parents pointed out your failings and shortcomings, they made you feel wrong, inadequate, lacking in intelligence and more. Their criticism of you will become your criticism of everything you do, think or feel. Those who suffer from being self-critical and often critical of others have the subconscious fear that they can not be who and what they are expected to be. Since you cannot be responsible for the expectations of others, this makes you feel powerless and frustrated. Constant criticism may have convinced you that the only way to prove that you are better than others is by showing up what you see to be the failings others. Criticism becomes a behaviour that seeks transfer the blame of not being good enough to others. This response becomes an attempt to prove a level of worthiness to qualify for love and acceptance. Avoiding failure and therefore not being good enough requires constant monitoring of everything you do and say. By finding fault with others, you get the satisfaction of believing that you are superior and right and that they are wrong.

The need to be without fault or failure can be so strong that you can convince yourself that your way is the only way to achieve the right outcome and that every other choice is wrong. You do not realise that you thereby ignore and dismiss the individuality of your own consciousness as well as that of others. Ultimately, your critical behaviour gives you no personal satisfaction because by invalidating everyone else you are alone and disconnected. Once you convince yourself that you should always be better than you are right now, you will always be disappointed in yourself. Accepting that being perfect is the only way you will be acceptable, you have trapped yourself in a circle of self-criticism and discontent from which there appears to be no escape. If what you achieve never feels good enough, it is likely you will judge others in the same way, and this will not make you friends.

Being self-critical is learned, you were not born with it. Once you accept that criticism defines expectation of who and what you should be, it causes you to be very sensitive to the critical comments of others. If this is your behaviour, one or both parents were probably critical and perfectionists thereby making you responsible for meeting their expectations, standards and values. You might take the same perfectionistic approach in your life and work, to avoid the embarrassment of being wrong and a failure. Your childhood experience may cause you to set standards for yourself that no one, including you, can fulfil. Your perfectionist attitude and a certain sense of superiority that can flow from this can then become a perfect platform for criticism. The fundamental reasons for your behaviours are your fear of being unworthy of the love, acceptance and trust should you fail the expectations of your parents. As an adult, you continue this dynamic with others in your life and work. By this time, you that you have to be perfect to be acceptable and valued.

Self-criticism resulting of unrealistic expectations creates fear of failure and shame for not being good enough. As a consequence, you tend to do everything with stress and anxiety. You may not realise that you are doing to yourself is what your parents did to you but now you could that person who is never good enough or always dissatisfied with your achievements. There are two phrases that if accepted as self-beliefs are very destructive: "I should always be better than I am" and "I have to surpass myself". On the surface, they appear to be the way to be successful, but if you analyse them, they are anything but positive. Both of these statements imply that no matter what you have achieved it is never good enough because you should have done better or outdone yourself. It also means that find it hard to celebrate your successes because you will find fault with them. If you live by this code, you are bound to be unfulfilled and never be content or happy. You will always be striving to reach a level of success that you move out of reach, because of what you believe. Regardless of your achievements, this will eventually culminate into thoughts and feelings that you are still not good enough and a disappointment to yourself and others.

Convinced that you are a failure who can only find redemption by being perfect, you are likely to justify your self-criticism as if it is the only way you can evolve and improve yourself. Your behaviour will commonly go to one of two extremes: You either believe you are imperfect and not good enough and accept it as a truth about yourself which is passive behaviour. Or you try and prove to yourself and others how perfect you are, which is aggressive or proactive. In both instances, you need to engage others to provide yourself with the proof you need to prove to yourself that you are smart, better or more significant.

Both strategies are intended to prove others that you are perfect. If you can convince them that you are, then in your mind, it must be true. What they come to believe about you becomes your belief about yourself. Regardless whether you have chosen a passive or aggressive strategy to deal with your fear, in both instances, you are dependent on others for validation that you are not who you fear you are. The need to be seen as such prevents you from seeing that you surrender your personal power to others by depending on them for what you need. Over time, in spite of your effort to prove otherwise, you will subconsciously keep creating situations where you find evidence that others are better than you. Your strategic behaviours cannot prevent your fears becoming a reality in your life.

MASTER OF YOUR INTENT

Obviously being aware of what your negative beliefs are and what intent they have, does not bring immediate change but is a definitive step towards it. Fear is the source for negative intent within our belief systems. We can only change our sense-of-self if we release the fear-based beliefs of which they are a part. Knowledge of the qualities that make up the beliefs systems that form our mind and understanding the process by which we create our reality is essential to learning how to do this.

The power and influence of intent are fundamental to everything we experience living in material reality. Nothing exists without the presence of intent that needs fulfilment because it underpins the very essence of creation and manifestation of everything that exists. We do not realise that the beliefs held by our consciousness have the capacity to be an instrument to focus our intent. Enhancing our mind with this skill would endow us with the ability to create and manifest a life of our choice.

You might say that 'Intent' has no judgement about its nature, regardless whether it originates from Fear or Unconditional Love, Acceptance and Trust.

Driven by its innate purpose to create, intent's only objective is to manifest "The Program" held by your beliefs.

If the program is one of fear, then your experience of life will reflect this. The many different faces of our fears will determine the events and relationships we will experience in our life. Naturally, intent from unconditional love, acceptance and trust will manifest a very different and positive experience.

Chapter 8

RELENTLESS NEEDS

Our needs and expectations are a major influence in our life because their fulfilment feels essential to our existence. The need to eat and breath is essential for our physical survival. Our innate need and expectation to exist in the state of unconditional love, acceptance and trust, is essential for the emotional survival of our consciousness and inner-harmony. These fundamental needs are a powerful and persuasive forces that influence our behaviour and attitude. When are positive in their intent, they support us by directing us towards actions and choices that lead to life experiences that evolve our consciousness. When fear underpins our needs and expectations, it changes the way we view them and how we act and behave to fulfil them. Fear adds a dimension of desperation to our needs, that is otherwise not present. The fear of being denied and unfulfilled pushes our thoughts, feeling, and behaviour to a level of aggression. The emotional state they create in us effects the way we go about satisfying these needs. How much our fear distorts our values, standards and integrity depend on how much our needs means to us.

Fear creates a level of desperation because it implies that you cannot survive, live, be happy, be fulfilled or complete and whole unless you can get what you need. Believing that you cannot exist without success, recognition, acceptance, appreciation and be acknowledged and so on, put emotional pressure on your behaviour to bring these into your life. For you, the consequence of existing without success is feeling you are a failure, going unrecognised, being ignored, being unacceptable, rejection, etc. You can behave passively and try and influence others through being the victim of your powerlessness to fulfil your needs. By creating guilt in others, you try and find a way to get them to satisfy your needs. Using aggressive and dominating behaviour, you may try and control other to achieve the same. The animation of fear in the expression of our needs and expectations will ultimately create undesirable experiences and results for yourself and with others. They become the basis for discord and conflict and finally anything but fulfilling or satisfying. Without resolution, they will cause us to repeat the same behaviours, reactions and responses over and again. Neediness of all kinds can be a persistent and controlling influence in all of our relationships and life choices.

The beliefs created by conditions our parents unwittingly set for us to qualify for their love, acceptance and trust, separate us from who we were meant to be — our authentic self. Besides starting out in life naively expressing who we are without knowing what that is represented by, we also engage our environment with the sense that we are wanted, significant, lovable, acceptable, desirable, trustworthy, valued and so on. We do not entertain any critical ideas or feelings about ourselves until our expectations contradict the way others treat us. When love and trust and other positive affirmations of our being are absent, we fear rejection, but they also become the needs in us we have to satisfy. If we are made to feel unacceptable through criticism and judgment, we will feel the need to be accepted. If made to feel worthless and insignificant we will develop the need to feel special, significant and admired. If we feel rejected and excluded, we will have a deep need to be loved, wanted and included.

The control that fear-driven needs have over our minds parallels that of our negative belief systems. To deny them will cause the intense emotional experience that is a product of their absence with us. The needs we feel have to be satisfied because we have the sensation that our very emotional survival depends on their fulfilment. Feeling that you are unlovable and unacceptable causes you to experience a sense of isolation from others that is intolerable, like a ship drifting pointlessly in the sea without a place to anchor. Circumstances, environments or personalities that were a part of the original experience that created them, will usually be the triggers that activate our unfulfilled needs. The feelings that neediness invokes will fuel your sense of urgency to respond and engage with these situations or people. At these times, your neediness will make you more than likely to be less discriminating and cautious in your self-expression and behaviour with others.

In those circumstances, we are presented with two choices — to act to fulfil our need or instead, do nothing. We always have the opportunity to respond differently to our fear based needs even though our feelings may try to convince us that there are emotional consequences if we do not. The threat of being be denied and not having our needs fulfilled can drive us to behave aggressively. Others may not even try to have their needs met because they are convinced that the lack the ability and power. They may use manipulation or guilt to get what they want but hardly ever aggression. These behavioural strategies create their problems, the effect of which will be felt by both parties. They both the fear that if they cannot fulfil their needs, they will feel the negative emotional consequences first experienced in childhood.

The exclusion from unconditional love, acceptance and trust remain our deepest and greatest fear affecting our emotional and physical survival and therefore, is our most intense and persistent need.

We tend to spend much of our time and effort in pursuit of satisfying our needs: the need to be loved, accepted, trusted, believed, wanted, trusted, acknowledged, appreciated, praised, listened to, heard, significant, exceptional, recognised, successful and so on. Our needs and expectations dominate our thoughts, behaviour and intentions in our life, relationships, work and social situations.

Fear can be the driving force of the need to be loved, wanted and as a consequence, we live in fear of rejection or abandonment. Whether you need to be acknowledged and validated, recognised and appreciated or be emotionally safe and secure, each has a matching fear-based belief that supports its existence. The fear of being abandoned, disbelieved, doubted, ignored, dismissed, invalidated, demeaned, belittled, worthless, insignificant, a failure, powerless and so on.

In response to meeting the conditions, we believe to exist; we develop behaviours to both to satisfy them as well to avoid the potential of negative consequences. When conditions are attached to love then even if we can meet them, it still would not be the love we expected to feel. Once love becomes conditional, it is no longer genuine love, and that leaves us needy and looking for love that is unconditional.

Therefore, the conditions we are expected to meet also create our neediness to be loved, accepted, for attention, validation that is unconditional. Once we have accepted that we cannot expect love, acceptance and trust without fulfilling certain requirements, we are in contradiction with our innate entitlement to receive and experience love, acceptance unconditionally.

Our reliance on strategic behaviour to satisfy our various needs will cause us to choose, behave and react in ways that are not representative of who we truly are. Fear is in control and distorts the intent and need for our behaviours. Even if others try to tell us that we are not rational or reasonable, it is unlikely to make much difference to us. We will more than likely justify and defend our behaviour in response to their comments. Once we are in fear of not having what we believe we cannot live without no explanation, logic or reasoning and no amount of intellectual dissemination of the situation will influence our minds. In spite of being told why our behaviour, attractions and choices are wrong or cause our pain and suffering, we will keep on doing the same thing. If we were to alter our behaviour and choices deliberately, we would still feel under duress because we would be acting in contradiction to our fearful intent.

However, fear-based needs are not only the domain of individuals we see as weak and vulnerable. Those who act aggressive, dominating and controlling, convinced that they are powerful are unlikely to admit that fear is the driving force for them. The fear of being powerless and without control is the reason for needing to be in power and have control. Having to prove that they are more significant, superior and better than others is a product of the fear of being worthless and of no consequence. The process of fulfilling needs does not necessarily suggest a passive, submissive approach. Aggressive and dominating strategies may give the impression of strength and power, but they are just as much a product of fear-based beliefs as submissive, subservient behaviour.

Our negative beliefs automatically create needs, feelings and behaviours that then form part of our sense-of-self.

- If you feel rejected and unwanted, you will feel unlovable and unacceptable to yourself and others.

How much love, attention and affection do you think you need to feel loved and wanted?

The Truth: It will never be enough (until you love and accept yourself).

- If you have a fear or shame of being a failure, you may feel the need to prove that you can be successful.

How big does your success have to be before you are satisfied?

The Truth: It will never be enough.

- If you are fearful of being poor and destitute, you will feel the need to have money and wealth for security.

How much will be enough to stop your fear?

The Truth: It will never be enough.

- If you have been raised to believe you are dumb and stupid and are now fearful that you are intellectually inadequate and an embarrassment.

How much education do you need to prove to everyone how smart you are?

The Truth: It will never be enough.

- If you are terrified of confrontation, what will you do to avoid conflict or aggression?

How much of life can you avoid before you have no life at all?

The Truth: You will avoid more and more of life's experiences until your fears become your emotional prison and you have no life at all.

The list is endless because just about anything in our perception can be fear.

THE WORLD TO EXPLOIT

Satisfying our fear-based needs by engaging others and the world is an automatic response for us. We try to deal with our fears by either confronting others with aggression or suppressing ourselves. Sometimes we do both, depending on whether we feel stronger or weaker than those with whom we are dealing. The belief held by parents that they are powerless in the world subconsciously teaches their children that the outside world is to blame for what we feel. When they are upset, angry or dissatisfied with us or others, their blaming attitude and vocabulary confirm that they are not responsible for what they feel and that others are to blame. They take the position of being the victim of their children by holding them responsible for how they feel. The guilt we accept when our parents repeatedly make us responsible for their feelings will eventually define who we believe we are, which creates our sense-of-self. Our parents and their fears and insecurities are the mirrors by which we innocently create our inner-identity.

The effect a fear-based self-perception has on a child can drive it towards either a greater need for self-sufficiency or to dependency and powerlessness. The innate drive towards independence still exists, but the pathway towards achieving it becomes highly distorted. Children naturally strive to be self-sufficient in every part of their life, initially by walking and eating on their own for example, or by choosing, thinking and reasoning independently. Self-confidence and trust in their mental, emotional and physical strength are essential for a child's development to be independent.

This innate drive to realise our independence to be self-sufficient creates the desire to acquire all the skills and knowledge we need to achieve this. If we fear that we are a burden and an imposition on our parents, it can drive us to try and be physically and emotionally independent before we have acquired the maturity, knowledge and ability to stand on our own two feet. The guilt we feel for being a burden cause us to want to prove that we do not depend and need our parents to support us. On the other hand, under the same circumstances, we may fall into the deep conviction that we are powerless to be independent because we are too young and then become very needy for support instead. It is possible to display both of these qualities dependent on the circumstances that are a part of their origin. Because these behaviours find their roots in our negative beliefs, neither is representative of the actual nature of the person who plays them out. In its most ideal state, our mind has no fear.

By the time, we have a negative sense of ourselves and the needs that go with them, we have already learned to focus outside of us to protect us from our insecurities and to get our needs fulfilled. Our issues put us under constant emotional pressure to be alert and aware of any threat to our well-being. We convince ourselves that only certain people, situations or things will keep us safe, make us happy or are a threat to us. When being with different people controls how we respond, react and speak we have proof that we do not feel free to be ourselves at all times and in all situations. Characteristically, over time, our choices and behaviours will fail to satisfy the needs and expectations we try to fulfil through others. Or, we find reasons to be dissatisfied or criticise what we have manifested in our lives. Once we begin to feel unhappy and disappointed, insecure or dissatisfied, the journey for self-fulfilment starts all over again. We do not recognise that we consistently return to the same negative place we have begun. We are under the illusion that if we make other choices, then next time everything will be different. Were we not so completely blinded by the negative beliefs we identify with, this would be obvious to us. We misinterpret the issues life presents us with by assuming that the causes are external and therefore others are responsible. Choices based on this understanding can therefore never be a permanent solution because we are trying to change others instead of ourselves. Consequently, we are dealing with the symptoms of our issues when we try to change what is outside of us, and we are not addressing the cause which is us. As a result, what we believe to be the solution to an issue is destined to fail and put us back to where we started. We are stuck in the perspective that our issues are a product of how others and the world behave towards us. As victims, we cannot and often do not want to see, that we are the keepers of our fears and the creators of our problems in life.

PARTNERS IN CONFLICT

Our choice of partner is not only determined by physical and emotional attractions but also by our emotional issues — our fears. Even though our relationships fail, we keep choosing the same kind of partner, causing us stress and unhappiness. Unsuccessful relationships can take on an obsessive quality, are often hard to close down and may linger for months or even years. Love that is unconditional does not create an emotionally negative experience and does not demand we suppress and compromise ourselves. If we accept that it is normal for love to be conditional, it will create emotional vulnerabilities, such as neediness and low self-esteem and others which will have undesirable consequences for a relationship. It is just as dangerous to believe that there is only one person that can make us happy, locking us into a narrow idea of what we expect love and relationships to be. Once we are committed to this belief, you will exclude other opportunities for love because, for us, they will not fit the conditions we set. This same attitude can also have the effect of making a relationship conditional to predetermined expectations which will set standards that will probably be impossible to meet. Probably, the most important thing to remember is, that your chosen partner, just like you, will bring his or her issues, expectations, standards and values into the relationship. And, that they, just like you, they believe that these are normal and justified.

The attractions that make two people compatible is complicated, but certain principles apply. The match between partners is not only based on positive elements such as love, sexual attraction and shared interests but also includes their fears and insecurities. The negative beliefs that are a part of your inner-identity play an influential role in the reasons for who you choose as your partner. If your 'perfect' relationship turns conflictual, you cannot come to any other conclusion that from the outset your perception of your partner was distorted. It is more than likely; it would have been the same for them in respect to you. However, because you chose to be with them, you cannot blame them for the issues in the relationship. This fact makes you at least half responsible for how your relationship is turning out. Understanding that you are the instigator of your relationships because they are your choice is a major step in finding a resolution for the issues you experience.

Even though it seems that we are attracted to someone because of the way they look, sexual attraction or the person they are, our negative and positive beliefs colour our perception of them. What we see and how it makes us feel is generated by the belief-systems we acquired in childhood as well as the convictions and unique nature with which we were born. Who we believe we are as a consequence of our past experiences determines the way we see them. Our perception of them is unique to us and who we think they are, may not necessarily represent who they believe themselves to be. If we do see some flaws in their behaviour or personality, we convince ourselves can that we can change them for the better. Sometimes we can sense the potential of what someone could be and convince ourselves that this is who they will be for us. We may then dismiss their issues as unimportant, because our need to be loved, wanted and accepted, is greater than our common sense. We do not see that fear distorts the perception we have of them.

The assumption that we can assure our happiness by finding the 'perfect' partner is another fantasy that does not deal with the reality of relationships. On the surface this appears to be the most logical thing to aim for but, the conditions that are a part of this expectation will reveal something very different. The reality is that what the perfect partner has to be for you, actually reveals more about you and your issues than it does about them. Breaking down the expectations of what you expect your partner, exposes many of your fears, shortcomings and insecurities. The conditions we apply to a potential partner are our way of dealing with our fear based issues and needs in relationships. Our search for the perfect partner ignores the existence of the fears and insecurities we have. As a result, we feel attracted to personalities whose issues dovetail neatly into ours. Instead of finding our perfect match, we set ourselves up for a difficult relationship.

If for example, you believe you are unlovable, unacceptable and unwanted, you are likely to feel undesirable and unattractive to your opposite sex. You will be self-critical and judgmental of your appearance and therefore expect others will not want you. The negative view you hold about yourself determines how you expect others to behave towards you. Your low self-esteem will cause you to expect that others will ignore you and not be interested in you and that they will see you as unattractive and undesirable. Your disbelief and distrust in your individuality and appearance, have convinced you and created the expectation, that no one will want or choose you and you will always be alone. Your conviction that no one would want to be with you makes you distrusting of anyone approaching you and without realising you exclude yourself from relationship opportunities that come your way. Your belief that you are unlovable and unacceptable intensified your need to be loved and wanted and making you long for what you think you can never have. In your fantasies, your ideal partner will be someone who sweeps you off your feet and makes you the centre of his attention with the exclusion of anyone else. He or she needs to make you feel that you are the only one they want and obsess over you, so you have proof that you are special and desirable. You have the need to be convinced by them that you are the only one to whom they are attracted. Any change in their attitude or behaviour can take you back to your fear that you are unlovable and unacceptable.

If you are fearful of unpredictable changes and emotional confrontation, your need will be to be with someone who is emotionally stable and protective but also non-confrontational. The person you attract has to be in many ways similar to you in respect to confrontation and change. The primary difference between you and your partner will be that they behave and speak as though they are in control when dealing with situations you tend to avoid. The fears that control each of you is similar and eventually one of you will realise that the other cannot meet expectations.

Parents who have a history of being denied and were forced to have to go without having their natural and basic needs met by their parents, often have difficulty accepting responsibility for the needs and expectations of their children. If in a co-dependent relationship, their neediness of one another may them exclude their children from love, closeness and intimacy. Their co-dependency implies that they need each other's love and that emotionally, they are takers and not givers of love and affection. At times, there may be discord between them, but they are unlikely to go their separate ways because the fear of being without each other is always greater than any conflict. It can be, that both parents are so focused on their need for each other and their fear of being denied, that their children come last and consequently feel emotionally neglected. Of course, as young children have no choice but accept this but they will grow up feeling that they are not entitled and denied, just like their parents. When they express their needs, expectations, wishes and desires, they are often made to feel guilty for expecting to receive what their parents felt denied. Their fear of upsetting them in this way creates guilt and makes them feel responsible and oversensitive for how others feel. They may begin to suppress and deny their entitlement to what they need, want or desire Instead they learn to give the needs of their parent's priority over their own, and put themselves last. This behaviour can later in life typify their relationship with others. Their sense of guilt causes them to live in constant fear that satisfying their own needs will cause someone else to be upset, disappointed or discontented.

Parents who consistently act as victims of their family history, life, others and circumstances, will unwittingly cause their children to believe that they are somehow responsible. Their children know no better but to think and feel that their unique presence, natural needs and expectations are somehow to blame for their parent's negative emotions and life experiences. The growing belief that they must somehow be responsible for what their parents, and in time others, feel, creates guilt. The reality is that their parents are controlled by the negative beliefs which they acquired in childhood, and are unaware of the consequences of their behaviour — for themselves and their offspring. Children may grow to be like their parents and learn to believe that they are the victim of life. If so they will avoid any relationship where they may be responsible for the expectations, needs or feelings of someone else. It is no surprise that they will be attracted to someone who is over-responsible because they feel guilty if someone is disappointed in them. Or, someone who is unwilling to accept responsibility or be held accountable.

There are obviously endless examples of emotional issues and shortcomings. However, distrust of your opposite gender is one of the most common. Distrust that is direct context with unconditional love and acceptance is somewhat different from not having trust with someone because you fear that they will lie or betray and deceive. Distrust and suspicion of love and acceptance, and consequently relationships, is on a more basic level of our sense-of-self. It is the fear of not believing that you are unconditionally lovable or acceptable because you do not love and accept yourself. Placing conditions on the love you have for yourself, you expect that conditions must exist in the love someone has for you. Your fear is that you may not qualify and can meet these conditions you have convinced yourself must exist because they are a part of you.

If your issues cause you to be attracted to someone with aggressive or passive aggressive behaviour, you will find that they will put their needs and expectations first and dismiss and invalidate yours. This dynamic will make your life as the more passive partner very difficult. Eventually, you will find the suppression of your voice intolerable this will increase the potential for conflict. What initially looked like security and stability becomes an emotional prison where nothing is your choice, and everything you do and want has to be justified and explained. Even though you know that the relationship is not what it should be, you may feel incapable of confronting the issue with your partner. Your lack of self-trust and self-confidence in who you are and what you are entitled to and deserve can make you feel helpless in respect your partner.

The fear of losing control and being powerless drives your partner's dominating behaviour which heightens his or her distrust in you and enhances their fear of abandonment. Despite their intimidating behaviour, fear will cause them to drop their aggressive, controlling behaviour as soon as they feel threatened with abandonment. Often, at this point, their fears, as well as their neediness and vulnerability, will make them say and promise anything to avoid rejection. To ensure you do not close the door permanently on them; they will agree to anything to ensure there is a way back into the relationship. Usually, they will change their behaviour and attitude and become attentive and caring. Once they feel safe and secure again, they will fall back into the same behavioural patterns that caused the crisis in the first place. The ability to change behaviour to suit their needs can cause breakups to drag on for a long time. Their incessant need for a partner ensures that even if you were to leave them, they would never be alone for long. The fears and insecurities in respect to the opposite sex will almost guarantee that they will behave like this with every partner. Often, they will make sure that while they are in a relationship that there are always a few other options available to them — just in case.

CONDITIONAL RELATIONSHIPS

We will delve into the complexities of relationships in much greater detail further on. For now, we should realise that fear driven needs will in time create issues and conflict in relationships. Each partner has the subconscious expectation that the emotional issues they bring into the relationship become the responsibility for the other to fulfil. Just by reading this you already know that this will never work in the long term.

When we cannot meet our needs, fear comes into play because we fear that we will be subjected to undesirable consequences. We learn very early in life to be in fear of rejection and criticism, guilt and being a disappointment for reasons typical of your family environment. As a result, fear is often the driving force behind our choices and decisions, feelings and behaviour. We channel our fears into every aspect of our life, particularly into intimate relationships. They are the force behind the reason why we repeat many of our illogical and irrational choices, decisions and attractions over and over again. They are also the cause and motivation for many of our socially unacceptable behaviours and mannerisms, which in many instances will determine how we see ourselves and how others perceive and judge us.

The question you need to answer for yourself is a simple one: Am I prepared to examine who I believe myself to be and the fears I have so that I can live without fear? Can you imagine what life would be like without your insecurities? What if you ceased to be a contributor to the conflict and difficulties that currently experience in your relationships and life?

A world populated by people who live without fear would be nothing like the world you know now. Imagine being in a world, where love, acceptance, trust and truth dominate, rather than fear, distrust, neediness and greed. Try and think of a place where invention and creation are mindful of the consequences on the well-being of all life. A world, where governments serve the people with wisdom and insight to the future, rather than serving short-term self-interest and fear. Imagine a society, intent on developing a higher sense being for its population, instead of being dominated by economic processes based on fear — power, control and material gain. That kind of world can exist just as easily as the distorted world you live in right now. All it needs is for a substantial portion of the total population to release the fears that prevented them from becoming who they were always meant to be. By giving expression to the beliefs that hold the positive intent that support these values. The capacity to manifest this lies primarily in the individual, not in the structure of governments or corporations.

We need to decide what kind of world we want to live in by first of all being WHO we were born to be. Without realising the strength of our conscious being, we will not understand how to apply our collective power in the world. Change starts by releasing the fears within us, and thereby not confer them onto our children. The reality is that it all begins with you and your relationship with yourself.

Chapter 9

THE ILLUSION OF BEING FREE

We adopt strategic behaviours in response to our fears, as a means to fulfil the needs created by the conditions we believe have to meet. Conduct that is spontaneous does not have a preconceived agenda and does not look for reciprocation, endorsement or approval. When we use dialogue, actions and responses as instruments to overcome our fear of not meeting these conditions, they have a definitive intent and therefore become strategic. When parents, respond and react with disapproval or criticism to us and our behaviour or self-expression, we feel compelled to alter our responses to avoid upsetting them. We assume that their reaction to us is our fault and therefore feel we must be to blame. By developing strategic responses, reactions and dialogue to meet the conditions they place on their relationship with us is also the method by which to avoid the consequences which we believe would follow should we fail them. They become an essential part of our survival mechanism throughout our life. Strategic behaviours are never random. Each has a definite intent and purpose.

Spontaneous reactions and responses are the mind's uncensored expression of qualities and attractions innate to our spiritual consciousness. They have the potential to create experiences that will evolve the awareness and growth of our spirit, mind and body. It can also be a response to our instinctive awareness to be safe from negative emotional or physical influences. The incessant intent to create and manifest, the desire to learn and know oneself in a relationship with everything our consciousness encounters in life, is innate in us. Being spontaneous in your expression does not require conscious contemplation to activate choices. 'Spontaneity' springs from an emotional space that is without fear, inhibitions shame or thoughts of negative consequences. Freely and unconditionally expressed, it rises from the comfortable sense of being supported by unconditional love and acceptance as the core sense of who you are.

We tend to have difficulty distinguishing impulsive behaviour from that which is spontaneous because they appear so very similar to a spectator. Impulsive behaviour is usually driven by fear-based beliefs and fulfils specific emotional goals; like getting attention or standing out from the crowd. In this respect, impulsive behaviour is strategic and often involves fear-based intentions. The fear of being ignored or overlooked, not feeling significant or meaningful and so on.

When we consciously orchestrate a particular intent to achieve a specific goal we tend to engage in planned strategized behaviour. We practice this approach in a very deliberate and contrived manner in business environments. But, for some people, this is the only way they can get through life. They feel the need to plan everything in great detail to remove any potential risk that they believe exists for failure, judgment or confrontation. On the surface, this may seem sensible and logical, but when you engage in this kind of approach to your work or relationships out of fear, you open yourself up to being vulnerable to stress and worry. The stress that comes from trying to anticipate every possible permutation for failure and disaster can be debilitating. The fear of not being in control of their lives and day-to-day relationships will dominate any decisions, self-expression or commitment where there is a perception of risk of adverse outcomes. Fear underpins their intent is to make their work and social environment as predictable as possible through planning every tiny aspect of the process to ensure success. Avoiding disaster and failure in this manner appears sensible until you that fear is running their life. Once you accept fear as a part of who you believe yourself to be, they have the habit of realising themselves in your life.

The majority of us rely on our strategic behaviours to get through life, and we would feel powerless without them. We do not realise the damage they do to us and others. We feel we have no choice but to rely on the success of our behaviour for our emotional survival — to be loved, to be accepted, and to be wanted, to avoid criticism and be powerless and so on. We are blind to the fact that negative beliefs and their intent, stop us from being the unique and empowered individuals we were born to be. Instead, the fear of being subjected to the consequences should our strategic behaviours fail us dominates our behaviour, choices and self-expression. We do not see that we behave act and respond in ways that are not representative of our authentic self. Neither are we aware of the negative impact out fears have on others and often more intensely on those who are closest to us. Strategic means contrived, insincere, distrusting, manipulative, misleading or covert. Our strategic behaviours are always of fear of failing conditions to love and acceptance that we perceive to exist.

The beliefs we create and accept, appear to give justification to all manner of fears and insecurities. Not surprisingly, considering the power that fear has over us, strategized behaviour is ever present in much of our self-expression. One of the reasons we so easily persist with this is that they promise to save us from what we fear by their potential to elicit a positive response from others and thereby avoid manifesting our fears.

Even though we do not choose these behaviours consciously, once they become our own, they become a persistent adjunct to our personality and a significant part of our lives. From childhood, we begin to learn how to behave to avoid becoming the victims of our parents discontent, criticism or anger. We feel them initially as a withdrawal of their love and acceptance of us. If our learned strategies are successful, they become our preferred way to get us out of emotional conflict and discord — initially with our parents, and later with others.

BECOMING STRATEGIC

All behaviour has intent, but only we are only concerned with that which is driven by fear. When your reactions, responses and self-expression without fear originate from unconditional love, acceptance and trust. Your unconditional approach to life and relationship will lead you in the direction of growth and self-development. Your motivation will be unconditional love, acceptance, trust, creativity, curiosity, the desire to learn and understand and so on. Expressed with unconditional love as its core value, the intent within your activities will steer your life in a positive direction, but changes when fear takes control. The primary purpose of your behaviour will then become strategic, to prevent your fears becoming a reality.

Even though the following may appear to be in contradiction, strategized behaviours have the potential to lead you to a path of personal growth and development. Not directly, but through the experiences, they create for you. Awareness and realisation of the reality of what motivates us to engage in a particular action or choice only seem to occur when they produce a failure or other problems in life. Only when we experience that they cannot support us, and we find ourselves in depression, constant anger, anxiety or even physical illness, we begin to question ourselves. Even though this puts us under enormous emotional pressure, it is also a reality check of where we are with ourselves in life.

Once we find ourselves in an emotionally debilitating state of mind because of the difficulties we have to deal with, we are without control over our lives. Often, for the first time, our emotional state forces us to look at what is going on in our minds to find the reasons for the emotionally confronting circumstances in which we find ourselves. Understanding of these negative experiences will indicate that fear underpins and drives our feelings, behaviour and choices. Recognition of the negative beliefs that are at the source presents us with an opportunity to make the first steps towards real change. Accepting responsibility for your actions and decisions and the emotional issues that motivate them, bring you closer to dealing with the causes of your problems. Your journey starts by developing the awareness and understanding of yourself, as the person who is responsible for the behaviour that leads to undesirable outcomes.

A child that spontaneously seeks to satisfy its curiosity is not driven by fear but engages in the act of exploring the nature of its emotional and physical being in relation with the environment it encounters. Significantly, it does this initially in the absence of fear other than the sense it has for physical survival. This first reaction to being in life shows that being without fear is not only possible but a natural potential of our consciousness. Unfortunately, a child's lack of awareness of its emotional and physical self, together with its dependence on support, care and protection, makes it also extremely vulnerable. It is aware of some but not all physical dangers, but oblivious to negative emotional influences, which become its greatest vulnerability. As a moving force in their child's life, parents may have the intent to love and accept their child unconditionally, but their fears and insecurities will get in the way, of making that a reality. It is unfortunate that the first casualties of their insecurities are their child's spontaneity and self-confidence.

Our sense-of-self forms progressively in the first 8 to 10 years of life, and becomes the foundation for everything we are and express after that time. What part, and how much of our sense-of-self is in harmony with unconditional love, and how much has fear at its core, is apparent in the way we behave, react and respond. The truth is that you cannot hide the nature of your sense-of-self from someone who has the awareness and clarity to see the fears that drive you. Should you act very confidently, when you are afraid, the lack of emotional balance you display will expose your fear to those who are aware. Your sense of yourself demonstrates its nature by the way you speak and use language, in your behaviour or respond, the way you move, your gestures and your posture. Even the nature of your health issues will expose the state of your sense-of-self over a lifetime. There are definitive associations between the negative disharmonious aspects of your sense-of-self, your behaviours, and your body.

The first strategic behaviours you are subject to are those of your mother, followed by those of your father. Her insecurities and the reactions and responses that they support, play a significant role in how you will see and relate to yourself and others in the future. Even should she have the conscious intention to be the perfect mother, tendency to be stressed, worried, unduly concerned and cannot cope, feels powerless and unhappy, dissatisfied and discontented, will undermine the positive development of her child's sense-of-itself. A child believes that it is the focus of its mother's worries and concerns and therefore also reason her negative emotions and feelings. Unable to distinguish itself from the emotional experience it has with its mother, a child begins to believe and accept that it must be the cause. When you were a child, you would have felt that the emotions, behaviour and attitude your mother displayed was about you and meant for you. Without knowing any better, you would have assumed that you were responsible for creating all of her stress, anxiety or unhappiness and so on. Consequently, that idea would have caused you to accept responsibility for them, even if you did not realise it at the time.

The expression of your authentic self, the needs and expectations essential for your survival, are initially spontaneous until you sense your mother's stress and anxiety, unhappiness or disappointment, fear and insecurity. With each new encounter, you become more aware of her negative state of mind, and this begins to influence your relationship with her. Your expectation was that the initial harmonious state with unconditional love would continue, but her behaviour and display of negative emotions became a challenge to that. Each successive exposure confirms your conclusion that somehow you must be the source, and therefore responsible for her stressed and unhappy state of mind. Subconsciously you begin to associate the spontaneous expression of your needs and expectations to her stressed and negative response. Your growing understanding that you must be the cause forces you to suppress your needs and expectations a little at the time. Withholding your natural needs and expectations and containing your behaviour is your attempt to avoid being the cause of your mother's distress. By now you are already accepting responsibility for her emotions. You also learn that a change in the way you present yourself, react and respond can lead to a different behaviour from her.

The obvious conclusions your innocent and naïve mind arrives at represent a child's interpretation to ensure its emotional and physical survival. Every fear-driven behaviour and intent by the parent also imply the kind of response required to avoid the threat that there will be negative consequences they hold.

- If your parent is annoyed by your presence, actions and responses, it implies that you should do your best to be invisible. You should avoid attracting their attention and becoming vulnerable to being blamed or criticised.
- If your parent is upset or angry because you ask for what you want, it implies that this expectation is not your entitlement or right. The response will compel you to suppress your wishes, desires, needs and expectations or become more aggressive in the expression of them
- If your parent becomes angry or abusive because you do not follow their rules and expectations, you are expected to obey without question, be submissive and compliant. You will suppress your intentions, free will, ideas, insights, conclusions, as well as your power and assertiveness, to avoid attracting anger and abuse.

There are an endless number of examples that will show that we adopt specific behaviours to deal with an emotional environment — our family — that does not accept us for who we authentically are as a person. We then believe that it is unacceptable to be who we are and thus become convinced that there is something wrong with us. The next phase is the suppression of our authentic self and a consistent effort throughout our lives to be what and who others expect us to be.

You also begin to realise that certain behaviours and expressions please your mother or father, and what will get you positive attention from them. In this case, suppression of your needs and expectations may get you a favourable response. Adopting the needs and expectations they want you to display will probably get you even more approval. Whenever your behaviour gets a positive reaction from either your mother or father, your mind recognises the pattern. Your awareness serves to lead you to adopt appropriate responses and reactions as a means to be loved and accepted — even if it is conditional. This process gives birth to your perception that your authentic self is unacceptable, and that strategic behaviours will make you feel accepted, loved and get you what you want. But, only as long as you can meet these conditions to the satisfaction of the person that created them in the first place.

Every response by a child to its mother's fears is to ensure it can maintain love and acceptance, trust and being wanted. A passive compliant child that pleases the parents to be loved and accepted will usually get endorsement and approval. A parent will judge a child to be difficult and challenging should it protest aggressively to the conditions set by its parent's behaviour. This aggression is its response to the threat of being separated from unconditional love and acceptance. The reason for the behaviours of both children is the same, but the contrast in their conduct puts them at opposites in the way their parents relate to them. In the perception of their parents, one is the good child and the other confronting and possibly obstinate. Neither child would be aware that it severely compromises its own emotional and mental well-being. In their fear of being abandoned or rejected, one child feels compelled to suppress itself to meet the parent's conditions and the other by aggressively demanding a response of love and acceptance that is unconditional. The outcome will be that the parents will treat each child according to the different conduct they displayed.

The strategic behaviours you now employ, are a direct reflection of the conditions encountered through the relationship dynamic with your parents. For a child, this will determine the nature of the belief systems that will ultimately determine its sense-of-self — in context, cause, intent and consequence. These elements will be explained in greater detail further on. They will be in of fear stepping outside the parameters defined by these new beliefs to avoid rejection and judgment, guilt and abandonment and so on. It may seem that an aggressively responding child is not fearful, but that it is acting in defiance of the consequences of its behaviour. However, fear is still the emotion that underpins the belief system that promotes its expression.

CONFLICT WITH YOUR SELF

Once a child begins to experience that it will not be loved and accepted for being its spontaneous, authentic and unique self, it feels instead that it has no choice but to suppress and hide it to be accepted. The negative response that their expression elicits a gradual process that causes an infant to feel fearful of its true nature and its spontaneous impulses. It is highly unlikely that a mother realises that her issues have this effect on her child's mind and sense of being. Believing that long as her conscious positive intent is the motivation for the interactions, she is convinced that what she is doing is right. Her general perception will be that it should feel loved, wanted and accepted by her because that is her intent.

The truth is that the emotional impact she has is much greater than she could ever imagine. Her issues, however, block her capacity to be more objective of her feelings, reactions and expression just as it is for any other adult. For example, she may not cope well with her new role as a mother, with unexpected issues or the responsibilities and demands that the child and motherhood place on her.

It is highly likely that it was the same for her mother when she was born. Even though she wanted to have a child, she may not have realised how its needs and expectations would challenge her and feel like an imposition on her. She may feel that everything in her life has become about her child and there is no space left for her. Her stress can create deep resentfulness of her baby as well as guilt for having these feelings. In many ways, she is reliving the same experience she had with her mother when she was a child. When she was young, it was always about her mother, and never about her. She feels that it would be easier if the baby did not depend on her so much and did not require so much care and attention. She is not aware that her child senses and knows it, just like she did when her mother behaved in the same way with her.

Even though she feels guilty about her selfish feelings, she cannot help putting her needs before those of the child and does so more and more as it matures. She does not realise it, but her child is growing up in the same way as she did and is likely to have the same issues. It will soon realise that its life, needs and expectations, are a burden for its mother. It will innocently take full responsibility by accepting the belief that its existence is a burden, and an unwanted responsibility. In an attempt to win its mother's love and affections, it has learned put its parent's needs before its own. As a result, its needs and expectation are now unlikely to be met.

The belief systems it has adopted out of its sense of guilt will effectively stop it from expressing its innate need for support, care, love and protection. It has learned that it is responsible for its mother's inability to cope, and feels guilt whenever she is stressed or upset. The child will also begin to take responsibility for her unfulfilled needs and the discontent of feeling denied. Part of its strategy to avoid being rejected by her or causing her pain is to remain sensitive to its mother's emotions and feelings. It also maintains a constant awareness of her fear-based needs and expectations. Learning how to read its parents' emotional state and knowing how to respond to it becomes an essential part of its strategic behaviour. It is in constant fear that anything it expresses or does may cause conflict with its mother or father. To maintain a "positive" relationship with its parents, it has no other choice but to suppress or be cautious in voicing what it wants and needs. The process of integrating negative beliefs takes about eight to ten years, but once it has incorporated them in its sense-of-self, the effect is powerful and complete.

The experience a child has of itself depends not only on its unique nature but also greatly on the emotional dynamic created by its family. The development of its sense-of-self depends on the kind of emotions, feelings and behaviours the mother and father display. The parents do not realise that they as individuals with their attitudes, actions and responses act as psychological mirrors for their child. Every word and interaction expressed by the parent cause the child to think that it is feeling and seeing itself. If the parent's sense-of-self were in harmony with their innate nature and therefore unconditional, they would also automatically connect to the intrinsic nature of their child. Being in acceptance of its original being without feeling a fear-driven need to change or reject it. If the parent's behaviours and attitudes are disharmonious because of their fears and insecurities, their child will feel that its authentic and spontaneous self is unacceptable and disapproved of by them. In that case, the parents will feel the need to impose new behaviours, values and standards.

Once these children reach adulthood, they still feel the lack of entitlement to have attention, ask for what they want and have their needs fulfilled. These beliefs can make them either become pleasers who put others before themselves to get attention without having to ask. Alternatively, they can become incredibly selfish by putting themselves before all others for fear of missing out. Their need for love and acceptance will be intense, and they may not cope well with the prospect of rejection or the expectation having to meet the requirements and expectations of others.

Pleasers tend to edit themselves before they speak to avoid being responsible for upsetting, offending, or cause any other form of negative response from others. If they instead use aggression to have their needs met, they may act in an uncaring manner without any sensitivity to what others may feel because they see themselves as the victim. Pleasers tend to keep their true feelings, thoughts and intents hidden to avoid potential confrontation or conflict. Because of that, you will never know what goes on in their minds, but their behaviour will always reflect their issues. Should either the pleaser or the aggressive victim become parents, it will be inevitable that the next generation will inherit their fears and insecurities.

LOST IN BEHAVIOUR

Achieving our emotional and physical independence through adulthood is a significant milestone in our existence because it fulfils both the innate intent of our consciousness and it is a necessary part of our emotional and physical survival. By defining ourselves as mature adults, we usually believe we have entered the realm of intellectual, emotional and physical independence, freedom, self-determination and responsibility. We expect that adulthood allows us to be masters of our universe and create our own destiny; at least, that is how we would like it to be. More than often the experience of life in adulthood is not anything like we thought it would be.

For many, this idealised vision already begins to crumble long before we reach adulthood. After experiencing intense emotional difficulties getting through childhood and then as teenagers, many of us struggle to create an optimistic vision of the future. Frequently, emotional issues have already spoiled our education and work opportunities. Once we are adults, our past already impinges on our future possibilities and limits our options in life. It takes a strong and wilful mind to take the steps necessary to overcome this.

Often, those have had a childhood without abusive or violent incidents or raised by passive parents will view their upbringing as normal or perfect. They do not realise that aggression, violence or verbal abuse are not necessary for fears and insecurities to be played out. Passively behaving parents who on the surface appear loving and caring may possess severe emotional limitations and be very insecure. Growing up with any fear, even if quietly expressed, still, has a negative influence on children. Many do not realise their issues until they are adults and engage in serious intimate relationships. Even though we may not be aware of it but our issues are present in every part of life.

The undeniable truth is that fears and insecurities will always manifest themselves in our lives; there is no escape from a fearful sense-of-self.

The notion of having had a perfect childhood will be a handicap if you want to resolve your issues because you are likely to look in all the wrong places for the causes. It is highly unlikely that your parents were perfect and had no fears or insecurities and therefore their relationship with you was unconditional. Assuming anything else leaves you with a difficult to resolve conclusion. If your childhood is not the origin of your present issues, then you have to accept that you were born with your fears and insecurities. Consequently, there is little you can do to change yourself because according to what you believe, they are a fixed part of you. Children are not born with the fear-motivated behaviours and attitudes they display as adults. These are also not caused by one event in your life like an accident, an intense emotional experience or a death in the family unless they occurred in the first eight years of our lives. It is more likely that your parents have fears and no matter how well intended and passive they may have been, they are the origin of your issues. Always remember that they too are the victims of their childhood experiences, and so being disappointed, angry or critical of them is not justified.

Do not think you are the only one with problems in life. Everyone has to face their fears in the process of living their life. Our issues appear in relationships and work, social activities and sport, but most importantly in our relationship with our self. Our fears may seem to be entirely different in each of these areas of life, but often they are a product of the same negative belief systems within our sense-of-self. For example, the issue of being unacceptable may appear differently at work than it does in relationships, or say sport yet the underlying reason can cross all of these.

When you find yourself back in situations with characters that mimic the original emotional conditions under which you accepted your negative beliefs, they will act as triggers that will cause you to re-experience your childhood fears. The feelings this will bring up in you will serve as a springboard for strategic behaviour. As you mature your responses will become more sophisticated, but it will still have the same basis and intent that it had when you were a child. Part of growing into an adult is to learn to socialise and to know how to interact in a manner acceptable to others. So, when your initial behaviour in childhood became unacceptable, you would have evolved new strategies that saved you from being judged or criticised. Such as passive-aggressive, assertive or manipulative actions and responses for example. Alternatively, you may use guilt and project yourself as the victim, thereby making others responsible for what you feel you miss out on or denied. You might get away with it in friendships, but in personal relationships, these behaviours commonly lead to problems and eventually conflict. Not so strangely, in a corporate environment or workplace, aggressive or manipulative interactions that get positive financial results for the company will often be rewarded, instead of judged as morally inappropriate.

Someone who is an aggressive perfectionist will find life similarly challenging. Their perfectionist expectations convert into criticism and judgment of themselves and others, which makes them appear demanding and hard to please. In their job, however, this behaviour can create a very different outcome. These personalities are usually very controlling as well as high achievers and hard workers. Perfectionists typically want their achievements to be based on their values and ideas of perfection and need to be in control of every aspect of the process they engage. Their need for recognition and approval to have their idea of perfection validated makes them vulnerable to being taken advantage of in working environments.

For fear of being judged as inadequate, they are unable to refuse any demands made on them, and always strive to meet expectations correctly. Always in fear of not doing anything well enough, and always self-critical and dissatisfied with their work, they toil long hours to meet the demands of their superiors. They tend to work hard to achieve more than what they are required to do. Consequently, they will frequently sacrifice their emotional and physical well-being and other things in their life in their quest for approval by being perfect.

These behaviours are tactical and highly sophisticated and always find justification and purpose in the environments in which they seek to be recognised. When your strategies get you what you feel you need such as recognition, reward and celebration, it becomes hard to accept that they could be destructive.

In fact, the prospect of giving up behaviours that will bring positive results can be confronting and create intense fear of being powerless. This fear can paralyse your intent to deal with your issues and the negative beliefs that underpin them. This issue is no exception for the perfectionist whose strategies creates positive outcomes at work, but for whom these same behaviours will cause problems in his or her relationships. Once fears control our intent, actions and responses the impact on our lives will always be negative. They will naturally be resistant to losing the emotional tools that they have learned to rely on to get what they want and need. Just like others who resist confronting their issues, perfectionists will always find justification for their behaviour and the beliefs that drive them. After all, they trusted in them to avoid failure, rejection or judgement, as well as to acquire success and recognition. The fear of living without strategic behaviours can make personal change a confronting challenge.

We do not understand the power and influence of our intentions when we interact with others. The success of our attitude and behaviour does not only depend on how others react but more profoundly on the belief-systems that support them. We base most of our understanding of the psychological dynamic between us and others on what our parents taught us through their behaviours. The emotional history of our family also reflects social, cultural and religious influences. Trying to understand yourself is hard when the only resources at your disposal are the distorted or simplistic notions about life and relationships you learned in childhood. These traditional beliefs and ideas may at times have a core of truth, but there is never a clear enough explanation to use them beneficially. More than often they only serve to distort the facts or provide an unsatisfactory explanation for human behaviour. Accepting them as truth can stop us from asking questions that would give us an emotional understanding of ourselves.

There is the general belief that we are not responsible for the events and circumstances to which we fall victim. Whenever we need to substantiate the reasons for a negative event, we assume that one party must be responsible or that it was an accident. Just about everything, the media presents us with implies that this has to be the case. The message we receive indicates that the victim is innocent and the aggressor is to blame or that others or the world are responsible for our experience of life. Our indoctrination of this idea starts at school and continues throughout our lives. This perspective acts as evidence that our self-power and control in life is extremely limited or in many circumstances non-existent. The belief in our responsibility for what others feel has become so deeply ingrained in our psyche, that to hold someone responsible for their unhappy or negative state of mind, will usually elicit a strong reaction of denial and an explanation that outside influences are responsible. If held liable for loss or disaster in life or relationships they will likely defend their innocence and find something or someone else to blame. Most are convinced that they would not, or could not, have possibly created unwanted experiences. The argument always sounds reasonable in that; Why would anyone deliberately do anything to oneself to cause pain and suffering?

The belief that our existence is subject to our environment or other is the main reason for our perspective on how we manifest our lives and life experiences. The concept that we are the creators of our personal and shared life experience is absent in almost every society.

The truth is that naturally, no one would consciously choose a life of unhappiness, pain and suffering. Our instinctive emotional and physical responses for survival are a part of us for that very reason. It proves however that there are emotional forces within us that motivate us to ignore our instincts and follow an alternative path of expression and choices that lead to undesirable outcomes in our lives. It is also true that we can only understand the actual reasons and causes for these negative intentions and the life experiences they manifest if we accept that we must be the source.

Regardless of the unique and different life situations, relationships and events we experience, we are the only consistent presence in all of them. From that fact alone, we can assume that we are the prime contributors to our life and relationship experiences. Add to this that every event and evolvement is a product of our choices and decisions, consciously or subconsciously, then there is positive proof that we are the originators of our life experiences. If further to this, you consider that each person has an individual experience of the same event, it becomes clear that we seamlessly create our reality. The truth is that individually, and collectively, we are always the creators of our experience of life. That puts the power and control of life directly into our hands.

When we say that we are not involved and responsible, it is because we do not know nor recognise the effect that the negative beliefs of our sense-of-self have on us and in the world. Consequently, we do not take into account the subconscious negative intent of our fear-based beliefs, needs, feelings and strategic behaviour. In doing so, we would know how we are involved in every one of our life-experiences. We would be able to accept emotional responsibility necessary to lead us to self-change and positive life. Gaining self-awareness and realisation of the nature of your subconscious mind is a major stride towards the transformation of your sense-of-self.

DEPENDING ON STRATEGIES

Once the illusions created by negative beliefs become the truth of who we are and determine our needs and behaviour, they will also control how we express ourselves. They also become the framework that we depend on for our emotional survival, and they have become, however flawed, our fundamental connection with love, acceptance and trust. As long as we meet the perceived conditions through our aggressive, passive or defensive strategic behaviours, we live with the promise that we will be loved and accepted, even if we do not recognise it is conditional.

Behaviour and attitude represent your most recognisable psychological expression for others and is commonly judged to be representative of who you are. The primary reason for this is that they — just like you — identify themselves by their behaviour, likes and dislikes.

Unaware your negative beliefs in control, you fail to recognise that your behaviour has become tactical and complement those with whom you are involved. The assumption is that, just like they do, your conduct and attitude represents who you authentically are. In fact, you are responding to the fear of being seen by others the way you believe yourself to be. It should be obvious that when fear controls your mind, it is not possible to give a voice to our authentic self. Having learned in childhood to anticipate that giving expression to your authentic self will provoke a negative response such as criticism and rejection you will actively suppress that part of yourself. The moment fear is active, you are not likely that you to recognise that these fear-based beliefs are illusions.

Even when we deliberately try to adopt new behaviours because we believe that these will be more effective in getting what we want or avoid confronting situations, we are still controlled by our subconscious fears. We hope our new form of expression will serve us better, and they may until they too will fail. When they do, the consequences of the fears that drive them will find realisation. You can only resolve your fears by releasing the beliefs that they are their source.

For example, learning behaviours and strategies so that you can confront and be assertive in negotiations or conflict, can be helpful and provide insight into the personal dynamics that take place in these conditions. Without understanding and dealing with the origin of the fear-based reason why you could not face potentially conflicting or aggressive confrontations in the first place, they will remain a part of your mind. You will just be a little better at managing them because of your newfound confidence in your newly learned strategies. The intent within your fear will not disappear, nor rest. If not dealt with, they will always be lurking in the background of your mind. There will always be a critical situation, for which you will not have the appropriate strategies, and then your fears will surface and take control, with the consequences to follow. The absence of fear of confrontation, conflict, argument or asking for what you want would allow you would deal with any negotiation with a different mind-set and subsequently get the result you want without stress or anxiety. You would learn the complexities of the dynamic of negotiations with confidence with the capacity to handle any situation.

Our inability to see who we are beyond our feelings, thoughts, perception and behaviour prevents us from understanding how they are a part of us. Were we to take an objective view of what the effect of our behaviour has on others and theirs on us; we would be more likely to make a step towards emotional self-responsibility. Unfortunately, the prospect of accepting that we are the source of our life experience usually triggers the fear of having to admit that we have faults, weaknesses and failings. We fear that by exposing shortcomings, we would be vulnerable to the judgment of others, and therefore instead resist acknowledging our fears. However, by accepting our fears — without judgment or blame — we put ourselves in a position of control take ownership of the source for our life issues. Our capacity to accept beliefs to support our survival indicates we also have the ability to change or release them. As the owners of our fears and the creators of our life experiences, we are therefore capable of personal change and cease to be victims of our fears.

Our biggest disappointment is not that we let others down, but how we are a disappointment to ourselves.

Self-acknowledgement of the reasons for your issues moves you towards self-realization and awareness. The next step is to look within yourself, at the nature of your sense of being by taking ownership of who you believe yourself to be — your sense-of-self. Your choice to accept responsibility for what you manifest in your life will be your first act of true self-empowerment. Possibly for the first time, you will claim back the power you gave to others and the world, and take charge over your life — the past, present and future.

Chapter 10

OUR GREATEST FEAR

Probably one of the greatest crimes ever committed against human consciousness, is the separation of spirit, mind and body as distinct entities, through centuries of empirical influences — laws, religion, commerce and science. The ongoing negation of the significance of the intent, validity and purpose and meaning of consciousness denies humanity as a whole an integrated understanding of the nature of our spiritual, mental, emotional and physical being. In the absence of this knowledge, we exist in a general state of fear and as a consequence live our emotional illusions as if they are a reality. Our distorted perception causes us to be lost in the material reality of the world because we have learned to rely on it to provide solutions for the emotional vacuum created by our fears.

Unaware that we are the originators of our life, we believe that the events we encounter and the people confronting us are the reasons for our stress, anxiety, disappointment or anger. These emotions will be present when you feel you cannot speak your truth, face your partner or boss with your opinions or feelings, needs or expectations, rights and entitlements and so on. These feelings are present in your anticipation of failure, or when you feel embarrassed or ashamed. You sense them when you expect to get something wrong and make mistakes or in your hesitation when making new choices. It can take a grip on your mind when sudden and unexpected changes or new events storm into your life. Its destructive force is active when you judge yourself for who you are and put yourself down. They drive you when you want to prove yourself better or superior to others. It is your motivation when you try to be the centre of attention or get others to like you and be your friend. It controls your behaviour and self-expression when it is your greatest concern that what you say or do will upset, offend or anger others. The reality is that in all of us fear rears its emotional presence in too many ways to ignore it.

IN FEAR OF LOVE

There is a core fear at the basis of all of our fears. We acquire our greatest insecurity at the very beginning of our life. The influence and control it will have over the way we will live our lives are enormous. The extent of its destructive effect on our consciousness depends on the intensity and quality of adverse influences of our childhood experiences. Its capacity to dominate our minds also relies on our suppression of the original and innate nature of our unique consciousness.

Once we have been forced to distrust and therefore reject much of our authentic self, we have no choice but to accept that love, acceptance and trust must be conditional. In our perception, this is the only kind of love to which we are entitled and can expect to receive. Our naïve understanding of the relationship with our parents now determines how we can act, respond and react to them. Their interaction with us has succeeded in generating distrust unconditional love and so on. The separation from the kind of love we expected and depended on even before we were born creates a division in our sense-of-self. Where first only unconditional love and acceptance resided, we suddenly have to meet conditions to be loved and accepted. Not surprisingly, with it comes the fear of failing this expectation. Conditional love and acceptance, etc., become the reasons and cause for our greatest fear because on every level of our consciousness we cannot accept an existence bereft of unconditional love acceptance and trust.

The state of internal separation conditional love and acceptance create in us, represent exclusion from our Spiritual Origin without which we cannot maintain a harmonious sense of being. We become like rudderless ships on the sea of our consciousness without any idea of who we truly are, lacking both purpose and direction. Without knowing and understanding the nature of our unique being, we cannot give our lives a meaningful direction. Our lack of drive and motivation or aggression and domination exposes our sense of insignificance and the feeling that our existence does not matter. Our negative behaviours and attitudes are evidence of this state of mind as are the consequences this have in our life. The fears held by our consciousness impacts on others and the environment and became indistinguishable from our sense-of-self. These core fears translate into behaviours, actions and choices which have a predetermined intent the consequences of which determine the state of our lives.

All of us innately sense that fulfilling the potential of our consciousness depends on being in harmony with our Origin and through this, we will know the eternity of our existence.

By living our lives in unconditional love — in the absence of fear — we can become aware and feel this harmonious connection with the essence of our spirit.

The need, desire and expectation to feel and experience love, acceptance and trust that are unconditional, are incessant in every human consciousness. Emotionally, it is the core driving force in our life but when absent, underpins the creation of our issues. In life situations, where love, acceptance and trust become conditional our emotional state becomes one of fear. Our subconscious naturally senses that we cannot exist without being at one with the essence of our spiritual being — unconditional love. Therefore, fear becomes the controlling force in our minds influencing every encounter in which love, acceptance or trust are involved which is virtually everything. The fear of living in the absence of our essence acts as a constant emotional compass for our highest state of being and represents an irresistible force in our consciousness. Our issues in life are a sign that we have strayed away from our path of spiritual development and growth and a warning to take account of the sense of who we believe we are. We need to think and act from a place of 'being' instead of defaulting to acts of 'doing' to resolve the problems we have with ourselves and in life.

We are in emotional disharmony and contradiction with the core of our being when unconditional love is no longer ours to have and feel. The childhood experiences that caused us to believe that we are not good enough, disappointment, a burden, too demanding, expecting too much, etc. convince us that we are unlovable, unwanted and unacceptable. Insecurities overtake our minds, once we accept these judgements to be true about who we are. To resolve this dilemma, we look outside of us to others to make us feel what we believe we are not. Convinced that we are unlovable or unacceptable, we want someone to love us and accept us to have proof that we are not who we believe we are. If we feel insignificant, we want to praise and recognition to prove otherwise. We become entirely dependent on others to provide us with what we feel is missing or non-existent within us. Our dependence on others goes hand in hand with our reliance on our strategic behaviours. They are the only way we know how to fulfil our emotional needs due to our separation from unconditional love and acceptance etc.

The positive outcomes from the use of strategies fool us into believing that this is the only way that we can get what we want. Nothing could be further from the truth. First of all, the fact that you need to use a strategy already proves that your conviction that you are not entitled to receive what you need or want. It leaves you with no choice but to repeat the behaviour over and again in every new situation, to try and create the same result. You will always fear that you will be denied if your strategies fail. In spite of the faith, you may have in your strategies, the negative beliefs that drive them will always be in contradiction to the essence of your being and therefore your authentic self. Ultimately this puts you consistently in a disharmonious state with your core values, with others and the world.

TRAPPED IN CONDITIONAL LOVE

Our negative personal beliefs separate us from unconditional love and do not support our authentic self and yet we cling to them without apparent rational reasons. All the unhappiness, pain and suffering in the world does not appear to be enough motivation to make us let go of the negativity that drives them. It seems that the emotional force that keeps us from releasing them must be greater and more influential than our desire and conscious intent to dismiss them from our mind.

If we are to understand the reason for our attachment to our fear based convictions, we need to appreciate the nature and power that it has over us. It is clear that all of us have great difficulty changing our behaviours, feelings, perception or pessimistic thoughts. You can try and alter any of these by telling yourself that you should not behave, feel or think a certain way but that is unlikely to stop them. Negative, pessimistic and destructive thoughts and feelings are almost impossible to dismiss or control, like unwanted visitors that refuse to leave. You can use various methods or distractions to make yourself feel different by but usually these are of little or no help in the long term. They have the potential to add to your problems by creating a self-critical mentality that reinforces your awareness of the issues in question and may cause you to go into denial and greater avoidance.

Avoiding your negative feelings and thoughts do not allow you to develop an understanding why and how you came to have them in the first place. Negative beliefs can exert so much emotional influence that they take control of every aspect of someone's life. The sense of powerlessness this creates can lead to creating justifications, excuses or blame to explain their state of mind and attitude in life. Even if they attempt to create changes in their feelings, thoughts or behaviour is likely they will soon return to their original state because it offers greater security to them. It is obvious that logic and reasoning based on our current understanding of the expression of human consciousness cannot provide an emotionally acceptable answer for the reasons we cling so desperately to our issues.

To illustrate this dilemma, imagine for a moment that you are going on a long journey by boat, innocently trusting that it cannot sink no matter what kind of calamity it will encounter. A big storm comes, and you are washed overboard without anyone noticing. Even though the boat is not far from shore, you cling to a piece of flotsam as you see your ship sail away. How important do you think that piece of debris will be to you if you are convinced that you do not have the strength to swim and reach the shore? Would cling on to it for dear life because you believe it is the only thing that will save you? Your fears and their strategized behaviours are just like that piece of flotsam.

When you do not receive unconditional love, the conditions you will feel forced to accept are an emotional trap. The reservations your parents place on their relationship with you, cause you to doubt and distrust your innate qualities and ultimately reject your unique and authentic self, little by little. Your subconscious rejection of your core values and unique, authentic self and the subsequent adoption of strategic behaviours, are your grasp for a means to make yourself loveable and acceptable to your parents. You do not realise you are sacrificing your authentic-self and what it will cost you in the future. These inevitable choices are your way to emotionally survive even if love, acceptance and trust will now be conditional. Your fear-based beliefs are like the flotsam you desperately cling to for your survival. It may appear like a good choice, but your emotional dependence on it will negate any apparent benefits.

As a result, you will develop an inner identity that may have very little in common with who you authentically are. Your newly acquired and distorted sense-of-self will now and in the future, determine who you believe you are. Whether you are worthy and deserving of love, acceptance and trust or not, whether you matter or not and are of value or not. The acceptance of conditional love will redefine the nature of your being by distorting your inner-perspective of who you believe yourself to be. This view will also suppress the potential of your intellectual and emotional resources, capacities, talents and abilities, etc.

Growing up with the emotional conditions set by your parents, you do not realise that your parents are two people out of billions on the planet and that their state of mind is unique to them and a product of their family upbringing. By accepting their version of reality, as your truth, you have unconsciously accepted illusions as if they represent the truth of who you are. Their negative beliefs are as much a distortion and an illusion for them as they will have become for you.

Once negative beliefs have become the only thing that you trust will support you, they represent your only resource for love, acceptance and trust. As a result, the only love you have learned to accept as real has to match the conditions held by your negative beliefs. If love were unconditional, you would probably not recognise it for what it represents and reject it. The conditional love you have learned to accept in childhood is the only love that you will know and trust because it is in congruence with your conditional beliefs.

FEAR, ILLUSIONS AND UNHAPPINESS

Fixated by a distorted sense of yourself, your altered perception will unconsciously create evidence that your fears and insecurities are real. You do not realise that you provide your own proof through the outcomes you create in life with your intent, choices and decisions. You are not aware that your negative belief systems determine the type of decisions you will make, that it shapes your attractions and resentments, thoughts and feelings. To you, it will feel normal to be the way you are. Your mind, distorted by fears, draws you into situations and brings you in contact with people that are a reflection of your sense-of-self — regardless whether your belief systems are negative or harmonious. If your fears influence your relationships, then you will be attracted to and attract those who have fears and insecurities that complement your own. Being involved with them will cause your fears and issues will begin to play out in their presence.

Believing you are not good enough, not what you think others expect you to be or not performing to expectations and so on will generate stressful and anxious emotions. In this state of mind, you will depend entirely on the success of your strategic behaviours for your sense of security and happiness. However, your fear of failure, embarrassment and criticism, for instance, will always be lurking in the shadows of your mind because you can never be sure that your strategic behaviour will succeed. If for example, you believe you do not matter, you will be drawn to be part events and with people that can provide proof of your significance. You may feel the need to associate with wealthy successful people because you convinced yourself that by association you would be special. But since these beliefs are a part of you no amount of external influences will change how you see yourself. The experience you create by mixing with people you believe to be significant is nothing but an illusion. No one can make you special but you. This about who you believe you are, and not about convincing others of who you are. In one form or another, we are all guilty of this because we all have fears that are represented by our negative beliefs. The negative beliefs you hold about yourself will cause you to get involved with others who allow you to prove the opposite to yourself to yourself. Should you feel unlikable and unwanted, you will choose to associate with those who display their interest and approval of you. Your passive approach to finding the resolution to your negative feelings is evident in your effort to avoid any people or situations that challenge your insecurities.

One of the most difficult things to fully realise is that every person around you is living with their version of negative belief systems. The reality is that everyone has issues and fears and therefore everyone employs strategic behaviours to survive emotionally in the process of living their lives. The seamless attraction we have or those with complementary issues to ours stops us from recognising that fear is in control and we are not. Our lack of awareness of who we believe we are as opposed to who we are meant to be, make our negative feelings emotions thoughts and perception and strategic behaviours natural to us. Many people find it hard to accept the idea that they could be different to who they think they are. They have integrated their issues so seamlessly, that the truth of who they are has become invisible. We do not see the wood for the trees because of our issues. Our minds are skewed to see life and living in the context of the beliefs we hold in our sense-of-self. They shape our perception and reinforce what we believe to be true within in us. It is easy to judge life situations by applying simple principles of cause and effect when you cannot see the deeper emotional forces at work within your own mind. But, by doing so you will blame others and see yourself as being innocent or a victim, and you would probably be wrong either way.

The most typical example for this happens every day in virtually everyone's life. For example, if person 'A' were to say something to person 'B' that they became emotionally upset about, others observing this would likely blame person 'A' for being responsible for how 'B' feels. Our reasoning is that because 'A' said something that 'B' was negatively affected by that 'A' must be guilty and "B' the victim. Our family environment and society teach us to believe that we are responsible and to blame for what others feel. This idea creates the impression that we all somehow have the power to give people particular feelings and create emotions in them. This concept also proposes that you as the victim of this, have no control or influence over how others affect you. People, who have negative beliefs that make them feel emotionally vulnerable and fragile are very likely to be easily upset over a variety of things. Does that mean that those who have done or said something by which they negatively affected are responsible? Or, could it be that the negative, fearful beliefs they hold themselves are the cause for what they feel? It should now be obvious that the latter has to be true, but that is not how we tend to see in our relationships.

Once you accept that you are responsible for what your parents feel and fear, every relationship you have as an adult will involve a degree of guilt by you. Fearful of being guilty should someone feel uncomfortable, challenged or criticised by what you say, you find yourself editing you express to protect others from their fears. Your subconscious strategy is to protect them from their fears but thereby demands that you suppress what you want to say, think or feel. Your distorted but well-intended approach does not support them in the way you think. By accommodating their issue with hearing your truth, you help them to stay in their fearful state and ensure that they never have to look at the reasons for them. You are in the same situation in that you do not have to face up to your guilt issues as long as you do not speak your mind.

It is a mistake to believe that you are caring and protective by accommodating their fears and accepting responsibility for their emotional reactions. By protecting them from their issues, you are creating an environment in which they will not have to confront their fears and insecurities. Your fear of being blamed and held responsible for the disappointment, feeling disrespected, feeling unacceptable or anger and so on in others will control your behaviour in all of your relationships. You may explain your behaviour as being 'protective and caring', but the underlying reasons are your fear of being blamed and feeling guilty. Your effort to avoid being held responsible for the negative feelings of others causes you to suppress your authentic self. Guilt will not allow yourself to express your spontaneous thoughts, feelings and intentions. You fear that by doing so, you will attract the same response that led to the original reasons for your over-responsibility. As a result, you do not deal with the guilt and consequential behaviour you feel in your dynamic with those who believe that they are vulnerable and fragile. They will never have a reason to change as long as you accommodate their weaknesses and insecurities and potentially will spend the rest of their life in fear. If you do not wish this for yourself then why would you allow this happen to others?

You may have always thought that negative events and encounters in your life were created by coincidence, random people or by misfortune. Every experience you have in life is a result of the manifestation of the intentions inherent in the beliefs that make up your sense-of-self. Intents are the most powerful force within our consciousness. Your sense of yourself, positive or negative, will always exert its intent through the beliefs it holds. The feelings generated by the intentions will drive you into passive or aggressive action. It does not matter whether a belief we hold is real or Illusionary, the intents they hold are the core emotional forces that control every aspect of your perception, emotions and self-expression and thereby create our life experience. Your life and the people in it, are always a reflection of who you believe yourself to be.

Whether we are aware of it or not, the innate intent and desire to exist in harmony with unconditional love, acceptance and trust are the spiritual forces at the centre of our consciousness. Our innate attraction to be at one with the essence of our spirit or unconditional love and acceptance creates an inevitable prejudice within our being. Once we deviate from this unconditional inner-state as our truth, we enter the realm of fear and insecurity.

Without unconditional love as a reference point for our consciousness, we would not recognise the difference between love and fear, good or bad and negative or positive emotions. On feeling these emotions, we would act them out indifferent to whether they represent something positive or negative. They would be feelings or emotions without any particular value or meaning. Being without a reference point for our state of being, we would have nothing to measure the emotional state of our consciousness. Our conduct would be indifferent to what we feel about ourselves and others as we would not be aware whether we act out of a negative or positive state of mind. We would not be able to differentiate between fear and love. The fact that we experience good and bad, negative or positive emotions and values are evidence that this reference point — unconditional love, acceptance and trust — exists in us is an innate and intrinsic aspect of our spirit-consciousness.

Chapter II

YOUR EMOTIONAL BODY

Were we in perfect harmony with our essence we could expect to live life without fear. Our Spirit, Mind and Body would operate in perfect harmonious synchronicity and make our existence an uplifting and expansive experience. This state of being would not only bring emotional and psychological benefits, but it would also promote a high level of physical health and wellness. For most people, this ideal state is unlikely to be a reality because we are wedded too tightly to fear-based beliefs. We do not realise that the negative emotional states are a product of our fears are detrimental to our emotional and physical health.

We are not only a product of the family paradigm in which we grew up but also of the culture and history of our race and nationality. Any experience we have in childhood that causes us to suppress our authentic self and disconnect from unconditional love will ultimately be in disharmony with our spirit as well as our bodies. Fear as an emotion creates adverse pressure on the body which is felt mostly in the stomach but then also affects various organs. The extent, intensity and duration of any fear play a significant role in how the body will react in the long term. Specifically, our bodies are a product of the genetic composition of that of our parents and the generations that went before. The past generational, environmental and psychological influences have a profound impact on our mind and our bodies. Just like our physical genetics, these fears and the illusions that support them are passed on from one generation to the next. Right now, your mind and your body are at the end of the generational chain of your family, but once you have children you will pass on both your physical as well as your emotional 'genes' to them'.

HOW THE BODY MEETS YOUR SPIRIT

Our bodies and minds have a metaphorical relationship where many of our emotional processes have a physical representation in our bodies. The built-in resilience of your body is a property of its innate intent to exist and express itself at the highest possible level of health. The immune system in concert with the organs to are employed to assure the body's highest possible functionality and well-being. The kind of emotional experiences you create in your life will determine that state of your feelings which will then impact your body positively or negatively. Negative influences can have a detrimental impact on particular organs such as the kidney adrenals, pancreas and liver, causing our immune system to spring into action. This natural reaction to anything emotionally disharmonious and therefore physically toxic ensures that we seek to orient our mind and body towards greater harmonious well-being and health. This response parallels with the natural reaction our consciousness has to fear by generating negative thoughts and feelings. These emotions are a sign that we are in a disharmonious state of mind.

The way your body maintains optimum health is very similar to the manner in which the mind directs you to your highest sense of being. Your consciousness seeks its highest possible state of being by guiding you to an existence without fear. The order of influence of the different elements that make up our physical and conscious presence is your spirit's influence over the mind and then the mind over the body. The natural disposition of our spirit-consciousness is to be in harmony with unconditional love and acceptance acts upon our body through the mind. Your body has physical reference points that have a context in its relationship with the mind. If there is a deviation from these, in our mind or our body, each has the resources needed to alert us that something is amiss. These inner-connections assure that the body is always entangled with our emotions. Whenever negative life experiences cause fear-based emotions, such as powerlessness, anxiety or stress, etc., it will affect both our bodies and minds.

We have difficulty recognising the profound connection that exists between our physical body and mind because the environment we grew up in convinced us that they are separate entities. We are prepared to accept that our headaches, stomach aches and back pain can come from the stress and worry of our life situations but we seek to address the physical symptoms as a resolution, thereby ignoring psychological causes. The skin — our largest sensory organ — has probably the most obvious metaphorical relationship with the emotional mind. One of the primary functions of the skin is to provide the capacity for feeling in a material world. Our ability to touch and feel gives us the means to be physically aware of the three-dimensional reality we live in and define the nature of our physical being.

The sensations provided by our feelings and emotions give us the capacity to be aware of our psychological environment. The sensory function of both our skin as well as every other part of our body is similar in their intent as our emotional self. Each makes us aware of how we relate to either a physical or emotional environment that we are in contact with or occupy. Energetically, the vibration or resonance of their intents is very similar, and this allows it to form a metaphorical relationship between them. In a metaphorical relationship between them, the intentions of our emotional senses are mimicked by our bodies. This connection also provides a pathway for emotional issues to manifest in our bodies the physical form of a disease. It is therefore not a surprise then that many pathologies of the skin are a direct result of emotional trauma, stress and fear and often appear when particular emotions are re-triggered.

Many of our chronic illnesses can be traced back to stress and fear related emotional states — cancer, kidney, liver, stomach and gallbladder issues for example. Even then, it is likely the focus of the treatment will only deal with the physical side of the problem. When a body is in crisis and requires urgent medical attention, this is entirely understandable, but that is usually as far as it will ever go. We tend to ignore the emotional aspect of our physical diseases, and therefore they go untreated.

Considering that the onset of most diseases is not well understood or unknown, the exclusion of the emotional mind as a considerable influence on our physical health does not make much sense. Acute observation of known physical responses to fear-related emotional states should make it obvious that our bodies do not exist in isolation of our mind or for that matter, our spirit. In our desire to understand the nature of our whole being we have separated them into discrete elements, which have over time become so partitioned by science and other influences that they are now generally viewed and dealt with as different entities. As a result, we do not recognise that every part of us functions as an integrated and interrelated whole. There is, however, a hierarchy in how our conscious being expresses itself into the three-dimensional reality of our world and our bodies.

Our spirit is the seat of our consciousness and holds the essence of our being and contains the benchmark for our existence— unconditional love, acceptance and trust.

Spirit consciousness contains the unique nature and qualities of our mind — our emotions, intelligence, talents and abilities, passions and desires, fantasy and imagination, attractions and fascinations.

We define the innate capacities of consciousness by our intellect, creativity, instinct, intuition, emotions feelings, beliefs, inspirations, potential, aspirations, curiosity, inventiveness, imagination, fantasies, talents and abilities, learning, memory, logic and reasoning.

We exist with the intent is to evolve, change, learn, experience, feel, to know, be aware, understand, to invent, create, and manifest

Our sense-of-self or ego is the container, if you like, of all of these elements, and its shape is defined by the belief systems that form it. Our minds comprise our self-beliefs, both positive and negative, which play a determining role in how we will see, feel and express ourselves because of who we believe ourselves to be.

WHEN THE BODY SPEAKS

The voice with which our emotional mind speaks through our body is not random in its effect on us but follows pre-determined pathways that represent metaphorical connections between body and mind. Every part of our body has one or more function, and therefore each carries an intent. In fact, since there is no part of us without intent, every part of our body can also be related to our emotional mind. The function of something also implies its intent and therefore its unique 'resonance', emotionally and physically. The different qualities of the intentions embedded in a belief-system possess an intrinsic resonance, just like the functional purpose of any part of our body. When expressing a belief-system that is harmonious in its emotional intent, it acts as a positive influence on those areas of the body, which have a similar functional resonance. These positive emotions will then promote greater health and well-being because it acts as an enhancement on the functional capacity of that part of the body. If a belief is fear-based, it will resonate out of phase with our core essence, and therefore also with those elements of the body with which it should be in harmony. The disharmony between mind and body will inhibit the functionality of the body, and this can over time result in disease affecting our physical health.

For example, if you feel stress or anxiety, it shows that your mind is in emotional conflict about issues related to powerlessness. These negative emotions will interact with your body and potentially create physical discomfort. The part of the body metaphorically representative of power is the area occupied by our sacrum and the organs in the space between your hips. The sacrum supports your spine and is the triangular bone that sits between your hip bones. Your body depends on the sacrum as a central support system between your hips and is the seat for your spine. Without it, you would fall apart and be physically powerless and immobilised. The sacrum provides your body with a platform for stable anchoring points for your muscles, which in turn allows spine and legs to have strength in their actions. The sacrum is also the location of your power or "chi" as referred to in Chinese medicine and martial arts. The belief that you are powerless and helpless result in feeling that you have no control over your life have the effect of weakening the core strength of the body. This relationship between our mind and body can lead to hip and lower back issues and also with the organs in that part of your body. In women, this emotional state can lead to problems with the uterus and ovaries. These physical problems can appear when there are emotional issues with powerlessness and inferiority in respect to their femininity or with creative and free self-expression. This response is not a certainty for every woman. Everyone is unique and we, therefore, respond differently to the same input or experiences.

Each emotional state such as powerlessness, indecisiveness and fear of free expression can find expression within our bodies. Depending on the particular emotional state activated, it can affect our lower back, jaw, teeth grinding, throat, the kidney-adrenals and so on. Each body part affected represents a physical metaphor with an emotional issue consistent with negative belief systems. Due to the complexity of the intents of our negative belief systems, and how these relate to our body, an issue will commonly affect various parts of our body. If fear based issues are persistent, the negative pressure on the metaphorically related aspects of the body will be incessant. These can be organs, body structure or different systems, such as the endocrine system. Should we persist in ignoring the signals generated by our state of emotional disharmony, potentially, our bodies will be the final place where the conflict between unconditional love and fear are played out. The result of not dealing with your emotional issues can eventually show up as critical issues with your health or in the well-being of your mind. How and when this vulnerability to our emotional issues will physically manifest, depends on the inbuilt resilience of your consciousness and consequently that of your body. Your physical response to your emotions is dependent on the inherited strengths or weaknesses of your physical genetics and those of the emotional 'genetics' of your sense-of-self.

The neck is a vulnerable but significant part of our bodies because it is physically responsible for carrying and supporting our head, which contains organs critical to our survival —our brain, eyes, ears, mouth, tongue, etc., (thinking, seeing, hearing, speaking, tasting, etc.)

Have you ever said to someone: "You are a pain in the neck"? Or that something in your life is a: "Pain in the neck". The reason for saying this is that you have the experience that certain people are a source of stress. When you suffer from neck or shoulder pain, you may not realise that your mind's perception of others, or certain responsibilities, or demands, maybe the source of your problems. You will find the cause of this issue in the way you see their behaviour, the task or responsibility. The situation forces you to deal with people and responsibilities of which you resentful. Fear-based beliefs may cause anger or aggression with what is expected of you, and this will determine how you view others or your responsibilities. You experience this emotionally as stress or anxiety because you feel that you have to force yourself to do something you resent, but feel powerless to refuse. This inner-conflict can then manifest itself, often immediately, as a contraction of muscles in the neck, compressing vertebrae and restricting blood supply. We feel pain in the neck and often shoulders, frequently together with headaches.

Stress does not affect everyone in the same way, even if there are some forms of physical expression of certain emotional issues more common than others. Whether your body will give physical expression to your emotional issues depends on your inner-perception and how your mind and body relate to each other in respect to your fears and insecurities. The fear of having to be responsible for something of critical importance is proportional to your belief in your powerlessness, incompetence and inadequacy and so on, to live up to these expectations. Your reaction usually mirrors a childhood in which your parents did not trust you to be responsible, and therefore you were not given the opportunity to develop self-confidence. When parents always think that they know better and do not give their child the chance to test the capacities of its emotional, physical, mental and intellectual resources, it will learn to trust in them instead of itself. Exposed to criticism for being a disappointment or to distrust in your capacity to be independent, you will have learned to doubt yourself rather than trust. Having to face responsibilities or dealing with matters that appear challenging, while these insecurities control you, will logically create stress, anxiety or fear. The solution does not lie in reducing or eliminating responsibility or the expectations of others from your life, or by employing better strategies. The permanent resolution lies in releasing the reasons for these fears which is your lack of self-confidence and self-trust in your emotional and mental capacities. You need to without the negative beliefs that underpin your fears to rediscover the innate trust in the unique mental and emotional resources with which you were born.

In the hierarchy of cause and effect within our consciousness, the emotional issues are responsible for driving the body into undesirable physical problems. If you release the emotional causes responsible for the stress you create, there is a high potential that the physical effects will also spontaneously release. The length of time emotional stress has been active, its intensity and the degree to which a disease has developed all play a significant role in its potential to heal.

MIND RULES THE BODY

There are much more examples of how our bodies respond to our emotional state. Most common is the queasy and sometimes nauseating feeling we have in our stomach when confronted by stressful events that overload our senses. Embarrassment or shame causes us to want to be invisible, but hyper-awareness of our predicament causes us to think that everyone can see our shame. As a result, the skin of our cheeks and ears flush with blood turning our faces bright red. Instead of being invisible, we have become highly noticeable to others, thereby increasing our sense of shamefulness.

When we are afraid to give expression to our truth, feelings, or point of view, our throats can become dry and tight. There are much more examples of how our bodies respond directly to our emotional state, but we need to realise that the metaphorical connection between body and mind operates on every emotional and physical level. That is not to say that there are no environmental biological or biochemical influences, or that we cannot inherit certain genetic predispositions. The emotional effects are recognised as epigenetic influences on our genetic expression and can vary depending on our state of mind, and the inherited strengths or vulnerabilities of our bodies.

The harmonious relationship between spirit, mind and body depends on the oneness of our mind with our spirit-essence. Any discord or illness any of these elements is evidence of a breakdown in the harmonious relationship between each of them. We tend to start life without emotional issues, and with our minds in harmony with their essence. The emotional state of our consciousness already acts as the primary reference point for the body's propensity towards its greatest possible health. We have no fear save our innate instinct for physical survival. The compromises we later make to meet the emotional conditions set by our parents cause the original balance between spirit, mind and body to be upset. By accepting these conditions, we compromise our trust in unconditional love which results in disharmonious influences on our bodies.

Chapter 12

CREATORS OF OUR OWN REALITY

The belief that we are creators of our reality is not an entirely new concept. However, due to our conditioned interpretation of relationship with others and the world, we do not understand the part we play in our life experiences. What follows is an explanation of how we use our emotional minds and energetic being to bring about our personal life experiences — individually and collectively. It will reveal how and why we attract distinct personalities and manifest certain events in our lives. This understanding will empower you to recognise the role you play in creating your life experiences such as intimate relationships, friendship, success but also stress, failure and other unwanted situations.

The reason why we have such an intense aversion to being blamed, held accountable, feeling guilty and other fears is because of our fear of being guilty and responsible for what we manifest in our lives. We protect ourselves from this by manufacturing countless reasons and justifications to provide proof that we cannot be held accountable for any conflict, disaster, failure, embarrassment, loss, etc. Instead of taking responsibility, we try to prove that we are the victim of others or circumstances. When others want to link us to a negative event or outcome, we are quick to come up with excuses and explanations that absolve us from any responsibility. Our intent is to usually exclude us and shift the blame to others, bad luck or unexplainable circumstances over which we had no control. Rarely do we put ourselves forward as the responsible party because of our fear of the consequences of being held accountable, criticised and judged. The beliefs that support this perspective blind us from seeing how we are directly, or indirectly, the creators of every experience in our lives.

Proving our innocence becomes our primary concern, particularly if it directly involves the core values of our spirit — love and acceptance, trust, being wanted and included. Relationships in conflict can generate fear and guilt, pain and anger and raises the stakes to emotionally intense levels. The fear of being rejected or abandoned because we do not meet the expectations of our partner is often at the core of our fear taking responsibility. In most circumstances, we can only retain their love and acceptance if we can convince others of our innocence. We do not realise that our responses and reactions are still those of the little girl or boy we once were — still in fear of judgment, criticism, rejection, failure, being a disappointment and guilt. In some respect, it is as if we have never grown up and time has stopped, and our little self is still in control of our lives.

We also learn very early in life that being found guilty is followed by some form punishment or reprimand, which then feels like rejection or abandonment. Even now as an adult, we continue to respond to these fears. You may release yourself from the guilt that you are responsible for pain and suffering in others, by finding justification for your behaviour. When parents avoid responsibility and blame, then by example, they transfer the need to avoid being guilty to their children. They subconsciously taught their children to avoid accepting responsibility, by displaying stress, anxiety or anger when avoiding being held accountable for their involvement in conflictual, embarrassing or other undesirable situations. The parent's reactions and emotions teach them who is responsible for what and demonstrates how to respond if confronted and held accountable. There is no doubt that children will always mirror back what their parents show them — good or bad.

We have great difficulty recognising linking ourselves to a negative event or outcome and understand how we were involved in the result. Our immediate view is that it must be related to what we did without questioning the nature of who did it. Should the outcome be positive, we often try and convince others that we are responsible in the hope we will be celebrated and praised. Most people are willing to accept the view that we are only responsible for our life in specific situations. In all other cases, they will proclaim that they are the victims of others, circumstance, childhood or even bad luck. While this perception is highly inconsistent, it is also convenient because it allows them to pick and choose when and how they are willing to be accountable or be the victim. If the process by which we create and manifest our lives were understood, we would realise there is no exception to our responsibility as creators of our lives. Whether it is obvious or not, we are connected to everything we experience in life and therefore responsible. This new understanding will prove that it is not possible to be an innocent bystander in the manifestation of your life.

Our negative belief systems — emotional issues — have the property of altering our perception, and creating strategic behaviours, with the aim of getting from others what we feel is missing within us. In other words, we believe that only an outside source can fill the emotional void that our issues create in us. We think we have to engage strategized behaviour to get others to accept us when we feel unacceptable to them. We convince ourselves that we have created the proof that we are acceptable, should our strategy be successful. But, any form of rejection or criticism will convince us that we must be unacceptable. Our dependence on evidence from others to provide us with a positive sense of ourselves holds us in a constant state of emotional vigilance with them. Fear keeps us in the belief that anything we do or say, can cause judgement and rejection proving that we are unacceptable, unwanted and not good enough. No matter how dysfunctional this appears to be; from the perspective of our need for emotional survival from a distorted sense-of-self, it is perfectly logical to behave this way.

DECEIVED BY CONDITIONAL REALITY

Everything in existence moves and changes in synchronicity with everything else and thus all elements, including all consciousness, are connected to each other and involved in the process we call life. We manifest every sensation and emotion we have in response to every experience in our lives, individually and collectively. We generate the thoughts and feelings and perception we have in response to an event or person or situation, which makes us the creator of our life experiences. We cannot experience life through the mind of someone else because their experience of the same event reflects their unique nature and the beliefs that have formed their sense of themselves. As a consequence, their perception, feelings and thoughts are very different from ours, and so is any event they experience. The relationship we have with ourselves and supported by our belief systems, create our experience of life and relationships. The emotional sensations we create by engaging in life originates from conscious or subconscious, positive or negative intent.

The influence of fear on your presence and behaviour will attract people and events into your life that will cause you to experience the original reasons for its existence within you. Positive or harmonious intent will always draw its mirror image into your life through your free association with others and the world. Manifesting our personal reality experiences is an inevitable part of being alive.

Our sense of who we are causes us create the emotional situations through the encounters we choose which seen from our perspective represent our life. When they are unhappy and undesirable events, they are confrontations with unresolved childhood issues. Our negative feelings are there to prompt us into the realisation that we are creating our life experiences from a disharmonious aspect of our sense-of-self. This emotional state creates the opportunity to address the belief-systems by which we make our choices and decisions. Unfortunately, more than often our immediate reaction to negative feelings is to reject or suppress them. We judge our fearful thoughts and feelings to be an accurate reflection of what we experience and then act and respond accordingly. Without confirming the basis for the thoughts and feelings we have in response to a particular circumstance, we cannot be sure of what we are facing. Recognising the capacity of fear-based beliefs to colour our mind's perception is essential if you are to be in control of your existence. The beliefs your mind hold about itself are not a fixed and permanent program. Our beliefs are the instruments by which our consciousness coalesces the intent that become our life experiences. Regardless whether our intentions in themselves are positive or negative, they will always find expression and become a reality in one form or another. The flexibility of our consciousness assures that our beliefs can be released and replaced. To release our undesirable convictions, we need to be exact and clear of what their structure is and why they are a part of us.

We do not consciously choose the reaction to what we feel and think. The underlying intent of the belief system that is subconsciously activated will determine our response to a situation or person. Unfortunately, from this lack of awareness comes the general view that we are not in control of our feelings and thoughts and ensuing actions and reactions. We respond to our feelings when, for instance, we expected success, but failure confronts us. What we feel, will take us into behaviour and reasoning that can cause us to be aggressive or defensive in our behaviour. Your emotional response can cause you to go into denial, justification, self-criticism or guilt. It all depends on the nature of the consequences attached to your negative beliefs. Rarely do we look at ourselves to see who believe we are to uncover the real reasons why our relationships or enterprises are unsuccessful.

Our consciousness feels in disharmony because the emotions generated by our fear-based beliefs detach it from unconditional love and acceptance. The fear of this separation becomes the reason we need to adopt strategized behaviours to find proof through others that we are not who we believe we are. Having accepted the belief that you are a failure, generates the need to prove that you are not or avoid the risk of failure at all cost. Both are an attempt to avoid failure becoming a reality as a life experience.

Negative beliefs create and illusionary sense of who you are. The convictions you took on in your childhood as being real are misconceptions about yourself and potentially many other aspects of life. If you never question them by interrogating every one of your feelings, thoughts and behaviours you run a better than even chance that your illusions are in control of your life and relationships. Avoiding responsibility or being aggressive, blaming and being the victim, pessimistic thoughts and expecting the worst, etc. are all evidence of living by your fears.

We tend to make excuses for our behaviour when others including ourselves are negatively affected by our actions, choices and attitude. Should this prove to be unacceptable to others, we may grasp at universal paradigms as an explanation and justification for our issues and problems. Statements such as: "Everyone has issues" or "It is okay to get angry", "No-one is perfect" or "Everyone needs love" are used to justify our behaviours, neediness or feelings. Should we to put our blame, justifications and excuses under close and critical scrutiny, however, we would realise that they have no real validity and we would have to accept that the real causes lie within us.

Our perception of whom and what is responsible for our life experience also determines how we view ourselves and the world. Our understanding of the roles we play is central to how we will choose to live life. It follows that if our fear-based beliefs distort our perception, our illusions determine our decision-making, judgments and conclusions. Surprisingly most of us live with this condition every day of our lives. When you have depended for most of your life on your fear-based beliefs for support, security and emotional survival, it can be difficult to confront them and let them go.

Questioning your negative life experiences from a position of self-responsibility will initiate a process of self-reflection that can lead to answers that can give you an insight into the beliefs your mind holds. The answer lies in seeking awareness and acknowledging the negative belief-systems at the source of your issues. Once you recognise them for what they are, you can engage in the process of releasing them.

We find it difficult to imagine that we would consciously choose or do anything that would make our lives miserable or painful. Therefore, we resist any implication that could prove that we are the responsible party. Even though it is unlikely that we would deliberately choose to create suffering, unhappiness and pain in our lives, we still are responsible for them. Unaware of the subconscious programming that underlie our choices, reactions and responses we can never be sure of our reasons and motivations. The trouble is that you cannot be aware of something of which you are not conscious. Without this critical knowledge of the subconscious programs by which you determine who you are, you are limited by what you are aware of and can see. The presence of a subconscious self may give the impression that all of us have an inner reality that is inaccessible and therefore unknown, but that is not so. We are born with the capacity to be aware of the nature of who we are — our sense-of-self, even though our fears try and direct our attention to the world outside of us.

Just like we may not be aware of the origin of the wind, but by the way, it touches our face and moves the leaves of a tree we know its presence. Were we to trace the wind to its origin and measure the conditions we would understand how and why it came into being. Similarly, our negative belief systems and their intent leave their impact on our lives through our feelings thoughts and behaviours and negative emotional experiences. We can find out their origin by understanding the process by which they came to be a part of us.

Our negative feelings, fear-driven needs and compensating strategies are all part of any life experience that causes suffering, anxiety, fear, insecurity, stress and emotional pain. We need to recognise that even though these are not desirable sensations, all feelings represent signposts that mark out whether fear and illusion or unconditional love are the foundations of our mind. That is not to say that our negative feelings are not a real sensation, it is just that the causes and reasons for their presence have no actual reality outside of us. Fear can fool the mind, through our emotions, into believing that we need to respond to the negative sensations it creates for our emotional survival. We engage our fear based needs and behaviours without any reflection because we have learned to identify with our negative state of mind as if it is normal. Convinced that these conditions exist, we automatically respond to them by applying our learned strategies.

Like actors playing out a well-rehearsed script, we react and act automatically to a situation that reflects our negative past. The trouble is that we, the actors, are so lost in the role, that we are no longer aware that we are acting. In the same way, we accept 'the script' written by the mind-set of our parents and the family paradigm as the truth of who we are. Once we take our role as our identity, we have effectively become what our family dynamic imposed on us. The state of being we evolve for our survival — our fear-based sense-of-self — will then determine how we will manifest our lives. We will unconsciously live our life by our parent's fears, beliefs, conditions, values and standards. Convinced that your 'script' represents who you are, you are unable to be anyone other than who you believe yourself to be. If challenged, you may even argue to defend the role you have learned to play and the illusions by which you live.

In living out a distortion of your authentic self, you will find that you will attract, and are attracted to those who are your emotional counterparts. Their presence in your life serves to give a sense of reality to your illusions, as you will to theirs. The fears and perceptions you share with each other are likely to be complimentary. Their issues and behaviour promise to fulfil your fear-driven needs and expectations and vice versa. A relationship can feel like a perfect match until discord leading to conflict starts to surface, and then you begin to realise what you thought was perfect is severely flawed. You will not necessarily recognise that your relationship is an emotional equivalent of the dynamic that existed between you, and one or both of your parents. The danger is that because you are not aware of this, you will blame your partner for the relationship going wrong. If you were to separate without understanding the causes for your relationship issues, neither of you would have learned anything. Potentially, both of you will repeat the same experience with someone else because you have not understood the role you played in the demise of your relationship.

We keep on recreating life according to a script that is individual to us, and according to the common consensus of what is true or false. The dynamic between people is a statement of who they believe they are as an individual and represents their version reality. Others, just like you, do not realise that their 'script' has altered the nature of their original self, and has come to redefine who they believe they are. Our acceptance of this is so complete that we will go in conflict to prove that our distorted version of reality is the correct one.

THE HABIT OF VICTIMHOOD

Life is full of experiences we believe to be inexplicable, unfair, unreasonable experiences:

- Take for example the girl who has always has had issues with her father. As an adult, she may find herself with a boss, co-worker or a partner who will be an emotional copy of her father. She is likely to relive her father issues with many of the men with whom she becomes involved.
- Or, the boy who as second child in his family was always blamed for everything that went wrong or for any conflict with his siblings. Even as an adult he is still living in the expectation of being guilty and in constant

fear that at work or in his relationships. Now, whenever something goes wrong, or someone gets upset, he fears being blamed.

- A man who as a child was subject to his parent's constant criticism, dismissal and invalidation of anything he said or wanted, now keeps on failing in all of his enterprises. He has learned to believe that he cannot trust his intellect, judgement and abilities. He believes everything he thinks or chooses may be flawed or wrong.

- The woman who was demeaned and abused as a child because both her mother and father favoured her brothers over her. As an adult, she attracts relationships with chauvinist males, where she is still subject to the same abusive behaviour she first experienced in childhood.

Our typical reaction to the story of the girl and her abusive, dominating and critical boss, would be to blame him for abusing her. We would see him as the aggressor, and her as the victim. In reality, however, she chose him subconsciously to be in her life as much as he attracted her through his business. In accepting work with a man who will confront her with the issues she inherited from her father, presents her with an opportunity to resolve them. However, this will only be the case if she recognises that she is subconsciously contributing to the interaction between her and the boss. If she blames him, convinced that she is the victim, she will miss the connection her emotional confrontation has with her past. Transferring the responsibility for her negative experiences renders her powerless to find a resolution, and surrenders the power over her life to him, and men like him.

Her aggressive, dominant boss will have unconsciously attracted her in his life because she may be representative of the childhood relationship he had with his needy and demanding mother. She made him responsible for her negative feelings, dissatisfaction and discontent. She controlled him through guilt making him feel powerless to refuse or disagree with her. The dynamic with his new staff member provides him with the opportunity to have a learning experience in respect to his issues. Although he may seem aggressive and intimidating to her, his dominating and controlling behaviour is nothing more than an emotional strategy to keep him safe from his fears.

The man who fears and believes that he is guilty of the negative emotions and reactions of others may get our sympathy but is likely to be judged for being oversensitive, insecure and weak. He is paralysed by his fears, stunted his self-expression and decision making. He lives in constant anxiety of doing or saying anything that will be judged as wrong or a failure and thereby attract criticism and blame. He will avoid change and initiate new ideas for the same reasons. He needs to get an endorsement from others for any critical decision before he makes committing himself. He is unlikely to be promoted to a position of responsibility because of his need to avoid being held accountable, blamed or accused dominate his mind. No-one, especially the man himself, will understand that his behaviours are a product of negative beliefs integrated during childhood. As long as his emotional issues control him, he will show himself to be very different from his authentic self and actual potential.

Were we to listen to the man with his failed enterprises, we would probably try and solve his issues by determining where he went wrong in his decisions and judgments and then proceed to give him advice on how to do it differently. In hindsight, it is easy to recognise what he may have done well or badly. In only paying attention to the business process that led to failure, we fail to see that his poor judgment or decisions are not the core of his problems.

The reality is that his fear-based sense-of-self, and the negative beliefs that underpin them, are central to his business failures. Potentially his lack of self-trust gives rise to his need to prove to others that he is knowledgeable and is competent. His fear of being perceived as being inadequate, insignificant or incompetent, stops him from seeing the flaws in his perception and reasoning. Needy of recognition, he has to become wealthy, powerful and successful as evidence that he is intelligent, capable, significant, in control and competent.

The same need to show his capacity for success, power and control may also incite him to take grandiose risks that could eventually cause his downfall.

The childhood of the girl whose parents discriminated against her reveals that she was judged to be inferior to her brother because of her femininity. The chauvinism of both her mother and father placed all their hope and pride in him, unaware of the lifelong consequences that both their son and daughter would suffer. Exposed to the preferential treatment received by her brother, she felt that her femininity made her unlovable, inferior, unwanted and a liability. To survive and attain some power she instinctively suppressed her feminine nature and adopted masculine traits to gain a level of acceptance from her parents. She finds herself subconsciously competing with her brother to get equal attention and validation from them. In her way, she tried to be everything she believed her parents expected her brother to be or more.

By proving she is academically superior or excelling in sport, she tries to prove herself to be worthy of her parent's love, acceptance and praise. All of her efforts will be to no avail if her parents remain in the worship of her brother. It is not unusual that even if he makes a mess of his life, and fails, he will still receive their support and adulation. He can do no wrong because his parents will manufacture excuses for his shortcomings for as long as they cannot let go of the perfect image they have of him. By the same token, their daughter can achieve great success in her business or profession without attracting any praise, validation or acknowledgement. Instead, they might even make her successes and achievements responsible for making her brother feel inferior and a failure.

These examples each show just one possible scenario that can come from the circumstances described. Each example reveals how being ignorant of your inner processes, not only causes you to sabotage your life, but it also makes you blind to any real solution. Relegating the reason for your problems to your environment does nothing but transfer the power over your life in the hands of others, thereby leaving you to be the victim. The reality is that you cannot control people and events in your life through strategic behaviours, by force or manipulation. At best, it will keep the consequences of your fear and insecurities temporarily at bay. The only way to be in control of your life is by examining the negative beliefs that define your sense-of-self. Once you recognise the distortions in "who you believe yourself to be", you will also become aware of the origin for your life experiences.

Each person in these examples does not feel they have any real control over the situations they have created and now have to confront. They are under constant stress for fear that their strategic behaviour will fail, with only one thing on their mind: to gain acceptance, love and trust. As long as they are in need of this from their parents, or later from others it does not matter if what they ultimately gain is conditional or not.

For each person to begin their journey of self-change, they need to make a fundamental choice: To accept ownership and responsibility for the life experiences they manifest — or blame their fear and insecurities on other and thereby making themselves powerless in life, and the victim of others.

LIFE WITHOUT FEAR

An intellectual understanding of how you create your reality does not automatically give you power over your life. However, your awareness will promote a new way of thinking that is an essential step in the right direction. If you want to have influence or control over your negative life experiences, you need to change the illusionary negative beliefs that make your life and relationships what they are right now.

- Releasing your negative beliefs (fears) will change who you are and start the process of revealing your authentic nature.
- Changing your sense-of-self will automatically alter your feelings, perception, thoughts, behaviour and choices.
- Your renewed realisation of your authentic self will create, attract and manifest a new life experience.

Achieving this is a gradual process, but as each illusionary part of your sense-of-self is released, you will realise more of your authentic self in life with obvious positive consequences.

Chapter 13

RESPONSIBILITY WITHOUT BLAME

Guilt is one of our most powerful and influential emotions. Our relationships become impaired, once we accept the belief that we are guilty or responsible for the feelings, needs or expectations of others. For each person, the reasons for being or feeling guilty will vary in detail for but the effect this has on their lives will be very similar. If you hurt someone with premeditation, your act of doing so makes you guilty. But, that is not the same as feeling responsible for someone's sadness, powerlessness, anxiety or worry. Your feeling of guilt for his or her emotions is unjustified. Many people suffer from living in a constant fear of feeling guilty of the negative emotional state of others. They cannot avoid feeling that somehow, they have to do something to save others from their negative state of mind, feelings or life circumstances. They experience an extreme sense of responsibility for the pain and suffering they witness. Guilt creates an automatic emotional response that causes them to feel that they must in some way be involved with what they see. That type of guilt is entirely different from being guilty of doing intentional harm. Guilt invokes a sense of responsibility or the blame for the negative emotional emotions or conditions suffered by others. This emotion does even require you to be directly involved with the reasons why they feel that way. The problem with experiencing these negative feelings, thoughts, anxiety or stress is that the emotional issues of others are beyond your control.

Extreme guilt can keep you in its emotional grip over a lifetime because you do not realise why you feel responsible for what others feel or experience. The behaviour that guilt brings out in someone is commonly seen as kind, giving and supportive. Even though feelings of guilt cause you to respond in a considerate and caring way, the core reason for your behaviour is guilt. The underlying truth is that the fear of being responsible for pain and suffering of others controls you. Your sense of over-responsibility makes it extremely difficult to say no or refuse when others expect you to meet their needs or demands. Guilt creates the idea that you must be somehow connected to the pain and suffering of others, even though this is not possible. Their feelings of powerlessness and helplessness are a part of their mind over which you do not have control.

Our sense of guilt is a powerful influence on our behaviour and act as a controlling element in our relationships, friendships and how we engage with the world. Guilt can cause us to be in a constant state of anticipation of upsetting or disappointing others. It demands that we are sensitive and conscious of to the emotional needs and expectations of others, their fears and vulnerabilities, and what will make them offended, angry, upset, disappointed, feel rejected or unwanted. Our fear of being responsible for their negative emotions, causes us to suppress who we truly are and what we think and feel. Instead, will try and act, respond and react the way we believe others expect from us. We rely on this strategy, to avoid creating conflict, being blamed and held accountable for offending or disappointing others.

When guilt is one of our primary issues, it can trap us in relationships where we are responsible for a partner who feels powerless and fearful. Once we are committed, and we feel we cannot meet the demands our emotionally dependent partner places on us, we will find it difficult to leave. We fear that by terminating the relationship, we will be responsible for the fear, pain and suffering our partner will go through.

Guilt can cause us to put the needs, wishes and desires of others before our own for fear of disappointing them, making them feel neglected or miss out. By giving them priority and putting yourself last, you believe you will avoid the guilt lest they feel upset, let down or denied. You might think that as long as you look after others, sooner or later your turn will come, but it never will.

Guilt will have us comply with the needs, demands and expectations of others, even if they are unreasonable and compromise our lives or come at the cost of our well-being.

Guilt will have us make choices and give support that benefits others, but cause us to sacrifice the fulfilment of the potential of our life. This behaviour may appear altruistic but when guilt is involved every action is a strategy to avoid guilt. Over time, our sense of over-responsibility can cause us to miss out on many of opportunities in life because we often realise too late that we lived with the wrong priorities for all the wrong reasons.

The many faces of guilt are confusing because they have the undesirable quality of parading themselves as socially praised or celebrated personality traits. Responsible and caring behaviour may collect praise and admiration from others, but that does not compensate for the long-term effect guilt has on you. If you are unaware of the underlying motivations for your behaviour, you will also not see how it affects your life. The approval you crave from others only serves to justify your actions and choices, even though you may deny yourself the fulfilment of your life potential. The suppression your spontaneous and authentic-self, thoughts, feelings, needs, expectations, goals and aspirations cannot lead to a fulfilling life.

It is important to realise that the actual dynamic between a guilt driven person and others also involves other emotional elements. So far, we have looked at the person with beliefs of over-responsibility for the negative feelings of others. Individuals who believe they are victims because they think that they are powerless, helpless in life. Who feel they are the victims of others, their emotions and feelings, aggression and confrontation, being denied, anxiety and stress and often of everything and everyone.

Their fears and insecurities cause them to be attracted to people who have a sense of over-responsibility or guilt. They need someone to be responsible for them, to save and protect them because they believe they lack the capacity power and resources to cope with their lives. In constant fear and anxiety that someone will confront them, start an argument, blame them, etc., they need to give priority to their safety and security. No wonder, that they are attracted to someone who cannot help to be the one to protect them from their fears because they perfectly match each other's issues. Their relationship dynamic fulfils the needs created by their negative belief systems. The over-responsible person feels that by supporting the victim, they satisfy their obligation to the victim. The victim has found someone to take responsibility for him or her; both feel a sense of satisfaction that will probably not stand the test of time. As long as they can maintain the relationship on that level neither of them will feel the need to change. Both will keep on playing out the beliefs that have come to define who they are to themselves and others until one begins to feel suppressed in their needs, or the other feels unprotected and denied.

Naturally, one can be giving, caring and sensitive to the suffering of others. Being there for others should never result in the suppression of who you are or cause you to give away your power or the fulfilment of your potential. Effectively supporting someone is often very different to what most people think is the right thing to do to take care of those who believe they cannot do so for themselves.

Usually, those who suffer from guilt, have issues with expressing their needs, wants and expectations. They have learned to believe that fulfilling their needs and expectations, wishes and desires, will deny others what they want. The natural need for self-fulfilment and expressions of entitlement is often judged as a sign of selfishness, being unreasonable or unfair. Someone steeped in guilt would feel selfish and greedy if they were not to respond to the neediness and expectations of those who see themselves as victims. Unaware that their behaviour is rooted in fear, they cannot disconnect from what they feel is their responsibility. The real intent is to avoid guilt and sometimes to gain acceptance and praise.

Guilt can drive you to convince others that you have no needs or wants wishes or desires. In childhood, you may have learned to be grateful for what your parents give you, and that asking for more makes you a burden, selfish or demanding. Your parents may have given you the message that whatever they do for you or give you comes at great sacrifice to them. You become convinced that you, therefore, should never complain or want or need anything. Later in life, you will still deny yourself the expression and fulfilment of what you want, need and desire. You can only have your needs met if you can justify them.

You reveal your guilt issues when you feel uncomfortable receiving a gift or when others do things for you.

If, you never ask for help, support or to be looked after.

If you never show others, you are sick or have issues, or are going through an emotionally difficult time.

If, you feel that your presence, needs and expectations are a burden to others

If, you never expect, want or need anything from anyone.

If, you suppress your feelings and emotions to avoid upsetting others.

You will find that if you have played out your guilt issues so consistently and convincingly to friends and acquaintances that:

Because you feel guilty asking anyone for support, there is never anyone there to help you when you need them. As a result, you have to do everything alone.

Of the belief that you are a burden to others, you feel guilty, and you tend to act as if you need to be invisible when in the company of others. You then get the sense that no one cares about you because no one approaches you, but do not realise that you have convinced them that you want to be alone and are fine.

You may find that you are always needed when others have issues but there is never anyone to support you in yours.

You see others having and doing what they want, while you feel as though you are always watching a situation with others from the outside. You then feel that you were missing out.

Overcoming guilt begins with the recognition that our sense of over-responsibility for the fears and insecurities of others is controlling us. Those who do not take responsibility for their life and emotion, are usually the trigger our feelings of guilt. Their behaviour has the strategic intent to make others responsible for their fears, insecurities, anxiety and stress. Acting like the victims, they manipulate the emotions of others by implying that they are responsible for how they feel. Those who are susceptible to this will feel guilt and respond by trying to fix something they are not responsible for and have no control over.

To an observer, it appears that those who give are being generous and caring, and naturally, the recipients are also likely to think so. Looking deeper into the giver's motivations might show that there may be more to this act than the obvious. For example, you may give to be liked and accepted or to avoid shame, which makes your gift conditional and your motivation less than altruistic. To be seen to be giving and appearing philanthropic can be a way to gain status or a sense of superiority. Even though the experience for the recipient may be the same, the giver's various issues and fears colour their gesture.

Guilt comes into play because of a sense of over-responsibility and sensitivity to the emotional plight of others. The fear of being blamed for being insensitive, selfish and uncaring supports their need to alleviate the worry, anxiety, and stress displayed by others. Their ingrained sense of guilt is a result of many years of being made responsible for the feelings and emotions of their parents and the subsequent fear of not being able to prove their innocence. The sense of powerlessness that flows from this causes them to be in empathy with those whose insecurities are similar.

To understand the reasons for your guilt it is important to recognise the nature of the beliefs of those who profit and benefit from them. Passive victims are in fear that their inner resources — emotional and mental resilience, strength and influence — are not sufficient to help them deal with aggression, confrontation, conflict and so on. Just living life, meeting the expectations or needs of others or the responsibilities they have in their job can feel overwhelming for them. They feel their powerlessness in many situations including relationships and believe they cannot live without support systems provided by others. As children, they may have been overprotective, or been criticised and distrusted and therefore never had the chance to develop confidence in themselves.

There are those who have also grown up with guilt issues but are vehement in their avoidance of blame and responsibility. They too are in fear of being powerless of being held accountable for any wrongdoing but use an aggressive response to deal with their fear. The potential of being accused causes them to be intense in their defensiveness. They will employ aggressive strategies designed to prove to everyone that they are not responsible. Blaming others, circumstances or being disadvantaged is their first line of defence. Should that fail, they will present themselves as powerless victims of everything in life. Even though they appear confident because of their aggressive and confronting behaviour, they will play the victim card if this does not succeed. As aggressive victims, they tend to blame and accuse others of every ill in their life just like passive victims do. At no time will they take responsibility for what they have created in their life as a result of their choices and behaviour. Their circle of friends usually consists of people who empathise with them or who give support, if for no other reason, then to justify their victim mentality. If challenged, they may pull together to justify each other's victimhood and validating their powerlessness in life.

Giving and receiving should not be tainted by guilt. In an ideal world, all giving is unconditional and joyful and devoid of conditions and expectations for both the giver and the receiver.

Guilt invariably involves others, even if your victim-thinking happens only in your mind. Accepting responsibility when the issue concerns others does not have to imply guilt or blame. It is fitting that those who are involved in an undesirable event hold themselves accountable for the part they contributed. If they do not then others should be prepared to do so. In the case of victims, their unwillingness to accept responsibility or not for their problems, sadness or stress should be irrelevant, because they are the creators of their issues. They need to have their role in manifesting a life of stress and anxiety explained to them with sensitivity to their vulnerable state. What matters to a someone who suffers from over-responsibility is that they do not take responsibility for the issues for which others must be accountable. The actions, choices and behaviour that has led to their undesirable experience of life and relationships are not under your control and therefore their responsibility. Redefining the difference between actual responsibility versus perceived guilt is essential for a clear understanding of what emotional guilt is all about.

The beliefs that underlie emotional guilt are so enmeshed in our perception that it appears in our use of language. At one time or another, we have all experienced someone getting upset by what someone else says. The general assumption is that we must be the reason because they had these feelings in response to what we said. Under these circumstances, those who observed the situation and feel the need to be protective of the perceived victim are likely to blame us for upsetting them. We have noted before, that it is not possible to create feelings in someone. The only way you can trigger negative or unpleasant emotions in others is if the basis for them already pre-exists as a particular fear or insecurity in that person's mind. Only then can referring to something that relates to it, may trigger negative and unpleasant emotions in them.

The nature of personal responsibility changes as we grow from children into adults. From the day we are born, and for 8 to 11 years that follow we cannot be entirely responsible for our own emotional and physical survival. Children need to gradually learn the concept of being responsible, accountable and learn self-discipline, by becoming aware that their actions and choices have consequences. It is unlikely that parents who do not take responsibility for their fears, insecurities, behaviour and subsequent emotions will develop these qualities in their children. Instead, they will pass their issues on to them.

The truth is that no one has the power to create emotions in others unless the reasons for them already pre-exist within the person. We are at all times and in any situation responsible for what we feel. Once our beliefs, which are the precursors for our emotions and behaviours, are activated by others or our surroundings, they will exercise a strong influence on us. In the absence of negative beliefs, we would not be affected by the emotional state of others. In fact, we will immediately assume that what do or say has nothing to do with us, and therefore, we do not take it personally. We may wonder why they are in an emotionally challenging state without necessarily feeling any responsibility for it. The question facing us is whether others should change to accommodate our fears or whether we should accept the responsibility for our fears and overcome them?

Were we to choose not to be accountable for our fears, we will transfer the responsibility for feelings, thoughts and behaviour to others. If we are parents, our children will be the innocent recipients of this as well. By default, they will come to feel responsible for the consequences for our fears. In later life, they will more than likely attract, and be attracted, to the counterpart to their issues in relationships. They accept the beliefs, values and standards they inherited from us as being representative of who they are as people. This inner-perception will subconsciously determine the life and relationships they will have. These negative beliefs do not allow them to be emotionally neutral when engaging in a relationship where guilt is the central focus between them and their partner. They will play out their guilt issues in whatever form they are a part of them, and so will their partner. Potentially, your children are likely to have the same life as you because of the negative belief systems they inherited from you.

WHEN GUILT DOMINATES

The reality is that you can only be responsible for those things you truly have control over. Even if you are not aware of expressing these issues, you are still accountable for what you create in your life and relationships. In emotional terms, this means that as an adult you are the only one responsible for who you are and what you manifest in your life — for your intent, feelings, behaviours and choices. Children are the only exception to this because without having developed a sense-of-self they lack the awareness of purpose, consequence and self-responsibility. They still need to depend on adult guidance, mentoring and support to learn. Once children reach the age of 8 to 11, they will have formed the foundation of their sense of self. From that time on, who they have learned to believe themselves to be, will now underpin all of their actions, responses and choices. The emotional chasm that often appears in teenage hood between parent and young adult is the result of the conditional behaviour that was imposed on them when they were younger.

Young adults are usually not aware that at the core of their conflict or discord with themselves comes from feeling powerlessness of being unconditionally loved, wanted, accepted trusted in childhood. They cannot see that origin of their issues result from the belief that they cannot be their authentic selves. They feel the internal struggle of trying to be who they were born to be but do not understand what prevents them from doing so. They are not aware that they fear to be who they were meant to be. Believing that they will become unlovable, unwanted or unacceptable, they suppress it and even fear being truly themselves. Even though they are becoming adults they are caught up in the strategic behaviours they have learned. Unaware of what controls and restricts their lives they believe they have to overcome the challenges with others and in the world, while the real battle they need to fight is within themselves. As a result, they may spend their life trying to overcome issues and problems over which they have no control.

Both parents and teenagers are usually not conscious of the deeper reasons for their differences. They do not realise that the conflict is just a symptom of what lies beneath the surface of the conscious emotional dynamic with each other. As they grow towards independence, they feel physically and emotionally more self-confident and self-assured, and will then give expression to their issues. This reaction can take the form of recalcitrance, anger, open defiance and so on. More than often parents are surprised and frightened by the emotional intensity of the reactions from their teenage children and usually cannot fathom why and how this is happening. The unawareness of their fears, limitations and insecurities blind them to the fact that they are central to the reasons for the conflict they now experience. This lack of awareness prevents them from appreciating the characteristics of their issues and the consequences these have had on their offspring. This kind of emotional blindness is a typical feature of our consciousness when fear is in control. In almost all instances, this perception will result in the belief that we are not responsible for what we create and manifest as a consequence of expressing our fears and insecurities.

The influence our fear-based beliefs have on our minds causes us to construct a perception and experience of reality that is false, but we hold to be true. This illusionary reality is so convincing to our senses that we will even fight for it in contradiction to logical argument. The fear of discovering that our sense of who we are is in some way invalid can be the cause of intense conflict and disagreement and longstanding arguments.

Dominating, controlling and often chauvinistic men are usually only attracted to passive compliant women. Women who feel inferior, powerless, needy and insecure will desire partners who appear to be able to protect them, support them and keep them safe. The wife of such a man may have a daughter who adopts her fearful beliefs, mentality and behaviour. If she fears to be like her mother, display an attitude and behaviour that is opposite to her. She may take on elements of her father's dominating strategies to protect herself from being powerless and a victim like her mother. By adopting many of her father's attitudes and behaviour to have the power and control her mother lacked, she runs the risk of becoming masculine in her self-expression.

In the same family, the son may take the role of protector of his mother to save her from the aggression of his father. He may subconsciously choose to suppress the assertiveness, aggression, power and strength of his masculinity to avoid being a threat to his mother like his father. In the future, this will cause him to be a passive and compliant male and potentially pleaser of women to avoid upsetting them or causing them pain. His future relationships will be with a powerless, insecure and passive woman, who has the need to be saved. Or, women with domineering and aggressive behaviours, but feel powerless and fear emotional confrontation.

CONDITIONAL PARENTING

The 'generation gap' is the name given to a conflict that families frequently have with their teenagers. When this discord triggers emotions in both parties, there is invariably blame on both sides. Parents will blame their children for being noncompliant, disrespectful or ungrateful and so on, for what they have done for them, and teenagers will blame their parents for whatever they believe to be the reason for conflict. Neither party has any clarity of reasons the conflict, although each is likely to blame the other for what they feel.

The parents will not be aware enough of themselves to admit that they have unknowingly imposed their fears and insecurities on their children. It is even more unlikely that teenagers will understand why and how they came to be subject to their parents' insecurities and what the effect on them has been. As confusing as the experience may be for parents and teenagers, the truth is that each is an emotional mirror for the other. In the conflict between them, parents experience the outcome of their fears and insecurities through the behaviour, reactions and responses of their children. Unaware that they are the origin of the way their teenagers act and behave, they do what they have always done more subconsciously which is to blame them for the conflict. Their teenagers will do the same because they have learned this from their parents. The deeper understanding is, that the process by which our consciousness manifests evolves, itself never fails to show us what we need to learn. Not recognising what our fears and their consequences are about, we cannot see what our life experiences reveal about ourselves. Both our experience of life and our sense-of-self are indivisible.

Real progress would be possible if both parent and child were to take responsibility for their state of mind and feelings, and accept that they both contribute to the conflict. It is important to understand that the parents cannot undo the consequences of having parented with fear no more than their children can make the instant choice of letting go of the emotional impact this made on their sense-of-self. The argument that "I did the best I could do" becomes feeble when your children go off the track and involve themselves in crime, drugs or alcohol. The damage they can do to themselves may last a lifetime. Eventually, most children grow up to be parents that their parents were to them, and thereby unconsciously affect their offspring in the same way as they were when they were young.

The reality is however that both parents and teenagers own and are responsible for their state of mind and the beliefs systems that form it. Only they have the individual power to choose to change who they are. Blaming each other or living in guilt or remorse will not make a difference to either party. Real insight and change are only possible if each accepts responsibility for who they believe themselves to be. If the parties are locked in conflict, engaging in frank communication, without judgment and blame might be difficult but is essential to finding a resolution that is lasting. Taking ownership of their feelings and issues would facilitate a new level of communication that would lead to closeness and understanding in their relationship with each other.

Living life in ignorance of the consequences of your behaviour, feelings, choices and intent, has to become unacceptable. At first, accepting responsibility for all the problems you have in life and relationships may be difficult. Once this becomes your new habit, you will come to realise that it empowers you because it gives you control over your life. Knowing your issues can point you to the negative beliefs that created them and provide you with the opportunity to release them. No matter how you look at it but you are not only responsible for the outcome of your choices, but also for the reasons that caused you to make them in the first place. Your sense-of-self is the definition for who you believe you are and this makes you responsible for the beliefs that determine your perception, feelings, choices, behaviours and intent and the outcomes they create in life. Ultimately, your state of mind can only be your responsibility because no one holds on to these self-beliefs but you. You cannot allow yourself to avoid this responsibility by making excuses, justification or blaming others.

As an adult, you are wholly responsible for what you manifest for your life experiences in relationships, friendships at work and life in general That is so in spite the fact that your family is at the origin of your issues. You are responsible because you are the only one with the power to release and change your negative beliefs. Fear will not leave by itself, and you cannot magically make it disappear by wishing it away. The reality is that you cannot control others and the world to make the world in which you will be safe from your fears and insecurities. Even if those, who are the origin for your issues were to change, you would still be the same person with the problems you inherited. It is up to you to take ownership of your negative beliefs and accept responsibility for how they cause you to feel, think and behave. Being responsible for 'who you believe you are' is a significant advance towards gaining control and power over your life. Your new approach will make you realise the conditions or expectations you place on your interaction with others and the world.

Any conflict arising in a relationship is the product of the dynamic between both parties and therefore, each carries responsibility for the part they experience and contribute. Commonly, one will blame the other for their pain or discontent to allocate guilt, and promote their innocence or victimhood. Even though both contribute, and there are no innocent parties, even if neither party are willing to accept responsibility for their part in the conflict.

The person that believes that their needs, expectations or security in their relationship, are the responsibility of their partner. They will choose an individual who is convinced that he or she will only have value and become deserving of love and acceptance if they can meet their partner's expectations. Their behaviour is a learned strategy to make their partner feel content, safe, loved and wanted so that they will receive love and affection and feel wanted and accepted. The issues each of them bring into the relationship are complementary. One partner is the aggressively needy one but does not take responsibility for feeling unlovable, unwanted and unacceptable, and the other partner believes it is their role to make them feel loved, wanted and accepted. They have learned to please and put them self-last as a condition for them to receive love and affection in return. Should the aggressively needy partner begin to feel insecure or unhappy, the other will try and do anything they can to fix it to avoid feeling guilty for disappointing them. Once guilt and a sense of failure take hold, the pleaser will feel that what they do is never enough and believe they are inadequate and guilty for not fulfilling expectations. As soon the guilty partner starts to give up trying to please, the other will feel neglected, abandoned and angry. They will feel the victim of not receiving the kind of attention they need to feel loved, wanted, accepted and secure.

They both lack the inner connection that would allow them to love, accept and trust themselves and each other unconditionally. To be ready to love unconditionally, one needs to have a strong sense of love and acceptance for oneself. Trapped by neediness and strategic behaviours, born out of conditional love, acceptance and trust, each looks to the other to find what they lack within themselves.

THE SOURCE FOR FALSE GUILT

Children interpret their parent's expression of emotion, attitude and their behaviour very differently to the way an adult would. An adult will draw their conclusions relying on experience and intellect but is usually unaware that they already function through the emotional filters of the beliefs that represent their inner-identity. A child has neither the experience nor the knowledge or an informed sense-of-self, to differentiate its emotional experience from the emotional reaction and behaviour of the parent. It is as yet not burdened by a host of negative belief systems that would act as filters and determine its perception, thoughts responses and actions. In the purity of its naïve and innocent consciousness, it is open and unconditionally trusting within the bounds of its instinctive need for emotional and physical survival.

A child will see a display of weakness, insecurity, worry, anxiety and unhappiness by one or both parents as an inability to cope with its need for love, support, care, nurturing, protection. This perception has profound consequences for its emotional and mental development. Subconsciously, the child feels the need to suppress its need for love and support to avoid being a burden to its parents. In the belief that it is an imposition to its parents, the child fears that it will be rejected and therefore not able to survive. It identifies itself by what it feels as a result of its parent's negative behaviour. Unable to distinguish its emotions from its authentic self it begins to determine its sense of who it is through its feelings. This response to its feelings also comes from the belief that it must be responsible for their stress and unhappiness. In taking on this responsibility, a child unwittingly accepts guilt for being the cause of the parent's negative emotional state as well as an identity based on guilt.

A child will sense if its parents are unhappy or resentful with each other even if it is not involved in this. It will not be able to determine whether it is the cause of their emotional discord or not. Even if parents were aware of their emotional issues and tried consciously to alter their behaviour so as not to repeat their childhood experience, it is still likely to have an adverse impact on their child. Even though a parent can consciously change how they act and express themselves, their actual emotional state would lack integrity, truth and sincerity and be incongruent with how they behave. A child will be subconsciously aware of this and receive contradictory emotional messages. It will be as if the parent is saying one thing but mean another. They may tell the child to function and be in the world without certain fears while they do not have the capacity to do so themselves. The parent's unspoken fears still find emotional expression within their behaviour and language. These contradictory and mixed messages will cause a child to doubt its innate and intuitive senses and sabotage its self-trust. The vulnerabilities this creates will diminish its capacities and strengths necessary for confronting life. It will default to using behavioural strategies of avoidance or aggression to ensure its emotional security. There are so many variations on this paradigm that it not possible to cover them all.

All of us suffer from guilt or over-responsibility to one degree or another. As children, we start to develop guilt issues almost as soon as we begin to interact with our parents. Given that fear is a part of everyone's mind you could say that it is unavoidable. In childhood, your ability to discern good experiences from bad, positive from negative is severely limited because everything in our life is new. We do not know who we are although we were born with a unique nature and qualities. We certainly have little conscious awareness of the world to which we opened our eyes. The absence of a definitive point of reference that we can use to know who we are and which represent the core values of our inner motivations handicaps our ability to understand ourselves. The lack of a base line for our consciousness prevents us from realising how the interactions between our parents and us have affected us. We naively accepted responsibility for the discrepancy between the innate expectation of unconditional love, acceptance and trust, and the conditional behaviour of our parents. Taking responsibility for something we never had any control over represents our first acceptance of guilt. We were not aware of what we chose, nor did we have any idea what consequences it would be for the rest of our lives.

By accepting the responsibility for the conditions our parents set, we become fearful of our spontaneous impulses and expressing our authentic and unique self, for fear that by showing them we will get a negative response. A display of annoyance or anxiety will cause us to feel and accept responsibility, convincing us that we are to blame — guilty. We might also begin to believe that we are selfish, uncaring and insensitive if our parents act as if they are victims of their responsibility for us. In these emotional family paradigms, the victim parent creates the expectation through their behaviour and expects consideration over everyone else in the family. His or her vulnerabilities become the controlling benchmark for the action, responses and self-expression of everyone else. Their fears will determine the family paradigm and dynamic that controls every family member.

The fear of being guilty of being the cause of this parent pain and stress or anger and abuse makes a child selectively monitor its self-expression and behaviour. This reaction to the fear of being of responsible will become a permanent feature in its life and acts as a severe constraint on the way it will be present in the world. When an adult, the guilt and the associated fear of causing pain and suffering in others will have the effect of attracting needy, vulnerable people because with them, they feel safe from their fears. If in addition to the guilt, they adopt the same victim strategies their parents displayed with them and will be just as sensitive and fragile, or as aggressive and abusive, as their parents were. Just like them, they will seek to avoid being held accountable for the negative experiences in life by shifting the responsibility to others or the world. The avoidance of guilt will become their priority in life.

THE INCEPTION OF FALSE GUILT

Here are some of the most common examples of family paradigms where guilt is the inevitable outcome:

A family where the father is emotionally shut down and will not be held accountable for his actions and behaviours. Feeling unable to express what he feels, he may resort to alcohol or become a workaholic to deal with his emotions and stress. Over time his emotional issues can take him into depression and make himself absent from the family or drink in excess. Failure and guilt, being a disappointment as a man is amongst his insecurities. Also, his fear of appearing weak and powerless by exposing his needs and feelings culminate in his issues with women. Experiencing a deep sense of powerlessness in life — he feels trapped in an emotional existence he believes to be real and believes he cannot change

His partner is insecure but aggressive in her demands and needs and is not afraid to let him know where he falls short of her expectations. His alcoholism and less than appropriate behaviour make him an easy target for her critical judgment and disappointment in him. His inability to respond in a meaningful way increases his sense of powerlessness and thereby his anger. Occasionally, in frustration, he may burst out in aggressive verbal abuse or even physical violence, only to feel the victim afterwards and withdraw to the nearest bar.

She feels justified in her judgment of him, but even though she blames him for being the problem, she lacks the self-confidence leave him. In reality, her belief in her powerlessness makes her needy and reliant on his presence in her life. Just like her mother, she fears facing life alone and feels she cannot exist without the support of a man. The prospect of facing the world on her own terrifies her, and this makes her confront him aggressively. She has trust issues with men because her father was an unpredictable and aggressive alcoholic. She does not completely realise that she married a man just like her father because in too many ways she has become the same woman her mother is.

What would you have been subjected to, had you grown up in this family, and how would that have affected you? If you were a girl, you would have your mother as the reference point for the development of your femininity. Your exposure to your parents' relationship and how your father relates to you will serve as a template for your future relationships. Their capacity to express love, affection and emotions will come to define how you feel about yourself, and how you expect others to feel about you. It will determine what your expectation of what a loving relationship should be. None of it can provide the prospect for a happy and emotionally balanced life. There is a lot more going on between the girl and her parents then what is obvious.

Though she is still a little girl, the disharmony between she senses her father and mother is a product of the repeated conflicts between them. The fundamental reasons lie in his issues with women and therefore also with his wife and her issues with men and with him. The little one perceives her mother as a victim in the conflict because, in their arguments, her father is the aggressively controlling one. She does not realise that subconsciously her sexuality resonates and aligns itself with that of her mother's and she, therefore, accepts her mother's fears and insecurities as her own. She models her femininity, in respect to men, on that of her mother's, and this is confirmed by the behaviour of her father to her and her mother. In adulthood, the sense-of-self she develops from her childhood experiences will determine the kind of men with whom she will choose to be in relationships. At her age, it is unavoidable that her connection with her father will be conditional to his fears, depression or anger because he controls the dynamic between them. It is also inevitable that she will change her behaviour and self-expression to accommodate her father's issues, if she wants a relationship with him, even if it is conditional and on his terms. By doing so, she subconsciously accepts responsibility —guilt — for his negative feelings, behaviour and attitude. Her issues appear as self-blame or guilt and will become a part of her sense-of-self in respect to all men. The beliefs she holds, as a result, will cause her to compromise herself to be in a relationship. In any conflict or confrontation with her father (or men like him), these beliefs will cause her to assume she must be the guilty or responsible one, and accept a position of powerlessness —just like her mother did.

She will deliberately avoid being open and expressive with her feelings, needs or desires for fear that it will provoke an angry reaction from her father or make him reject or abandon her. Just like her mother, her passive-aggressive strategic behaviour is to complain indirectly about all the things she is unhappy with, misses out on and cannot have. She will now and in the future also be the one that will compromise and withdraw if her father or partner gets aggressive with her. She only feels free and safe to express her discontentment and show her disappointment in him in moments when he feels powerless or inadequate —just like her mother did. Her guilt issues in respect to her father and learned from her mother will reappear later in life, because she will be attracted to and attract men like him. Her mother's belief that she is the innocent victim of her father is likely to become hers concerning men. She confirms her victimhood by being convinced that men are the cause of all her issues, fears and unhappiness. It will be unlikely, that she will look within herself and take responsibility for the reasons for this and be accountable for them.

Even though the mother behaves like the victim in the relationship, her negative attitude and consistent dissatisfaction and unhappiness dominated the family paradigm. Her neediness and discontent receive priority in every family situation, thereby ignoring her daughter's needs, fear and insecurities. The mother's neediness for attention and affection, her powerlessness, inability to cope and her dependence on men to fulfil these expectations, make her selfish. This mindset was already present before her daughter was born and compounded by her mother's inability to cope with the demands and responsibilities of motherhood. She felt that her daughter's needs displaced her own and felt unable to give her daughter the love and attention she was entitled to receive. She felt emotionally under-resourced and powerless to deal with the fundamental needs and expectation of her daughter and this amplified her fears and self-doubt. Her daughter, sensing her mother's fears and anxiety, believed that she was the cause and therefore automatically accepted responsibility for her mother's stress. This guilt stops her from holding her mother accountable for not being emotionally present for her.

The suppression of the authentic, spontaneous and unique self-begins very early in a child's life. In her case, the inhibition of her original nature and her acceptance of the belief that she is responsible and guilty for her mother's negative emotions, powerlessness and dissatisfaction, went hand in hand. Her-suppression of her issues, needs and expectations had the effect of intensifying her unfulfilled neediness to be loved, to have attention and to get what she wants. As a result, she cannot help herself being needy in her behaviour. She fears to ask directly for what she wants for fear of being guilty of being a burden. Without realising she emulates much of her mother's behaviour, for similar emotional reasons. She resorts to complaining and nagging as an indirect means to get her needs fulfilled. She subconsciously completes an emotional circle, which sets her up to repeat her mother's life with a man like her father. She will finish up living a life of powerlessness and guilt which is what she always wanted to avoid.

A boy would have a similar experience to the girl but would likely, adopt the same masculinity from his father. By modelling himself on his father, he will also take on many of his fears. He will form his sense-of-himself from the constant exposure to a dissatisfied insecure mother, who is powerless in life, and a frustrated, angry father who feels he can never be and do enough and feels burdened by his family. Initially, his mother has the most influence over him. His is need and dependence on her for her love and acceptance, translates into pleasing behaviour that has the intent to keep his mother happy and content. He is likely to become frustrated by the guilt he feels when she displays her discontent and unhappiness because he feels powerless to satisfy her needs. All this sets him up for the same future relationship as his father. His beliefs about women are modelling on his father's conviction that a man has to be responsible for the happiness and satisfaction of women to be loved and accepted by them. Consequently, he will attract and be attracted to unhappy, needy and dissatisfied women. The over-responsibility for the negative emotions of women have become a part of his sense-of-self, and determine the type of relationships he will choose. Their issues allow him to play out his guilt issues about them.

If his father is abusive and neglectful, he may become defensive of his mother and feel contempt for his father's aggression, intimidation and use of his male power. This perception of a man as a powerful abuser can cause him to suppress his natural masculine assertiveness and sexual nature to avoid appearing as a threat to his mother. Alternatively, he may take on his father's values, standards and behaviour and adopt a chauvinistic attitude that makes him look down on women and see them as inferior. Consequently, he will blame them for everything that he believes to be wrong in his relationship with them.

Both the girl and boy have learned that the conditions incorporated in their guilt are those by which they will be loved, accepted and trusted. Until they acknowledge the part they play in their relationships and deal with the belief systems related to these issues; their lives are likely to remain the same.

EMBARRASSMENT AND SHAME

We cannot talk about guilt and responsibility without addressing embarrassment and shame. Shame and embarrassment are closely related to guilt but are not an intrinsic part of our consciousness. We acquire these characteristics from the environment in which we arrive as a child. Babies, do not care if they are stark naked and urinate in public if they have food on their faces or demand that their needs are met, even under the most challenging circumstances. Shame and embarrassment are learned from others, family or culture.

We acquire shame and embarrassment by accepting responsibility for the shame others feel but for which they make us responsible. When blamed for causing embarrassment or shame for the first time, we usually have no idea of what it is all about. We are accused, of something we cannot immediately relate to but realise others blame us something over which they are angry or upset. Guilt overwhelms us because even though they told us that we are the reason for the embarrassment, we do not necessarily understand why and how. The behaviour of the other person and the insistent nature of their blame soon makes it clear we must be guilty of something terrible. Initially, we cannot fathom the connection between the embarrassed adult and us or what we did or did not do that triggered this aggressive reaction towards us. We begin to feel however that we must be responsible for something that is seriously wrong cause we have become the centre of ridicule, blame or anger. Unaware of what it is about us that causes this adverse reaction, we can only conclude that the reason for the shame is who we are — our presence. Once the so-called error in our expression or behaviour is pointed out to us, and it is also made clear why we are the embarrassment. Even though still unable to intellectually understand the reason, our emotions which are a combination of feeling shy, wrong, guilty and a failure as well as public judgement, cement the belief that we are an embarrassment. We begin to assume responsibility without knowing what the real reasons an emotional issue are. We have learned to become ashamed because others have made us responsible for their sense of embarrassment. These values will over time evolve into self-beliefs of shame that then form our sense-of-self. We quickly learn to blame others for our feelings of the shame or embarrassment in the same way they did it to us.

Our physical reaction to shame— blushing — attracts the attention from others just when we wish to be invisible and unnoticed. Becoming the centre of everyone's attention only serves to reinforce our sense of guilt, even though the last thing we want, is to be seen as the embarrassment. It becomes evident to a child that it cannot defend its behaviour against the accusations of an adult and therefore it has no choice but to accept the blame. In the future, whenever he or she experience shame, they are likely to blame others for feeling embarrassment, just like the person who created the shame in them in the first place.

Our learned and adopted fears and insecurities will come to the surface in the form of behaviours and feelings, but this usually gives little if no indication as to how they are a part of us. The belief that others are responsible for what we feel is engendered by the way our parents raised us and causes us to believe that we are not liable for our life experiences. When we try to find the cause of our issues, we can only see that others must be the reason for our shame or anger, to feel offended or sad and so on. We have been trained to look at what others appear to be doing or saying to us and to judge that to be the reason for how we feel and think in response.

The influence shame and embarrassment can have over our state of mind are evident in some cultures where sentences of extreme punishment are committed on those believed to be responsible for embarrassing, shaming or offending others, the family, community or religion. Murder and disfigurement of women are still a frequent occurrence in some locations in the world, with shame and embarrassment as the most common motivation.

Believing that we are responsible for the thoughts, feelings and emotions of others, would result in accepting that others must be guilty of causing the repertoire of negative emotions we feel, including shame and embarrassment. By not holding yourself accountable for what we create in our lives, this interpretation of the reasons and causes for what we feel, think and how we behave, will be perpetuated by the next generation.

Chapter 14

CONDITIONAL RELATIONSHIPS

Falling in love is one of the most emotionally intense and overwhelming experiences in life. Our relationships or the potential for one can dominate our entire focus and interest in life. In many ways, intimate love relationships are central to human existence and paramount to the continuation of our species. We do not exist in isolation from others or the world and have the need for a partner and have families and friendships in our lives. Experiencing our sense-of-self through the dynamic of our relationships is essential to evolving our consciousness and the nature of our spirit. On an emotional level, relationships serve to create mirrors that allow us to see who we believe we are and who we should not be. The same will be true for them in their relationship with us. Nothing exposes the truth about us more than the emotional kaleidoscope that reveals itself within us when we fall in love and enter a relationship.

Relationships between people range from casual, to friendships and to being close and intimate. All relationships are a place where many of our critical issues, central to our emotional and sometimes physical survival, will be played out. If it were as simple as falling in love and living happily ever after, we would not have the conflict and unhappiness that lead to separation and divorce. The reality is that being happy and fulfilled in relationships is amazingly difficult for the majority of people. We are convinced by our negative experiences in childhood that for a relationship to be successful, we either have to surrender our own needs and expectations or make others give up theirs for us. However, compromises of this kind are never a solution for the issues that we bring into a relationship. Treating an intimate relationship as if it should function as a negotiated contract might appear sensible and logical, but this will rarely lead to a solution for the dissonance between partners. This almost business-like solution can make a relationship an ongoing negotiation over power, need fulfilment, values, standards, setting and respecting boundaries of behaviour and so on, but is unlikely to lead to enduring emotional success.

Many believe that conflict and relationships naturally go together because often from childhood, they have not known it to be any different. It is true that being in a relationship almost guarantees that sooner or later differences appear which can become the sites for hostile emotional battles. Most people believe that a successful, harmonious relationship is a matter of making the right choice of partner. Just the same, very few would be prepared to admit that they are the reason why their relationships fail. The fact that you are the common factor in your relationships proves that the finger of responsibility it firmly pointed at you. Each time you enter a relationship your emotional issues and those of your partner come into play. It is inevitable.

You will only understand why your relationships evolve in the way they do if you understand who you are as a partner. You can begin by looking at your behaviour and by becoming aware of your thoughts and feelings when you are in a relationship. If you want to recognise and accept responsibility for your contribution to the issues in your relationships, it is essential that you get to know 'who you believe you are' really well.

ATTRACTIONS AND DESIRES

Our desire to be in an intimate relationship occupies our emotions and focus well before we get involved. Our sexual interest and focus on appearance always feel as if they are the central driving forces in our search for a mate. Even though they are a significant part of our focus, once we have met someone, other even more influential aspects of our consciousness come to the surface. Whenever there is a prospect of meeting a potential partner we tend to become self-conscious of our appearance and how we believe others will see and judge us. Worried that we will not be good enough, we already fear rejection before it has happened. We commonly measure our self-esteem and our potential for attracting a partner by the confidence we have in our appearance and behaviour with the opposite sex.

You are likely to believe that you have nothing to offer to a prospective partner if you can only see yourself in a negative light. Your negative beliefs about yourself set the stage for any encounter with your opposite gender because you will expect and anticipate rejection or judgement from the outset. Your conviction that you will not be chosen or wanted because of who you believe yourself to be will control what you will say and how you behave. If this is how it is for you, remember that you have learned your critical view of yourself from the way your family raised you.

Ironically, we often acquire our negative beliefs from those who have the best intention to teach us right from wrong, good from bad. The problem is that our parents are teaching us these values without the awareness of their fears and insecurities. As a result, what they try and educate us is often based on behaviour and perceptions distorted by fear-based beliefs systems. Believing that by critically telling us what we do wrong, how we fail and disappoint them they think that we will somehow know what to do right and to trust and feel confident in ourselves. In practice, their criticism delivered with the intent to teach us has exactly the opposite outcome for us. We begin to feel insecure, self-doubting, develop low self-esteem and become fearful. Parents do not realise that they unconsciously teach their children the same beliefs, values and standards they learned in their childhood, unaware that their fears have distorted them. They feel the need, to remind their offspring through criticism and judgment, that everything they do or express is in their perception and by their values or standards, wrong or a failure. It makes no difference, whether they do this passively or aggressively, the result will be the same for the child. Its choices, perception, judgment or behaviour will be wrong, and theirs is deemed to be right. Instead of presenting their children with positive guiding input, that would allow them to develop self-trust and self-confidence, their criticism and negative comments create the perception that there must be something wrong with them. In spite of the intent to be a supportive force in their child's life and make it feel confident and loved, the way they engage it creates the direct opposite outcome. Their constant focus on the negatives they perceive in their child is a direct reflection of their perception of themselves.

The way their communication is personalised through direct or indirect blame, criticism or judgement imprints the child's mind with what appears to be the truth of its shortcomings of who it is. These comments on what is made out to be its failings then become the child's perception of itself — the definition of who it is. These negative self-beliefs will begin to occupy its mind and become the basis for future attitudes, intents, emotions and behaviours, with inevitable outcomes.

Few parents realise that the way they communicate their expectations can be adverse for their children. A child may appear to be compliant and successful because it is meeting the expectations of its parents, but that may not be the child's experience. The expectation our parents have of us, do not necessarily reflect our passions and desires, even if we do not know how to articulate them. In fact, our zealous need to please our parents and to be loved and accepted by them will cause us to comply or fit in with what they want us to be or do. Following their expectations of us can cause us to deny discovering our own. Without the chance to see what our potential, talents and abilities, passions and desires are, or having them dismissed, can be fatal to finding our passions and fascinations in life. As a consequence, we may please our parents by entering a profession they value, but we may thereby also deny ourselves doing what we want in life. Our natural creative talents and abilities can be lost to ourselves and never find a voice in our lifetime. Living life in fear of the judgments of others can deny us the experience through which we could ultimately fulfil our life potential.

Should you feel and believe that you fail living up to your parent's standards, values and expectations, you may well be convinced that you are 'the disappointment' and 'a failure' to them as well as to yourself. Parents, who have specific ideas of what their child should be in their life do so generally with the best of intentions. They are also likely to dismiss and invalidate anything that does not conform to their perception of what that should be. As a result, a parent may never find out the talents or abilities and passions and desires of their child. Even though your parents create the expectations they have of you, they will hold you responsible should you fail and disappoint them. Unfortunately, it very is likely that you will naively accept the responsibility for their disappointment in you. You will assume that you must be guilty because you failed them and disappointed them by not being or doing what they expected from you. At no time will it occur to them that they are the creators of these expectations and that you cannot be responsible for them. As a child, these expectations are interpreted by you, as conditions for acceptance and love. In fact, you will accept that you are 'the disappointment' and 'the failure' as a part of your identity.

People who have no trust in the strength, value, significance and capacity of their mind will either be passive and lack confidence and avoid, or be aggressive and try and prove to everyone that they know everything and is always right. Both strategic behaviours are a product of a lack of self-trust and self-confidence. Unfortunately, when they become parents, they will unwittingly play these issues out on their children through their behaviour and attitude. They will still feel the need to prove to themselves that they are right and knowledgeable by making their children wrong. Their criticism, judgement and 'know better and more' attitude promotes a lack of self-confidence, self-belief and self-trust in their children. They will feel they can no longer trust and depend on their inner resources and the capacity of their mind, to cope with issues and life in general. If the parent shows in their behaviour and attitude that they are fearful of responsibility, meeting needs, expectation, conflict argument or confrontation they are modelling their fears in life to their children who may then adopt them as being real and something to fear. Regardless, whether their approach is aggressive or passively critical, neither will produce self-trust and self-confidence in their offspring.

By repeatedly invalidating their children's thinking, judgment, perception, behaviour, ideas, choices, etc. they actively teach their offspring to distrust and disbelieve themselves. Criticism, being constantly corrected or made to feel wrong makes them fearful of being a disappointment and a failure. The insecurity this creates leads to the fear of making choices, decisions and commitments and other avoidance behaviours. To prove they know more and better they regularly overrule and correct their children's understanding, explanations, decisions, etc. This form of criticism, no matter how well intended, will prevent them from developing trust and confidence of their intellectual, mental and emotional capacities. Parents may have the intent to teach their children knowledge, values and standards, but their methods undermine their confidence in the mental tools necessary for fulfilling their potential in life. They have learned to be fearful of making decisions and choices and distrust their thinking, judgement, reasoning, perception and their ability to conclude. They will feel not good enough, inferior, inadequate, hopeless, powerless and the list goes on. Every level of expression of its emotional, intellectual and creative mind is adversely affected. Under these psychological pressures, any child will potentially grow up convinced that it is emotionally and intellectually inferior. Either way, it has no trust its judgement, knowledge and in its capacity to think and reason independently. Some will rely initially on their parents and later on others, to get through life. This scenario can also result in a child becoming demonstratively independent. It will act and behave as if it does not need anyone to support it and has a need to prove that it knows everything and does not need any advice from others.

Living with the expectation that you know, understand and have the skill to do something before you have learned or understood it is, of course, ridiculous, but that is often exactly what a child learns to believe. Parents who through their behaviour need to prove they are right and all-knowing will frequently and unwittingly create the impression that they expect this from their children. They need to convince everyone including their children that they know 'everything' and that others do not. They do not realise, that through this behaviour, their child believes that it should have understood something before learning it. Without being taught to understand it, a child will conclude that it must be dumb, inadequate and hopeless for not knowing it. The parent's need to prove they know more than a child by asking it to know something that is beyond its education and experience of which to be aware. This kind of challenge places an unrealistic demand on a child's intellect, knowledge and competency, which assures that it will fail. Once it has internalised this experience as its sense-of-self, it is left to face the future with fears that will continually undermine its confidence in its mental capacities. They will be the mental 'tools' by which it is expected to fulfil its potential, be successful and create happiness and abundance in the future. The outcome is not hard to predict because usually, the difficulties will already have begun by the time a child goes to school. Children with these issues often have the experience that the education system does not run far behind the all-knowing and infallible parent in the way it "punishes" children by failing them, for not performing to the curriculum's expectations.

Criticism and judgement come in many forms — it can be indirect and subtle, by continually correcting everything a child chooses or how it expresses itself and by treating it as a disappointment, a failure or a mistake. Alternatively, by directly criticism and judgement, being labelled as stupid, hopeless, incompetent, and so on. Creating expectations that a child cannot meet is also interpreted as a form of criticism. Children feel the effect of all these different forms of criticism but as adults do not necessarily remember the source for their lack of self-confidence, self-criticism and judgement. The more passive and subtle the dynamic between parents and children is the less likely they will be aware of the reasons for their issues once they have reached adulthood. Collectively, every demeaning, critical, judgement and correction will form a child's belief of who and what it believes itself to be. The outcome will reveal itself in their behaviour by either acting as if they know everything to convince others they are intelligent or accepting that they will always be wrong and fail. Regardless of which strategy they employ, both will live in fear of failure, criticism and judgement.

DEVELOPING A CONDITIONAL SENSE-OF-SELF

Every child is a unique conscious entity, and what appear to be qualities in common with one or both parents in respect to their behaviour or physical likeness, are not an indication of the actual nature of its consciousness. The character of a child demands that it grows and learns in its own unique way and at a pace that befits this. The environment they grow up in presents them with a perception of reality to which they have to conform if they are to survive emotionally. They do not realise, that what they see and experience through their parents and in the world, will determine who they will ultimately believe themselves to be — both negatively and positively.

A child's innate drive and desire to spontaneously express its natural, authentic self will usually put it in conflict with the fear-based needs, values and standards held by its parents. The preconceived assumptions they have made about how it should behave and what it should choose, want and respond, etc., will be made the child' responsibility. Should a child's behaviour not conform with these expectations, its parents are likely to respond with criticism to correct the child and become what they believe to be right and proper. Their offspring, however, will interpret this as a rejection of who they are. More specifically, it may feel convinced that they are a failure and disappointment, unlovable and unacceptable, not good enough and inferior, etc. When a child response is disagreeable, stubborn or obstinate, it is trying to survive the emotional pressure from its parents to change from being its authentic self to their idea of who it should be. Not understanding the reasons for their child's behaviour, they automatically blame and criticise the child for being difficult, unacceptable and noncompliant. The issues the child's parents inherited from their parents deprive them of experiencing their child's most natural and powerful state of being. Instead of enhancing its unique characteristics they seek to inhibit and change them to suit their fear-based needs and expectations. Little do they realise that they reject the authentic nature of their child by expecting it to accept emotional conditions they brought into the relationship from their childhood.

The need to be loved and accepted and the pressure of their innate emotional and physical survival instincts forces most children to agree with the emotional constraints created by their parent's fears. The fear-driven dynamic between parent and child will cause its unique qualities to go unrecognised and dismissed. The impact of not being acceptable will manifest in every aspect of its life.

When a child's attraction and fascination are outside the parents' interest or frame of reference, they are often squashed or just ignored and invalidated. Even though a parent may believe that a child's passions and desires are a struggle to realise that does not mean this it is unachievable for their child. Unintentionally, the parent's fears and limitations become the restricted and often fearful world that they force their children to accept. Their biased perception may not allow them to appreciate the potential, talent and ability in their children. They may have an attraction for artistic pursuits and show no interest in physical or material achievements, or it may be the other way around. Once they have learned that their talents, abilities and interests have no value to their parents, they will repeat the same behaviour their parents taught them. When as adults trying, and find their passion or desire, they will dismiss and invalidate them just like their parents did. As a result, later in life, it cannot decide what it wants to do, not realising that it has learned to dismiss what it originally wanted and by which it was excited.

A child can be late in finding its passion or fascination and therefore needs time for self-discovery and self-realisation. Stimulation, exploration, time and space give it room to let its imagination and fantasy roam freely, creating the opportunity to discover its desires, attractions and dreams. A child needs the emotional space to develop its talents and abilities, at its own pace and in its way, to discover its capacity to be creative in dealing with the complexities of life. Open minded guidance and support and space for experimentation and failure are essential to finding its unique direction. Exposure to criticism and judgment will only cause it to believe that it is not good enough, a failure or a disappointment. Childhood is a critical stage for our perpetually evolving minds, and each aspect of the emotional environment of our family plays a determining role in forming our inner sense of being.

Most parents are the victims of their issues just like we are, and usually, do not realise the impact this will have on their offspring. Every time parents expose their children to their disappointment and sadness, depression and negativity, worry and stress and so on, their children feel the effect consciously and internalise it subconsciously. Their negative sense-of-self and the emotional state it creates in them will prevent them being the confident and positive guiding forces their children need them to be.

The expectation to be responsible for a life other than your own is a significant responsibility, and for some parents and this can be an overwhelming emotional challenge, particularly when they have never experienced love and affection, feeling wanted and accepted themselves. Potentially they may feel emotionally under-resourced and unable to cope with the emotional pressure created by the needs and expectations of their new-born. These feelings can emphasise their own unfulfilled needs and make them feel denied and unfulfilled. It is extremely difficult for someone, who was never loved and accepted unconditionally to love themselves, to give unconditional love and receive it in the same way. In these cases, the reservations parents place on meeting these needs and expectations of their child cause it to believe that its life and presence are a burden and an unwanted responsibility to them. The innate need their child expresses to experience and receive unconditional love, acceptance and trust, can be felt by its parents as a demanding them to sacrifice their own need for love, affection. The physical and emotional need for support expressed by their child creates a victim mentality in its parents, causing their child to believe that its existence is a burden, and its innate expectations are an intrusion on their lives. It will feel that it has no choice but to suppress its need for love, acceptance, support, care and protection, etc., as the only way it can have a relationship with their parents. Often, the guilt and obligation the child feels for the mother's or father's pain and suffering will cause it to try and fulfil the parent's need to be loved and accepted. By giving their needs and expectations priority over its own, and by giving love, affection and attention to its parents in exchange for love, acceptance, validation and acknowledgement in return. Adults who grow up like this can be excessively protective of one or both parents.

We need to remind ourselves that we are all born unique and different and that our emotional issues are a legacy from childhood. First of all, it is important to intellectually accept that our issues are not and will never represent who we truly are. The part of you that feels the negative emotions and experiences adverse outcomes is, in fact, more representative 'the real you' than that part of you that gets lost in these fear-based emotions. By accepting that your issues do not define who you authentically are, you can at least be sure of who you are not.

BLINDED BY ILLUSIONS

Anything you believe or feel about yourself based on fear is an illusion and cannot be representative of your authentic self.

Once we are adults, we do not realise that the emotional footprints our childhood has left on our sense-of-self will continue to control our behaviour, choices and perception. Its influence proves that the family legacy of negative beliefs still defines who we believe we are, and therefore our sense of emotional reality. We need to explore our family history to understand the complex nature of our issues and behaviours in our relationships. We each interpret the negative and positive dynamics of our families differently because of our unique characteristics. If for example, our family of origin the family is emotionally turbulent or violent, then there is visible evidence of negative influences. Knowing this, we can assume that these emotional experiences would have affected on our minds adversely.

Passive dysfunctional paradigms played out in families are much harder to recognise because open confrontation and conflict is extremely rare or never occurs at all. On the surface, a family can appear harmonious and peaceful because of the passive and suppressive emotional strategies with which the parents control the emotional space. The parents unconsciously play out their issues through passive behaviours and attitudes that have their roots in powerlessness and victimhood. They give the impression that they will be negatively affected by the free and spontaneous expression of the behaviour, needs, expectations and emotions of their children. The mother or father make their children feel responsible for what their fears and do not want to deal with by acting like victims and consistently putting their vulnerabilities on display. Fears and insecurities determine their actions and responses, and these become the instruments with which they control their emotional environment.

Children will quickly develop reciprocal behavioural responses to avoid the guilt if they were to upset their parents. They learn to fear giving expression to anything that they now believe will cause stress, worry and concern in their parents. Becoming independent very early in life is one way they can avoid being a burden to their parents. Compliant and submissive behaviour by the children to prevent the potential for conflict and disagreement can create a façade of peace and harmony. This false picture of the family may not only be for the benefit of outsiders but also for the sake of all family members because it accommodates the parent's ear of aggression, conflict and confrontation. Not knowing any different, each family member could well be under the illusion that they are part of a perfect family. The reality is that each unconsciously practices self-suppression to avoid being confronted by their greatest fear — being guilty of upsetting another member of their family and creating an emotional confrontation. In adulthood, they will practice the same behaviour with others, and their fears will determine the kind of partner they will choose.

That sort of background makes it difficult to get a clear understanding of the origin of your issues. Parents who are passive powerless and fearful of confrontation unconsciously solicit protection and support from their children. By taking responsibility for their emotional problems they also accept the guilt for how and what their parents feel. In adulthood, their sense of emotional over-responsibility makes it challenging to see their mother and father objectively. Often parents will create the perception that they struggled and sacrificed themselves for them. The guilt this creates makes it difficult to accept that their parents are the origin of their issues in life. This conclusion leaves them to accept that they must either have been born with their fears and insecurities or that the world is responsible for all their ills. In both cases, they would have to accept that they are powerless and have no control over their life. Neither of these options will take them to a place where real change and a permanent resolution is possible. Understanding the reasons for our fears will not be achievable if we allow guilt to stop us from being objective of the relationship dynamic we experienced with our parents.

Depending on the gender of the child, the influence a parent has over a child can be broken down into specific areas. If a girl, she will instinctively model her sense of femininity on her mother just as a boy will model his masculinity on that of his father.

Their interpretation of the sexuality same gender parent will profoundly influence their definition of the nature of their femininity or masculinity. Depending on whether a child feels empowered or disempowered by the example of their same gender parent, a child will either try to reject or embrace it. This choice will depend on its unique nature and how it will serve its emotional survival in respect to its gender. The kind of intimate relationships it will have as an adult depends on the way the child's opposite sex parent related to the same-sex parent and the child. The strategic and emotional behaviour the parents display to each other, and their child will determine the sense-of-self it will adopt. Constant exposure to the parent's negative interactions and self-expression between each other and their children enmeshes a child in their gender-based fears and insecurities.

The inner-perspective a girl or boy develop because of the relationship dynamic between their mother and father comes to define their sense of their femininity or masculinity. If these are fear-based, this will show in every part of life, but most intensely in their intimate relationships. Our subconscious needs, feelings of distrust and powerlessness, shape our expectations of close relationships and subsequent experiences and so will our disappointments.

The lack of awareness of what drives our behaviour, feelings and choices, make it very difficult to recognise that we have issues and how they affect us. Initially, our feelings often lead us to believe that we have found the perfect partner, only to discover later that we cannot live with much of their behaviour, habits or attitude. The inherited issues related to our opposite gender make it difficult to be objective in relationships. We see qualities in our potential partner that are a reflection of our own emotional needs born out of fear-based beliefs. This perception initially creates the illusion that they will fulfil our needs and expectations and are a perfect fit for us. In the early stages of the relationship, we do not see that we are matching issues rather than just positive qualities. From their perspective, the story is the same in that they see their needs fulfilled through us, and also do not realise that these are a product of their issues. Sooner or later this will bear out when conflict and discord arise from mutual dissatisfaction and discontent.

When a relationship fails, both parties commonly believe that they have justifiable reasons to blame the other for what went wrong. The accusations can be many, but they often include being deceitful or deceptive at the early part of the relationship. One will hold the other responsible for not being the person they first met or that he or she deliberately misled or manipulated them. Rarely are the real and fundamental reasons for the breakup — their fears and insecurities —recognised and addressed.

MISLED BY FEELINGS AND ATTRACTIONS

Our consciousness has a simple consistency:

It will only be able to recognise and understand the issues of others once it has realised and transcended its own.

Issues manifested by your negative beliefs alter your perception and feelings by creating false insecurities, needs and expectations. Negative emotions have the capacity to make unfulfilled needs, expectations and vulnerabilities appear genuine, and this will cause you to be attracted to someone whose issues seem to be able to protect you of yours. As a counterpart to your problems, their emotional experience of you will in many ways equal your own. For example, ego-driven insecurity is attracted to ego-based confidence — ego-driven vulnerability and powerlessness are attracted to ego-based power and strength — a passive, insecure victim will attract an ego-driven, controlling individual, and of course vice versa., Often, it may not be as recognisable and clear as this because other issues can muddy the water, but this kind of pattern consistently appears in just about every relationship.

At the beginning of a relationship, both parties tend to become so overwhelmed by their feelings for each other that the real and more fundamental motivations for the attraction go unnoticed. The love and lust for one another become the priority for emotional and physical satisfaction. At this time, there is no awareness that there may be other and deeper reasons for their mutual attraction. Together with love, they have also activated the needs and vulnerabilities generated by their separate negative belief systems. The altered perception create by this makes them feel as if they are a perfect fit for each other and makes each more desirable to the other. Mutual attraction can consist of many different emotional aspects of which love takes centre stage, but fear can distort them to the point where love is no longer the core value in a relationship. It is a consistent characteristic of relationships for each partner to have issues that complement each other and match. This concept is in the same vein as an aggressor finding a victim but also vice versa. Or, a passive partner finding a dominant and controlling partner. In each case, the behaviour of one is complementary to the others. Once a couple gets together the complementary nature of their fears will generate the feeling that one will fulfil the needs of the other. In the bliss of the initial phase of their encounter, they will not be aware that a big part of what they experience with one another is an illusion of their own creation. The way their issues interrelate and correspond so perfectly serve to make it feel real and genuine.

Time is inclined to expose cracks and flaws in relationships, and often it does not take very long for these to become serious points of conflict which if unresolved, can destroy a relationship. For anyone who recognises the dynamic in play, the outcome is predictable, but for those playing out their fear, the warning signs are all but invisible. Often sometime after the 'honeymoon period' is over, disappointments, dissatisfaction and criticism are felt or expressed. When partners do not deal with the fundamental causes of any discord between them, other measures such as changes in behaviour, are unlikely to bring lasting resolution. Failing to see that the issues of one, mirror those of the other, they will resort to blaming and accusations to deal with what each feel. Unaware of the part each play in bringing the conflict about, they do not appreciate the responsibility each has for the fears they brought in their relationship. We miss the opportunity to learn and grow from the experience when we do not recognise that our issues are the primary reason for our conflicts. As a result, the conclusion of a relationship can be in stark contrast to the initial emotional experience we had when we first met.

Relationship issues do not prove that you 'are the failure', but you make it hard for yourself if you do not understand the reasons for your attraction to a particular type of character with whom you consistently have issues. You cannot change your relationships without changing yourself, and that is not possible without you being aware of what the issues are in the first place.

Relationships are an essential part of the process of living life not only for procreation but also because they have the capacity to show us graphically who we believe we are. The interaction between partners does not only have the ability to reveal our fear-based illusions but can thereby also provide the opportunity to discover who we authentically are. Only you are responsible if you keep on choosing the same problematic relationships over and over again without questioning yourself. Your consistent presence in all of your relationships with different partners, points at you being the responsible party. By not accepting that you must be the central contributor to your relationship experiences, you are destined to repeat them. The emotional pain you suffer as a consequence of failed relationships is an alert to take stock of who you believe you are and acknowledge your fears and insecurities.

Remember the core of your issue is not about what you do or choose but who you are as the one making these choices and engaging in certain behaviours. Blaming others makes you the victim of others or the situation without resolution. Blame and accusing or criticising others is your subconscious attempt to avoid responsibility for your choices. Based on what you believe, feel and think, you are the one who decides on the kind of relationship you want to have. Your choice of partner will show if fear is controlling you or not. You need to understand your emotional processes to see why you choose relationships that are unworkable. Developing clarity as to why you have the attraction for personalities that lead you to pain and unhappiness, is essential if you want to know what it is you need to let go off, to change.

Intellect and logic alone cannot undo the reasons for this distorted perception and the illusions it creates. Uncovering the nature of your sense-of-self by releasing your negative beliefs is the only way to raise your clarity of insight, and bring you to understand your fears. Changing the core nature of your sense-of-self by releasing your fears will remove distortion from your perception, feelings and behaviour. Without it, manifesting a life that fulfils your potential on a personal level, as well as in an intimate relationship, will be extremely difficult if not impossible. Emotional issues will always act as a restriction in your life — in relationships, self-fulfilment and success.

TRAPPED IN CONDITIONAL LOVE

Love and physical attraction alone is not the basis of the desire for a potential partner. The nature of our sense-of-self plays an undeniable part in shaping the context of our desires. Once our self-beliefs are involved, so are the fears we harbour about ourselves and others. The fear-based beliefs that form our subconscious identity will ensure that the object of our desire will be a counterpart to our issues and insecurities. That we do this without any awareness, insight, thought, planning or understanding should be truly alarming. Without fail, out of hundreds of potential choices, we will choose the very person who represents a perfect counterpart for our fears.

It may not occur to you that your potential partner will be going through a similar experience because your insecurities cause theirs to be hidden from you. The dynamic between the individual issues you both bring into the relationship will cause them to become the reasons for disharmony and conflict. The interaction between a passive victim and an aggressive, controlling person will remain conflict fee if each will stay in their designated roles. As long as the victim accepts the aggression and does not confront it and the aggressor is satisfied that they are in control the relationship will be emotionally stable. The moment the victim protests or refuses to play their part or the aggressor loses interest in the victim the dynamic is out of balance and conflict will surface.

Typically, in a room of full of people, you will be attracted to a particular kind of person. You may also have noticed who you are interested in; others are not. You may think that their looks and behaviour are the main reason for your attraction for them, but it is the emotional energy their presence radiates that will win you over. Their emotional state of being has to complement yours to make them — in your perception — the "right" person for you.

For example: If you need to be the saviour in relationships, you have to engage in behaviour that makes you appear supportive, stable or indispensable but also non-confrontational and protective. Your strategy is designed to prove your strength and worthiness to be loved and wanted. With this approach, you will be attractive to partners who have a need to be saved — who feel unlovable, unacceptable and are powerless, needy and insecure. It goes without saying that they will be attracted to the one who will save them.

If you are a person who has insecurities and feels in many ways unlovable, unacceptable and powerless to support yourself in life, you will be attracted to someone who appears strong and independent with the capacity to support you without having any expectations of you. Your strategy may be to give love, affection and attention to be loved, saved and protected. You do not realise that your reliable and safe partner has learned to present him or herself that way to his parent to avoid being a burden and unwanted responsibility for their parents. Instead, they try to be supportive of their mother or father and make them feel safe from their fears. They have learned that by doing so, they will get attention, acknowledgement and acceptance even if it is conditional. It also makes them avoid feeling guilty of causing for causing their parents stress, anxiety and worry. Just like you expect your partner to do this for you.

You could say these two are a perfect match for each other because their issues are complementary, but eventually, their union is likely to result in conflict. When the reliable partner becomes tired of meeting the endless expectations of his or her weak and vulnerable mate and withdraws, they will feel abandoned and deserted. The now fearful, disappointed and powerless partner is likely to make the other responsible for what they feel. The 'stronger' of the two now begins to feel that they are re-experiencing their childhood guilt and blame all over again.

Should the weaker partner change and become empowered, develop confidence in himself or herself, and no longer need support and protection, the 'strong partner' will feel redundant and useless. Each of the two people in this example has an agenda inspired by their fear-based issues. Even though each compliments the negative beliefs and associated strategies of the other, their relationship fears will ensure that they will surface in the long term. If they were to look at themselves and each other objectively, they would realise that each mirrors the fears and insecurities of the other. The real difference lies in how they deal with it individually — one does so by using passive, victim behaviour, and the other by being dominating and controlling.

If for example, giving and receiving love in your family was conditional, then relationships will become a provisional process for you. Fear and distrust, in respect to love and acceptance, will form an inevitable part of your life. You will attract and be attracted to partners who through their issues are also conditional in their giving and receiving of love, because of their distrust issues. The behaviour in individual personalities can be obsessive, in the way they express love and attention and in their effort to convince someone that they should be the only person in their life. Relentless communication and contact can be used to make their potential partner believe that they are the only one for them and that there is no-one else for them but you. Their fear of rejection, abandonment by the opposite sex or being alone is extreme. However, because you believe that you are unlovable and unacceptable, you have the need to be loved and wanted. This vulnerability causes you to feel needy for someone to convince you that you are lovable and wanted. Your lack of self-esteem and combined with your trust issues with men demands that you expect an excessive level of persistent attention before you will accept that someone is interested in you. Only an obsessive person will give you the kind of exclusive attention to satisfy their need to be loved and because of their fear of rejection.

Your fear of being hurt by rejection or abandonment will stop you from realising that your partner is completely enrolled in a relationship strategy — to give love and to receive it, to pay attention and to get it and so on. By receiving the sort of interest and care you crave, you to respond positively to their behaviour and you become convinced that they are trustworthy and sincere with you. The emotional experience creates the sense that you can trust and believe his or her love and attention, including the dialogue that supports it because of their persistence. The need to feel loved and wanted, and your attraction to this kind of attention, is usually enough to make you blind to what is your partner plays out and the motivation for your reaction to this. Your desire to be convinced that it is safe to love and commit become the security for your overly attentive partner. Unfortunately, once they have won you over and feel secure in the relationship things will usually change. Inclusive, with all their other fears, they do not cope with the incessant demands, needs and expectations that your need for reassurance places on them. The emotional expectations they have created in you, with their exclusive attention for you, becomes a trap for them. No partner can maintain this level of attention without feeling that they compromise his or her own need for love and validation. At this point, they feel it is their turn to receive rather than give 'love'. Their change in behaviour will look to you like a withdrawal of love, affection and attention and this sets your alarm bells ringing. Your fears are well founded because your relationship has now reached a critical juncture. Your fear-based neediness to receive love and acceptance far outweighs your capacity to give these unconditionally.

People who actively, obsessively and strategically "give love to get love" often need to convince themselves that every member of the opposite gender will desire and want them. Their behaviour with their opposite sex is geared to get the response that will 'prove' that they are attractive and desirable to them. They may have lots of so-called 'friends', many of which are potential partners, waiting in the wings should their current relationship fail. Their deeper insecurities may cause them to be extremely jealous of other males or females in your circle of contacts and friends. This jealousy can cause them to isolate you from friends and others through subtle criticism. They will also try and sabotage your connections by non-participation in activities with friends, to force you to choose between him or her and your friends and make you feel guilty. To quiet their fears, they need to 'own' you exclusively in every way and control your life. One way to achieve this is by being critical of your friends and acquaintances and forcing you to choose them over others. The real problem lies with you because, without your fears and distrust of men, love and acceptance, this kind of partner would never have been desirable to you in the first place. Even though you are not aware of it, but you need to be loved and safe and secure in a relationship, have set you up for a lot of pain, unhappiness and frustration.

Once you are conscious that your fears affect your objectivity, it is wise to become more aware of your interactions with the opposite sex. Try and recognise the kind of fears and insecurities that drive your choices, behaviours, needs and feelings. Carefully monitoring these would make you more aware of your deeper motivations and the potential consequences of your attractions and dislikes. The innate need to love and be loved, including sexual attraction is naturally major influences in any personal relationship. You will only find a reliable level of stability and objectivity in relationships when unconditional love and acceptance are the core values of your relationship with yourself. Never forget that the emotional attractions created by the intent of your negative beliefs have the capacity to turn your fears and insecurities into a real relationship experience. Finally, unconditional love and acceptance and feeling wanted starts within you, with yourself.

WHO IS TO BLAME?

Just imagine that every one of your failed relationships was a crime scene. Would you not be suspicious if the same person turned up each time? Do you realise that even though your partners change, you are the only one who is consistently present in every one of your relationships? Obviously, that cannot be a coincidence. Who do you think would be the prime suspect in all of your failed relationships if you are the common factor? The feelings, attractions and subsequent choices that bring you into these relationships are yours and yours alone. However, you are always responsible for your attraction and decisions in spite of the fact that you may be unaware of the influences your negative sense-of-self has over them. You can choose not to accept responsibility for your relationship failures, but in doing so, you also decide not to be in control over your life. You can only create the opportunity for change, and take charge of your emotional life by taking responsibility for what and how you contributed to your relationships choices. By questioning whether fear controls your attitude, needs, attractions and behaviour, you will begin to realise the distortions by which you live. Releasing the negative beliefs that support them allows you to discover the power with which you were born, and embrace your authentic self.

The greatest difficulty we have creating loving, functional relationships comes from our lack of awareness of who we believe ourselves to be. The lack of understanding we have of our consciousness is a severe handicap to our ability to appreciate who we believe ourselves to be versus our yet undefined authentic self. Our reticence to acknowledge the negative beliefs we hold about ourselves makes us often unwilling to take responsibility for what they represent. The additional problem is that we will only discover who we were born to be once we release the negative beliefs that are the container for our fears. We cannot avoid what we feel and believe about ourselves in our relationships with others but, by accepting responsibility for our feelings, emotions, choices and behaviour, we would not fall into blame, powerlessness and subsequent victimhood. Unfortunately, we tend to throw ourselves into relationships like lemmings running over a cliff, with the kind of desperate commitment that would leave a casual observer breathless. We tend to believe that what we see in someone and feel about them represents the truth of who they are, even if others do not share our perception. We are not aware that what we see in someone else, are be a product of the beliefs that make up our sense-of-self and can distort our needs and expectations. Sometimes we see the potential of what someone could be — rather than who they are right now with all of their emotional problems. Once fear distorts our perception, our expectation of who someone is and how they will be in a relationship will be misleading.

Our judgment of potential partners is usually hopelessly flawed due to the issues we have. As a result, we tend to follow our feelings and attractions regardless of the advice we receive, because we fear missing out on satisfying our fear-driven needs. The interesting part of this is that many have a sense that something about the object of their passion is not quite what who he or she appears to be. Both the lack of certainty and the fear that it will interfere with the fulfilment of their desire to be loved, make them dismiss these instinctive warnings. In hindsight, you may recall these moments of awareness and wish you had listened to it. The reality is that you can consciously override common sense to fulfil your needs, but it will not save from your negative beliefs eventually influencing your relationships.

Considering that the attraction both parties have for each other includes their emotional issues, it is no surprise that conflict ensues over time. The way we experience conflict in a relationship causes it to feel genuine and actual. When conflict and negative confrontations put both parties in a highly emotional state of mind and may become aggressive or completely powerless, they are both subject to distinct differences in perception and awareness, needs and expectations, etc. The intensity with which couples fight over these differences is a consequence of their fear for emotional survival. The problems they believe to be at the centre of their conflict are usually the symptoms of an issue rather than the core reasons. Only self-examination of the emotional issues they each brought into the relationship — will reveal the truth of what is going on between them. Unfortunately, blaming one another will only lead to further argument and separation and less meaningful communication. By making each other responsible for the anger, frustration or disappointment they feel, they avoid accepting responsibility for their part in it, which is exactly the opposite of what you should be doing

Hold this thought:

At the most fundamental level of our spiritual being, we are all one without being the same. At this core level of our being all consciousness melts into one unified concept of being:

One Greater Consciousness which encompasses the potential for every possible state of unique being.

The nature of unconditional love, acceptance and trust are the foundation of this fundamental unity of which we are all a part. When these essential emotional elements are absent, all of our life experiences become conditional, and we then live in fear of everything that flows from the conditions we believe and perceive to exist.

THE STORY OF "SUSPICIOUS DISTRUST" AND "THE CONVINCER."

A woman who believes that men cannot be trusted will inevitably be attracted and attract those who are a counterpart to this issue. Her conviction that they will betray, deceive and disappoint her, will cause her to look for someone she can prove to her that he is dependable, reliable and trustworthy. Her consistent state of suspicion and distrust makes entering relationships a confronting and challenging process for her. She finds it difficult to find men she feels she can trust.

The reasons for her issues will stem from childhood because her mother would have been distrusting of men. Her father may have been a charismatic philanderer, a flirt and a good talker with the need to prove to himself that women want and desire him. Even though her mother was continuously critical and complained about her father, she never left him. Her mother was far too needy and fearful of being alone to make that choice. Besides, her father would always talk himself back into her mother's life, and her mother would always accept the promises he made. She, just like her mother, regarded her father, and later in life other men, with distrust, something she has never been able to let go off.

A man who has trust issues with women grows up in a similar family. Early in life he will be exposed to his parents' relationship issues and witness some of their conflicts. Through his mother's complaints and discontent, he will often have an early awareness of his father's indiscretions. His mother's persistent suspicion of his father makes him feel judged as a male. His sense of over-responsibility for his mother's fears has the potential to make him feel guilty without there being any real cause. His mother's distrust of men also affects how she conducts her relationship with him. She often wants to know his whereabouts and the company he keeps which feels to him as if she is interrogating him and this only reinforces his feelings of guilt. Driven by his innate need for his mother's love, he seeks to placate his mother's distrust of him by telling her what he believes she wants and needs to hear. He begins to realise that this is the only way he can be free from her oppressive and controlling behaviour. Unconsciously he adopts a style of communication that has the intent to convince her that he would never hurt or disappoint her. This kind of dialogue becomes his way of taking responsibility for his mother's fear and insecurities. His strategic communication style has the intent to prove that he is not like his father or men like him. He wants to convince her that he will protect her by shielding her from anything that could upset her or make her feel insecure.

The beliefs he takes on from his childhood experiences with his mother develop his understanding of how he should relate to women and define what they expect from him. As an adult in relationships, it feels natural to him to be secretive about his life to avoid upsetting his partner. He has learned only to give out information will avoid causing disappointment or discontent in his partner and still will get him what he wants. This learned behaviour is the only way he knows how to give love and to be loved, even though it is very conditional to his needs and expectations.

He bears his mother or women no direct malice because he perceives them as being the victims. The potential of being guilty of causing them pain is in constant conflict with his emotional need and desire to feel wanted and accepted by women. His well-meant ways will unfortunately always result in them getting hurt and victimised which leaves him feeling misunderstood, unloved and unwanted. On the surface, the issues will look like deceit and distrust, but the real reasons are the negative beliefs each brought into the relationship. He has learned to present himself as trustworthy and emotionally dependable to convince women that he will not hurt or deceive them, while afraid of the responsibility and restrictions that a commitment to a relationship would place on him. At the same time, he lives in constant fear of not being lovable, wanted and acceptable to women. She will feel entirely justified in her feelings of distrust and therefore believes it is up to him to prove he is different and can meet her expectations. The only way out of this dilemma is for both to release the reasons for this kind of an impasse, which are the distorted beliefs each holds in respect to their opposite gender. Their negative beliefs are responsible for the unrealistic expectations each has of the other and need to be released to see themselves and each other differently.

Their relationship will have a chance to be successful if they change who they are to themselves before they place any demands on each other.

Women who distrust men are the daughters of the same kind of mothers and fathers that these men once had. Listening to their mother's stream of suspicions and accusations as they were growing up, and exposed to their father's often secretive and covert behaviour, girls become convinced that men cannot be trusted or believed. Boys will unconsciously model themselves on their father while the girls model their femininity on their mother. They unknowingly adopt their mother's belief systems about men, relationships and love, and incorporate these into their sense-of-self. They see their father and as a consequence, all men, as deceivers and liars who do not keep their promises and cannot be trusted to be supportive, dependable or faithful. She adopts her mother's strategic behaviour of suspicion and distrust and is inquisitive and controlling in relationships to quiet her fears.

Now, as an adult, she constantly demands that the partner in her life proves his trustworthiness to satisfy her suspicions. However, her neediness to be loved and have a man in her life, just like her mother, defeats her every time. The only relationships she attracts are with men who seem to have the power to make her believe that they are true to their word and would never hurt her, but then do the exact opposite. At the onset of the relationship, men make her feel that she the centre of their passion and that she is the only one that matters in their life. Greedy for proof that will validate and endorse her need for love and acceptance, she is likely to succumb to his promises. She does not realise she is the perfect counterpart for a convincer and that she is in fact attracted to his type of personality because of her neediness as a result of her issues. Her belief that she is unlovable to a man and her distrust of the love from men makes her also intensely needy for it.

Her vision of the world locks her in a perspective where men can never be trusted which has been proven by her experience of relationships. She does not realise that out of all the men she encounters that she will feel attracted to those with a charismatic, over-confident and articulate manner. This particular kind of character will find himself subconsciously drawn to her because her need to be loved and wanted, makes her appear vulnerable. Once they are involved with each other, she will not be able to resist looking for more security in the relationship. She will start asking questions, which he experiences as being a mirror of his restrictive childhood and this will cause him to become evasive and secretive. His response only serves to bring back the suspicions her mother had with her father, and before she can stop herself, she is asking questions that sound to him like an interrogation. What follows should have been predictable for each of them, had they understood the emotional baggage with which they left home.

Once they are adults, both the girl and boy suffer the consequences of distrust in love and relationships. We all have the innate desire and need to be in relationships whether they are close and intimate or friendships, but issues become unavoidable we are ruled by our fears. A distrusting person feels inherently vulnerable to betrayal and deception, rejection and abandonment and will seek proof from their partner that they will be safe from this. It does not occur to them that they are the problem, but instead, may impose their need for proof of trust in others to assure their safety from deceit.

THE STORY OF "NEVER ENOUGH" AND THE "TIRELESS PROVIDER."

Women, who believe they do not have the capacity and intellectual and emotional resources to live without support, fear taking responsibility for their own lives. They feel being powerless and helpless to support themselves and therefore believe that they need to depend on a man to survive. Often their sexuality and capacity to attract men become the currency in their relationships and life in general. The significance of their physical appearance features prominently throughout their lives. In families where the mother has the belief that men are indebted to her, her daughter will grow up believing that they owe her support and care. Convinced of their entitlement to hold men responsible for their needs, emotional and material security, they tend to have an air of discontent and dissatisfaction with virtually everything in their life as if nothing is ever quite good enough for them. The significance of their entitlement underlines their criticism of everything and everyone that does not meet their expectations. Their behaviour is designed to give an impression of superiority and is their strategy for dealing with their fear of not being significant enough, and to show that they are never satisfied with what they receive. They convince themselves that their sense of entitlement makes their behaviour and demands entirely justified. Their fear of the perceived consequences of being denied can drive them to go to any length to get what they want. She is high maintenance because her fear of being less than others by being without material and emotional security rules her emotions, perception and behaviour. Her fears ensure that she is the only priority in her life and everyone else runs a distant second.

Men that are attracted to women with this kind of issue come from families that have mothers with these characteristics. The males in the family learn very early that to be worthy of their mother's love and affection, they need to be able to meet her high demands and expectations as providers, and caretakers of women. In many ways, he learns to emulate the dynamic between his father and mother. When they are young, they are expected to meet their mother's emotional needs, but as they mature into men, these become material and financial. In this family dynamic, the father and his issues are just as a significant influence on him as that of the mother. The father's problems with self-value and significance in respect to women causes him to be attracted to his partner's pretentious behaviour. She gives him the impression that she is a woman with high expectations and values, and a prize for any man she deems good enough. Having her glamour in his life makes him feel that he stands out and is more significant than other men. Unfortunately, he takes great pride in his ability to keep up with her neediness to display material wealth at great cost to himself. His boasts and need to prove his superiority as a man serves as an example to his son, who is likely to try and prove his worth as a man in the same way.

Their daughter will relate to her femininity according to the role her mother plays out for her and with her father. Her father and mother set the standards and values and promotes the belief systems that will determine what her future expectations from men and relationships will be. The behaviour of both her mother and father will convince her that all men are like him and are responsible for saving her from her insecurities, by providing for her needs whatever they may be. Her father, true to his role, will in all likelihood believe that he has to give his daughter everything she desires so that he can win her heart. If he were not to meet the needs and expectations of women in his life, he fears not being worthy of their love. He has learned to accept that their dissatisfaction, discontent and unhappiness are a product of his shortcomings and so guilt is a strong driving force in his motivation to please. His fear of disappointing them makes him extremely vulnerable to their criticism and judgement

The behaviour between mother and father is the lesson by which both son and daughter will in time learn to define their respective sexualities. The boy will accept that being responsible for his mother, and later women is an inseparable part of his masculinity. The girl will emulate her mother's sense-of-self to become just like her. They both learn that the promise of their strategic behaviours is to be loved and accepted but have no awareness that all the conditions they set for each other distort the sincerity and truth of their relationships. Love for both is conditional and failure to meet the expectations they have of each other and will result in the belief that ultimately love will be denied. The potential absence of love and acceptance drives the fear that motivates their behaviour. In adulthood, he is unlikely to confront her for her unreasonable demands, needs and behaviour because she will make him feel inadequate as a man for failing her. He will believe that her dissatisfaction and disappointment is always his fault. She will not ever be satisfied and content with her life because her real desire is to feel that love, trust and acceptance is unconditional.

Her neediness to have a man provide for her and his need to be the provider to be deserving of her love makes them interdependent. In the long-term, emotional stress and pain will often be inevitable in this kind of relationship dynamic. All family members live in fear and guilt, and the only solution they believe they have available in their emotional arsenal is to meet the conditions each set for the other.

Neither feels they can exist alone because they are both needy of their emotional counterpart to feel they are lovable, wanted and significant, even if it is conditional.

Women and men with these issues have insecurities with emotional and physical intimacy and the tendency to use their sexuality to attract each other. Because of this, they will never be long without a relationship. Her fear that she cannot survive without a man results in a desperate need to be in a relationship. Once she has a partner, she is in constant fear of being rejected or abandoned. This issue will be very similar to that of her male counterpart. A man could lose meaning and purpose in the latter years of his life if he focussed all of his efforts on satisfying the expectations of his partner while his own remained unfulfilled. From the very beginning his passions, desires, talents and abilities would always have been second to the needs and expectations of his mother, and later to those of his partners.

This kind of relationship lasts as long as he remains the tireless supplier to his partner's needs and expectations, and she feels satisfied and secure enough to stay with him. Their relationship is only as strong as his need to create the lifestyle she requires for her ego, and her fear of being rejected and having to face life on her own.

WITHOUT FEELINGS WHERE IS LOVE?

There are many who, to one degree or another, have an issue with showing their feelings and emotions and dealing with those of others. The causes for this can sometimes be cultural but are usually for personal and emotional reasons to do with fear of guilt, embarrassment or shame. This fear of revealing one's emotions and feelings openly and freely, generally also leads to the need to avoid emotional confrontation and an attraction to those who have similar reasons to suppress them. The unconscious intent is to avoid being confronted by sincere and honest, or extreme emotions, such as anger, sadness or pain and then be required to reciprocate.

Instead, to avoid being exposed to emotionally intense or aggressive behaviour, their potential partner needs to be emotionally predictable and stable. The need to be secure in the knowledge that they will never be aggressively confronted or challenged in a relationship. However, this also means that they cannot make any emotional demands or have expectations of one another, or hold one another accountable when there is conflict.

They may be attracted to people who are frank with their emotions and opinions, but the prospect of sharing a life with someone like that is too confronting because it demands that they respond likewise. It is common for one partner to be a little more assertive and confident than the other, but this is often more product of the differences in their coping strategies for the same fears. Neither will openly show what they truly feel and as a result, issues, when they arise, are never actually resolved. Avoidance of any negative emotional situation or conflict is their strategy in relationships and in life, which makes confronting their issues an extreme challenge.

The reasons for this behaviour can be traced back to their family upbringing. Growing in an environment, where the expression of emotion, often except happy or positive feelings, would be frowned upon and passively or actively suppressed, he learned to suppress his feelings. Showing the need for love and affection can frequently generate an extreme reaction in this kind of family paradigm. Only emotions that will not offend or confront are allowed to have a voice. In some family dynamics, members can only be present and engaged if expressing light-heartedness, happiness and optimism, thereby creating unrealistic emotional relationships between parents and children. The result is a family environment that is lacking in sincere and truthful communication. Children can only openly express a small range of feelings causing them to fear any other emotion they experience within themselves. They cannot show anger, aggression, discontent or question anything to do with their mother or father for fear of provoking a negative response that will make them out to be the guilty party. Children from such families are often insecure and live in doubt as to whether they are lovable, acceptable or wanted. Their parents never freely show their love and affection for them or any other emotion that may offend or cause them to feel uncomfortable or confronted. Instead, everything emotional is conditional to their fears and insecurities. Without the self-confidence, that expressions of love, physical affection, attention and interest would give their children, they are left to question whether they matter at all to their parents.

When parents are unaware of their negative beliefs — fears — concerning the expression of feelings and their issues with unconditional love, they often assume, that by physically caring for their children, they are giving love. They may have the intent to love, want, accept and trust unconditionally but their child has no emotional or physical evidence that their parent feels that way about them. Without the experience, it needs to affirm that it is unconditionally lovable, acceptable and wanted, it is in doubt that its existence has worth and matters.

The avoidance strategies played by their parents — passively or aggressively — result in different forms of guilt for their children. Their behaviour implies that they cannot cope with the emotional needs and expectations of their children. In turn, in the belief, that they are responsible for creating the stress and fear their parent's display, their children suppress their own needs and emotions subconsciously, to avoid feeling guilty for being responsible for their parents' negative feelings. Their parents' behaviour convinces them that they must be an emotional burden and thereby learn to feel guilty for expecting and needing love and affection. They learn to believe that to be taken care of and included they have no choice but to suppress their innate need and entitlement to be unconditionally loved and accepted. Subconsciously this expectation will influence every future relationship.

Not knowing any different, children accept the pervading family paradigm as normal. Their naivety causes the need to develop a sense-of-self based on fear of expressing feelings and emotions. Potentially, in constant fear of offending or upsetting others, they will spend their life trying to anticipate how others will feel and what they think or want to know what they should or should not say or do. They edit their choice of what to say or not to say for their fear of upsetting others. They cannot express their emotions and feelings spontaneously, for fear of being guilty of causing a negative response or reaction in others and provoking the potential for rejection, criticism or blame. The limit of their self-expression will always depend on their perception and interpretation of the emotional vulnerabilities and potential aggression in others.

Children who have not experienced physical and emotional demonstrations of love, acceptance and trust become adults who never feels free to express the need to experience this. The question is: If no one has ever shown you that you are entitled, worthy and deserving of love and are therefore lovable and feel confident to give and receive love, then how will you conduct yourself in a relationship and what kind of relationship would you choose?

Relationships formed by suppressed emotions, driven by guilt either become bland or fail. The lack of emotional fulfilment for each partner will make the more aggressive partner will look for a resolution, which will be unsettling if not confrontational for the other, passive partner. Whoever takes the assertive role in this confrontation will be seen to be responsible for the breakup and thereby leaving the passive partner to appear to be the 'innocent victim'. Resolution for the issues of each partner lies in releasing the beliefs that underpin their fear of experiencing, receiving and expressing unacceptable emotions. The characteristic of these emotions may be positive or negative. They will only feel safe to show their feelings and emotions once they have released the fear of being blamed for the adverse reactions of others. Assuming there is love between them, the absence of these damaging beliefs would change their relationship dramatically. Their changed sense-of-themselves would lead to a transformation in perception, needs and behaviour, that would serve to bring them closer to being the spontaneous emotional spirits they were always meant to be.

The fear of unconditional love, acceptance and trust creates an emotional void, that unless dealt with will remain a source of pain throughout one's life. Our innate expectation to be in harmony with our essence will assure that we will always yearn to fill the emptiness that the absence of unconditional love leaves.

CHANGE WITHOUT FEAR

Even though our families are the origin for how our sense-of-self develops, we need to remember that our grandparents subjected our parents to the issues they inherited from their families. Blaming them for what you are going through will not resolve anything for you. Persisting in holding them responsible for what you feel, will in the long term keep you powerless to change because you perceive the cause for your problems to be outside of you. It will also leave your family issues unresolved in you. You need to take ownership of your issues by accepting that now, as an adult, you are the one holding on to the causes as a part of your sense-of-self. As an adult, you can no longer claim that anyone is 'doing it' to you.

By accepting this responsibility, you also accept that you are the origin of your problems in life. This choice allows you to regain control over your life and take back your power, instead of being disempowered by the belief that you are the victim of others and external forces. This change in perception is the most significant you can make because it will transform your perspective of yourself and life, as you know it. By accepting responsibility for your issues, you are ready to objectively explore your past, your emotional family history in respect to yourself.

Becoming aware of your behavioural patterns that are responsible for conflict, unhappiness and discontent and so on, is the first step in understanding yourself and others. The knowledge you acquire can bring you to realise why you feel the way you do in those situations. Everything you learn and see will be a piece of the puzzle that will ultimately lead you to discover the negative belief systems that are at the source of your problems. Knowing that your fears distort your sense-of-self, and by becoming aware of how you relate to others and the world, you will begin to see who you believe yourself to be in a different light. You will not like what you see but remember that what you have realised about yourself is NOT who you were born to be.

Even though by forcing yourself to behave differently, you may have had some positive results, this kind of solution difficult to maintain. This approach does not address the core reasons for your issues. Over time it is unavoidable that your fear-based beliefs will manifest anyway because that is how fear affects our lives. Real transformation comes from changing who you are and not just by a change in behaviour. Releasing the false beliefs, you identify with, rooted in fear, will change who believe yourself to be — your sense-of-yourself. Changing who you are will automatically transform your perception, what you do and how you think, act, and respond. A new inner-identity will also change whom you are attracted to, and who will be attracted to you.

Changing who you are, makes for a new relationship with yourself and this alters the dynamic of your relationship with others. Your accountability for any potential negative contributions to the relationship will prevent many issues and reasons for conflict arising. It will be the same for your partner. Remember that your current partner is your choice and is a result of your attractions, needs and expectations, none of which you can hold her or him accountable. If they turned out to be unlike the person you thought they were, you have no choice but to take responsibility for your distorted perception of them. You need to be responsible for deceiving yourself because they were this way from when they grew up. Your negative or positive belief systems hold the key to the nature of your attractions, expectations and desires in relationships. These are 'the programs' that shape your perception of the person you are attracted to and ultimately choose. Your negative belief systems have the effect of blinding you from recognising that their behaviour is strategic because they are complementary to yours. The reality is that they are a part of the attraction you have for one another. No matter what nature your negative beliefs are, you will find or bring out issues in your partner that compliment your own. It will be the same for them as it is for you. Although it may initially be hard to accept, no one but you can be responsible for the experience you have of your relationships and life.

If you are in the middle of a relationship break-up, you may find it difficult to accept this point of view, particularly when both parties are emotionally affected. Each has their unique response to a breakup, but whether passive or aggressive, guilt or blame —both are likely to believe that the other is responsible. Once fear controls your behaviours, you cannot escape the consequences — you will not be able to and neither will your partner. Whatever pain, anger or resentment you may feel, they are a direct result of your emotional processes even though the situation with your partner may have triggered them. You will believe yourself to be the victim in the breakup if you feel vindictive because you want your partner to suffer for what they have done to you. Even though you may feel convinced that the conflict is your partner's responsibility, the reality is that you are doing it to yourself. Your conclusion prevents you from holding yourself accountable and accepting responsibility for choosing this relationship in the first place. By refusing to accept that your emotional problems are responsible for your current life situation, you have no other recourse but to blame others for what you feel. You are certain to repeat your relationship story with similar personality types until you realise that you are the one who must change.

Resolving conflict within a framework of self-responsibility requires complete emotional frankness by both parties. Instead of confronting issues when they reach a crisis they should be addressed the moment they become apparent. By communicating your personal experience of the situation without blame, you can stop disagreements from growing out of control. Try and explain the motivations, feelings and intent for your behaviour, actions or choices and let your partner do the same. Your focus needs to be on understanding your part in it as well as your partner's experience of the situation and their way of thinking. Speaking with emotional clarity and honesty is far more likely to create positive results than blame, avoidance, accusations. Telling your partner what you think they want to hear to avoid conflict will only postpone the situation to the next time.

You will find, that your efforts to discover the causes for the fears, that play out as discord in your relationship, will reward you with answers that have the capacity to bring you much closer to each other. You must remember that you cannot take this approach independently of your partner and that they need to be prepared to address their relationship issues with a similar frame of mind. Speaking openly and truthful from the heart about what nature of your negative contribution to the relationship, will get you positive results. Sometimes the outcome may not be what you would expect it to be, but remember that both of you can only flourish as spirits in a relationship based on truth and honesty. You may not always totally understand the basis for all of the feelings, thoughts and behaviours that represent your part of the issue or those of your partner. But, by giving expression to what you do know and understand, you create steps towards resolution and growth. It all comes down to being self-responsible in life

EMOTIONAL 'GENETICS.'

It should be apparent from our examples that that is unavoidable that we pass on our beliefs to the next generation. The emotional imprint we receive in childhood becomes the template for how and why we live our lives and create relationships and will raise our offspring. If we do not release our fear based beliefs before we have children, we pass on the emotional patterns inherited from our parents to them. Unaware of the true nature of our being and in the absence of any understanding of the process by which we manifest our life experiences, there is no other outcome possible. The conscious and subconscious belief systems of the parents become those of their children, and in the absence of real change, they are doomed to repeat this process when they become parents. Only you can disrupt this generational repetition, by changing who you believe you are and seeking to live life in the absence of fear, as your authentic and spontaneous self. Your unique, different and spontaneous authentic-self, is the most powerful representation of your consciousness and the best example of how to be as a person for your children.

It is possible to recognise negative patterns of beliefs from the type of behaviour that is displayed. Behaviour, can on the surface appear to be very functional, but also strategically disguise someone's real intent. For example, actions and responses designed to be very confident and absolute in expression can hide fears of not being good enough or the fear of being weak. This type of behaviour seeks to convince others of the opposite and is most successful with those who are passive and uncertain. Overconfident behaviour can be an attempt impress others and hide a lack of self-trust. The examples are endless. The problem with strategized behaviour associated with negative beliefs is that if we do not transcend them, their effect on children may ensure that they will persist for generations to come.

In that respect, your emotional family tree is in many ways more interesting than your genetic one. Consider that who you will attract as a partner, and the person who is attracted to you is an emotional reflection of each of your parent's fears. If you were to trace the issues and insecurities of each family member to previous generations, you would realise that your emotional family tree will show particular emotional patterns. If you also combine this result with that of the 'genetically-emotional' tree of your partner, you would discover many common qualities, which prove that these attractions appear to be almost inevitable. Once you recognise the patterns of attraction and the cause for conflict, it gives the impression that you have little or no control over your life. It may seem that it is your destiny to perpetuate these patterns, but this is not true. Repeating your family's negative emotional heritage will be inevitable, as long as you remain ignorant of the truth and in fear of facing the fears you hold.

Separation from our authentic-self appears to be a gradual process where each subsequent generation finds itself further removed from their inner truth and spiritual reality. Our misconceptions and illusions not only affect our lives but also that of others. The impact on society is even further reaching because of the influence we have as a collective with our unresolved fears and insecurities. Sharing our illusionary fears with others gives them a sense of reality and truth which makes them believable. Potentially these distortions have the capacity to become "new truths" by which a society then makes its rules, by which we have to live and survive. The creation of distorted values and standards does not necessarily happen in a lifetime, but it is an ongoing process that we can measure in generations, over many hundreds of years.

EMPOWERED BEING

Changing the world starts with you, and therefore, without exception, each person has to take responsibility for what they manifest in their life. There are no shortcuts or simple solutions that magically make issues and the feelings and behaviours that go with them disappear. Reclaiming your power as a creative and manifesting consciousness is essential to fulfilling the potential of your authentic and unique being.

Positive results are hard to create when your negative beliefs are in contradiction with your goals and sabotage the fulfilment your potential. You may think that the difficulties you experience as a result of this are with others or the world, but in reality, the conflict is with yourself. Your negative self-beliefs are the actual barriers to the achievement of your goals and aspirations.

We tend to believe that only our conscious thoughts and choices create our experiences in life. Undesirable or painful events are mostly judged to be outside our control, bad luck or deliberately created by others. Nothing could be further from the truth.

We manifest our lives incessantly through the intent of the beliefs that determine our sense-of-self, consciously and subconsciously, negative or positive. We do so as individuals and as a collective population. Whenever our fears are activated, they will by their very nature, seek to dominate our mind and make themselves present in our lives. Realise that whenever it seems that your issues appear in your life that you must be manifesting the experiences from your fears in the most effortless of ways.

The effort required to create a fulfilling and happy life experiences is the same as what you use to manifest adverse experiences in life. You produce positive life experiences by living life in the absence of a fearful sense-of-self, supported by beliefs that are in harmony with your essence, with the same effortlessness as you did your issues and problems.

The process is easier than you might think because it all depends on who and what you believe yourself to be in respect to yourself, and the world. Looking for your life solutions beyond the obvious will take you to the source of your limitations and releasing these will create the space for your authentic and unique self to become present. Each change will contribute positively to the foundation by which you manifest your life.

We are unaware that 'who we believe we are', our sense-of-self, operates on an individual and collective levels. The power the intent of our sense-of-self has over us as individuals also influence our society and the world as a shared consciousness. The negative or positive emotional consequences of expressing our sense-of-self are present within us and are visible all around us. Prisons, armies, poverty and starvation, unequally distributed wealth, discrimination of all kinds, drug taking and all forms of abuse are manifestations of human consciousness living in illusion and controlled by fear.

Chapter 15

THE QUEST FOR HAPPINESS

The quest for personal happiness is at the top of the list for most people. At first glance, this seems to be logical because who, after all, would not want to be happy? Happiness tends to appear for only short periods in life and rarely do we meet someone who is in a constant state of happiness or bliss. So why is happiness so important to us and should we not ask why and what is behind this quest for what most think is the nirvana of life?

Before we can go any further, consider what the nature of true happiness is so that it can become a reference point in understanding our relationship with it.

The dictionary defines happiness (as in "emotional state") as a state of well-being characterised by emotions ranging from contentment to intense joy.

However, it does not explain when and how you might experience happiness. A more spiritual description of happiness might be as follows: We feel true happiness:

– by living life in a state of unconditional love, acceptance and trust with the freedom to express the power and potential of your authentic self unconditionally.
– by living life true to the essence of our spirit in the absence of fear.
– by being in a state of unconditional harmony with the essence of our consciousness and the nature of All That Is – Universal Consciousness.

Anything less becomes happiness that is conditional to the absence of all manner of fear. Our desire to find happiness is intertwined with our innate drive to exist in harmony with the essence of our spirit. Achieving this harmonious state connects us with the actual source of happiness and joy. Our feelings can be extremely deceptive, making it possible to have emotional experiences that parade as happiness and joy but are in reality poor facsimiles. Without knowing what real happiness, bliss and joy feel like, we lack a meaningful reference point to recognise it.

Our unique nature makes the general idea of happiness different from one person to another. While one feels happy watching the sun go down, another feels it by seeing their favourite sports team win. One will find contentment and happiness helping others, while another will only be satisfied when they get what they always wanted. You may be happy not to be fired from your job or not getting killed in an accident. A lottery win may keep you smiling for a long time because of the way it changes your life. At long last finding a partner to share your life with may well keep you happy for a while. Finding your way out of a critical predicament will probably do the same thing. Going on vacation after a year of slogging it out in your job may be your version of happiness, while others believe that getting blind drunk or high on drugs is the way to feel 'happy'.

Obviously, there is any number of examples for what happiness is, which only illustrates that on the surface, our idea of happiness is very individual and contextual. Chasing this kind of happiness is very different from the happiness experienced by being in harmony with the essence of our spirit. We do not want to face the fact that much of our idea of happiness depends on the issues we have. The security of food and shelter can be a source of feeling happy for the homeless and displaced, just as power is to the powerless and wealth to the poor. In the awareness that we create our own life experiences, it follows that our concept of happiness often depends on escaping what we fear.

Whenever we avoid our fear of pain, suffering, loss, guilt or blame, we are likely to feel happy. This kind of happiness is a product of the absence of fear, loss, guilt, powerlessness, anxiety, worry, pain and so on, and is a result of escaping from what we fear.

On the physical level, this can be job security over unemployment, having a holiday and freedom over constantly having to work and bear responsibility or just having a secure income over having to survive from day to day, and so forth.

On a more emotional level, it can be having power and control instead of being powerless and helpless, having a choice in life over having to do as you are told, or feeling loved over being rejected or abandoned and so on. Each time you achieve the positive over the negative you are likely to feel happy, but it is unlikely to be an enduring state. Regardless of feeling elated, the reasons why you manifest negative experiences in your life in the first place are still a part of you. You may convince yourself that your positive emotions — feeling happy and a sense of relief — are an indication that you have dealt with your issue but that is just an illusion. The emotion you experience is produced by external circumstances and not a sensation from your inner-self. Without releasing the reason for the negative, this will not be enduring and what you felt is not real joy or bliss.

Using strategic behaviours to achieve happiness is fraught with pitfalls. Its success depends on accommodating, controlling or influencing those around you and this may not work. The fear of being rejected, disappointed, unwanted, failure and being denied and so on, drives your strategies, and this ensures that your happiness will always sit on the edge of failure. Feeling happy will be entirely dependent on your capacity to maintain control and influence over the way others react and respond to you. Your dependence on their positive response to being happy makes it very likely that sooner or later you will fail. The intent created by fear will always win out, and as a result, you will deny yourself happiness because of your issues. If strategized behaviour is your only means to get what you want then repeating the same action or response is your only option. You will always be in the hope that you will succeed and in fear that it will fail you. The problem is that in your perception, the fundamental source of happiness lies outside of you because you are dependent on how others respond. Holding the belief that your strategies can give you control over happiness is just an illusion.

If for example, you believe you are unattractive, undesirable and not good enough, you will probably think that no one would want to be with you. Assume for a moment that you discovered a strategy to make yourself appear confident to the opposite sex and use it as a means to convince them to like you. The successful implementation of this idea will cause you feel happy in the belief that you have found a way to be interesting and attractive to your opposite sex. However, you are now worried that they will lose interest in you if they discover who you really are. You still hold the belief that you are not good enough because of who you believe yourself to be. Even though your behaviour lacks sincerity, you have no choice but to continue with your strategies for fear that if you do not, you will be alone with no one to love or want you. You may be 'happy' each time your strategy works, but your fear of being found out to be the inferior person you believe yourself to be will always be lurking in the background of your mind. This kind of happiness is strategic because it depends on conscious behavioural choices to manifest.

Confusing relief or escape from loss or disaster or anything we fear or cannot cope with, as happiness, joy or bliss confuses our perception of what matters in life and what is real and what is false. Elevated feelings of relief from suspense and fear of disaster, pain or failure is not true happiness even though they are welcomed and embraced. Not being the victim of a negative experience or event should never be described as real happiness because it binds us to be strategic in life. This perspective can cause us to choose strategies over confronting our fears and dealing with the belief systems that support their presence in us. We need to be able to recognise and make a distinction between happiness or joy and feeling relieved or safe and secure.

HAPPINESS WITHOUT FEAR

Language may contribute to the problem when we try to put our feelings of happiness, joy, elation, bliss and exuberance into words. When we think of all the different shades these feelings can have, we may find that the vocabulary used to express feelings of love, joy and happiness are limited in many cultures. In English, the words 'happiness' and 'love' are readily used in any number of the circumstances.

Happiness as a result of experiencing love by giving or receiving it can become complicated when we try to distinguish the love for a friend from the love we have for ourselves, our partner or our children. Even though we may know what our interpretation of the meaning and intention of the happiness is, communicating this precisely to others are not so simple. They cannot be inside our mind to know what we think and feel. Consequently, the finer layers of what we feel get lost in translation because we cannot find exact words to express these nuances in our feelings of love and joy, and therefore happiness.

True happiness comes from being in harmony with our spirit through being at oneness with the unconditional love, acceptance and trust with All That Is and oneself.

This concept of happiness refers to the core foundation of this feeling in our being and is new emotional territory for most people.

How would you answer the following questions?

How would we experience life if our state of mind were harmonious within, with others and the world?

What would it be like to live life without fear, powerlessness and distrust, and accept accountability for everything we create in our life?

How would we express our sense of being — emotionally, physically and intellectually — if we were openly truthful, spontaneous and free, suspending all judgment and criticism of ourselves and others?

How would we experience and conduct our intimate and other relationships in the absence of fear and guilt?

What would be the nature and quality of our parenting in the absence of our fears and insecurities?

How would we raise our children and what would be the focus in their education if the evolution their consciousness was a priority?

What would the nature of our health care be, if we understood the connection between spirit, mind and body, and our energetic being?

From what kind of vision would we create a world society if we had a mind that is emotionally self-responsible and feels connected to everything?

With what kind of economic structures and laws would we govern and support each other's existence, if each of us were authentic and unconditionally loving, accepting and in trust of ourselves and others?

What kind of world would our eyes see if they were uncorrupted by fear?

FINDING HAPPINESS WITHIN

You might say that happiness and joy come in different layers of which the internal harmony between mind and spirit forms the core. Once we achieve a level of inner-harmony that is more dominant than our fears, our experience of pleasure and happiness will be greatly enhanced. The emotional resilience that is an inherent characteristic of our consciousness will diminish the negative impact that our remaining fears may have on our perception, thoughts and emotions.

Fulfilling the potential of our authentic self by living life unconditionally — in freedom and absence of fear — is central to finding true and consistent happiness and joy. This kind of happiness comes from the achievements that support the growth of our mind and spirit. They do not depend on the recognition or adulation from others or having to prove one's superiority over others. Instead, inner-change expands our consciousness and leads to the greater fulfilment of our spiritual potential.

The only triumphs that matter in life, are those we achieve within ourselves: Through fulfilling our potential by releasing our fears and expressing our authentic self unconditionally, we will manifest our experience of life in the full awareness of our responsibility as creators of our existence.

All creative acts of manifestation begin and end with ourselves. An original thought, supported by the intent of our beliefs, with the will to bring it into reality through the application of the mind and all its faculties, becomes an act of creative manifestation. All creative acts and the results they achieve are both a learning experience and a mirror for who you are. Your responses and reactions to any outcome are a reflection of the nature of your belief systems — your sense-of-self — and the level of inner-harmony you have at this point in your life. The way the balance tips for us, between fear-based and harmonious sense-of-self, is the determining factor for the presence or absence of happiness in our lives. When it leans towards inner-harmony with our essence, everything in life is sweeter.

HAPPINESS BY AVOIDING SUFFERING

Your life happiness is not a product of escaping or avoiding your fears and therefore should not depend on relationships, material security or need fulfilment. Sharing oneself and contributing to others in the process of self-fulfilment, and learning from their unique perspectives is a substantial part of discovering inner-happiness. Once we live our lives from this context, our happiness cannot fade or disappear in the face of negative external circumstances. Instead, we would manifest a world, in which nature and experience would correspond to the new intent of the harmonious belief systems within our sense-of-self.

We need to stop blaming personal unhappiness on others or circumstances in our life and begin to question the nature of our mind to understand why we create the events that cause us to feel that way. Were we to take this approach we would give ourselves a chance to go to the root of our issues of unhappiness. For instance, once we feel 'unhappy' with our job, we will find a million things wrong with our work environment and the people with whom we share it. Holding our workplace responsible for our dissatisfaction, for instance, gives our discontent an external cause and justification, and allows us to convince ourselves that we are not the problem — work is. Regardless of the many reasons why work can be an unhappy experience, your choices have put you where you are right now. The question you should ask yourself is what the core reasons for your choices are because the answers would show that you to be the cause. Unresolved, the consequences of the beliefs responsible for your decisions will appear in other places but a similar context in your life until you confront them.

Every choice you make in life whether for work or relationships is a product of your mind-set coloured by the beliefs you hold — positive or negative. Your choices in life will always place you in environments where your issues will manifest. Your understanding of negative encounters also represents an opportunity to overcome the fear based belief systems that underpin these experiences.

Remember that your experience of life is a product of the innate and incessant creative intent of the belief systems that make up your sense-of-self.

You resent your career but do not know what else to do with your life. You hold onto the idea that your parents invalidated your interests, passions and desires and you blame them. Their rejection of your interests, talents, and abilities convinced you that what you were attracted to and excited about, is worthless and insignificant. You may not realise that you reject and invalidate your interests and passions because your parents did because they convinced you that they have no value. Now you have chosen a career that pleases your parents but does not please you. In your mind, meeting their expectations at that time was more important to your emotional survival then insisting on exploring your talents and interests. Doing what they expected from you was your way of making yourself acceptable to them and the condition you believed you had to meet.

Fear of confrontation, being held accountable or fear of failure may represent another reason why you do not like your work environment. Your emotional problems may cause you to perceive others in your workplace as aggressive and critical, demanding and judgmental of you. The issues you have, are all within you, so you do not have to look very far for the culprit who created your problems. The question is: Do you have the courage to face yourself without fear or judgment and accept the reality of your beliefs to transcend them?

HAPPINESS AND RELATIONSHIPS

Those who depend on relationships to find their life happiness are likely to be disappointed. Relying on someone else, to have your emotional needs, dreams and expectations fulfilled is bound to fail. This kind of happiness is usually the product of a heart that does not love and accepts itself and seeks to feel love and acceptance through being loved by another. This version of love is always dependent on what someone else is prepared to give, and makes us feel powerless, emotionally needy and vulnerable. The expectation that another should complete what is missing in oneself is learned through the example our parents set for us in their relationship with each other, and how they related to us individually. Your experience of their expression and understanding of love becomes your definition of what love is. You will seek to recreate the same conditional love, acceptance and trust you were exposed to by your parents, by choosing a partner who will fulfil this subconscious requirement in you. The person you are attracted to will naturally have complementary issues to your own, which will be a facsimile of those of your parents. The process that is life will ensure that you will replicate the conditions you believe to exist for love, acceptance and trust in relationships.

Happiness that comes as a result of one person compensating for the fears and insecurities of another will usually be short-lived. Someone who feels weak and insecure will be attracted to someone who appears to be strong and in control as a resolution for their fears. Their choice of partner will be someone who has learned to be loved and accepted by strategically presenting themselves as strong, capable and dependable. In reality, it is their way of dealing with their fear of being unlovable and unacceptable, and this will complement the fears of the weak partner. Unfortunately, the idea that one can compensate for the other's fear and insecurities is an illusion, and therefore an unrealistic expectation for both. In time, the more aggressive or assertive partner will give up because they feel there is no end to the dissatisfaction for which the other holds them responsible. Eventually discontent will lead to conflict, as each is likely to blame the other for what they feel is missing. Happiness will have left the relationship a long time before that.

We have a better chance of achieving consistent happiness if in principle, both parties accept responsibility for their emotional experiences in the relationship, even if how and why is not clear to them at the time. Should there be conflict, then each will take responsibility for their own feelings and look within themselves for the reasons for their part in it. Open and truthful communication over the emotional matters that are at the core of their issues will allow them to support each other in finding resolution within themselves. By helping each other through fears and insecurities, they will develop a deeper understanding of one another, and make their relationship more intimate, rather than less.

Working towards happiness and what we share with others is an inner process that asks us to investigate all and any reasons for the fear-based conditions we place on love, acceptance and trust in ourselves and others. Our fears create critical emotional limits and processes representative of our fear-based beliefs. These will always lead to unhappiness and discontent. With closer observation, we will invariably find that our conditional self-beliefs mimic the conditions that our parents acted out between them and with us. Letting go of these negative beliefs will alter our thoughts and perception, and change our feelings, behaviour and choices because we — our sense-of-self — will have changed.

The moment we open our eyes to this new world, we embark on the journey of finding happiness within, through existing in greater harmony with our spiritual essence. Every time we release fear, we allow more of the essence of our spirit to come to the surface and reveal new aspects of our authentic self. Each progressive change brings us closer to our spiritual being and allows us to find greater expression for our incredible potential. Every time we release an issue in its fundamental form we are in greater harmony with our essence, and this is what will create a new level of genuine and consistent happiness within all of us.

Chapter 16

POWER WITHOUT FEAR

These are some of the explanations for the meaning of the word power:

Power is the capacity or ability to direct or influence the behaviour of others or the course of events.

Power is a measurement of an entity's ability to control its environment, including the behaviour of others.

Authority is the right to act in a specified way, delegated from one person or organisation to another.

Power can be seen as evil or unjust, but the exercise of power is accepted as endemic to humans as social beings.

The use of power need not involve coercion (force or the threat of force). At one extreme, it more closely resembles what every day English-speakers call "influence", although some authors make a distinction between power and influence — the means by which power is used.

The problem is that none of these explanations of power takes into account the psychological state of the individual wielding it. None of it explains that the potential effect they will have on others, or the environment will depend entirely on their issues, fears and insecurities. These will always distort the values and standards, integrity and principles the use of power and the consequences.

An individual's egocentric sense-of-self does not dissolve because they are in a position of power.

When we say, power corrupts, it is not that power as such is to blame for altering a person's mind. The issues or fears within the individual who acquires power will cause them to misuse and abuse it. The need to be powerful and in control will only seduce those who believe they are powerless, and this will corrupt them.

Someone with fears and a distorted sense-of-self will be tempted into using and abusing power at their disposal. Consequently, it becomes a resource to satisfy their need to feel powerful and be in control or overcome other personal issues related to powerlessness. They will always find justification for their actions and choices that are consistent with their fear-based mind. This kind of personality tends to be selfish and will often act in total disregard of the consequences this has for others and the environment.

It is not surprising that power and control have become important values in today's society where most people feel rendered powerless in life by the systems and process to which they have to abide. For many, it seems nothing can be attained or achieved without having these two elements. The fact is that those promising changes often use the words power in many of their slogans and control, is confirmation of this. Their acquisition promises to give you the capacity to get all the things you want, wish for and desire. The power to have what you want in life and "Control Your Destiny" through personal power is a seductive idea. Most of us assume that if we have control over every tiny aspect of what we and others do and think, over their behaviour and choices, we will also be in control of the outcome. Our experience of childhood convinced us that we have to be in control to get what we want when we want it. On the other hand, we can develop or inherit strategies that promise to work and achieve positive outcomes. Unfortunately, this approach to being in control of your life will, over time, fail us in one form or another.

The strategic approach to life tends to ignore the greatest influence of all — YOU as the instigator and creator of your life experiences. We do not see that what your life will be and how you will experience it, will ultimately be determined by who you believe yourself to be. What you do and how you do it may initially bring you a level of success, but you cannot stop yourself expressing your negative beliefs — fears — and the intent they hold. The process of living your life manifests the nature of who you are automatically and brings it into existence as an emotional or physical life experience.

The thought that we can acquire anything by knowing strategic "how to behave in a particular situation" appeals to those who believe in magical solutions to overcome their fears and insecurities. The logical part of us is always looking for that one concept, strategy or idea that will take away our fears so that we can get what we want or need. For those reasons alone, the idea of being in control and having power is a prevalent notion.

Should the acquisition of power and control be the primary goal in life, you might be wise to look very carefully at your reasons and motivations. From your perspective, it may seem normal to strive for this, but potentially you may have negative grounds for this desire. Without knowing the actual nature of your sense-of-self, you will not recognise the negative consequences your quest may have for yourself and others.

Before we go any further consider these statements:

You only need power and control, if you are in fear of being powerless and without control over your life.

Only those in fear of powerlessness and without control need power, control and the domination over others to feel empowered and in control.

The general notion of personal power is the ability to get whatever you want, when and how you want it, regardless of external influences or the effect, this may have on others or the environment. We tend to believe that should external forces prevent us from achieving our goals; we need to become more strategic and tactical, more aggressive or assertive in the application of our power and the exercise of control. This paradigm disregards the nature of human consciousness and the consequences this approach can have on others and the world.

Extreme versions of this such as the use of violence, threat, torture and fear as weapons to control individuals or a population, are justified by those who resort to these methods. Many people believe that this behaviour is unacceptable and in many cases unwarranted. Our judgment changes, when same sources of power convince us that we need to use these methods for the greater good and our welfare and protection. The same fears and insecurities that had us reject this kind of violence now cause us to sanction and justify them. They form the perception that we are no longer isolated and therefore safe from this sort of threat, and generate the fear that we could be the victims. By playing on our pre-existing fears and insecurities and sense of victimhood, the emotional state of a population can be manipulated to manufacture consent. By convincing a fearful population that particular actions and choices are an absolute necessity for their security and safety, and by creating alternatives that are made to be obviously shocking and unacceptable, they can extract approval and consent. Believing it to be in defence of our own survival and security and that of others, we are usually prepared to accept inhumane and cruel methods. We do not even realise that we thereby corrupt our personal and innate values and standards, integrity and principles. Unfortunately, the idea that; 'the end justifies the means' and 'we have to sacrifice for the greater good' is still very much alive, and used extensively and inappropriately when individuals or institutions seek power and control.

Naturally, we are entitled to defend ourselves if our life or well-being is under threat but what if the perceived threat is a product of deception, reinforced by our fears and insecurities which are at their core illusionary? In many cases, these misconceptions are the result of generations of fear-based beliefs. Are violence and aggressive control still justified if the reasons for our fears have no foundation in truth, or the reasons for them have long dissolved in history? There can only be a basis for an enduring peaceful resolution, if these are questions are answered by both sides of a conflict.

THE BEGINNING OF POWERLESSNESS

How and why do we come to feel powerless when at birth we seem to be without fears and insecurities?

How does our sense of powerlessness become a part of us and why it has such influence and control?

Even though we are helpless to survive independently at birth, we do not feel controlled by fear or powerlessness. A baby shows no concern that it has no "power and control" over its survival in the new world it has entered even though it will call out if in discomfort, not fed or kept clean. By all account, it is clear that there is an inborn trust and expectation that it will be loved, taken care of and protected. This inner confidence has to be innate as it appears in all babies. It is unequivocal in the expectation that the environment in which it arrives, will support, love, want, accept and trust it unconditionally. This sense of confidence in its survival originates from its instinct and the unconditional and naive state with which it is born. This dependence without fear also forms a substantial part of the bond it feels with its mother. The unconditional nature of its original sense-of-itself becomes the only reference point by which it can develop an awareness of the quality of the relationships it experiences with everyone and everything.

A child is driven by the innate intent to develop and evolve its physical and emotional independence not only as part of a physical survival strategy but primarily to acquire the capacity to fulfil the multifaceted potential of its creative consciousness. The process of living becomes its journey of self-discovery, self-expression and an opportunity to evolve every element of its unique and authentic self. In just about every instance a child will begin this process with trust and in the absence of fear. Fear and powerlessness only become a part of its mind when there is a consistent conflict between the conditions set by the parent and its innate expectations. Should it become aware, that its authentic and unique self cannot meet the conditional expectations of its parents, it first feels a sense of powerlessness. It has the innate trust that it will be unconditionally loved wanted and accepted has been disappointed and can no longer be trusted. The security that it felt it could depend on for its emotional survival has been taken away by the condition the parent demand it meets if it is be loved and accepted. Separated from its source for emotional security it feels powerless and insecure. By accepting the conditions set by its parents and fulfilling their expectations, it can reconnect with them. Now love, acceptance, trust and being wanted have become conditional and require a designated response to avoid rejection. Once powerlessness gets a hold, the fear of failing to meet these conditions becomes its faithful companion and will dominate its development throughout its life.

Transcending the emotional environment of its family is the first and probably most difficult part of a child's journey in life. The ground-rules for emotional expression and interaction have already been determined by the parents' insecurities and limitations and leave a child no choice. Any fears or issues they inherited from their families will become a prominent part of the emotional paradigm that characterises the relationships between all family members. Every negative belief a child takes on as its sense-of-self, invokes another version of powerlessness.

Your sense of powerlessness is the real reason that you feel overwhelmed or cannot cope being confronted by a verbally aggressive person, being rejected by your lover, feelings demeaned by criticism or being ignored and dismissed. The relationship you have with your power or powerlessness will determine how you experience your life and relationships. Although it may not be obvious, using dominating or controlling behaviour to be in control of your life is just as dysfunctional as being passive and powerless.

The parent's subconscious rejection of their child's authentic-self severely compromises its faith in unconditional love, acceptance and trust. Failure to meet these expectations creates inner conflict because it feels powerless to be accepted unconditionally as its authentic self. Each time it cannot meet the conditions set by the parents, its sense of powerlessness deepens.

The constant pressure to conform, convinces it that giving in to its parent's expectations is the only way it will be loved and accepted. Compromising itself to meet these conditions, it is unaware of giving away its power, initially to its parents and later to others. Gradually, it learns to depend on outside approval and endorsement to be accepted and acceptable. Every new dependency on others creates more needs in a child and causes it to experience powerlessness in different ways. In maturity, this will prevent it from living life to its full emotional and physical potential. Personal powerlessness goes hand in hand with not being in control of your life. Nearly all of our fear-based issues contain this emotionally disabling element. Rejection and abandonment make us feel powerless to be loved and wanted. Being judged and criticised makes us feel powerless to be good enough, to be acceptable and so on. Our response is to become strategically passive-powerless or aggressive-powerless

LIVING IN POWERLESSNESS

Your fears are proportional to your sense of powerlessness and vulnerability to a perceived threat. Once you believe that you lack the strength and resources to survive or cope with an overwhelming emotional or physical confrontation, you will experience the fear of being powerless. It has less to do with the size of the threat than it has with your perception of your own power and capacity. Fear will dominate your mind if the threat or confrontation appears to be larger or stronger than you believe you are. In the case of a physical threat this can be justifiable, but even under these circumstances, our self-perception plays a significant role in respect as to how we will respond to it. The evaluation needs to be very different when confronted with strictly emotional fears because these are illusionary. The perceived consequences and their effect on us have no basis in reality. Our experience of rejection or blame, shame or criticism and so on, will not cause us to suffer real injuries or terminate our existence.

Living in the belief that you cannot survive, confront or overcome a range of emotional issues will make you commonly fearful of living life. The consequence of rejection and abandonment, anger and aggression, making 'wrong' decisions and choices, initiating new ideas and potential failure, expressing your feelings and speaking your truth and so on will not kill you even though it may feel that you cannot deal with the outcome.

Your need to avoid negative emotional experiences, and your inability to do so consistently and successfully, will have the effect of making you feel fearful and powerless. The fear of the consequences of being powerless and without being in control of your life will distort your choices and interactions with others. Issues of this kind are more common in people than one would think. The fear of having to confront the negative emotional experiences can spiral into an ever-greater avoidance of engaging in life. The emotional stress associated with this can develop into a greater dependence on strategic behaviours, and reliance on the support of others. The influence and power of fear can become such an intense emotional and physical experience, that once the self is overwhelmed, it can cause an emotional shutdown that can affect the function of the body. The fear of total powerlessness can generate fatigue, and discomfort in the digestive system. What started out as avoidance behaviour due to stress and fear can become a source of physical problems.

People with these fears unconsciously choose to become passive-powerless in their behaviour which reveals itself in the way they live and conduct relationships. Their anticipation that their responses, actions and choices will elicit an adverse reaction from others, results in suppression of their spontaneity and emotional truth. They are trying to control the emotional dynamic between them and others in every encounter, to avoid criticism, blame, conflict, guilt and so on. By being pleasing others and accommodating them, they can appear to be ultra-caring and considerate, but in reality, this is a behavioural strategy to ensure they will be accepted and avoid any negative confrontation. This behaviour also serves to hide the stress and anxiety with which they live.

The sort of people they are likely to attract and be attracted to, have had a need to be pleased. They fear being offended, criticised, rejected, judged, denied, refused, dismissed, etc. and can not do what they want or be who they want to be. Typically, they are aggressive-powerless individuals, who feel safe using demanding and controlling behaviours, because they sense that someone who is a pleaser will not deny them. They are subconsciously attracted to 'pleasers' because they will neither refuse nor confront them or hold them accountable for being demanding and selfish.

Those who are fearful of the negative emotional consequences of their choices and decisions tend to think that others or circumstances force them to behave this way. Although the fear is theirs, they believe that others and the potential of adverse outcomes are to blame. The truth is that subconsciously, their fear causes them to surrender their power over their emotional life to others, and the world around them. They commonly hold others responsible for any negative circumstances or experiences in their life, by behaving as if they are the victims. Their sense of powerlessness does not allow them to address their issues directly. As long as they believe themselves to be victims, they do not accept responsibility for their existence and instead blame others. Each time we avoid taking responsibility for our fears and insecurities we do so to postpone the consequences we fear. However, the process of living life will inevitably present us, progressively, with ever bigger and more intense experiences of our fear-based beliefs.

Powerlessness plays a role in every fear we hold. Together with related negative emotions, it drives us into developing strategic behaviours as a counter-measure to our fears. If we are passive by nature and feel powerless to be loved and accepted by our parent, we will try and avoid rejection by whatever means at our disposal. We may use avoidance strategies and never to display behaviour that might trigger a negative response. Or we may choose to engage by being submissive and accommodating, to please and gain approval. If our fear is intense enough, we can be driven to use aggressive, controlling and confronting responses and reactions to be in control. Our aggressive strategies are intended to challenge those who we believe do not love and accept us and to try and elicit a response that will prove to us, as well as to them, that they do not care about us. All these strategies have a use-by date and will sooner or later fail.

In the course of all this, our parents unwittingly keep proving with their fear-driven interaction that our spontaneous, authentic self is not wanted, lovable or acceptable to them. This kind of rejection will generate the feeling that we can never be who we were born to be and still gain their love and acceptance. Confronted by our parent's conditional behaviour, we feel we have no other choice than to be who we were authentically born to be and rejected or abandoned. Or, accept the conditions placed on us, change our actions and responses and be included and taken care off.

When parents feel that who we authentically and spontaneously are is in contradiction with their expectations of us, they seek to change us to suit their sense-of-themselves inclusive of their fears and insecurities. The expression of our authentic and unique nature raises all manner of issues in them. They, therefore, demand we change to accommodate their fears which they express by putting conditions on their love and acceptance of us. Our ultimate compliance with their expectations of who and what they want us to be convinces us to dismiss and suppress our authentic nature, and our spontaneous-self. Instead, our own need for their support and approval and their fear-based behaviour coerced us into accepting self-beliefs that do not represent our authentic nature. Even if we behave according to their expectations, there is no guarantee that the approval and acceptance we seek will be permanent or given at all. Hence, we are always in fear of losing love and acceptance, and experience rejection.

In reality, all we want is to fulfil our innate expectation to be unconditionally loved, accepted, trusted and wanted. The only way to arrive at that state of being is to release the beliefs that convince us that we are not lovable and acceptable, and do not qualify to receive it.

Living life subject to fears that create feelings of total powerlessness and helplessness makes for a terrifying existence. It is easy to refer to extreme cases and forget that many exist every day with constant fears, stress, anxiety or panic. Passive-powerless people are mostly subjugated by their fears and tend to use avoidance strategies to survive. They are also most likely to become the target for aggressive-powerless individuals who deal with their fears by being controlling, intimidating and dominant over their passive counterparts.

Aggressive-powerless personalities can be in positions of power and control and may try and overcome their fear using behaviour that appears confident, sometimes intimidation or use guilt. Their family background often promotes the value of competition to prove who is better and use dialogue designed to show they know better and are right. Those who are similarly minded are drawn to trust and have confidence in them. Powerless-passive people, however, are attracted to this kind of person because they lack self-confidence and determination. Without trust in their power, resources and abilities, they choose to be led, rather than take responsibility for their life — decisions and choices. The need for one to appear empowered and in control and the fear of being powerless in the other makes for a co-dependent relationship.

FROM POWERLESSNESS TO ANGER TO VIOLENCE

Anger is an emotion we are all too familiar with because at one time or another we have all been at the receiving end of it, or felt and expressed it. Every time we find ourselves in a state of emotional powerlessness, there is the potential that we will respond with anger and aggression, or with avoidance and repression.

Anger, aggression and powerlessness are emotions that are all inter-connected. Some will not ever dare to give expression to their anger because they have learned to believe it to be wrong and unacceptable. Fearing that showing anger will lead to rejection and a loss of love and acceptance, they strategically suppress it. All emotions require resolutions because if unexpressed anger can, over time, result in unpredictable and extreme aggressive outburst of aggression over circumstances that does not to warrant this behaviour. Consistently internalised negative emotions such as powerlessness will ultimately demand and find expression. If not emotionally it may find expression in your body and manifest as physical health issues.

Your family is the source of any beliefs that convince you that you are powerless and have no control over your life. In a family dynamic, there are two ways that a child can develop a sense of powerlessness and both can be present a simultaneously. Being exposed to one parent who is aggressive, intimidating, dominant and the other who acts as if a passive, powerless and a victim will create a sense of powerlessness in a child. One parent overpowers the child, and the other creates guilt for which it cannot be responsible.

Emotional intimidation, anger or guilt will overwhelm a child's capacity to respond to protect or save itself. Repeated exposure, therefore, can cause it feel completely overwhelmed and powerless. To survive the onslaught, it may use passive avoidance or become aggressive, to protect itself. Neither of these behaviours will save it from the emotional damage to its sense-of-self.

Parents who are in fear of taking emotional and material responsibility usually perceive themselves to be the victim of the demands and needs of their partner and children. Their strategic behaviour can either be aggressive-defensive (blame), passive-defensive (guilt) or they may adopt total avoidance as a strategy to prevent a confrontation with their fears. Regardless of the behaviour employed, they will act as if they are the victims those who depend on them and blame for being the 'aggressors'. Even though their children's needs and expectations are normal for their age, they will withhold and suppress these to avoid being the reason for their parent's anxiety and stress or anger and resentment. Their greatest fear is rejection and emotional abandonment. Assume, that they must be guilty and emotionally responsible if the parent gets resentful whenever they express their needs and wants, they feel they have no other choice. In truth, a child cannot be responsible for the parent's feelings because they have no control over the pre-existing fears held by them. Unfortunately, these issues and insecurities become the child's powerlessness and guilt for wanting and needing support, care and protection. As an adult, this guilt manifests as a lack of entitlement either paraded as independence and self-sufficiency or total helplessness.

More than often it is the male in the family who is the aggressive figure and the female partner is the passive one, but it can just as easily be the other way around. Women tend to be emotionally dominant and controlling but not physically threatening. They control emotionally by a display of vulnerability, anxiety and stress, while aggressively complaining about their dissatisfaction and disappointment with their partner or their lot in life — by being the victim and powerless. This kind of parent sees themselves as a victim of their children's needs and expectations, and that their offspring are the cause for their discontent.

In this context, a parent can use aggressive and dominant behaviour to avoid perceived blame and accountability, often acting as if they are beyond reproach to hide their own feelings of powerlessness and inadequacy. Trying to prove that they are all knowing and never wrong, they expect to be listened to and obeyed. To cope with the emotional pressure created by the fears, they live with; they may use ways to avoid what they feel by finding relief in other ways. For example, consuming alcohol in excess or just being absent from the family. When held accountable for their behaviour, it is not uncommon that they default to anger and aggression or behave the victim. Their belief that they are powerless, helpless victims of the demands and expectations of others, circumstances and the world can make them respond either way.

Unfortunately, it is a reality is that children exposed to this kind of emotional paradigm, have a definite potential to become just like the parents that raised them. Children exposed to fear-motivated behaviours develop the need to be constantly aware and alert to be prepared for the unpredictable aggressive or powerless responses of their parent. Avoiding being the target of aggression becomes an essential part of its behavioural strategies in relationships. A child will adopt strategies to avoid being held responsible and accountable for the negative feelings and behaviour of its parent. Often, it will adopt similar behavioural strategies as those role-played by the parent. It learns to believe that aggression or avoidance is an effective defensive mechanism against being blamed and accused, or feeling guilty and to blame. Unconsciously it becomes just like the parent.

The assumption that parents naturally want the responsibility for the family they create ignores many of the reasons why people are attracted to form intimate relationships in the first place. A person's issues play a decisive role in the attractions they have for a partner and therefore these fears and insecurities make themselves most apparent in intimate relationships. These beliefs are taken on in families where conditional love, acceptance and trust are the currency between each family member. The interdependence this creates is challenges the capacity of each to love, accept, trust, support, care and protect and so on, unconditionally. Even if it is not an issue as yet between partners, their children will usually challenge everything that is conditional in each parent with the expression of their needs and expectations. This emotional environment brings their fear-based beliefs in the parent's sense-of-self to the surface as behavioural strategies begin to fail.

In the reality of life, aggressive-powerless victims feel a subconscious attraction to those with a passive-powerless sense-of-self and vice versa. Ironically, they complement each other perfectly because the root of their issues is powerlessness and so one is an emotional mirror of the other.

CONTROL WITHOUT POWER

By now you may be confused about how anyone can have any power and control over their life at all. It is important to know how to make the distinction between the power within and a sense of power that comes from outside of yourself. If you can only feel safe and secure by using strategic behaviour to have power and control over others or the world, it is very likely that you are responding to the fear of being powerless and being without control. Your behaviour, driven by your feelings, is a manifestation of your fear of being powerless and not having control over getting what you want. Whatever the circumstances that may be responsible for activating these issues, your need for strategic behaviour, intended to ensure that you are in control, proves that you are not self-empowered. That is not to say you cannot be proactive in your behaviour and choices but it does mean that your inner motivations and intent come from the fear of being powerless and without control. If this fear is at the core of your behaviour, any resultant experience of power and control is, in reality, an illusion. Your capacity to have power and be in control will always depend on the environment in which you can strategically play out your fears — a passive-powerless emotional environment.

DOMINANT CONTROL

Should you fear never getting what you want, being insignificant and of no consequence, you may have a high need for recognition and feeling special. Instead of becoming a pleaser, you may adopt controlling and dominating strategies to prove to others that you are significant and entitled to be accepted by them. Your need to resort to strategic behaviour will create constant stress, for fear that they will fail, and you will be judged to be worthless and insignificant. This behaviour is a product of the same fears that make others passively compromise themselves and become pleasers to gain significance and be valued by others. These differences demonstrate passive or aggressive attempts to resolve comparable, of not the same, dysfunctional belief systems.

By understanding the relationship between behaviour and the negative state that underpins it, we can identify specific emotional characteristics about ourselves and others. Powerlessness underpins both passive-powerless and aggressive controlling behaviour. The attraction that aggressive, powerless individuals have for passive, powerless personalities reflects a dynamic, which fulfils both their emotional needs. One uses proactive strategies to have power and control, and the other avoids and surrenders and gives their power and control away. Each finds reality in the expression of the fear-based beliefs they individually hold.

Passive-powerless people tend to use pleasing and putting others before themselves as their strategy to fulfil their need to avoid confrontation with rejection and judgment. They will attract aggressive-powerless individuals who find their sense of power by engaging those who are passive pleasers. Both were powerless to be unconditionally loved and accepted by their parents, and as adults by others. Both ultimately compromise their authentic self and finish up living life subject to the emotional whims of those to whom they are attracted.

TRUE PERSONAL POWER AND CONTROL

The simple truth is that the human mind can be persuaded to accept or believe almost anything. Our minds have enormous flexibility and capacity for change. This inbuilt mental versatility also means that we are equipped to change who we have been convinced to believe we are. We are naturally capable of changing the nature of our sense-of-self and recovering our unique, authentic origin. Our negative beliefs are founded in fear and are therefore illusions and not real.

Whether we know it or not, we continually and incessantly create our own sense of reality. The intent held in the beliefs that form your sense-of-self controls the unique focus of your mind, which then determines how you express and perceive your world. The intents in your beliefs are the directors of your mind and as a consequence, your life energy.

You as the originator of your intent — positive or negative — are actually in control of your life experiences through the beliefs that form your sense-of-self. You, as the keeper of your own beliefs, are the one who has the power to be in control of your existence.

You have not realised that you are already managing your life. It may not feel like that is the case because you are convinced that others and the world are responsible for what you experience. Accepting ownership of your negative beliefs and responsibility for the outcomes they create, is your first step towards taking control. You can begin to be real and truthful with yourself by letting go of being the emotional and behavioural strategist you have become, by beginning to deal with a multitude of issues that limit your life. It will create the freedom to take stock of your fears, insecurities and negative or self-destructive behaviours, leading you to understand the beliefs that are at their core. Each step constitutes a move to take charge of the nature of your own being and the acquisition of the real personal power with which you are innately endowed.

Once you have taken ownership of your sense-of-self, you need to decide which beliefs you are prepared to accept as your truth and based on fear, are therefore negative and illusionary. By doing so, you are not just taking control over your belief systems, but are automatically taking control over the negative intent that originates from them. Releasing these beliefs will then alter the intentions of your sense-of-self and the kind of life you will manifest and experience as a result. You are also opening the way for your unique, authentic-self to resurface and become the dominant voice in your self-expression.

Your sense-of-self contains both negative and positive beliefs, the balance and intensity of which is different for everyone. Letting go of a disharmonious or negative way of thinking gradually moves the overall balance of your intentions towards being positive and harmonious, creating a happier, more positive life experience. Each change contributes to a greater sense of well-being and a reduction in anxious, stressful and fearful emotions. Depending on the issue you are dealing with and the system of beliefs you release, you will see an improvement in a particular area, or there will be an overall improvement in your state of mind. The influences these changes have over your life will astonish you as will the way others will change their perception of you. You will come to realise that your fears are the only restriction on the fulfilment of the potential of your consciousness.

The capacity of your personal power lies within your sense-of-self. As your sense-of-self reaches greater harmony with the essence of your spirit, you will become aware of your confidence in every aspect of your being and self-expression. The power to create the life you want lies within you, and you do not need to have power over others or anything else in this world to attain it.

The personal power to create and manifest your life potential through the nature of your authentic-self lies in accepting the nature of your spiritual essence — unconditional love, acceptance and trust.

Unconditional Love and Acceptance are the only real source of power for any human consciousness.

Each person has the natural power and entitlement to live life as their unique and authentic self.

We are born with the innate capacity and resources to fulfil our different potential, without restricting, diminishing or controlling the lives of others.

Our existence is intended to be harmonious and cooperative with that of others and complement and support the evolvement of each consciousness.

COLLECTIVE POWERLESSNESS

The nature of the world we live in today is almost exactly opposite to the ideal world we imagine. The fear that dominates our planet has its roots in the powerlessness of every individual and causes us to distrust of ourselves and each other. Without any awareness and understanding of the process by which our consciousness creates our life experiences, we are left to deal with life controlled by our fears. Consequently, most interaction between people is strategic and not based on love, acceptance and trust and therefore are not present as the person they were meant to be. The illusions they share creates a collective experience that they believe to be real and genuine. In some respects, they may as well be walking in their sleep. Humanity lives in a state of fear that has become so much a part of the fabric of life we consider it to be normal.

Although we have learned to believe that others and the world cause our fears, their origin resides within us. What we experience in the world is only a mirror for the many layers of fears we individually and collectively hold within our sense-of-self and act out in the world.

THE STORY OF FEAR

Fear's powerful intent to get you to respond to its message is extremely persuasive because it seeks to trigger your fear for emotional survival, and then take control of what you will manifest in your life.

Fear is like a sly friend who tells you that he will protect you from danger, which in reality does not even exist because it is an illusion. By convincing you that your emotional or sometimes physical survival is at stake, it capitalises on your emotional vulnerability and insecurity. Fear deceives you into believing that your feelings of anxiety, worry and stress are real to make you give in to the emotional pressure it creates. By surrendering your power to your seemingly protective friend, fear now owns and controls you and whether you like it or not you will be doing its bidding.

It promises that if you rely and depend on your strategic behaviours — aggressive or passive — you will avoid that any of your fears become real.

Fear has made the illusions it has created in your sense-of-self seem like reality. Fooled by your emotions and feelings, you cannot help but dance to its tune.

If you want to take control over your life, you need to conquer your fears by realising that they are illusions, and then take the steps necessary to release the beliefs they control.

Some notes about power, control and powerlessness to think about:

Aggressive-Powerless strategic people will only feel powerful by being in control of those who are Passive-Powerless.

Passive-Powerless people exist in the constant need to feel safe and seek to be protected by those who appear to be strong and in control — those who are Aggressive-Powerless.

Genuine Personal Power can only exist in the absence of fear.

Genuine Personal Power is NOT a product of control over those who are weak and fearful.

Genuine Personal Power comes from being in harmony with your spirit and does not need control over others or the world.

Genuine Personal Power does not fear the loss of power or control because it resides within.

Genuine Personal Power naturally serves to empower others.

Chapter 17

TRANSCENDING FEAR

The experience of pain and suffering, fears and unhappiness are such a common feature of life that we do not question how we get to have those feelings. How we deal with negative events depends mostly on how internalised how our parents coped with their issues in life. Their fear of confronting aggression, unexpected changes, conflict, responsibility, the needs of others, for example, will determine our reaction and response to these emotional elements in life. Their actions and responses with you teach you how to behave to comply with their expectations of you. Conforming to their fears is an almost automatic response. Your trust in your parents and emotional survival instinct causes you to accept any of their fears as being real and valid. Learning how to avoid what we fear by taking on particular behaviours can give the impression that dealing with life is nothing but a strategic skill or trick. Even though that is not true, many who believe that it is the way how life works. When a behaviour fails, we immediately seek to replace it with something more effective. This reaction appears logical until you examine the primary reasons why our strategies will ultimately fail. Our strategies can never permanently hide our lack of self-confidence and trust in the capacity, power and integrity of our sense-of-self. We can also not avoid being creators of our life experiences, whether we do it from fear, or unconditional love and acceptance.

Our reaction to negative emotions sets the stage for our thoughts and behaviours. Should we be subject to emotional pain or sadness, our first reaction is to try and avoid it or suppress or dismiss it. Dealing with emotions that are intense becomes challenging when they threaten to overwhelm us. Once we are caught up in negative emotions, our thoughts, behaviour and perception will all be affected. Emotions can feel so encompassing that they can take total control how we will act and respond. Depending on their intensity, our feelings can drive to withdraw or suppress passively or to become extremely aggressive and confronting. If what we feel lacks in impact, we might just complain or criticise, but we will always react in some way.

Activities that we engage in for pleasure can also become a means to escape from what we perceive to be a threat to our well-being. We are usually so convinced that what we feel is the issue that we do not realise that what our emotions represent the symptoms of our problems and are not the cause. By not confronting the origin for what we feel, the kind of experience you are trying to avoid will in time repeat itself. As long as you act and behave from belief systems that are fear-based, you will continue to manifest them as life experiences. The strategies you have developed to deal with your issues, have to be continually used to escape the consequences of your fears. The key to developing a clearer insight is to understand your perception and that of others. Your beliefs determine the perception of what you believe to be real or false, genuine or an illusion. When fear is not of a physical threat but a threat represented by an emotional state such as rejection, criticism, feeling inferior, powerless for example, they cannot destroy you. The problem is that you believe they will and that gives them emotional power over you. Allowing your feelings to be in control is accepting that the consequences implied by your negative belief systems are also real. That is why you resort to being strategic in your behaviours to survive something that has no reality. Your fear that they might fail adds to the insecurity you already have. This condition is the same for others as it is for you.

The most common ways to deal with an unwanted experience is the transfer of responsibility to others using blame or aggression and disassociation through emotional and physical withdrawal. Individuals who cannot cope with their emotions may use these behaviours to deal with their life issues. They try to resolve them by disconnecting from everyone, excessive partying, casual relationships, sex, sport, 'medicating' themselves by drinking alcohol or taking drugs. Whether you will choose avoidance over confrontation depends on the nature and intensity of your feelings of fear or powerlessness. Your sense of powerlessness relates directly to the belief systems of your sense-of-self — powerless to be lovable and loved, acceptable and accepted, wanted and so on. Any or all of these can make you vulnerable to rejection, low self-esteem, stress, pessimism, aggression, abuse, sadness and so on. Once you have chosen avoidance over dealing with your issues, you may use whatever works for you to try not to feel the negative emotions that come from your fears.

THE TRUTH ABOUT LOVE AND FEAR

It is quite common to be resistant to therapy for emotional issues even though there is deep suffering. Often, in comparing ourselves to others, we fear that the admittance or acceptance that we have problems is proof of inferiority and inadequacy. We try and convince ourselves and others that we know what we need to do to overcome our issues. Frequently, we only consider asking for help when everything we have done has failed, and we have arrived at a point of complete powerlessness. Even then we can be extremely reluctant to accept support. We can be even more resistant to the idea that we are responsible for creating our negative experiences. It is the only perspective that makes a real solution possible.

When you cannot see that you are the originator of your emotional issues, you are likely to look for the cause outside of yourself just like your parents would have. If your parents suppressed their feelings, your avoidance behaviour is liable to be the same. You may suppress or deny your negative feelings to avoid dealing with who or what you believe to be the source. In the course of your life, this behaviour may become intolerably painful.

Pretending that what you feel is not an issue or does not matter, is an invalidation of your authentic sense of being. You convince yourself that your negative feelings do not affect you because you have learned it is unacceptable to show what you feel. By doing this, you close the door on your senses and innate awareness of what is a disharmonious emotional state in you. Your denial also diminishes the value and relationship with your emotional being. You may not realise that there is only one door through which your feelings flow, and that closing it will cause you dismiss or diminish positive as well as negative emotions. Denial proves that you have become fearful and distrusting of your emotional nature — positive or negative. Unfortunately, once in denial, you are not likely to question your state of mind and try and uncover the reasons for your behaviour.

VICTIMISED BY BELIEFS

The greatest source of pain and suffering are the fear of rejection and abandonment, guilt and shame because they will control the dynamic of all of your relationships. If the behaviour or dialogue by your partner, friends or even strangers is construed to be criticism or judgement, rejection or abandonment, it will immediately trigger related negative belief systems in you. The same goes for guilt and shame; each is a very compelling and influential, emotional force that can drive human behaviour to extreme levels. Your interpretation of their behaviour or words confirms for you that the beliefs of being unwanted, unlovable and unacceptable in its various forms, are about to become a reality. Your response can be one of high anxiety or even panic but also anger, aggression or sadness. Once these intense feelings overwhelm your senses, you will either be prepared to meet almost any condition at any cost or feel the need to aggressively confront or blame others to protect yourself from your fears.

We are not aware that because we exist, we are by definition lovable, acceptable and wanted at the core of our being. We would not be in existence if we were unlovable, unwanted and unacceptable.

Every spirit consciousness comes into existence through an act of creative manifestation, founded in unconditional love and acceptance, belonging and trust. This expression of the self is the source of our being and represents the natural state of our consciousness from which we cannot separate.

They are innate psychological reference points that are truthful and consistent and provide us with inner guidance.

The origin and very nature of our consciousness made us a creation and a creator, a manifestation and endowed with the capacity to manifest.

The fact that we exist is in itself proof that we belong and therefore matter. Any notion that contradicts this is just a belief and does not represent spiritual reality. As part of our capacity to create and manifest our reality, we can use our will as a force to drive our intention to fulfil our potentials. The mind has the inherent ability to accept or reject any belief, which has the effect of altering the characteristic of our intent and changes our perception, feelings thoughts actions and choices. If we accept that love, acceptance or trust are conditional and make it our truth, we will create and manifest from a state of fear. Assimilation of our parent's fears makes them ours and thereby their illusions become who we believe we are.

You lose the ability to be objective when you allow negative feelings to dominate, and your capacity to be rational in respect to your issues becomes questionable. Even if you have an understanding that your parents did not want or love you, you will not necessarily realise that just because they did not want you, it does not mean that your life or existence is unwanted. Your parents are, but two individuals in a world of billions and they are the only ones that you had this experience. By accepting your parent's treatment as your truth of who you are, you are allowing it to define your identity. You assume that you must not be lovable, acceptable or wanted by anyone else either.

Logically this does not make any sense at all, but our almost childlike emotional mind makes its own rules. However, it does mean that your parents' capacity to love and accept, support and be involved with you unconditionally, was limited by their fears and insecurities. Now, as an adult, the problem is yours to deal with because the distortions lived out by your parents have become self-defining beliefs held by you and no one else. At this time, you are just as lost in fear-based illusions as your parents were when you were young and maybe still are. Only an open-minded examination of your emotional origins will lead to a greater understanding of the reasons for your fears, and allow you to recognise the beliefs that have held you in their painful grip for too long.

THE ORIGINS FOR NEGATIVE EVENTS

It is hard to accept that external forces are not the cause of the failure, conflict, argument, disappointment, pain, resentment and suffering, etc. Once the beliefs that make up your sense-of-self distort your perception, feelings and behaviour, it is hard to know what is true and what is not. The energy you give out as a person depends on the state of your mind, and this will determine who you will attract to become involved with in life. Your state of being will bring people and events in your life which will be complicit in making your fear-based issues a reality. In this sense, nothing that happens in your life is an accident; the people you attract play out their sense-of-self in concert with yours. Everyone's self-expression carries the intent shaped by their sense-of-self. The events in which each of you participates will be a product of the fears each party brings into the equation. There is no escape from the fact that intentions held by the beliefs that define our mind will manifest regardless of whether they are negative or positive.

Since the origin of our fear, suffering, anger or resentment are an intrinsic part of our sense-of-self, no one but us can take responsibility for the beliefs we hold. While this may sound harsh, it becomes evident that we are responsible for generating the quality, nature and intensity of our pain in life. Accepting this, allows us to see that we should not blame negative events or others for what we feel and experience. Just as unconditional love and inner-harmony are the basis for happiness and joy, so does conditional love, acceptance and trust create the fears that drive disharmony and inner-conflict, and become the source of pain and suffering. Our sense-of-self holds the key to our negative or positive life experiences. Our perception that others and the world are the cause rather than us is a handicap to personal change and a distortion of reality.

Probably one of the wisest statements ever made is:

Do not try and change those things that you cannot change (i.e., others and the world) but change that which you can (i.e., yourself).

This saying applies to the way we create life because you cannot change others or the world to accommodate your fears and insecurities. You may not realise, but you are already trying to do just that with the strategies you use to evade your fears. You try to change the response and reactions from others by presenting yourself in a way that you believe will make you lovable, acceptable, trustworthy, dependable, etc., to them. With these strategies, you also intend to avoid the adverse outcomes implied by your fears. Spending all your effort and energy trying to change others does not change you, or subsequently, your life experiences. Regardless of what strategies you apply — passive or aggressive control, manipulation or any other kind of influence, — you will remain the person you believe yourself to be. Even if any of your strategies have success; it will be just with that person, in that moment and for that situation. You will have to spend your life repeating your effort over and over, under the constant pressure of fear of failing.

The only real control you can have in life is over yourself. More specifically, over the beliefs that determine for you who you are. By releasing the beliefs that do not support your authentic self, your true nature, you change your identity. Once you remove belief systems that distort your perception, thoughts and feelings, you transform the energetic vibration of your being. When your consciousness has a different presence, it will realign itself with those, with whom it will find harmony. As the creator of your life, through your sense-of-self, you are born with the capacity to change who you are by releasing the negative beliefs systems that define it. The reality is that you have the ability to be in control over your issues, pain and suffering by letting go of fear, and by accepting the true nature of who you are.

IN LIFE AND DEATH

Feelings of abandonment and grief are a natural emotional response when we lose a loved one to death. How we experience and process such a shocking event in the long term is not entirely dependent on the emotional bond with them. Under these circumstances, our belief systems play a significant role in the way we emotionally process our loss, and how we will continue to live life in their absence.

Our personal beliefs about the nature of consciousness and life also define our perception of death. If you hold the belief that life is inherently physical and the presence of our consciousness depends on the existence of our bodies, then death is a step into a place of non-existence. If that is your belief then losing someone makes their departure extremely painful because, for you, they went from being into nothingness. Their interaction, involvements and confrontations with you dissolve into memories as their life comes to a permanent conclusion. When there has been pain and suffering, throughout someone's life, it often appears that they died without ever experiencing any joy, benefit, pleasure or happiness.

The belief that you will also eventually leave this existence and go from being someone into nothingness will not only determine the perception of your eminent demise but will also influence the way you will live your life. This kind of belief system creates the understanding that purpose and value are limited to the procreation of the species. Asking the question why and how we exist become meaningless. Living becomes a process without direction or a sense of higher purpose and meaning. This state of mind denies its self a future beyond the term of its physical existence because we think that the body generates our consciousness. What you believe to be true for yourself, you will hold to be the same for others, and this will add to the sadness and pain felt at a time of loss.

The concept of spirit, mind and body trilogy sees the process of death as an inevitable part of its eternal journey, as a natural transition of the conscious self to another level of being. Without spirit, neither mind nor body would exist because it is the core essence of our conscious being. The mind is the vibration of our awareness of self and the knowing of our state of being. The body is a vehicle for our spirit and mind in material reality and is essentially a creation of spirit-consciousness. Our consciousness is intimately bonded to our bodies. Our sense-of-self connects emotionally with the body through metaphorical patterns that can vibrate either in or out of harmony with it. As a consequence, anything that happens in mind will also find expression in the body, and all of its workings. As our bodies come to the end of physical functionality, death creates the transition essential for the spiritual expansion of our consciousness and our evolvement beyond physical reality.

The origin of our consciousness or spirit is a source of endless religious, philosophical and scientific debate. Since each demands its' own particular proof, you need to look within yourself to access your inner-knowing for what is right for you. Being objective in your judgment is extremely difficult considering the concepts and beliefs of your culture, inherited religious beliefs and the society with which you grow up. By allowing your intuition and inner senses to lead you to your truth, you will come to an individual understanding of what your issues are.

Once you recognise that our spirit and mind are intimately related to our bodies, it may be easier to accept that our spirit is who you are and continues to exist after death. Surrendering our body by releasing spirit and mind from their physical bondage recognises the continuation of our spirit-being. Acceptance of this transition from the physical to a non-physical state of being can alter our perception of death as an end of existence, and change how we see the departure of a loved one. Death is as much part of the ongoing journey of their spirit as it will be of ours. Every life lived is a learning experience to expand the infinite nature of our consciousness. Although most cultures teach that death is a grave, undesirable event, the transition into our next state of being should be a celebration of the life lived by the person on their journey to evolve to a greater state of being.

EMOTIONAL SUFFERING

When tragedies occur in our lives, there are no glib solutions to deal with the emotional pain and suffering we feel as a consequence. We often hope that the passage of time will create emotional distance between the event and us, but many regularly live their pain over and again to one degree or another. To avoid the pain, some will change their lives through making new determinations to deal with their loss. Emotional support of others is desirable, but usually, over time, this will fade as family and friends return to their own lives. Ultimately, we are left to face our tragedies alone because we are the only ones that can do this for ourselves. Even though particular strategies will be effective to allow us to continue our lives with some normality, they do not necessarily deal with the reasons why the pain may have taken on such an enduring form.

There will always be an emotional distress when separated from those we love, by death, or even severe illness. The fact that each of us can have a different experience of the same or similar event shows that there is no simple answer for dealing with the pain of loss. Our issues related to rejection, and abandonment, powerlessness and being unwanted for example, play a decisive role in the way we will experience trauma and the stress of loss. Someone who loses their partner and fear being alone because they feel unlovable, unwanted and unacceptable, will feel very differently affected than someone who does not have these issues. The need to have someone in their life and therefore their dependence on their partner to be loved and accepted makes them extremely needy and fearful of abandonment and therefore extremely vulnerable and sensitive to suffering loss. Their emotional security and identity rely on the presence of their partner, whom they depend on for the fulfilment of their needs. Their absence can plunge them into an abyss of fear, loneliness and unhappiness. Their fears and insecurities serve to intensify the experience of their loss, and this will exacerbate and prolong their sadness and suffering.

An event such as this can take them back to re-experience their childhood fears, which were compensated for by their partner when they were alive. Overcoming them would of course not change the fact that they have lost someone dear to them. Inner-change will, however, alter their self-perspective and therefore also how they will feel about their loss and this can potentially can make it bearable or even cause them to hold on to fond memories. Life and death are intrinsically connected and natural elements of the existence of everything including us. Everything changes and transforms, and physical death is a natural aspect of consciousness existing in material reality. As much as we want to experience life, without pain and suffering, we must accept death as the natural course taken by all living consciousness on its continues journey of evolving it being.

Someone with a harmonious sense-of-self will deal with emotional trauma very differently than someone who is insecure, needy, dependent, powerless and so on. The beliefs they hold about themselves, life, death and dying are from the point of self-power and eternal existence. This awareness helps them to accept the journey of the departed and continue a meaningful path in life. Whether one chooses to have a new relationship or a different direction in life or not, becomes a matter of choice and should not be a product of fear. Life does not have to become an ongoing journey of loneliness, misery and pain.

Someone who goes into depression or becomes suicidal after a significant financial loss shows that they already have their sense-of-self-worth, and identity rolled up in material wealth before the event. If you become emotionally distraught by the breakup of your relationship you are not likely to look at how you contributed to it. If you attract events or people in your life that cause you pain or anger, powerlessness or guilt, you need to accept that because you are the constant factor in all of them, that you the source of your issues. There are an endless number of examples of these. Your understanding will allow you to define a clear difference between the authentic pain of loss and trauma, and those created by your pre-existing emotional issues.

While under stressful circumstances it may be difficult to examine your state of mind, the reasons for doing so are extremely relevant and legitimate if you are to find inner peace. Those who cannot cope with traumatic emotional events are very likely to have pre-existing belief systems responsible for intensifying the experience. Dealing with unresolved emotional issues related to emotional loss or trauma can make a significant difference to your perception and feelings. You do not need to worry that a changed self will make you an uncaring or insensitive individual. Your grief will still be sincere but releasing the cause of these issues will exclude that part of your emotions which were really about you, and not about the one you lost.

Chapter 18

FANTASY AND IMAGINATION

So far, our focus has only been on belief systems being the source for the creation and manifestation of our experience of reality. They are the crucial and deterministic elements in the process of manifesting our experience of ourselves in life, but there is much more to the innate capacities of our consciousness that make this possible. The faculties that give us the power to manifest our lives per the beliefs, which make up our sense-of-self, are an inherent part of our consciousness.

We are born with the incessant drive to create and manifest our beliefs, thoughts, fantasies and imagination in the world, to experience the nature of our being through our experience of life. The desire of our consciousness to evolve by learning and knowing, understanding and experimentation are never ending. All of this, feeds the all-encompassing force within all consciousness to expand the nature and capacity of its being and to evolve towards its ever-growing potential. Consciousness is always in evolution and always seeks to become more than what it is. Its sense of who and what it is to itself determines the direction it chooses to achieve this. When consciousness creates negative versus positive experiences, our emotions and feelings will notify the mind that it is manifesting life from fear (conditional love, trust and acceptance) rather than unconditional love.

Being conscious that the essence of your spiritual being is present in all of your beliefs and feelings, behaviour and self-expression is the only way to be aware that you are manifesting a harmonious existence. Being in harmony with yourself is the only way to be in harmony with the world and others and to exist without fear.

Anything invented, built and achieved by man started out as an idea, inspiration, fantasy or imagination. Anything that is a physical creation, an idea or concept begins as an energetic construct of the mind, initiated by our imagination. Application of our intellect and judgment, choices and actions, talents and abilities, competencies, skills and commitment can bring what was an inspired idea into physical reality. Whether it is the pyramids or a box of matches, a mathematical equation or a painting, they all start within our mind as a creative concept or inspiration.

Imagination and fantasies are essential elements of our life tools which, when driven by our innate desire to learn and manifest, can result in astonishing outcomes. They are the source of new ideas and concepts that can transcend current perception. Without them, we would not have had the advances in every area of our existence that are now a regular part of life. Imagination and fantasy give us the means by which to tap into realms of creative contemplation that transcend the limits of convention and accepted logic. They allow the mind to bend laws and rules of reality established by conventional knowledge and logic, and go beyond norms that act as limitations and restrictions in the mental, physical or emotional world. They serve to challenge our perception of reality and what is possible to transcend accepted convention. These faculties are incredibly precious aspects of human consciousness because they assist us in our quest to evolve, grow and expand the nature of our being.

Each of us has the capacity for fantasy and imagination, which is especially evident in young children, whose minds flow effortlessly and freely between reality and fantasy. When fantasies and imaginings are encouraged, children learn to use them as a place of experimentation and to test the veracity of their imagination against the reality of the physical world. You might be surprised to learn that children are innately aware of the differences between their imaginings and reality without feeling that they have to dismiss them as invalid concoctions of their minds. Each has value in context with the intent behind their creation, and this connects them intimately to the another. Because of this, dismissing them could damage to their trust in the creative capacity of their minds. Invalidation of their fantasies and imagination diminished their confidence in natural psychological abilities they were born with and invoked distrust in their mental resources. The doubt created by ridicule or other forms of invalidation can severely affect a child's capacity to become a confident creator of their adult life. Fantasies and imagination are a resource that allows consciousness to find a creative outlet for the fulfilment of its potential beyond accepted norms.

The nature of your sense-of-self plays a central role in the expression of your fantasies and imagination. Your trust or distrust in these innate capacities will affect any creative ventures your mind considers to undertake. Your relationship with your creative impulses and desires, talents and abilities can be a resource for the achievements of your aspirations. Your rejection, doubt or distrust in your creative imagination will act as a restraint on your inspirations and creative self-expression and ultimately, the life experiences you will manifest for yourself.

SUPPRESSING YOUR CREATIVE SELF

It is easier to suppress the natural creative capacities you were born with than what you might think. When we first display, and express our creative imagination in play, storytelling and games, they are often not accepted by parents who may have fears in respect to this. Their dismissal, criticism or comments can make us feel wrong about the voice we give to our spontaneous fantasies and imaginations. We learn to reject and suppress our creative thoughts and ideas because of our parent's disapproval. It is likely our parents had the same experience in their childhood and did the same to us as was done to them. Without realising it, they parented us the way they were.

People who lead a powerless and restricted life will often need to convince their offspring that life is harsh and remorseless because that is what they believe life to be. They do not realise that as the creators of their life, they are responsible for having this experience. They see a world in which there is no place for fanciful imaginations and fantasies because, in their view, this will only lead to disappointment, pain and suffering. Their fears create a life that it is difficult, a struggle and full of hardship. They do not realise that even then, they use their creative imagination in concert with their negative beliefs to paint a gloomy negative picture of reality and the future.

If you grew up with parents whose issues and therefore fears consistently created adverse experiences in their lives, you would come to assume that this is how life is. Their belief that it is a struggle will become your expectation in life. Growing up in a family with a pessimistic attitude to everything in life may cause you to use your fantasy and imagination to escape from the terrible world you come to believe exists. On the other hand, you might reject your fantasies because you have allowed yourself to be convinced that they are unrealistic and have no place in the harsh reality of life. Locked into the pessimistic perceptions inherited from your family, you believe the perception of reality your family presents you with is true. You would not know that your parent's version of the world and others are a product of what they believe to be real and consequently, not knowing any better you cannot imagine that what they present you with could be different. By negating your own imagination, you inadvertently invalidate that of others, if for no other reason than to be right. Even though you may not actively discourage your children in their fantasy play, your pessimistic behaviour and attitude would transfer the pain you feel in living 'a life of struggle' to them. Others may judge you for being cynical and pessimistic, but in your perception, you believe yourself to be a 'realist'.

Pessimism, negativity, and adversarial perception of relationships and the anticipation of disaster, they all have the capacity to dominate our lives. The fact is that all fears tend to undermine our faith in the whole creative process that is life. If driven by fear, imagination and fantasy project negative potentials into the present and the future. Pessimism can colour even the past with sombreness. Highly creative personalities i.e. artists of all kinds, who have fears and issues tend to express their creativity with a pessimistic slant that encompasses their pain and suffering. It is romantic to think that their pain is the source for their art, but more than often they only feel comfortable or safe to express what they feel through the voice of their artistic abilities. Their art becomes the language by which they communicate their pain or anger or any other emotion. Deeply affected by emotional issues, they may show their true feelings through their artistry. In this respect, art also can be a therapeutic bridge to find free emotional expression for those who have difficulty giving a voice to their feelings. Art can be optimistic, revealing and inspiring or an instrument to enlighten and this also shows the nature of the artist

ESCAPE FROM REALITY

Consciousness is amazingly gifted when it seeks to survive in the face of perceived fears, limitations and restrictions, and in the absence of love and acceptance. It will use any psychological tool at its disposal to ensure its emotional security and the most powerful of these is strategic behaviour. The nature of our negative beliefs and the manner in which we acquire them, steer us to become strategic. They become the means by which to retain our relationships with our parents and later with others and the world. They delude us into believing that we will be loved and accepted by meeting conditions that only exist in our minds. Once we have adopted these behaviours, they become our means to overcome our fears in life.

Our fantasies, dreams and imagination can become a strategic tool to escape fears and insecurities, disappointment and restrictions, instead of being the source for instigating new life experiences. Families that promote negative, pessimistic and restrictive ideas and beliefs through passive or aggressive behaviour, push their children to find ways to survive emotionally. Each child will feel restricted and controlled by their parent's emotional issues without realising that they cannot be responsible for them.

Our mode of escape can take many forms from sport, books or computer games, alcohol, drugs, sex, intellectual pursuits, money and so on. Escape from suppressing your natural impulses and desires potentials and aspirations, fantasies and creative imagination because of fear, can alienate us from engaging in life and work and from socialising with others. We may withdraw and emotionally want to disconnect to avoid confrontation with others which is really about avoiding confronting ourselves. Consequently, we then become alone and lonely. By reacting aggressively to being suppressed, we find ourselves in constant conflict, and that too does not bring us happiness and peace. Without realising it, we will come to accept our patterns of behaviour as normal, as if part of our personality. Our lack of self-awareness can lead us to become the same as our parents, and potentially repeat their pattern of life and relationships.

LOST IN FANTASY

Under emotional suppression and in fear a child may look for psychological escape by withdrawing into fantasy and imagination. It can seem the only place where it can feel free to be who it wishes to be and have what it desires is by creating an imagined existence without restrictions and limitations. In your fantasies, you are the creator of an imagined reality, that you control and in which you are safe. Some children try to compensate for the fears they inherited by separating their fantasies far from reality. The disparity between real life and your imaginary existence can be so wide, that you may believe that you can only ever be who you want to be in your fantasies and imagination. Remember that we create our own existence no matter what. Believing you can never have what you want in reality creates the intent that you never will. In your fantasies, you may have loving relationships, enjoy immense success and live in great abundance even if you hold the belief that you are not lovable and acceptable, not entitled and unattractive, not good enough and dumb.

Once you convince yourself that you can only have what you want by being in your fantasies, dreams and imagination, you have set the stage for how you will manifest your life.

The consequence of this kind of belief system is not easily seen but can have an extremely restrictive effect on someone's capacity to fulfil their potential. The context and intensity of this issue vary enormously from person to person. In adulthood, they will not make an effort to bring fantasies and imaginations to life because they are convinced that they what they want in reality. This conviction stops them from taking action to fulfil their aspirations and hold them in a constant state of avoidance. Dreaming them becomes an escape without the potential for failure, stress or anxiety. Avoiding confrontation with their fears, they often live life feeling denied and unfulfilled.

Those with this issue are usually not aware that they are the cause for many of their frustrations and disappointments in life. Without converting their imagination and fantasy into decisions and actions, life cannot turn out to be anything else but a disappointment. Convinced in their expectation that their wishes and desires, hopes and dreams will never be fulfilled, they cannot project an optimistic future for themselves. Another child, similarly made powerlessness because of the rejection and judgement of its fantasies and imaginations, may rebel with anger and aggression, and fight for its right to express its creative self openly and freely.

Everything we manifest in life and the world starts as a creative projection manifested by our fantasies and imagination before it ultimately becomes a reality. By accepting our negative beliefs as truths, we may stop our creative ideas from ever being realised. Without making an effort to understand why this is our experience of reality, it is likely that we will have disappointments in life.

Potentially, people with this mind-set tend to make their fantasies disproportionally ambitious. As a result, their expectations become so incredibly outlandish that they have no possibility of being realised. Imaginings of romantic relationships with extremely wealthy, successful and handsome men or beautiful women, becoming famous or successful may sound like obvious fantasies but are more common than you might think. In most cases, they are not actively involved in anything that could lead them to make their fantasy a reality. By imagining a life that they cannot make real, they emphasise their belief in their shortcomings and failings. Putting their dreams far beyond the reach of their capacity to manifest them gives them justification for not doing anything to create a life that approaches these ambitions. Naturally, they will spend a life of dreaming and waiting rather than involving themselves in the process of fulfilling their life potentials. Consequently, the outcomes they experience will be will be a faithful reflection of their fears and confirm that they cannot have what they want in reality.

Even though we are born free to believe, think and behave any way we want, the emotional forces that raised us, determine how we will act, behave and express ourselves in the world. Every quality that defines the nature of our consciousness plays a role in the manifestation of who we are in life, and what our life experience will be. Our fantasy, imagination and dreams will always play a significant role in our creative capacity to project and manifest our future existence. If we were to release these emotional restrictions and restore our innate capacity for fantasy and imagination, then we will be able to turn our dreams into reality. There are no limits to the inherent capacity of your consciousness other than the fears you hold in your sense-of-self.

Considering the perception of 'who we believe we are', determines our limitations, it not surprising that we tend to dismiss the proposition that we should naturally be experts in the process of manifesting our lives. This perception makes it seem impossible to have control over our lives, even though this is entirely achievable. The capacity to be the conscious creative force in the manifestation of our reality is innate in every one of us. There is no doubt however that to be an 'expert' creator; you need to strive to become the 'master of your consciousness'. For this, you need to, first of all, develop a clear and intimate understanding of the fears held by your own mind's sense-of-itself. A 'master' would engage in the process of creating life in the absence of fear, with complete trust in the purity and power of his or her being and the expression of its intent.

This understanding should explain why strategic behaviours have only temporary value as a solution for our fears. We should only use them as a stopgap and temporary fix but never trust them to be a permanent support system. In the process of becoming a master creator of your reality, you have to deal with your fears. Every release will bring you closer to that goal. Fantasies and imagination are essential tools for a master creator in the process of inventing and initiating new life challenges so that his or her consciousness can evolve. Through manifesting intent, they allow you to project a potential for a different life into the future. By forming a clear and well-defined idea or plan for the future that you can apply in the present and engage in activities directed to make them a reality, you are creating your dreams and aspirations. You are also making progress to becoming the master creator of your life.

Chapter 19

LIVING YOUR UNCONDITIONAL POTENTIAL

Who you believe yourself to be and the feelings this creates in you will determine the choices that will lead you to experience your unique life journey. When we encounter emotionally challenging issues, and our current strategies fail, we usually respond by trying to replace them with new strategies with the intent for a better outcome. However, we should always see this as a temporary, stopgap solution. The fact that the outcome was not what we expected should have prompted questions about us, as the decision makers and instigators. It improbable that a new approach will resolve the fundamental causes of why we failed in the first place.

If you want to address your issues at their core, you have no choice but to explore the nature of your mind. Your preoccupation with changing what you do needs to stop and instead you have to focus on changing who you are. Achieving real personal change requires a transformation of your sense-of-self which you can accomplish by releasing the negative beliefs that cause you to manifest your fears and insecurities as life experiences. You may believe that the reason for a conflict is what you do or how somebody else responds, but you are looking at the symptoms of the issues that each party plays out through their strategic behaviours. Both of parties attempt to avoid the consequences that each of them believes exist should the fears they hold become a reality.

DEFINED BY FEAR

While it may be difficult to become unconditional in the absolute sense, but you can be sure that every time you release a fear-based belief, you are bringing yourself closer to that goal. Before you can do that, you will need to examine everything about yourself — your perception, thoughts, behaviour, feelings, choices and responses to others. All these elements come into play as you create your life experiences — positive or negative.

You may find for example that many of the things you want from life or others are aspects that you believe to be absent within you.

- If you have the need to be accepted by others, it is because you are not acceptable to yourself.
- If you have to prove that you are unique and significant to others, it is because you believe that who you are does not matter.
- If you need others to love you to prove to you that you are lovable and acceptable, it is because you believe yourself to be unlovable and unacceptable.
- If you need the attention from others and get upset when they ignore you, it is because you think your presence and existence are insignificant and do not matter to anyone.
- If your constant fear and anticipation of being blamed and accused, convinced that whenever someone is upset, or things go wrong, you must somehow be guilty or implicated.

Your strategic behaviours have the intent to get proof from others that you are not the dysfunctional self, you believe yourself to be. If you think are unacceptable, you may try and prove that it is not true by getting others to accept you. You have the idea, that if this strategy succeeds, that their acceptance of you constitutes proof that you are acceptable. These strategic behaviours have the intent to convince others that you are lovable and acceptable, significant or extraordinary, etc., and to prove to yourself that you are not who you believe yourself to be. Understand, that the only reason for employing a strategic behaviour, is so that you can hide the negative self — you believe yourself to be — from others by creating evidence that the opposite is true. You have accepted the illusion that by convincing others that you are significant, you have proof that you are. You can apply this to feeling unlovable instead of lovable, feeling unacceptable instead of acceptable, feeling guilty instead of innocent or not responsible and so on.

The obvious problem is that you will be dependent on others for an affirmative response to your behaviour, to what you say and how you react and respond. There is always the fear that your strategic action may fail. If it does, you fear that others have recognised that you are insignificant, not good enough, stupid, powerless, fearful and so on. Controlled by fear, you are unlikely to realise that your dependence on others for a positive response, gives them power over you because of your negative view of yourself. You are dependent on their affirmation of your strategies to feel positively validated. Any success your behaviours achieves will be short lived and in the real sense, illusionary. The result will only appear genuine and real to those involved and not to anyone else, not even you. Every time you feel the same insecurities, you will have to play out your strategies over again, driven by the same fears. The only people you will be able to accept that your behaviour represents the truth about you, are those who have fears and insecurities, which in many ways match your own.

Your approach to protecting your issues can be either aggressive or passive, and for some both (but not simultaneously). Behaviour and dialogue are the most common ways you can try and convince others that you are significant, intelligent or competent, etc. Alternatively, you may identify so completely with your negative beliefs that you believe that they represent who you are. Unable to be anyone other than who you believe yourself to be, you feel as if you are a victim of yourself. Once you accept that this is who you are, you also feel helpless to do anything about it because it feels pointless to try. When you believe that you are a powerless victim, is hard to see that what you hold to be true about yourself is just a belief and not carved in stone. Even though your beliefs may define who you are, they can be released or changed.

If you always live being unhappy, disappointed and sad, you will try and focus on those things and situations that you believe will bring you joy and avoid those that will not. Your mother or father (or both) would have modelled these issues through their behaviour and attitude.

They mark their pursuit of happiness by expressions of dissatisfaction and discontent. You will sense a lack of self-fulfilment, with each other and life. Their pessimistic beliefs convince them that they will never be happy, content or satisfied and that their expectations will go unfulfilled. These fears cause them to give disproportionate attention to anything that disappoints them or makes them unhappy or sad because it proves that they are right and victims of life. This reaction to any disappointment only serves to emphasise their despondency to their children who begin to accept this as being a real potential for themselves and their lives. Their parent's belief that others and the world are responsible for bringing them fulfilment and happiness become their expectation as well. By accepting this as their truth, they will not appreciate that what they want can only be created by them. A profound sense of powerlessness colours their perception, which makes them pessimistic of ever finding happiness and contentment in life. Constant exposure to the helplessness, pessimism, disappointment, dissatisfaction and discontent of their parents will set the children up to believe that this is how life is and what to expect in their future. By accepting this as truth, they will try and do anything possible to create fulfilment and happiness through others or accept that they will always be powerless to have their expectations met. In both cases, disappointment and discontent will fill their lives, but each will act and behave differently in response to the same issue. Your belief that you will never be happy and satisfied may cause you sidestep anything in your life that has the potential to make you stressed, sad, upset or disappointed. Alternatively, you may obsessively engage in activities chosen to make you feel good, even if it is only of a temporary nature. In both situations, each tries to distance themselves from their fear based feelings through their actions and responses. Instead of directing their attention to what is going on in their minds to discover the causes for what they believe, feel and experience, they have made themselves dependent on others and the world to feel safe from their fears; just like their parents did.

If you are a victim of aggression, rejection or the manipulative control of your parents, it is likely that this has caused you to believe that you are powerless and have no control over your life. The belief that you are powerless is a result of having every aspect of your behaviour and expression controlled by one or both of your parent. Their need and expectation that you were the child they expected you to be were made to be your responsibility. Born to exist as a different consciousness, you would never be able to accommodate what they wanted you to be particularly because fear and insecurities have distorted their expectations of you.

Your unique nature makes you unpredictable to them and triggers their issues even though at your age, you can only be spontaneous and sincere. Your parent's attitude and response to you reveal whenever your behaviour contradicts whom your parents believe you should be. You will learn that the only way they will accept you if your responses, actions, choices and attitude corresponds with their needs, expectations, values, standards and does not provoke their fears and insecurities. Their reaction to your behaviour implies what they demand and expect from you, which can come through criticism, judgement, blame, rejection, guilt, annoyance, impatient, etc. Your parent's response to you causes you to feel and believe that your authentic self is unacceptable and unwanted. The message you receive is that you will only be loved and accepted if you comply with every need and expectation they have of you. They leave you no choice because whether they intend to or not, these are the condition they place on their relationship with you.

If you failed to be who they expect and need you to be, you are likely to attract their criticism, blame, anger, aggression, guilt or abuse. You are made responsible for your parent's inability to accept you as the person you were born to be because fear and insecurity control them. Their feelings of disappointment, discontent, frustration or anger or any other negative feelings related to their issues, are blamed on you, while you are still unable to speak up for yourself.

Should your parent be passive-powerless and act as if they are victims of others and life, they will still transfer the responsibility for their fears to you. It does not matter whether they are passive or tend to be aggressive either way you will be made responsible for what and how they feel and think. In both scenarios, the transfer of responsibility for your parent's issues to you makes you believe you are the guilty party. Your way of dealing with your emotional guilt is to either adopt passive or aggressive strategies to survive emotionally. Your fear of being powerless may be so intense that you react by emulating the behaviour of the abusive parent to avoid being a victim. On the other hand, you may have accepted the belief that you are powerless as a truth about yourself. Your sense of helplessness can cause you to wait for approval and get permission to do or have what you want. You will also try and avoid doing or saying anything that may provoke an adverse response from your aggressive parent and later from others. You may be attracted to or become a follower of someone who you believe is powerful and significant because of your belief in your powerlessness. Their display of power influence and control gives you a sense of strength, significance and value by association.

You will need to depend on strategies when you are with others if you believe yourself to be insignificant, of no consequence, not entitled and not deserving. Aggressive, confronting and attention seeking behaviour will ensure that you will always be the centre of everyone's attention. Or, by acting passively, by being compliant and non-confrontational make yourself emotionally 'invisible' to avoid being noticed. Secondary behavioural strategies in response to this kind of belief system can be — developing extreme independence, not being able to ask for support, help or for what you want and the need to prove that you are emotionally mentally and physically self-sufficient. Besides having a childhood history of feeling ignored, forgotten and blamed you may also feel that you are a burden to your parents and an intrusion in their lives. Their lack of interest in your needs, expectations, feelings, issues, fears and involvement in your life, convinced you that you are uninteresting, insignificant and that your existence does not matter. Their lack of desire to connect with you feels like a dismissal of your authentic and unique self and everything that represents for you, and therefore you believe you do not matter. Once you accept that you do not matter and your life is of no consequence, you will lose the motivation to live life to fulfil the potentials with which you were born. The constant cycle of negative thoughts and feelings created in you can make you fall into depression because it continues to raise a sense of insignificance, worthlessness, powerlessness and subsequent pointlessness.

The reasons for these family paradigms are many. Parents who feel the pain of being denied love, attention and acknowledgement in their childhood can resent giving the attention, love, and affection they missed out on, to their children. We would like to think that our parents loved us unconditionally, but the reality is that their fears prevented them from being unconditional in their relationship with you. Just like others, their fears and insecurities become most evident by living together and parenthood. Unfortunately, their behaviour ensures that their issues become ours because by denying us the unconditional love, acceptance and attention we expected, results in making us just as fearful, needy or insecure as they were. Consequently, we are likely to repeat their patterns of behaviour, their choices and potentially their lives.

The way out of repeating these patterns of generational negative belief systems is possible for everyone. It requires that your first response to any negative emotional experience is to look at yourself; your behaviour, attitude thoughts, perception and feelings to discover your part in its manifestation in your life. Arriving at an objective understanding of the nature of your belief systems if you do not judge, blame and criticise itself or others. You must try and be as open minded and unconditional in your analysis of yourself and the behaviour of others as you can be. Only then will you discover and understand the causes with clarity. Fear will distort and kind of action, response, reaction, expression, feeling, perception or thoughts. Once fear is involved it will warp your emotional perception, feelings, behaviour and awareness and what you believe is true and real will be in many ways an illusion. You bring yourself a step closer to finding causes for your fear-based illusions and misperceptions if you can recognise that your response comes from a distorted perception of the situation. When you search deeper, you will begin to see the form in which you hold the negative self-beliefs in your sense-of-self that are at the source and the cause for what you experience in life. It will lead you to understand that the fear-driven conditions you subconsciously place on your relationships and living life control your mind.

In time. You will become aware that only you can be responsible for your issues because you are the one holding on to the fear-based beliefs that create them.

In childhood, your need for emotional survival gave you no choice but to accept the conditions set by the fear-driven behaviour of your parents. They demanded your compliance to quell their insecurities. Your naive mind did not allow you to judge or realise the reasons and causes for these emotional experiences and so you accepted them as being real. Their behaviour convinced you of who you are, how you should be and behave to be acceptable to your parents and later others. Consequently, you either lived by their rules, expectations, values and standards or you were in constant conflict with them. In time you came to accept their judgment of you as being representative of who you are and this perception evolved into your identity. Now, these fear-based beliefs and their associated feelings and behaviours act as your emotional survival mechanism in relationships and life. The sense that you can survive without them is the reason why hold on to them, and why you fear to engage in life without them. Since you are the one holding on to them, you are also the only one that can change who you believe yourself to be by releasing these negative beliefs.

Our negative beliefs do not attach themselves to us; our childhood fears of being rejected and abandoned causes us to hold on to them and treat them as if they are essential for our survival. We are convinced that it is the only way that we will be accepted, wanted and loved, and we cannot see that it is entirely conditional.

THE LIES FEAR CREATES

Fear holds the promise that if we accept the conditions, it sets for our emotional safety and security to be true, we will be protected from the consequences if we were to ignore it and receive love, acceptance and trust. Fear never reveals the actual consequences of what will happen if you accept what it wants you to believe. It convinces you that as long as you respond to its call, you will be safe from abandonment and rejection, criticism and judgement, shame and unhappiness, loneliness and exclusion, and so on. Fear convinces you that love, acceptance and trust can ever be unconditional and persuades you to accept that the conditions you have to meet are inevitable and unavoidable.

When we are still children, our need to be unconditionally loved, wanted and accepted and our total dependence on our parents in the first years of life, makes us feel that we have no other choice but to assume that being loved, wanted, and accepted is conditional. We already believe that we have no choice. Without this emotional connection, we feel that there will be no-one to support our existence and survival. At this time of our life, our emotions determine our behaviour and choices, and therefore we feel that we have no choice. When we come to a point where we believe ourselves to be on the verge of being rejected, abandoned, excluded, deserted or so on, the emotion we feel is our first taste of fear. It is the first time we can no longer take the expectation of being unconditionally loved, accepted, wanted and trust for granted.

Once fear takes a hold over us, we can no longer think, feel, perceive and behave with real clarity. Our fear created by the absence of love and acceptance that we assumed was unconditional takes control. With it does our conviction that we have to meet conditions and expectations to recover some if not all of the unconditional love we lost. When our change in behaviour receives a positive response from our parents, it feels as if they restored their love and acceptance for us. At the time, we do not realise that we are being taught to meet conditions that suit them. We are being trained to respond in a particular way to their fear-based issues. By responding with behaviour that waylays their discomfort or inability to cope, we naively take responsibility for their fears and insecurities. Whether they are aware of it or not but parents expect that their children behave and act according to expectations, many of which are a product of their fears, and do not recognise the emotional compromise they demand from their children.

Being dependent on our strategic behaviours means that we have accepted that we have to meet conditions to bring love and acceptance back into our lives. We do not realise that we give our power and control away to others because we depend on their positive response to be loved, accepted and wanted. Our dependence on our belief and consequently others to approve and endorse our behaviour and attitude makes us powerless. We make ourselves subject to the judgement of others by giving them the power to determine whether we meet their conditions or not. They will decide whether we are lovable, acceptable, wanted, desirable, good enough, intelligent, significant or not. We need to see that our fears render us powerless and cause us to lose control over our lives. We hold on to the illusion that the strategic behaviours we have learned to employ, give us power and put us in charge. Nothing could be further from the truth, as they are misrepresentations of who we truly are — our authentic self.

Due to the way, our psychology has evolved the nature of our beliefs over the ages, our personal and collective awareness and perception of ourselves and others have become severely restricted. The aim of authentic personal transformation is to expand our consciousness so that we understand who we truly are and live a life that fulfils our potential. We need to reconnect to the essence of our inner-being to reclaim the value, power, significance and worth of the mental, emotional and spiritual resources with which we came into the world. The results of releasing negative beliefs are life-changing and permanent in how they transform your experience of life. The absence of fear as a part of your inner-identity alters the sense of who you are, as well as your behaviours, feelings and perception, and therefore how you believe others will perceive you. It is ultimately unavoidable that everyone has to contend with the fears they hold onto, and can do this by becoming aware of the core reasons for them, the impact they have on us and how they implicate us with the insecurities of others. Without real change, our emotional functionality in relationships and life will depend on the ongoing effectiveness or failure of our strategic behaviours.

THE INTERNAL BATTLE TO CONTROL YOUR MIND

Fear is constantly in a contest with unconditional love and acceptance for control over your emotional mind. If the absence of unconditional love is our deepest fear, why do we not just unconditionally surrender to love, acceptance and trust and thereby resolve all of our issues? It should be obvious that we have extreme difficulty doing exactly that from the way we end up living our lives. There are emotionally compelling reasons to explain why we not only have significant issues with confronting, recognising and accepting our issues but also why we are reluctant to release them.

The reasons are explained here in the approximate order in which these emotional barriers tend to become a part of us.

Distrust of our authentic self is a major obstacle when we want to change. Our strong identification with our fear-based sense-of-self and our dependence on it for our emotional survival through our strategic behaviours convinces us that we will be powerless without our fears. Without them, we feel vulnerable to everything of which we are afraid, left without a sense of who we are. Our parents' distrust and dismissal of our authentic self and its unique and different qualities because they did not fit their expectations, norms and values caused us to invalidate it to get a measure of their love and acceptance even if it was conditional. Their fears and insecurities of anything that is different from what they held to be true or right caused them to judge our spontaneous, unique and authentic-self to be wrong and unacceptable. Without a clear set of standards and values to draw from, we have no choice but to accept the values and standards shaped by their fears and to accept them as our 'truths'. We then naturally begin to fear to express our spontaneous desires, expectations and needs and hide and suppress our authentic-self. Even though their negative state of mind will contradict the innate nature of our authentic self, our need to emotionally survive gave us no alternative but to accept the conditions our parents placed on their love and acceptance of us. Our unconscious choices have brought us into a state of mind that makes us fearful of being our authentic self and expressing our authentic nature. Instead, we have become dependent on fear to live life in the safety of rejection, criticism, shame, failure, being inadequate, etc. each of which is essentially an illusion. Once our mind has reached this point, we are convinced that if we were to express our unique, spontaneous nature and think, want and feel, we would provoke conflict or aggression, criticism or judgement, anger or resentment, powerlessness or guilt, and so on. Once we are adults, we still believe that we will invoke the same responses from others as we did from our parents as young children. We have unconsciously chosen for our fear to be our protector and friend.

Emotional neediness and the feelings our fears create are compelling forces that will cause us to reach out for our strategic behaviours as the only psychological tools we believe will protect us from the negative consequences implied by our fears or lead us to fulfilment. We do not realise that the real love and acceptance we seek is unconditional. Our conviction that there is a particular need that we have to meet separates us from grasping the reality of what is going on within us. The fear of having to live without feeling lovable, acceptable, wanted, trusted and so on provides the impulse to search for ways to fulfil these needs. Under constant pressure from the fear of not having the unconditional love and acceptance we feel we cannot exist without, and the fear that our strategies will fail us, causes us to live life in a persistent state of anxiety. The fear of being rejected or abandoned and alone, not having a family, being unhappy and disappointed, missing out or being ignored, being unnoticed or never being fulfilled, feeling worthless and so on, are all different forms of neediness with fear at their centre. Each will create their brand of stress that drives us to resort to strategic behaviours.

We become so conditioned to believe that love, acceptance and trust are conditional that we usually will not even recognise or accept unconditional love if we fell over it. Strange as it may seem, but unconditional love can become so foreign to us that if it should cross our path that we tend to treat it with suspicion and distrust. The belief that love is conditional makes the absence of these conditions strange experience, and in some ways very challenging. Being unconditional in love and acceptance can feel uncomfortable because it demands you to be unconditional in return. The expectation that you reciprocate in kind confronts you with the conditions you hold in respect to love. The expectation that you should be completely unconditional is likely to bring up many if not all of your fears, which will prevent you from being who you were born to be. If you have a partner, who genuinely love and accept him or herself and is, therefore, is not needy of love and acceptance, it can make you feel vulnerable and insecure. The absence of their neediness of you can make you feel as if you do not matter or are not enough for them. The feelings this can create in you can take you into the pain of abandonment and rejection because they do not need your love and do not depend on you to be acceptable, though they do want to be with you. Your insecurity and fear of not being lovable and acceptable and therefore hold onto rejection and abandonment issues, create the condition that you need them to need you to love them so that you can feel secure in the relationship. If your partner were just as needy and co-dependent as you are, then the relationship may initially seem perfect, but over time it is likely that cracks will appear in the trust you have of each other. Fear is the driving force of emotional neediness and distrust and doubt will always creep into the mind when there is a chance that the other party might not meet these expectations. Surrendering the conditions created by fears that you believe real, is like giving up the protection from the pain and suffering experienced in childhood.

So instead of choosing unconditional love, we find ourselves settling for living in fear — conditional love, acceptance and trust. We are subconsciously drawn to be with people who carry issues complementary to our own. The fear of existing in the absence of love and the fear of loneliness intensifies the neediness for a partner, in our lives and shuts our eyes to the emotional causes for our negative feelings. Our neediness will control our behaviour and responses such as pleasing and attention-seeking for example, but can also drive controlling and dominant behaviour.

The fundamental problem with neediness is that it always represents an expectation from others. By being needy, you transfer the responsibility for what is missing for you within yourself to others or a partner. Your counterpart will likely be someone who learned in childhood that they would only be loved and accepted if they take responsibility for the needs and expectations of their potential partner. They need to prove to you that you are lovable and acceptable by putting you before themselves and giving your needs and expectations priority over their own. Eventually, this will create resentment because they will feel that you ignore their needs. At the same time, your neediness and discontent will remain persistent and can feel endless. Your sense of feeling unfulfilled will cause to feel dissatisfied and disappointed in your relationship. Hearing you complaining and discontent has the effect of making your partner feel that he or she can never please you because they are somehow not good enough. Both parties can only resolve the problems between them if they individually release the core reasons for the issues revealed by their behaviours.

Fear of being powerless in the world can be so intense that just living your life can feel like an overwhelming confrontation. When controlled by these feelings, you are likely to try and avoid engaging in anything that looks like as a potential challenge, risk or threat. The belief in your weaknesses and vulnerabilities creates an existence, in which you are the potential victim of misfortune, threats and aggression. Powerlessness and being vulnerable can be experienced more intensely in an intimate relationship, which can become the battleground for the survival of emotional self. Your strategies may be passive or aggressive — either in avoidance of anything that creates stress or fear — or — cause you to resort to aggressive or manipulative behaviour to gain power and control. Either way, your fearful, negative or pessimistic outlook on life or unrealistic positive outlook are a reflection of your fundamental fears. Trying to avoid being seen as weak and powerless ensures your dependence on your strategic behaviours to maintain the outward illusion that you are powerful and in control. Unfortunately, this will also cause you to avoid facing your emotional issues and dealing with the core reasons for your fears. Any failure to maintain emotional control over your life will be likely blamed on others or circumstances and justifies being more aggressive, cautious or mistrusting. You do not realise that by not accepting responsibility for your fear-based beliefs, you create justification for maintaining your sense of powerlessness.

Your fears will always try and sabotage your attempts to find their origin. To protect yourself from what you feel afraid of, you turn your attention to everything and everyone that could be a threat. Your belief that the reasons for your fears are external will keep you focused on your environment, which ensures that you will not look within yourself for the reasons for your state of mind.

Your dependence on your strategic behaviours and your trust in them become the only means of which you can have power and control to be safe from your fears, and get what you want in life. However, it also keeps you in a state powerlessness. The conditional relationship with your parents taught you that if you get it wrong, you will be blamed and suffer the consequences. However, at the same time, the conditions they set also imply what you need to do to qualify for their love, acceptance, trust and so on. If you fail to meet them by not being who they want and expect you to be, you will feel powerless to have control over your relationship with them. As a child, it will feel as if you are forced to choose between being your authentic self and suffer judgement and rejection, or you have to do, be and behave according to their expectations of you. Neither choice is beneficial for you as the first creates the risk of rejection and the second demands that you give up who you feel you are and become someone who is not authentic. Your innate need for unconditional love, acceptance and trust represents your emotional survival but poses a challenge to your parent's fears and insecurities. The behaviour and attitude the express represent the conditions they place on their relationship with you, which they have learned to accept as real from their parents. Just like they did in their childhood, you are likely to give in to the conditions they now place on the way they expect you to be, behave and respond. It will feel to you as if there no choice because you need to have some form of love and acceptance, even if it is conditional. But, not every child will necessarily submit to being forced into accepting responsibility for its parent's fears and then engage in behaviours that it feels do not represent who it is. Some will become the children that we perceive as problematic and contrary because they refuse to submit to the parent's fear-based ideas, values and standards.

The fear of being seen to be wrong or imperfect, a failure or inadequate, responsible or guilty and so on, by others can make acknowledgement and take ownership of your issues feel like an admittance of guilt, inferiority or not being good enough, if not ashamed. You feel that accepting that you have fears, issues, insecurities or shortcomings and so on is a contradiction of what you are trying to prove to others through your behaviours. You want to appear strong, powerful and in control, as someone who has total self-confidence and trust. Failing this, you fear that you will again feel like the child who was insecure and self-doubting, because what you experienced in childhood. You have probably adopted the same strategies your parents used on you — by making others wrong and yourself right to give yourself an air of superiority, and thereby hide your insecurities. Potentially you are your own worst critic and beat yourself up for not being who and what you believe you should be. Your desire to be perfect in the eyes of others can be so intense that admitting your flaws becomes a virtual impossibility. Instead, you completely rely on your strategic behaviours to create an image of yourself that you want the world to see. Unsurprisingly it has the result of making you live in fear and stress, that they may ultimately fail you and expose the negative self you believe yourself to be.

At work, the pressure of being seen as perfect may cause you to work yourself into the ground to make sure that you do not fail the expectations of others because that would mean that they would be aware of your weaknesses and insecurities. Your excessive commitment might make you the performance star in the workplace; it will be at a high emotional cost to yourself because you put yourself under a lot of the stress and anxiety. This same approach will fail dismally in relationships where your desire to be seen as perfect causes you to present yourself as you believe your partner would want you to be. In the long term, you cannot maintain this presentation of yourself, which is a product your perception, contrived by the fear of not being good enough. Your contrived idea of who you should be for your partner lacks sincerity, sensitivity and spontaneity and does not represent who your authentic self. The absence of a genuine connection makes it unlikely that your partner will reciprocate positively. Even though you try hard to be the perfect partner, your relationship will probably not be.

No matter whether you took on passive or aggressive strategies to survive your childhood, should they fail, it is likely that you will try and find new and better strategies to regain control over your life situations. You do this automatically because it is what you have learned to do. Alternatives are invisible to you. You do not see that the negative emotional state the circumstances you find yourself are in are a reflection of who you believe yourself to be. You have been to taught to think; 'What do I have to do to ....', as a solution to any emotional problem. This way reasoning is a restriction on your ability to overcome life and relationship issues because it keeps in the process of 'doing' and does not allow you to get to a state of 'being'. As a result, the prospect of letting go of these instruments of power and control — your strategic behaviours — feels like an unacceptable proposition. In your understanding of how life works and because you are unaware of alternatives, you would feel powerless without them.

When we focus our attention on releasing fears by letting go of the beliefs that support them we have the intention to achieve a new state of being. Moving from the concept of 'Doing' to solve your issues in life to embracing an authentic state of 'Being' requires a substantial shift in understanding and perception. Trying to transcend life's problems and challenges through 'Doing' is essentially an attempt to control forces outside of you, to overcome a problem or confrontation. The acquisition of a new state of 'Being' is attained by releasing the fear based beliefs which intend are responsible for manifesting these challenges in your life in the first place. Each time you have to resolve your life problems you need to call on strategic 'Doing' again because your fears remain a part of you.

Once you have released your fears and elevated you conscious "Being', the intent that brings these issues about in your life, no longer exists. The strategy of "Doing' does not bring about wisdom, it only accumulates knowledge, while the attainment pure 'Being' is the essence of wisdom and a pathway to the evolution of your spirit-consciousness.

Unfortunately, the motivation to look at oneself only comes after suffering emotional pain, stress and consistent failure of your strategies. We usually need to run out of 'Doing' options before we are prepared to consider that we are the reason and the source of our life issues.

The prospect of being unconditional in love and acceptance poses enormous emotional challenges because it demands that we live life in the total absence of fear. Unfortunately, our issues no matter how small or large, are all a product of fears caused initially by our separation from unconditional love, acceptance and trust and are compounded by the fear that our strategic behaviours will fail. Even though emotional conditions restrict our expression in life, we are deeply attached to the identity created by our negative beliefs responsible for them. When fear, distrust and suspicion causes us to adopt passive or aggressive behavioural strategies which have been lifelong companions that kept us safe from rejection, judgement and getting into trouble, the prospect of letting them go can make you feel extremely vulnerable. Letting go of the very tools that kept you safe and secure can make you feel powerless in life.

Unconditional love in the form of unconditional acceptance and trust, are so terrifying because we have learned to feel helpless without our fears and strategies. We want a guarantee that the outcome will be according to our expectations before we become unconditional, but that in itself would be a condition. No one can say that it is easy, and that is why we should not expect that becoming unconditional is the same as flipping a switch. It is a process, where each time you release more fear-based beliefs your levels of being unconditional become greater.

The fear of the consequences of being spontaneous makes us contrived in our behaviour and responses. One of the major benefits of releasing your fears is the return of spontaneity lost in childhood. Fear will always make us question our initial impulse to be spontaneous, resulting in behaviour that is false. Doubting our spontaneous impulses can also make us question our instinctive and intuitive actions, creativity and inspirations and therefore dismiss them. Fear will cause us to become calculated and contrived in our self-expression, by making us question our perception, interpretations, judgment and choices. Soon our lack of self-trust and self-belief will turn into fear which will take control over our lives and make our decisions for us. Fear separates us from existing within our own power and makes us hide our spontaneous and unique, authentic self. Ultimately fear will stop us from being at one with unconditional love, and be connected to Everything That Is.

You can see that potentially, there can be quite a few bridges to cross on your journey to real change, but if you take a good look at each of these obstacles, you will realise they all are a part of the illusions you have been living in all along. You will find that they are all interconnected and overcoming one, supports transcendence of the others. The reality is that there is nothing more motivating than fear, pain, stress and suffering to create the emotional motivation necessary for personal change. It is also true that setting out on this journey before your life hits a crisis point can save you from a lot of anguish.

DEPENDENCE ON STRATEGIES

Emotional strategies have a role in life because they give us results in the short term, but their success always depends on how others respond to their particular application. Regardless of the outcome, you achieve with your strategies, your relationship with yourself and with others will stay conditional and rooted in fear. As long as we stay strategic, we will always find reasons to justify our behaviours.

Over time, the process of living life will present us with progressively more intensely confronting events and situations that represent our fears, until eventually, our strategies will let us down. At the time, we may think that we have failed, but the event is a fear-based version of ourselves that we have been trying to avoid by being strategic in our lives. Each adverse experience is a reflection of our emotional issues or a mirror of who we believe we are — our negative sense-of-self. If you are fearful of criticism, you will tend to experience any comment on your performance or contribution to mean that you have failed or are not good enough. If you fear confrontation and you are held responsible for what you did, you may feel attacked and vulnerable.

There is always the potential that we will experience emotional or physical health issues by suppressing or hiding the adverse psychological effect from negative life experiences. In life, there is no escaping the emotional impact of the consequences of the process by which we manifest our reality. This outcome is as accurate in the negative sense when we live in fear, as it is in the positive sense when we come from a state of inner-harmony.

We are often not prepared to explore the nature of our minds for fear of that we will discover all the terrible shortcomings and failings of who we believe ourselves to be. However, if we choose not to confront our issues before we reach these physical or emotional extremes, the negative consequences will be inevitable over time. Without accepting that we are the instigators and creators of our own life experiences, it is doubtful that we can achieve a permanent change in our sense-of-self and fulfil our potential.

STRATEGIC RELATIONSHIPS

Usually, those who are looking for the perfect partner do not realise for what they are asking. Unaware of their issues are bound up with this expectation, they do not appreciate that their idea of the perfect partner incorporates their fears and insecurities. Someone who feels powerless and vulnerable will automatically look for someone to protect and support them. If you are in fear of being trapped in responsibilities or unable to cope with them, you will try and find someone who is over-responsible and has no expectations of you. If you are aggressively controlling in your life, you will want a partner who is passive compliant and will not challenge or confront you.

We unconsciously seek out and attract partners who compensate for our insecurities and whose issues make us desirable to them. Of course, as a part of your conditions, they also have to be good looking, financially well off, have a sense of humour, be intelligent, socially engaging, trustworthy and so on. Those who depend on their relationships to make them happy, feel safe and fulfilled, also a tendency to believe that their appearance is their most valuable asset if they are to find the partner of their dreams. Usually, in denial of their issues, they rely heavily on their appearance, to attract and be attractive to the right partner. How others may judge their appearance can become the focus of obsessive attention because it is the only part of them they feel that they have any direct control over.

Once you are convinced that others are the cause of your relationship difficulties, it is logical to believe that only the 'perfect partner' will make you happy. Reality paints a very different picture because instead of attracting a partner, who will save you from your fears; you will attract someone whose issues are complementary to your own. Your expectation that your partner makes you feel lovable, acceptable and wanted, also includes your subconscious need that they protect you from your fears and insecurities. The consideration that your partner may have needs, expectations and issues of their own does not figure in your idea of the perfect relationship. The belief that your partner's only desire and focus in life should be to make you happy is an unrealistic romantic idea that is unlikely to be sustainable. Your own issues will guarantee that your partner's issues with themselves and with you will surface in the course of time, which will potentially mark the beginning of your discontent.

It is quite common for both partners to have the same underlying issues but play these out using different strategies. One will use passive strategic behaviours while the other lean towards more proactive, aggressive or confronting strategies by comparison. In relative terms, this makes one appear capable and strong and the other vulnerable or weak. Subconsciously, each depends on the other to compensate for their issues and create emotional security. This exchange of apparent power and the dependence each has on the other, can function reasonably well for a period. Sooner or later, however, one or the other will begin to feel that the power and support are not genuine or enough, and question the nature of the relationship.

Couples who are both fearful of confronting aggression, difficulties, obstacles, etc. in life are a good example of this. By sharing their fear of confrontation, guilt, conflict, judgment, powerlessness, rejection and so on, they share a similar fearful perception of the world. As a result, their issues and fears and the avoidance strategies they both employ to deal with them, are likely to complement one another. Everything to do with living life generates fear in them, including openly expressing ideas, beliefs and emotions. Even though they are both passive, one may take a more dominant role by, for example, using logical reasoning to justify why certain avoidance strategies are perfectly sensible to be safe from the world. By knowing what to do and how to do it to avoid confrontation, the more aggressive partner makes the other feel safe. Their fear-based inter-dependence places severe restrictions on the sharing feelings, emotions, choices, decisions, opinions, etc., for fear that one will cause anxiety or stress in the other. Their anticipation of adverse outcomes makes them cautious in the way they relate to each other. They exist in constant fear of causing conflict and that upsetting one another will result in rejection or abandonment. Their insecurities have turned their 'perfect' relationship both into an apparent safe-haven while in reality, it is an emotional jail. Their sense of self will not evolve to its potential in this environment, and they are unlikely ever to know what it would be like to exist in the freedom of expressing their authentic self. No one should aspire to this kind of relationship.

FALSE NEEDS AND EXPECTATIONS

It is not simple to create the life you desire if your issues control you. First of all, you need to remember that — consciously or subconsciously — you always manifest your life experiences. We tend to think that the only time, we deliberately put strategic plans in place to achieve certain goals, that we actively do something with a specific intent. This understanding is misleading. The intentions that are a part of the beliefs that form your sense-of-self can be active every moment of your existence. Your subconscious intent seeks to find fulfilment with much greater vigour in every moment and aspect of life than you are aware. The fear-based intents propagated by your negative beliefs can and will override your consciously planned and created motivations. Positive or negative, your intentions will attract, create and manifest life experiences that fit the of the beliefs that are their origin.

Going after what you want and desire because you think it is essential to your life, may seem normal until you question your motives. Without being conscious of why specific needs such as wealth, possessions and power are so significant in your life, your pursuit may prove to be destructive or even irrational. The needs and feelings that make them so prominent for you might have their origin in fear of missing out, being denied, being insignificant, ignored, worthless, powerless and so on. Even though these fear-based beliefs are nothing but illusions, their emotional influence can control how and where you will spend your energy and effort in life, in short, they have the ability to determine your intent.

Knowing that all of us have emotional fears of some description, it is sensible to question your needs, expectations and desires. Your aspirations could be fear based, and consequently, the way you go about realising them can have undesirable consequences for yourself and others. It is therefore important that you make yourself aware of why your need for something is so intense, and to what extreme are you prepared to go to get it. Understanding the motivations for your needs, desires and what you do, will show you if you are responding to greed or ego or some other distorted perspective. Justifying the purpose your actions and behaviours because you see others doing the same, is misleading because you do not know what their motivations are.

If you are powerless, you will believe you need to have power,

- if you are poor, you will aspire to be wealthy,
- if you are a failure, you want success or to have someone successful in your life,
- if you are lonely, you want to have a partner,
- if you feel vulnerable, you want to be in control and invulnerable or protected, and so on.

By not questioning the motivation for what you want, you risk that your aspirations or desires are distortions based on illusions created by fear. Trying to create the opposite of these negative beliefs is a habitual response to avoid what your fear. Your reaction to what you feel will be — what do I have to do: to be successful, to be strong, to have a partner, and so on. Because it is strategic, our choice of a solution does not change anything, because you remain the same person. Even though you may have manifested wealth and established a position of power in your life, you continue to have to depend on the success of your strategies to hold on to them. Despite giving the appearance that you have transcended the issues of your past, you have only changed what is outside of you but not who you are— your sense-of-self. The same applies to those people whose avoidance strategies have kept them from confrontation and conflict. Whether you like it or not, in spite of the perceived success of your strategies, negative beliefs still control your emotional state of mind. Over your lifetime, the consequences of your fears are likely to reveal themselves in other areas of emotional life in the form of stress, anxiety, depression, pessimism worry and so on. They can also make themselves known in your body through all manner of physical symptoms.

We commonly want to have those things we were denied in childhood and do the things we were not allowed to do. We want to give a voice to that part of us that was suppressed, criticised and judged, or made out to be a disappointment. The problem lies in how we go about reclaiming our freedom, our power and ultimately our authentic self. We live in a world that has us convinced that we need to do the opposite of what we fear to change our life experience and then we can have what we want. It appears that regardless of how we interpret our life issues, just about everyone follows similar patterns of response, which is to discover new strategies to avoid the potential for adverse outcomes.

The sense of who you believe yourself to be would have developed very differently had you grown up in a family where the parents were unconditional. You would not have acquired fear-based sense-of-yourself. Instead, you would feel self-confident and empowered by your authentic and unique self. Free to follow your inspirations, talents and abilities without concern for failure, you would have the opportunity to fulfil every aspect of your potential. You may discover that you have more than one passion in your life and many talents and abilities to which give expression. You can be certain, that in the absence of fear, neediness, powerlessness and so on, your life, relationships and future would be very different.

HOW TO BE AUTHENTIC

The journey to find yourself assumes that you have lost who you are and therefore you must find who and what you truly are to be able to change and evolve. The good news is that you cannot lose your authentic-self. On the other hand, to expect your original nature to reveal itself like a 'Jack-out-of-a-box' is an unrealistic expectation, and unlikely to happen. Add to this, that you have learned to fear, suppress and hide most of what represents the authentic-self, it becomes difficult for you to establish who that is. You have spent most of your life actively suppressing your authentic-self because your parents rejected it for being unacceptable. The fears that determine you sense-of-self are also responsible for your rejection of who you truly are, and your lack of awareness of who you are meant to be. Without the aid of emotional reference points, it is hard, if not impossible, recognise what part of you represents your authentic self, and what does not.

We respond to this by disassociating ourselves from the authentic nature of our being. With the passage of time, our authentic-self will be buried by fear driven beliefs, needs and strategies, before we ever had the chance to realise its true nature, capacity and power for ourselves. Now, we no longer trust it to bring us the unconditional love, acceptance, emotional security or self-fulfilment it initially promised, and to which we felt innately entitled. Instead, we have learned to put our faith in our fears and strategised behaviours with the expectation that they will keep us safe, and get us what we want and need. Unfortunately, there is no greater illusion than to believe that fear will save you from creating a negative reality for yourself and others.

Describing the actual qualities that would make your authentic-self recognisable for you is not possible, other than to confirm that it is in harmony with your spiritual essence and that of All Consciousness. The authentic self is not so much a fixed state of being than it is a representation of a collection of qualities of consciousness, which are unique to you. Everything that makes up your authentic-self exists in a state of greater potential and contains the capacity to evolve into something more than what it is. Its destiny is not predetermined, but it has qualities and abilities, leanings and biases that will cause it to develop in its unique way, under your auspices. The potential intrinsic in our authentic self, together with our innate drive for creativity, self-expression, inventiveness and capacity to formulate intent, makes it the most potent aspect of our psyche. There is also no limit on the way or how far it can evolve because that depends entirely on us. "FEAR" as a concept and an emotional state of mind, is the critical limiting factor in your discovery and development of your authentic-self

Your fear-based beliefs have buried your authentic-self and overlaid it with behaviours that have the intent to make you loved and accepted to others, even though it is all conditional. This focus ensures that your true self is seen to be unacceptable by you and never given a voice. Even though your authentic-self reflects your authentic spiritual identity, your negative beliefs, feelings and strategies are now your resource for survival in the world and therefore dominate your perception. Nevertheless, even though denied presence and self-expression, your authentic-self is still the essential nature of your consciousness and will always remain a part of you ready to be re-discovered. The consequences that are implied by your fears are the very reason you do not allow yourself to be authentic. Your negative beliefs and behaviours are like are like a fortress of negative emotions, which keeps your safe from the consequences of your fears, but simultaneously keeps you its prisoner. Even though your fear-driven convictions portray themselves as your saviours, in reality, they restrict, contain and control the expression of who you authentically are.

TRANSCENDING YOUR ILLUSIONARY SELF

Becoming your authentic self, without dealing with the fears that caused you to distrust and suppress it in the first place, will probably be unsuccessful. Your conscious desire to be your authentic-self contradicts the intent contained in your negative beliefs. Your fear-based intent will warn you that accepting your authentic-self will recreate the fears of your childhood all over again. Guess which of these will win out? Since you have learned to mistrust much of what is your authentic self, you need a different approach to bring your original being back into yourself.

Your dependence on your fears and their strategies to survive in your life makes it highly unlikely that you can instantly switch from your fears to being your authentic self. Overcoming fears, in this way, are extremely difficult to achieve, without an emotional reference point that allows you to recognise which of your beliefs or illusionary and which are not. The two things you can be sure of is that your authentic-self does not come from fear and that the absence of unconditional love and acceptance is fear.

The secret to becoming your authentic self is simple:

Release all fear, and your authentic self will automatically begin to reveal itself.

Once you start the process of releasing your fear-based beliefs, your authentic self will show the nature itself layer by layer, through the way you think, feel, behave, respond and choose. It will change your perception of yourself and others, and what will manifest as your life-experiences in relationships, work and in life in general.

After you let go of certain fears, the next step is to accept and trust any newly discovered aspect of yourself. However, you need to be mindful at all times, that your newly uncovered qualities are not unresolved fears. You may not always immediately recognise those beliefs represent your essence. If fear is a dimension of any new aspect you discover about yourself, you can be sure that it is not your authentic self. Only then can you trust these emerging aspects of yourself, and give them full expression. In time, you will go through this process without feeling uncertainty, because of your growing awareness of what is fear-based and what is not.

Most people believe that their authentic-self has to be the opposite of their issues which distorts purity of the intent, inherent in the authentic nature of your being. Feeling powerless and helpless in life will make you believe that your authentic self will be powerful, dominant and in control. Feeling insignificant will cause you to think that your authentic-self has to be very special and unique in the eyes of others. The point is, that if you are convinced that once become your authentic self, your life will be total opposite to your current experience of your fear-based self, you will likely be disappointed. It is true that once you release your fears, the related issues will dissolve, but it does not mean that this will manifest as the extreme opposite of who you believe yourself to be because of the fears you hold. In other words, you will not automatically rise to become a recognised dominant figure from being a passive compliant victim, because you release beliefs related to your fear of being insignificant, powerless or a failure. To believe that once have released your fear of commitment, intimacy, and giving and receiving love, you will immediately fall in the most amazing and perfect relationship, is unrealistic. Life and particularly relationships are complicated. In the absence of your fears with the opposite gender, and with love, acceptance and trust in relationships, you will have the potential for this to be manifested by you. You will attract and be attracted to the person that matches your new sense of being.

Understand that now, the changes you have made are within you. Transforming your sense-of-self has changed the potential of what you will choose to manifest in your life. The biggest transformation of your sense-of-self is the absence of fears and neediness of all kinds, and how this alters your idea of what you want out of life and relationships. The other significant change comes from realising that you have choices you could not even imagine you could have, or make, because of the absence of your fears. Instead of fear deciding for you, now you do.

You will only feel and experience giving and receiving unconditional love, acceptance and trust, in the absence of your negative beliefs. There appears to be no shortcut to this because for as long as fear dominates the mind, it will always prioritise your fears for the sake emotional survival.

Chapter 20

OUR CONDITIONAL MIND

Undoing the negative impact of your childhood will take us through all manner of mental and emotional stages. Even though we try and avoid negative and painful emotions, our feelings are essential to our understanding of who and what we are. Our emotional experience of life is critical to the growth and survival of our consciousness. We would not be aware that there is very wrong within us until we experience intense and sometimes enduring negative emotions. Without feeling the many different forms of pain or happiness and joy, we have no way of knowing whether we are manifesting our life experiences from our essence, or from our fears. In the absence of negative feelings, there would also be no motivation to try and resolve the inner conflict that creates them. We would not care about the consequences our fears manifest for us and others. Negative emotions are an indicator that what we experience is a result of actions and choices which are in disharmony with our essence.

Commonly our immediate response to negative feelings is to find the source for what we feel outside of us rather than within. It usually does not occur to us that who we believe we are is the problem and therefore the key to a solution, limiting how we deal with emotional issues.

By working on the symptoms of a problem instead of ourselves, we remain deluded that we are resolving our life problems. It is precisely in this way that our parents tried to change us to deal with their fears and insecurities. We, just like them, have learned to believe that we can solve our issues by changing others and the world. However, you will ensure that your negative beliefs will not be passed on to future generations by transforming your sense-of-self.

Fear of being separated from unconditional love will always trigger our emotional survival mechanism. By raising the acuteness of our awareness, we pay greater attention to anything emotionally threatening. It is an innate defence and survival strategy for our consciousness that serves us well. The same is true on a physical level for the body. The trouble starts when we lose the capacity to differentiate between a real threat and one that we create in our mind in response to a fear-based belief, that we believe to be real. Once we cannot differentiate an actual threat from a self-created illusion, we have lost touch with what is real and what is not. In that case, fear can dominate our perception, behaviour, emotions, our view of reality and what we experience. Without knowing what is real or false, our illusions will be in control and potentially condemn us to a life of fear and insecurity.

A distorted perception makes our fears feel real, and this will usually override any sensible reasoning or responses. If we were able to access the causes for our feelings, we would have a more objective and responsible perspective. Giving in to your emotions without any consideration why you feel them in the first place, will ensure that you stay in old patterns and learn very little. It is important to understand the source of your feelings and try and recognise what contribution you made to a negative event.

Obviously, it is unlikely that you will accept responsibility if you start out with the belief that you could not be involved in your life events. But, it makes more sense to assume that you must be in some way responsible if you cannot resolve your negative feelings and experiences by blaming others for rejection, criticism, disappointment, aggression, feeling powerless and vulnerable. If not anything else, you are the constant figure present in every negative event or circumstance in your life. It makes sense to accept that you must be involved, even if you are not clear on how and why that is so, rather than to think that you had nothing to do with it. Painting yourself the victim of others or circumstances will do nothing to advance your personal growth. Blaming others makes you the victim, and therefore causes you to take a position of powerlessness. However, this will not address your issues, and you are likely to perpetuate them in the future.

You must not be judgmental or critical of yourself or others on your journey of self-discovery. There is nothing to gain from self-blame, guilt or blaming others because they do not reflect an act of self-responsibility. Blaming yourself does nothing but demean your view of who you are which is opposite to what you want to achieve. Indulging in this approach to finding a reason for your life circumstance, will only distort your perception even further, and make it harder to understand what it takes to change your life.

When seeking to determine the nature of your negative beliefs, you may wonder how you can be sure that the conclusions you come to are, as unbiased and objective as possible. The notion that one can be truly objective when making personal judgments is misleading. Even if you are without fear, your perception will always be affected by the unique nature of your mind. Resolution for your issues does not, in fact, rely on your capacity to be objective as much as it does on your acceptance that your present understanding of what the causes for your issues are, has been learned in childhood.

The reality is that your issues are a product of fear and therefore illusionary because they contradict the unconditional nature of your spirit. Beliefs containing fear do not represent the qualities inherent of your authentic-self. If you fear to be a failure, it is because you believe you are good enough to be acceptable to others, including yourself. Should you feel unlovable to others, it is because you believe you are not good enough to qualify for love. If you feel powerless in life, it is because you fear that you do not have the power, capacity and resources to cope with the challenges that life presents you. Your childhood interpretation of the negative emotional events created by the dynamic between you and your mother and father have formed these beliefs, but that does not mean they are real. However, by comparing childhood relationships and experiences with your current issues, the negative beliefs at the origin for your issues will become evident.

The standards and values you can apply to test whether your findings represent positive or negative belief systems are as follows:

- Any behaviour, response, action, choice or feeling that has FEAR at its core is a product of negative belief systems that form your sense-of-self.

As soon as you recognise that fear is involved in your feelings and behaviour, you indicate that you are dealing with a negative belief that you believe to be real but is not. Fear is always a negative influence no matter what justification or reason you give to the contrary.

- Any behaviour or response, action or choice or feeling motivated by Guilt, Shame or Self-Blame is a product of negative beliefs — Fear.

Unless you are guilty of knowingly and with premeditation causing pain and suffering, your feelings of guilt have no real basis in reality. Guilt, shame and self-blame are products of feeling over-responsible for the issues, emotional pain, embarrassment and suffering of others. You are most likely to experience guilt with people who perceive themselves to be victims and powerless. Their behaviour can be aggressive in making other responsible for their issues and to prove that they are the victims. Or, they can also present themselves as passive, powerless victims. The core reasons for your response to them will be in your childhood with a similarly affected parent.

- The only truth that counts in your search for emotional truth is your perception and experience of an event or relationships.

In searching for the truth about your childhood, your version of what happened to you is the product of your interpretation of events and represents the emotional experiences that shaped your sense-of-self. Only the conclusions you drew from the dynamic between you and your parents can explain the nature and reasons for your behaviour and feelings, choices and perception. Your version of events caused you to form beliefs about yourself that are now limiting your expression in life. The negative beliefs that make up your sense of self will always hold the key to the reasons for your behaviour and feelings. Asking others for their perspective of your upbringing can provide you with helpful points of view, but they do not necessarily have to correspond to your own experience and understanding. Sometimes it can verify what you already believe to be true and at other times someone else's opinions will be at odds with your own. Ultimately, you can only accept information which corresponds with your perception and which you, therefore, believe to be true. Even if it were distorted and not true to fact, it is still your version of the truth and therefore has formed the basis for the negative beliefs you took on board. The focus has to be on what you believe to be true according to your experiences, rather than discovering 'the truth' according to someone else. Typically, everyone will have their version of what that is. If you come to the right conclusions, they should reveal the negative beliefs you hold and are responsible for driving your feelings, actions and behaviours.

- Parents who fear that they parent their children the way their parents did with them, may consciously express the intent to be loving and accepting, but do not realise, that their behaviour and attitude sends a contradictory message to their children. The issues they inherited, stop them from their expression of love and acceptance being genuine. Saying that you love someone is not the same as a true show of love and affection. They can find it hard to be unconditional in accepting their children and showing love, affection. Their fear of showing emotions and feelings of love, affection, emotional sensitivity and empathy, contradicts their conscious effort to connect emotionally with them. Their fears sabotage their intent to give love and be emotionally close and intimate. Often, they can be physically caring and supportive and even say they love you, while their actual behaviour and attitude around the expression of emotions and feelings contradict this. Sensing the awkwardness of your parent's responses, you felt that the expression of your expectation for love and affection were somehow inappropriate and wrong. When this is the case, you were left in confusion how to express love, affection, closeness and intimacy as well as your fears, issues and insecurities. The reality is that when it comes to love, it is hard to give to others what you have never received unconditionally.

Most parents will say that they accept and love you unconditionally because that is their intent. You need to recognise that if they set conditions due to their fears and insecurities, you would have experienced their love as conditional. The result is that a child will believe that it is unlovable and unacceptable until it has met these conditions, regardless of what the conscious intent of the parent might have been. Fear of revealing feelings and emotions to others denies a child the actual physical and emotional sensation of being loved, accepted, feeling special and wanted. The emotional void this creates demands to be filled. The consequence will be that once the child becomes an adult, it is likely to behave in the same manner and experience the same emotional difficulties as its parents did. The absence of love and acceptance from the parents denies a child the experience of being unconditionally loved and accepted. Being denied what it feels innately entitled to has the effect of making it feel and believe that it is unlovable and unacceptable and so on. Feeling unlovable it cannot love and accept itself and consequently, to act with unconditional love and acceptance towards others. Instead, its need to be loved creates an empty well that yearns to be filled up by the love from others, which then causes it to be selfish and needy. The intent to love and accept cannot replace the actual act of being unconditionally loved and accepted. The same can apply to any emotional state for which children require confirmation, such as: being supported, being praised, being trusted and being able to trust, expressing truth, being listened to and so on.

- You must be truthful with yourself about your issues. By being in denial about your contribution to any negative events in your life, you deny yourself the opportunity to change your life and your future. Even if your part in it is not entirely clear to you, you need to approach your issue with the understanding that you must be involved. Only then will you begin to look in places that will show you why that is so.

- Do not put any conditions or limits on your search for inner-truth, or the process of your change. Limiting ideas will ultimately become restrictions that will hold you back from finding your truth, and being who you were always meant to be. Bite the bullet if you have to face issues that you find extremely confrontational and follow through. In the final analysis, the negative emotions you feel are an expression of beliefs which are nothing but illusions, and so, in reality, there is nothing to fear. The emotional intensity behind your avoidance of dealing with issues is usually proportional to the fear of the negative consequences you believe they may create in your life. Release your fears, and the outcome will be more than you can imagine.

- Do not set expectations or standards and conditions, as to how the results of change should appear in your life, or in the experience of yourself. Starting out with pre-conceived ideas of what your changes should look like or how they should appear in your life may cause you to miss recognising the positive effects on your life. Consequently, you will not appreciate the value and significance of what you have achieved. Without knowing who and what your authentic self is all about, you will discover new aspects of yourself that have been foreign to you since childhood. Allow yourself to be amazed by experiencing this 'new' self.

DECIPHERING YOUR ILLUSIONS

The level of control that negative beliefs have over you depends on your fear of the consequences, should you be unable to meet their conditions. Feelings, perceptions and behaviours that come out of fear are your guides to the source that created them. On face value, it always seems that the person or situation you are afraid of is also the cause for your fear, but that is not true. Even this aspect of your perception is a product of beliefs. By blaming something or someone, you may think that you have found the reason for your issue when this experience is really an illusion of your creation.

Fears of all kinds are driven by a variety of negative beliefs in unique contexts and with different consequences. The first step in your search for your emotional truth is to take a deep look at the reasons for your emotions and behaviour. The nature of an event and the emotions of those who are involved are essential pieces of information that can lead you to understand the nature of the beliefs that brought the situation into being. Connecting current events and outcomes with historical ones in childhood can help you to recognise the original experiences responsible for the negative beliefs you still hold.

If for example, you have a strong reaction to criticism then you can expect to find the reason for your behaviour in your earliest experience of this with one or both parents. If you suffer from fear of rejection and abandonment, then you may assume that your relationship with your mother and father was extremely conditional. The relationship between them also deserves investigation, because it will expose you to their issues and insecurities. You will find that differences in your perception and that of others, make reality and the truth not always as clear cut as you would like it to be. Just work with what you find, apply the rule that it must be false if fear is involved and trust your intuition.

The belief that an emotional issue has to be the result of a traumatic or critical event in childhood or later in life can be erroneous and misleading. You start manifesting your life experiences from a very young age — around 10-12 years, and this becomes more telling as we become teenagers— 12-21 years, and more conclusively so in adulthood. It follows that once our foundational belief systems are acquired — from 0 to 8-10 years old — at which time we gradually and subconsciously incorporate them as a part of our sense-of-self. However, they do not stay unnoticed, as they will reveal themselves through our choices and decisions, actions and reactions, and so on. Our beliefs lead us to attract and be attracted to certain personalities and situations throughout life, and these encounters create our negative or positive life experiences. Even though these outcomes are a manifestation of the intent held by our beliefs, that does not mean that a traumatic experience later in life is the origin for emotional issues. If you feel disempowered and without control over your emotional or physical security, you are likely to suffer from the belief that you are powerless and vulnerable in life and lack trust in yourself. This experience can make you passive, anxious and submissive or an aggressive, angry and controlling individual. Your beliefs and associated feelings and behaviour will be a strong influence on the way you will go through life. When you mature, any situation or circumstance that threatens you emotional or physical security will be an intense experience for you but not necessarily for someone who does not harbour these fears. As such, you may think that the situation is responsible for your issues while the origin lies in your childhood.

The search for the right answers lies in discovering a truth that can in many ways only be unique to you. Your truth distinguishes itself from others in that it is entirely based on your perception and experience as it was at the time. The nature of the personality of the person involved, being a family member or sibling, is not the point of your search for the causes of your issues. You also do not have to establish the absolute or shared truth of a particular event that affected you, even if such a truth even exists. Each family member is likely to interpret a situation or event differently, while the effect it had on your mind is the only thing that matters. If for example, your parents favoured your brother or sister over you, their experience of your mother or father or both would be very different from yours. Not receiving the same level of attention would make you feel ignored and forgotten and cause you to believe that you are unlovable, unwanted or do not matter. Your sibling would think they were special to your mother and father. Even if later in life, your parents were to assure you that they loved you just the same, your belief that you are not lovable will continue to influence your perception of yourself and how others see you. Your issues with love and affection prove that the original reasons for your beliefs are still active within you, regardless of time and maturity.

The initial perceptions you took on as a child remain the foundation of the belief systems that now make up your sense-of-self. Once you can accept that the conclusions you draw based on your perception are accurate to the best of your knowledge, you are ready to put it into a form that is representative of a self-belief. In the final analysis, your conclusions are not open to judgment by others. They may think, for example, that your parent is good and kind because they did so much for every person in their circle of friends and acquaintances. You, however, may have experienced them as being selfish and uninterested, because they felt it was more important to be involved with others, they ignored and neglected you. To you, the only version of yourself that is of value in your process of change is the one you perceived as a child. There are many reasons why each sibling in a family is likely to remember their relationship with their parents very differently. The original nature of your unique being and order of birth, gender and favouritism, are strong influences who you have come to believe yourself to be. Add to this the individual emotional issues your mother and father brought into their relationship and the family unit, and you can see how each contributes to make childhood different for each sibling. The perception of outsiders to a family only reflects what is real for them, but you cannot allow their view to invalidate your interpretation and understanding of your childhood.

OWNING YOUR FEARS

Taking ownership of your issues can be challenging even if you intend to be serious about change. Not many would readily accept the idea that we are the origin of all of our life issues. Self-change can only start once we take the view that we are the creators of all of our life experiences without exception. Assuming responsibility for your problems is a big turnaround in perspective after you spend most of your life blaming others and the world. This view can be particularly confronting if your strategies are predominantly dominating and controlling. You are likely to believe that you will be powerless and defenceless without your aggressive approach. Being in a position that is dominant and controlling can create the assumption that you must be superior to others, which then can make it difficult to admit and accept that you have flaws. You would have to acknowledge that you are acting out of fear rather than any other justification.

The problem that passive, strategic individuals have with taking responsibility for their issues, is different. They are often deeply affected by guilt and therefore perceive some positive personal value in accepting responsibility and blame for the negative emotions of other. Overwhelming guilt controls them, even though in actuality they cannot be responsible for what others feel. Their sense of over-responsibility causes them to try to avoid situations and contact with people where guilt may become an issue for them. They edit all of their communication with others to avoid upsetting anyone or attracting criticism or blame. The process by which life manifests creates the exact the opposite experience for them. Their sense of guilt sub-consciously advertises their apparent willingness to accept responsibility for the issues of others. Their attitude causes them to attract, and be attracted to individuals who fear taking responsibility for the problems and dramas they create in their life. They strategically avoid any emotional responsibility for their fears, anxiety and stress and being held accountable. This kind of person intuitively senses that their newly found friend will never confront them because of their fear of being guilty of causing negative emotions in others. The fear of being blamed assures their new partner that they will never be held responsible for anything that causes conflict or argument. Each is just a mirror for the other concerning their issues with guilt and blame.

On the positive side, the assumption of guilt by an over-responsible person can make it easier for them to seek help. They act and behave as if victims of their pain and suffering and thereby attract the support from others. Understanding the mental processes and beliefs that underlie their problems is a significant step towards emotional resolution. Letting go of negative beliefs will liberate them from their burden of guilt and allows them live life without being controlled by the fear-based emotions of others.

UNDERSTANDING LIFE'S PURPOSE

If you cannot see how and why you are involved in every aspect of your life experiences, it is hard to accept that you are the creator of them. The causative triggers for any event in your life are very individual and commonly not easily fathomable by others. You cannot depend on others to confirm for you what is real or not in your life when your perception and awareness are central to the way you experience life. It can be difficult to accept that we do not live in an accidental universe and that nothing happens by chance. You cannot feel truly connected to others and the reality in which you exist if you cannot even relate to the nature of your sense-of-self. The awareness of your inner being is also the pathway to deeper connections with the essence and complexity of all consciousness which forms experience that we know as physical and emotional reality. When you begin to realise that all of the consciousness is connected and relates to one another, it is also simpler to accept that reality, and the events we experience cannot happen by chance. We can only experience the sense of who we are and being conscious and alive through our feelings, thoughts, action, responses and reactions with who and what we encounter in the material world. The sensations that this dynamic creates in us is what makes us feel that we exist and are alive. At the core, the manifestation of our life experiences is both an individual and a collective expression of who we believe we are and fundamentally the result of interconnected consciousness. We do not act in isolation of others, but it may feel as if that is the case. The intent expressed by one individual has an impact on all others even if you are not conscious of it. Our general lack of self-awareness makes this significant element of consciousness hard to recognise and appreciate.

In childhood, we have been indoctrinated to believe that in most instances, our emotional experiences are a product of outside forces. We manifest the dynamic between ourselves and others without any conscious thought or intent and react and respond in ways that feel normal and natural to us. The truth is that the process of creating the reality we experience through our sense-of-self is an inseparable and incessant part of all consciousness. The potential to be in or out of harmony with itself depends on the positive or negative nature of the beliefs that form your sense-of-self. Regardless of what beliefs control your mind, you are always an interactive influence within the overall state of universal consciousness. When you are an intrinsic part of Everything That Exists, you cannot opt out of the responsibility for your life when your existence is dependent on being a part of all that is Consciousness.

The intent within human consciousness will attract and be attracted to others whose consciousness resonates in harmony with it, regardless of whether the dynamic is negative or positive. The interaction between them will bring about events, which will reveal the true nature of their specific intents — positive or negative, unconditional love and acceptance or fear.

The deeply personal nature of any creative act by our consciousness makes it difficult for an outsider to fathom the intents and motivations for the manifestation of a particular event because the core values of the behaviour that supports it can either be sincere or strategic. It is then difficult to see what the true and what is not and what the real issues are when they are acted out. Strategic behaviour serves as a disguise if fear is the motivating force behind its intent. Also, an observer is likely to have issues of their own of which they are unaware, and these will act as filters and distort their perception of the persons involved. All these elements make it difficult, if not impossible, for many to understand the deeper motivations and intent for someone's behaviour, and the life situations they create.

Without any real insight into the fundamental emotional forces at play, we often try to explain the disasters experienced by others by looking for guilty parties associated with such events. We may label the situations as accidents or misfortunes or judge who are the aggressors and victims. If this is your approach to problems in your life, it is predictable that your first impulse will be to reject the idea that you are the creator of your own life, and are therefore responsible.

The most common approach used to try and prove that we cannot be the creators of our own negative reality experiences, is to list various disasters in which many suffered, or lives lost their lives. The deeper reasons for involvement in a horrific accident are often utterly incomprehensible to an observer. From their perspective pain, suffering and death occur indiscriminately and without apparent reason and purpose. The victims of a disaster can be of any age or gender — from babies to the old and infirm. At another level of consciousness, those who are involved in a disastrous event may well understand and be aware the reasons for their participation. Excluded from knowing the deeper nature of the mind and consciousness of those who are involved, it is hard for observers and survivors to comprehend the reasons for this. Much of this requires our understanding of the nature of consciousness, death and life, and our responsibility for what the expression of our consciousness creates. The actual reasons for being a victim of a disastrous event are difficult to argue because the chairs for those who might be able to provide the relevant information are empty. It helps our capacity to deal with life and death if we can accept that all consciousness is interconnected, and transcends physical and material life. If we can come to see that everything that is in existence is the product of intent of a greater consciousness and that we are actively participating creators, we may realise that every experience and event is of our individual and collective making.

It may serve you to appreciate that your existence goes beyond the physical lifespan of your body and your spirit-mind is on a path of infinite evolution.

FROM ISSUES TO NEGATIVE BELIEFS

We need to delve a bit deeper into our state of mind and family dynamics to understand why our negative perceptions take a particular form. Understanding how and in which way the mind is influenced by them so that we can develop clarity about their nature and intent. The clues to appreciate the qualities of our negative belief systems are within us as thoughts, feelings, perceptions and reactions and responses. There is more evidence to be found outside of us, in events and experiences, people and situations we are attracted to and attract. Negative experiences are the most obvious place to begin because they are a clear sign that we are manifesting from a place of fear.

The personality and behaviour of your friends are also a good indicator of your state of mind, because like attracts like in the negative sense, as well as positive. Your friends do not only reflect your interests, but they will also mirror or complement your issues, fears and insecurities. Throughout this material, there have been examples how certain negative traits will attract others who match them, and the friends you make are no exception to this. Objectively re-appraising your friendships can be useful in discovering more about the nature of who you are. Doing this may be unappealing to you, but it is a necessary part of your learning process and self-education.

The good news is that you cannot fail because every new understanding and realisation is a triumph for your authentic self and the essence of your spirit. You will find that your path to self-realization becomes easier as your clarity and insight progressively grow thereby taking you to a new level of awareness. Once you understand the nature of the different elements that make up your negative beliefs, you will also appreciate why they are such a powerful psychological force in your mind.

THE ELEMENTS OF NEGATIVE BELIEFS

The structure of a negative belief system is complex because it contains the elements of overall intent, cause, context and consequence. Each part of a system of beliefs plays a decisive role in determining how, where and with whom a belief system will become activated, and what kind of consequences this will have for us. Some of the previous examples show what to look for when exploring your psychological family history. Going beyond the obvious is essential if you are to discover the causes, and in what context and consequence our fear-based beliefs operate. Once you recognise how each element works with all others, you will be able to understand the basis for their influence and potency in your life.

Appreciating the contribution that each aspect makes to the structure of your negative belief systems is important when you want to release them. You cannot let go of a negative belief you neither own nor understand and appreciate in detail. Trying to release belief systems by using their most contracted and basic form such as — I do not love myself / I am unacceptable / I do not matter / I have no value — does not work. While the general intent of a belief system is sometimes easy to recognise, this form is not accurate and detailed enough to address the unique reasons why it has such a hold over your emotions, perception and behaviour. In other words, it is too general in concept to have any real meaning or context if you were to try and release it.

Our minds are already extremely sophisticated in our earliest state of consciousness and register a vast amount of detail in an abstract form. These early emotional and physical impressions relate to the essence of our spirit-consciousness and instincts for emotional and physical survival. As we mature, they will become an integral part of the function of our minds. From the outset, our perception, responses and reactions are influenced by how we experience them emotionally. Our yet un-evolved mind is a receptacle for every bit of emotional and physical information it is exposed to but lacks meaningful reference points necessary to be discriminating and make sense out of it. A child's primary frame of reference is its innate expectation and entitlement to be unconditionally loved, wanted, accepted, to be able to trust and its survival instincts. Unfortunately, at this stage of its life, this innate intention of its consciousness has as yet not been validated by its parents through their behaviour and attitude. These elements need to be expressed unconditionally by its parents so that they become the child's perception of who it believes itself to be. The emotional and mental dynamic parents create with their children is the mirror by which their child will know who it is. This experience is essential to its consciousness and when internalised and accepted becomes a positive part of its sense-of-itself.

Even though being raised with unconditional love and acceptance is vital to a child's evolving spirit and mind, it does not provide it with an instant understanding of the nature of the reality in which it just became conscious. Nor does it give a child the insight and wisdom to deal with the life experiences to which it will be exposed. In a deeper sense, these innate reference points serve a much greater and higher purpose in its consciousness. Its enduring influence maintains the intention to aspire to ever higher levels of evolution of our consciousness. The presence of unconditional love, acceptance, trust and being wanted will always remain the essence of its conscious being and an eternal emotional reference point for its mind. Regardless of how the child will turn out in life, and no matter to what level its consciousness has evolved, this reference point — the essence of its spirit — will remain central to the nature of its sense of being.

Unconditional love, acceptance, to trust and being trusted, being wanted and so on, will always be the core reference point for your understanding of what part of your sense-of-self is supportive of harmonious existence and which is not.

CAUSE, CONTEXT AND CONSEQUENCE IN NEGATIVE BELIEF SYSTEMS

Emotional issues are a product of beliefs held as a sense of yourself that contains conditions founded in fear. These views include the threat that there will be adverse consequences if you do not meet these conditions. You then use your strategic behaviours to try and avoid this from happening. Appreciating the value of intent, cause, context, and consequence in belief systems is crucial for your understanding of who you believe yourself to be.

Take for example that you were to hold the belief that you are unacceptable.

THE PRIMARY INTENT within the belief is to convince you that you are unacceptable because of who you are. You, therefore, expect that others will see you the way you see yourself and that you are therefore unacceptable to others. If you believe you are unlovable, unwanted, undesirable, ugly, unattractive, dumb, worthless, insignificant, do not matter, etc. the same applies. What you believe about yourself you will expect that others think about you. This conviction is the very reason why you use strategic behaviours because you either want them to see you differently, you want to avoid their judgement or to protect yourself.

THE CAUSE is a product of a particular set of emotional circumstances in which an issue was initially experienced, realised and accepted. The cause can be an aggressive, dismissive, irritated, annoyed, critical, your actions or responses, the expression of your needs or expectations, wanting love and affection, needing validation and attention, etc. When parents repeatedly respond to you in a way which contradicts unconditional love, acceptance and feeling wanted and trusted in childhood, you will begin to see your expression of yourself as the cause of conflict or discord. Some examples of this are judgment, rejection, being treated as if you are a burden, being ignored, being invalidated and blamed, being criticised and judged, having your needs and expectations dismissed and so on. It comes down to not being unconditionally loved, accepted, trusted, wanted and celebrated for who you truly are — your authentic self. The cause will always relate back to the issues your parents have and the strategic behaviours they employ to deal with them.

THE CONTEXT is a product of the unique circumstances and personality types involved in the emotional events that were experienced by you at the inception and formation of your negative belief systems. Even though our consciousness defines and records these elements, the lack of a dependable frame of reference prevents a clear realisation of who is responsible for what and why. The only reference we have is the absence of unconditional love and acceptance. When trying to make sense out of its emotional experiences, the naivety of a child's mind limits its ability to make value judgments. Restricted by its unevolved awareness, lack of life experience and a frame of reference for its emotions it can only record and internalise its experiences in an in a cohesive form. What it will ultimately accept and believe to be real and genuine is determined by its innate need for survival of its emotional being and physical self.

THE CONTEXT within a negative belief represents the kind of situation, and the type of personalities and their emotional intent and expression, involved at the inception of your negative belief systems. These contextual elements will still be active later in life, and manifest similar if not the same emotional issues. They are the circumstances and conditions which act as triggers which are unique to you and that have become an intrinsic part of your negative belief systems. When particular circumstances reflecting the context by which you came to internalise your negative beliefs are activated, they will define your perception, feelings and behaviour within the framework of your fear-based beliefs.

For example: If the father or mother who raised you were controlling and domineering, your involvement with people with similar emotional characteristics are likely to trigger the same emotional response you had with them. Men that grew up with emotionally needy, dependent and insecure mothers and have learned to be protective and responsible for her fears and expectations, will attract women with similar issues and exhibit similar behaviours. Similarly, women who were raised by controlling and dominating fathers will find themselves attracted to controlling men. Or, to avoid being controlled, they will show a preference for passive personalities.

Should both your parents come from a family background that denied them and made them feel guilty for expressing their needs and expectations, they are likely to be selfish and self-centred or behave as if they have no needs and expectations. A selfish parent and the parent who has an issue expressing their needs will create guilt in you for having needs and expectations because both feel burdened by them. Both are likely to feel and believe that they are denied and cannot have what they want while feeling simultaneously powerless and incapable of getting what they desire. The selfish parent will aggressively dismiss your needs while the passive parent will act as if the victim of them. Their weaknesses and insecurities make them behave in a needy, selfish or sacrificial manner thereby causing guilt in their children for having needs and expectations. Their response to this can make them aggressively needy and be demanding for fear of missing out or act like victims for being denied. As a consequence, a child may feel compelled to deny its needs and expectations and instead put others before itself as a way to avoid feelings of guilt. This upbringing can cause you to believe that others are more entitled than you or envious of those who have more than you. Without realising you may either strategically always put yourself first in order not to miss out. If you had parents who demanded priority as a condition of their acceptance of you, then you may put yourself last because of your lack of entitlement and guilt feelings. You are likely to become a pleaser and put others ahead of your needs and expectation at the detriment of yourself. In the end, you could turn out to be just as needy and selfish, or feel as disentitled as your parents.

THE CONSEQUENCE is that once you believe that you are unlovable, unacceptable, unwanted undesirable, insignificant, etc. you will be criticised, judged, rejected and abandoned and so forth. This conviction causes you to expect that if you do not comply with the conditions set by your parents, you will be rejected, abandoned and alone and unable to survive. Believing you are unacceptable, unwanted, unlovable and so on, can have other consequences such as being ignored, dismissed and forgotten, not feeling entitled, deserving, significant or welcomed and wanted. It all depends on the context you acquired fear-based beliefs. Your negative self-perception can make you feel powerless and helpless or a failure and disappointment. It all depends on who raised you and how.

Understanding the cause is extremely significant because it can lead you to understand how negative beliefs became a part of your sense-of-self. Your insight into the causes will also reveal why you create unwanted outcomes or events and why they affect you the way they do. All causes responsible for establishing negative beliefs share similar emotional elements. Every event or encounter that underwrites the formation of negative beliefs will contain any of the following derivatives of fear: exclusion, abandonment or rejection, criticism or judgment, embarrassment or shame, blame or guilt, powerlessness or helplessness, vulnerability or inferiority. There are much more, but these represent the most common emotional elements of fear based causes, that result in negative belief systems.

When the behaviour and attitude of your parents are adverse to your presence and natural expression of who you are and your innate needs and expectations, you develop the fear-based belief-systems that will later dominate your life. The dismissal of your authentic and spontaneous self is the origin of the experience of these negative emotions, thoughts, perception and behaviour. Their reaction could be in response to your appearance, gender or presence, or just that you are different from what your parents expected or needed you to be because of the expectations created by their mind-set. Even though their issues are responsible for the manner in which they treated you, your need to survive the rejection of who you are will cause you to take responsibility for them. You will unconsciously internalise the experience of their behaviour as conditional beliefs which then become your sense-of-self. Your desire to be loved and accepted will automatically become the cause for developing strategic behaviours that seek to meet these conditions. As a consequence, your negative beliefs and associated actions and responses will then determine your attitude towards yourself, and others. You may justify your negative state of mind by becoming a judge and critic for yourself, turning negative behaviour into a virtue, or taking the role of the justified aggressor or a vulnerable victim — none of this will represent who you truly are and meant to be.

THE ULTIMATE INTENT OF YOUR BELIEFS

Together, intent, cause, context and consequence have the capacity to turn a belief system into an incredibly powerful psychological instrument for the expression of our consciousness. The axe our minds wield in its process of creating its reality is both conscious and subconscious. Although the focus has been on negative beliefs, to show you how they influence and control your life, the power and influence of beliefs also operate in the positive sense.

The power and influence that gives negative beliefs the capacity to manifest undesirable life experiences are also present in positive beliefs. An unconditional belief-system allows us to manifest positive events and relationships.

Cause, context and consequence are elements that contribute to the distinct nature of the intent of any belief system and the environment that will trigger them. Jointly, they define what will enable a belief-system and what it will create if the implied conditions are met, or not met. Without the internal reference point of unconditional love, acceptance and trust, you might well be utterly indifferent to what a belief system creates for you in life. Emotions like fear or love, anger and resentment and so on, would cease to have any meaning and be discernible. Potentially, you would not be able to appreciate what their nature is, because you will not be able to differentiate a negative emotion from a positive one, nor would it matter to you. An event, regardless of the impact or outcome, would be just that: an experience without emotional context. Only threats to your physical survival would elicit a response for survival from you.

Your spiritual foundation rests on unconditional love, acceptance and trust and this provides the context in which fear and powerlessness, distrust and non-acceptance, acquire meaning and make an impact on our lives through the experience of our emotions. On deeper levels of your consciousness, you are always in awareness of this, and the intent this holds creates the emotional differentiation, that allows you to recognise, and experience, any event, encounter or relationship as being a reflection of unconditional love, acceptance and trust, or as being of fear.

Whenever you find yourself back in the emotional context of an issue, you revert to the child you were at the time when these events first occurred. Your naïve acceptance of the truth of what you learned to believe, ensures that you will go back to the same childlike behaviour that you have now framed in adult justifications and strategies. Once our childhood fears take centre stage, our intellectual, logical adult reasoning and perspectives tend to go missing.

In actuality, our belief systems are like interchangeable 'tools for the mind'. A system of beliefs provides our mind with a clear focus that contains intent that we can bring into reality through the energy produced by our consciousness. The nature of beliefs also defines their intention, and that means that negative and fear-based believes will create negative emotional events, and positive, harmonious beliefs will manifest as positive experiences. We have the opportunity to evolve our consciousness either way, but only if we realise that fear-based beliefs are limiting and will hold us back. We need to release them to transcend the effect they have on our lives if we are to evolve our consciousness and expand our awareness. Our individual and collective reality will change in significant ways once we transcend first our negative childhood beliefs and then our limiting social and other structured belief systems. To that aim, we need to focus our efforts first on dealing with our childhood fears, so that we can release them at their origin. Not doing this can result in creating an existence that translates into a life of unhappiness and disappointment, and causes us to pass these same negative beliefs on to our children.

Once we have incorporated negative beliefs as a part of our sense-of-self, we will without exception manifest WHO WE BELIEVE WE ARE — our fear-based self — rather than our authentic being.

The Consequences implied in belief systems articulate the basis for your fears. They represent the outcomes that we fear will become a reality, should our behaviour fail to meet the conditions we are convinced exist. The fear of being judged, criticised or punished for being a failure, inadequate and unacceptable is a part of your sense-of-self because you believe that you do not meet the expectations or conditions set by your parents. At the time, you do not realise that they behaved that way to you because of their fears and insecurities. For example: being made to feel guilty and responsible for upsetting your parents or others because you are blamed for being insensitive, uncaring and aggressive, causes you to blame yourself and take responsibility for how they felt. Or, being told that you are unwanted and unlovable because you are a nuisance and a burden to your parents. As a result, you now feel that you cannot need want and expect anything for of fear of being a burden or too much trouble and consequently judged, rejected or deserted and then alone.

Once you recognise that there is a particular consequence you fear, you can begin to trace how it became a part of you in the first place. Try and remember in what emotional environment and circumstance this became a fear for you. You may have a fear of being alone and being without your friends, not realising that it proves that you have abandonment and rejection issues. So, how and when did these fears become a part of you? You may avoid confrontations with others and tell yourself that this is a good thing while in reality, you are terrified of having to deal with aggression, disagreement and conflict. Ask yourself, what kind of aggressive confrontation, were you exposed to in childhood and by whom? You were not born with these fears, and so you need to question the dynamic of your childhood relationship with your mother and father, to find out the causes for your fears. Uncovering the emotional issues your parents had at the time, and by discussing the childhood experiences your parents had with their parents, can reveal many of the reasons why they behaved the way they did with you. It may show how they acquired the fears and insecurities they played out as your parent. This kind of conversation could be a good process for them as well as for you.

Consequences go hand in hand with the conditions contained in negative belief systems. Here are a few brief examples that show how children can respond to outcomes implied by the conditions set by their parents' fearful sense-of-selves:

A mother who is afraid of failing, making mistakes and getting things wrong will also fear to be unable to meet expectations. She is likely indecisive and not deal well with the pressure of having to be responsible for raising a child. She will have little or no idea how to respond to situations and problems created by her new-born because for her every choice feels critical and essential, and therefore creates a crisis. Confused and overwhelmed by the possibilities of every decision, her inability to set priorities, causes her to physically withdraw and emotionally disconnect to hide from the potential of failing her child, and potentially attract criticism and judgment. Often, she will try and get advice from others to make sense out of her indecisiveness, but then is still unsure of what to do.

The emotional scenario that she lives by is a product of her negative belief systems and is only true in her perception. Her lack of self-trust and her belief that she is vulnerable and powerless gives her a victim mentality. She needs to release the negative beliefs responsible for her sense of helplessness, vulnerability and lack of self-confidence, to have a different perception of herself and manifest a new life. In the absence of her fears, she will rediscover trust and confidence in the innate power, capacities and mental resources with which she was born.

If your mother had displayed this behaviour, then the following may apply to you:

The causes of your issues are a product of the fears your parents inherited from their parents. Once your mother accepted that she did not have the ability to meet the conditions her parents set for her, she took the blame for failing them. In doing so, she believed that she had to be the failure, and unlovable, unacceptable, the disappointment, unwanted, weak, powerless, vulnerable, incompetent, incapable, untrustworthy, dumb and so on. The conditions created by the fears with which your mother's parents raised her predetermined what your childhood experience was going to be. As a consequence of the fears she inherited, she felt that she could not cope with the responsibilities of motherhood and life. She could only give love and acceptance and trust to the point where they did not challenge her fears and insecurities, and that made the only love she could give you to be conditional. As a result, you came to believe and accept that your authentic self and innate needs were a burden and imposition on her because you were convinced that they were the cause of her stress and anxiety. You concluded from her behaviour that you were the cause of her stress and anxiety, worry and unhappiness and therefore that you must be unwanted, unlovable and insignificant, do not matter, etc.

The strategic behaviour you adopted to compensate for your fears fall into two types: You accept that you are accountable for the needs, expectations and feelings of your mother and others and adopt behaviours that please and accommodate to be accepted. On the other hand, your fear of 'being the guilty one' can make you take on an aggressive attitude that ensures that you are not going to be held accountable or responsible for anything that others expect or need from you or suffer, feel or experience. You will be more likely to blame and accuse others than to accept responsibility. Regardless of whether a child's behaviour falls in the first or the second category, later in life the negative beliefs that support these behaviours will become the cause for its life issues.

The context of your beliefs represents the interaction with people with whom their particular issues produce a specific emotional dynamic, that mimics the childhood experiences which created your problems. You could say that they are using the same dysfunctional script your parents used when they raised you. In the context of our example, they are indecisive, emotionally disconnected, fearful, anxious and insecure, have issues with emotional expression, feel powerless, act as victims of life and the world, worry and cannot cope.

The consequences of the belief in this case are:

The fear of being guilty of causing pain, suffering and insecurities in others. Suppression of your authentic self or the fear of imposing your needs and expectation on others.

Attracting anger and resentment from others if you express your needs and expectations.

The fear of being blamed, accused, held accountable and responsible.

The side effects of these belief-systems are the inability to refuse and just say no, fearing confrontation and speaking your truth.

The general fear of being spontaneous and authentic in your presence and behaviour with others, and a fear of upsetting or offending others.

Understand that once a parent or parents through the emotional dynamic with you, convince you that they are the victims of your basic needs and expectations, you cannot help accepting that it is your fault. Their issues convince them that they are powerless and vulnerable in life, and cannot cope with their responsibility for your life, your expectations and emotional demands. Instead of taking responsibility for their issues, they transferred it to you by holding you accountable for what they feel in response to having to be there for you.

As a consequence, if you are a girl, you may become just like your mother, Or, feel fearful of being like her, try and be the opposite of what she is by being entirely independent, self-sufficient and without needs or expectations. Should you be a boy, then the interaction between you and your mother causes you to be oversensitive and excessively caring for fear of being the reason for her pain and suffering. Your guilt driven attitude with your mother will cause you to become attracted to women just like her. Subconsciously you have taken the belief that behaving this way is a condition to being loved and accepted by women. The women you are attracted to and who want to be with you are needy and insecure, and you will want to save and protect them. Or, they will appear to be independent and self-sufficient because you do not want the responsibility of having to protect them from their fears. Your issues will prevent you from seeing that their behaviour hides their fear of being seen to be needy and dependent. The third option is to be in complete avoidance of all intimate relationships, for fear of having to be responsible for the needs and insecurities of women.

The intent and cause, context and consequence are core elements of every belief and are of particular significance in respect to negative beliefs because of how they control our lives.

A basic version of this belief system looks something like this:

Because my mother is always worried, stressed and unhappy, upset, fearful, powerless, helpless and cannot cope

- I have to live in fear, be worried and concerned —
- That if I express my presence, my needs and expectations, wishes and desires, fears and insecurities —
- My mother will get upset, worried, stressed, unhappy, stressed and anxious (and so on). —
- And that will be my fault; I will be to blame, I will be the guilty and responsible —
- And so, because of that, I have to suppress and hide, never show and reveal, never expose or demonstrate —
- My innate need to be unconditionally loved, and wanted, accepted and trusted, supported and cared for, saved and protected, acknowledged and validated, listened to and heard, endorsed and approved of, considered, appreciated and praised —
- I have to hide and suppress my authentic self and my power, my truth, my true nature, my spontaneous self and so on —
- To avoid being guilty, responsible and to blame for my mother's pain, anxiety, worry, concern, stress, unhappiness, sadness, disappointment and so on —
- Because it is always my fault — I am always to blame — I am always the guilty one.

There are many variations possible, but many of the core elements always remain the same.

A father who will not tolerate being contradicted, disagreed with or having his ideas and values challenged, may use aggression and intimidation to be in control. He cements his need for intellectual and emotional superiority by being critical and dissatisfied with everyone around him. At the same time, he never takes responsibility for any of the issues he creates through his actions, behaviour and choices. He believes he is always justified in his decisions, behaviour and responses and blames others and the world when the outcome fails or is not to his liking. He becomes indignant and responds with anger and aggression when held accountable, to create the impression that he is perfect and never wrong. Often, he will see himself as sacrificing his life, freedom and opportunities by having to be the provider, partner and father, as the man in the family.

When he is in a negative state of mind, he is provoked by anything his child does, and he then responds with resentment, anger or critical blame. His child learns to live in fear of finding itself at the brunt of his or her father's anger and abuse. Under pressure of the unpredictable behaviour of its parent, it subconsciously develops an acute awareness and sensitivity of his habits, his moods, reactions and responses to be ready to protect itself. emotional. The child's fears sharpen its senses, and the moment its father is in the vicinity, its awareness goes on high alert. In this kind of environment, a child will commonly avoid being present to avoid attracting the attention of its father as a part of its survival strategy. Under these circumstances, a child cannot experience feeling loved, wanted and accepted by its father. Instead, it will learn to distrust him and try and avoid him and others like him. It learns to live in constant state of fear of the potential consequences should its strategies fail to help it avoid the unpredictable aggression of its father.

The father's issues are generally: fear of being powerless, denied, inferior, failing, being wrong and incompetent. He may feel burdened by the responsibility for his family and restricted because of that. He has to prove he is more intelligent and knows more than others because he feels inferior and inadequate. He fears to have to be responsible for the needs and expectations of his family because his inability to meet them would expose him to be the incompetent failure he fears and believes that he is. Potentially, in his mind, having to satisfy these needs and expectations will deny him fulfilling his desires, wishes and expectations, and restrict his freedom.

For the child, being yelled at and accused by an aggressive grown up, and not knowing why it is the target this kind of behaviour, serves to make it feel truly powerless and helpless, and ultimately guilty and responsible. The consequences are manifold: fear of physical and emotional violence and abuse, fear of being demeaned, criticised, blamed and put down. Everything about the attitude and expression of the father tells it that not only it is to blame, but also that it is a burden, stupid and inadequate and more. It is possible to recognise the father's negative beliefs in the issues he creates in his child through his behaviour and attitude.

The father delivers his emotional abuse in a way that makes the child responsible for his anger, disappointment, criticism and rejection.

The child knows no better than to internalise the blame and criticism as a negative part of its sense-of-self. The feeling that it is responsible leaves it no other choice but to accept it father's words as the truth of who it is and that it is to blame. His actions and responses to the child are a complete contradiction to its expectations of unconditional love and acceptance and cause it to feel rejected, unwanted and dismissed instead. By now, it will hold the belief that it is not good enough and a failure, a disappointment, unlovable, unacceptable, an unwanted responsibility, unwelcome, and so on.

It has the choice of one of two strategies to overcome its fear of the consequences of not being who it should be for its father. It can adopt the behaviour of its father and potentially become aggressive, critical, confronting and a bully. Alternatively, it can become passive and use avoidance strategies, which are likely to be very much like its mother's behaviour. By relying on passive avoidance strategies for its survival in the belief that it is a powerless victim in life, can make it vulnerable to become the target of bullying.

The context is, in this case, are people and in particular men, who feel they need to be forcefully aggressive, dominating and controlling deal with their fears. These are their strategies to get what they want, desire and need. They believe they have to present themselves as knowing everything, never being wrong and never fail. They deeply resent being held accountable, because they are always justified in their behaviour, attitude and decisions. In their world, everyone else has the issues, except them. If assertively confronted and held responsible, they commonly revert to the basis of the negative beliefs they hold about themselves, and then act and behave as if they are the victims of everyone else.

People with these beliefs and aggressive behaviours are attracted to those who have the same core issues, but who display passive, powerless behaviour. Their insecurities allow them to freely play out their dominating and aggressive strategies through convincing themselves that they are right and superior and others are wrong and less. Without consciously realising it, those who are passive, powerless choose environments in which they will expose themselves to these aggressive dominating personalities

The consequences are that in both cases, whether passive or aggressive in behaviour, we live our lives under pressure of all manner of fears and ultimately rejection or abandonment. We will always feel that we cannot survive the withdrawal of love and acceptance. We will try and avoid all this by suppressing our needs and expectations, wishes and desires, by hiding our feelings, fears and insecurities, power and spontaneity — by not being our authentic self.

A basic version of this belief system which includes the elements of intent, cause, context and consequence, looks something like this:

Because my father is always aggressive and angry, abusive and upset, can never be pleased, and is always unhappy and disappointed, critical and judgemental, etc.

- I have to live in fear and be worried and concerned that if I express my spontaneous, authentic self, my power, my truth, my needs and expectations, what I want and feel, etc., —
- My father and others will be angry and resentful, aggressive and upset, abusive and critical of me — violent and judgmental, offended and disappointed in me, —
- And so, because of that, I have to suppress and hide, never show and reveal my personal power, my authentic self, the capacity of my intellect and potential, my talents and abilities and creativity — my emotional strength, my truth, needs and expectations — my feelings, desires, hopes and dreams, etc., —
- Because it is the only way I can avoid being the victim, the cause and the reason for my father's aggressive anger, resentment and abuse, —
- Because it is always my fault, – I am always to blame, – I am always the guilty one.

Once you can see the intent, cause, context and consequence within the beliefs you hold, you are getting ready to let go of your conditional beliefs — your fears.

Something to be aware of: Our attachment we each have to our fears contributes to the collective fear and distrust that humanity lives with every moment of every day, the consequences of which are evident all around us. If we were only prepared to recognise them for what they are for us, individually, the change in us will initiate a transformation on a larger scale and begin to eliminate much of humanity's self-created suffering. Taking individual responsibility for your issues by addressing your fears makes a significant contribution to changing the collective. Real and definitive change in the world has to start with us, you and me, and this makes taking responsibility for what we manifest in our lives an act of much greater importance than it may appear. We cannot escape the inter-connection between of all of our consciousness. As long as the emotion, that we call fear is in control of how we manifest our lives individually, we will not change the destination that our collective fears are taking us. The absence of unconditional love, acceptance and trust, and the subsequent presence of fear are such negative influential forces in our emotional lives that collectively, they control our human destiny.

Chapter 21

UNCOVERING SELF-DECEPTION

You need to become a 'forensic' investigator of your childhood and present life, to discover the negative aspects at the centre of your sense-of-self. Up until now, we have accepted our perception, thoughts, feelings and behaviour as proof of nature of an encounter or event. In other words, we observe others and the event and make judgement of what they do and what has happened and make decisions about its significance and meaning to us. We make assessments about what we look at and see, but we do not question the observer, which is you. If your camera took distorted pictures, the first thing you would do is check the lens. The conviction that the experience you have through your perception is an accurate and real representation of what is happening stops you from questioning yourself. Your beliefs are the lenses through which you see life, others and the world. More than that, because they control your perception of everything you encounter, they also determine the experience you have of everyone and everything.

We do not realise how they can mislead us and cause us to misinterpret the nature of our experiences. Feelings can cause us to believe that something is true while it is an illusion created by a fear-based belief-system. Our unquestionable trust in our feelings and thoughts allows us to justify our perception and behaviour. To break this habit of blindly responding to our thoughts and behaviour, we need to first of all question our feelings, because they act as primary instigators for our responses and reactions.

It can seem as if our feelings and behaviour conspire against us to keep us in a state of powerlessness and fear, but that is not true. It is relatively easy to recognise erroneous feelings by appreciating how they affect you and others.

If what you or the other person feel is in anyway negative — anxiety, worry, stress, powerlessness or feeling insecure, pessimistic, anticipating disaster, etc. — beliefs driven by fear are in control.

You are also responding to fear, if your interactions with others or situations make you feel angry, aggressive, judgmental, critical and blame or accuse others and so on.

Should the behaviour you display in response to your feelings benefit you, but intimidate, hurt or be a disadvantage to others, it is highly likely that you are acting out of fear.

Feelings that are a product of fears will always result in disharmony within yourself and with others. Once you see yourself capitalising on the weaknesses and insecurities of others as the only way to feel powerful or safe, superior or in control, you can be sure that your fears are dominating your mind. It shows that the emotions that initiated your strategic behaviour had to come from fear because of the intent displayed in your response. The need to be in control or dominant, avoid responsibility or confrontation and so on, is proof that negative beliefs dominate your expression in life.

In the act of playing out your issues with others and in the world, you will probably not realise that your behaviour is all about you and no one else. Fear makes you selfish and self-centred regardless of whether your strategies are passive or aggressive. Fear makes you focus all your efforts and energy on your emotional survival because it has convinced you that it is at risk. It becomes "all about you" even if you are pleasing others because even then the only reason for your pleasing is to be liked and accepted, or to avoid blame and guilt. All fear-based behaviours create a negative dynamic between you and others, which brings everyone's negative beliefs into play.

Should any life situation trigger negative feelings and thoughts they are proof that your fears have taken control, through the negative beliefs that make them appear real for you.

Feelings such as: being unlovable, unwanted, unacceptable, feeling judged, entrapped, anger, resentment, guilt, insecurity, powerlessness, submissiveness, inferiority, inadequacy, exclusion, rejection, abandonment, worthlessness, embarrassment, shame, dismissed, invalidated, anxiety, stress, worry, and so on.

If you look closely at the dynamic of a negative event between you and a partner, friend or even a total stranger, you would recognise the similarities in the issues being played out. Even though each of you may be using different behaviours, they are mirrors of comparable, negative belief-systems. By one playing out their issues on the other, each turns these beliefs into a real experience for themselves. Your understanding of the dynamic between yourself, your partner, your parents and others will make it easier for you to recognise what issues you have taken on in childhood. Your need or habit to go into specific behaviours over and over again because you are in fear that you might be confronted by consequences with which you cannot cope. Your behaviour and the feelings that underpin them are an indication that they are strategic and fear-based. Be prepared to question the validity of your feelings at all times until you understand yourself better by knowing your fears because their ability to deceive you is always present.

Always be conscious and aware of your negative emotions, 'WHEN' you feel them and in 'WHAT' context you feel them so that you may realise the reasons 'WHY' you feel them. The same applies to your thoughts, responses and reactions: 'When' you experience negative thoughts, in 'What' context you think them, to understand 'Why' you think them.

Once you recognise that fear underpins your thoughts, feelings, perception and responses, you analyse your reasons and motivation in the context of the experience. It is important also to identify the consequences you believe you would be subject to should you fail to meet the conditions your negative beliefs imply. Pay attention to feelings of aggression and anger, criticism or judgement, abandonment or rejection, being ignored or forgotten, being unlovable or unacceptable, not being good enough and so on. Making notes of how you feel, behave and think can be very useful, because these allow you to relate them back to your childhood. It gives you the opportunity to analyse and compare all the elements involved, and correlate them to what you may be going through at this time. It will add to your capacity to develop greater clarity and understanding of your sense-of-self. Also, be aware that as it is for you, so it is for others, including those with whom you share the experience.

NEGATIVE LIFE EVENTS

The things that upset us in life can frustrate or make us angry always represent issues within ourselves. Your impatience with other drivers in traffic, annoyance with a work associate, your criticism of yourself and others, they all point at you being the issue because you are the central figure in all of them. Dependent on the fears you hold as your sense-of-self, every encounter can turn into a negative event. Imagine you are repeatedly overlooked by shop assistants, causing you to feel insulted and frustrated. Who is responsible? The obvious answer would be that it must be the person serving you. Off course they may need to be more observant to see whose turn it but there is more to this than what the eye meets.

Ask yourself: Why does this happening so frequently to you and with so many different shop attendants — is there perhaps a secret conspiracy against you? You may note that you are the constant figure in all of these encounters, which is evidence that somehow, you must be involved. The question is: How do you usually behave around others and what do you feel? When you are in a social group do you honestly want to be noticed and approached, or do you like to take on a cloak of invisibility, and avoid contact? Do you fear to have to express your feelings and opinions or meet the expectations you believe others have of you? Are you worried that others will recognise and notice all your shortcomings and failings? Any or all of these could be the reasons why you may have developed the strategy of making yourself unnoticed in the presence of others to avoid being approached. But, the moment you walk into a shop and expect to be served, you think that your intent to be invisible to others. The truth is that you cannot be surprised that you have created a reality experience consistent with your negative beliefs and subsequent behaviour in your desire to protect yourself from being noticed and approached.

The power of your energetic being, expressed through your mind, has greater influence than all the muscular strength your body can muster. Your consciousness radiates the presence of its energetic being continually. It does not have an on or off switch. The quality and nature of the energy, which your aura transmits, depends on your state of being, which is defined by your sense-of-self. Your belief systems play a dominant role in determining the nature of the energy of your mind, which can speak 'louder' than your voice ever can. You "radiate" who you are through your energetic being. Your 'transmission' influences the dynamic between you and others to the extent that it can trigger their fears and insecurities before you exchange a word with them. Your presence alone can be the trigger for them to react and respond with strategic behaviours. All this can happen without any specific or related dialogue. Such is the power of the presence of our consciousness and its dynamic interaction with others.

The second aspect of the energetic presence of our minds is how it affects the way we move our bodies, how we gesture and posture. Each feature something about us, which others unconsciously sense. They unaware of tuning into our energy, as well as our physical state of being through the perception created by their sense-of-self, subconsciously. It is a part of their emotional and physical survival instinct. No matter what kind of interaction you have and with whom, your belief systems and theirs — positive or negative — will play leading roles in the energetic, psychological and physical dynamic of your encounter.

CONDITIONED BY FEAR

Fear is an intrinsic part of negative beliefs, and like a virus, it will contaminate everyone with whom it comes into contact. Its effect is like a contagion, in that once it infects you, it wants to be in control and take you over even if, in the end, it might sacrifice its own existence. Fear is neither kind nor benevolent and does not care about those who believe they have to depend on it to be safe.

The human response to fear that originates from a psychological belief is distinctly different from that of a threat triggers our physical survival mechanism because they are very different from each other. A. Once a physical threat has proven to be harmless, we are no longer afraid and probably ignore it. We have much greater difficulty dealing with the psychological fears contained by the beliefs that determine our sense-of-self. Beliefs such as: being unlovable, unacceptable, powerless, incompetent, insignificant, and so on. Psychological fears are a creation of the mind, a product of perception and interpretation, and are only as real as you believe they are. Our conviction in their reality alters our perception so that it can no longer distinguish the truth from the illusion. Once fear-based beliefs rule our minds, this deception goes unnoticed by us. Even though we acquire our fears in childhood, they continue to control our lives, because we delude ourselves that we cannot survive without them. Every time fear confronts us; we do not realise that we are looking at a distorted part of who we believe we are. Our fear of not qualifying for the unconditional love and acceptance we expect from our parents convinces us to accept the conditions they demand that we meet. Subconsciously, to be accepted and survive emotionally, we change who we are and our behaviour to accommodate our parent's issues, fears and insecurities. The emotional discord you experience internally is the fear you feel from believing you were unconditionally lovable, acceptable and wanted to a potential state of rejection or abandonment. Being in disharmony with your essence creates the force behind your need for emotional survival. Through the emotional experiences with our parents, we learn to accept the idea that we can only find love and acceptance by getting others to accept, love and want us. This conviction will then dominate all of our intentions, behaviours and feelings because we believe our emotional survival depends on it. At this point, we are flying emotionally blind because fear is in control and we have become passengers of its intent.

Your perception of reality takes on a veil of truth beyond which you will find it difficult to see any possible alternatives. Once fear is in control, you will unconsciously and selectively ignore any information that contradicts your particular version of reality. With your perception corrupted by negative beliefs and convinced by what your thoughts and feelings, you will not recognise that your interpretation of the dynamics between yourself and others is a product of your mind. You are likely to give your version of reality the ring of truth by surrounding yourself with people — friends and acquaintances —who share your fear-based beliefs and values or complement them. Those who hold similar belief systems are naturally attracted to each other, to endorse on another's perspective and world view but also to avoid being confronted by belief structures that contradict their own. Once fear gets a hold of your mind, the illusionary security it provides puts you in conflict with those whose beliefs challenge your perceived version of reality. Your friendship circles will reflect this.

Every element of an emotional experience is part of a mosaic that forms a picture of the nature of your sense-of-yourself. You do not need to worry about positive experiences because they will always support you but any fears need to be recognised and understood if you are to change. Most of us get to the point where we begin to realise that our strategies are failing us and our issues become intrusive, painful and limiting experiences in life. You can benefit from this critical period by dealing with your feelings and fears. Try and go back to your earliest memory of your experience of the same negative feelings and context in your life, preferably before the age of ten. That is where you will find the answers for the causes for your current state of mind.

Recalling the emotional dynamic that was active at the time between you and the parent or person involved can be the source for uncovering the information you need. Recognising the fears and insecurities of your parents will support your journey of self-realisation. The kind of dialogue, your parents exposed you to, is usually very significant because it reveals the nature of the issues of the speaker. As a child, you would have taken these words literally and not recognised the intent behind them. Being called derogatory names as a child can cause you to label yourself for life. Labels such as stupid, hopeless, useless, worthless, and not good enough, a failure, a disappointment and so on, become the words by which you will identify yourself later in life. If your parent expressed their criticism or dissatisfaction with you openly, then remembering these moments makes it easier for you to establish the nature and context of your issues. Even if they had the best of intentions, parents could still have a negative emotional impact on their offspring. Do not feel you are judging or condemning your father or mother by exploring your emotional history with them. Be as objective as you can be.

Parents with high expectations of their offspring may not realise that potentially they may be imposing their values and standards. Their demand that their child fulfils their vision of who it should be and what it should do may well dismiss or ignore their children's innate talents, passions and desires or needs and expectations. A child is likely to feel that these same expectations are a criticism of who it is and what it wants and desires. Should the child resist being steered in a direction that is not its own, the parents can make them feel guilty for not fulfilling their expectations. Children can feel guilty and ungrateful when parents portray that they sacrificed themselves for them. Their sacrificial attitude can cause their child to believe that must be a burden and an unwanted responsibility. It is challenging for many parents to accept that their child has interests, talents, abilities or aspirations are valid even though they may be completely different from their own. A sports-focussed family may have a child whose interests are not physical and therefore does not excel in these areas. An academic family may have the reverse or have an artistically, musically or sports minded child. If the unique and innate gifts that a child brings into the world are not accepted and acknowledged, it may feel that it has nothing to offer and contribute and see itself as having no value or worth. Note that parents who force their children to conform to their expectations were treated similarly in their childhood.

Parents tend to blame their child if it does something they get upset about because they never reflect whether they are the one with the issue. By not considering that they have the issue and not the child, they transfer the responsibility for their resentment to them. No wonder they cause their children to believe that 'who they are' is the problem, and not 'what they do'. It is not uncommon for children to think that they must have been emotionally 'faulty' or 'dysfunctional' when they were born, because of the way their parents treated them. The manner in which our issues become a part of us and the way we interpret and record them, make us feel and believe they are an intrinsic part of who we are, and are therefore unchangeable. This understanding creates the reasoning that adopting new behaviours and thought processes, is the best way to try and change our lives and to help us cope with our fears. Fortunately, our minds are immensely flexible and resilient, and we have not reached anywhere near our emotional and intellectual potential. We were born with the capacity to change completely the sense of who we are by releasing our limiting and delusional beliefs.

Emotionally damaging processes such as criticism, transfer of guilt or neediness, etc., can be hidden in behaviour, physical expression or unspoken expectations. For instance, parents who have an issue showing feelings and emotions may never articulate love and affection, discontent and criticism, or other emotions openly. They may use facial expression, behaviours or obtuse comments to ensure that they communicate their fear that their children confront them with an undesirable emotional response. Regardless how veiled their communication may be, as their child, you would learn very quickly how to interpret the subtle intent behind this behaviour. You would soon know and be aware of what will get their approval and what will not.

When the suppression of any display of emotions is a substantial part of your family paradigm, you will experience this behaviour as being normal. This dynamic is usually indirect and deliberately non-confrontational and obscures the harm it does. The effect on a child will be emotionally damaging because it is denied the emotional experience that it is lovable, that it mattered, that it is interesting and so on. The child's feelings will not receive consideration, be heard or validated unless they meet the criteria of the parents. Your parents fear of not being able to cope with any emotions that cause them stress or anxiety prevents you from being freely expressive of your feelings. Your fear of upsetting your parents becomes your fear that anything you say will cause a negative response by others for which you will feel responsible. Should you have adopted their fears and insecurities concerning emotional expression, you will find that your relationships often turn into emotionally confrontational experiences. You have come to believe that putting your feelings and emotions, needs and expectations on display is inappropriate and an imposition on others. As a result, you contrive to be emotionally appropriate by being restrained and controlled in your encounters with others. Avoiding guilt by suppressing what you feel, need and want will cause you to attract and be attracted to partners who suffer similarly fears. Once you are enrolled in this process, you do not realise that being emotionally sincere and honest is a struggle for you.

A NEW PERSPECTIVE

It is not easy to look at a behaviour or attitude you have accepted as normal with new eyes and realise that in reality, it does not support you in being your authentic self. By taking a critical view of feelings and behaviour and relating these back to your family history, you can discover the links, that will lead you to the core reasons for your issues. Accepting that your childhood was not perfect and that you hold onto fears that drive your negative feelings, behaviour and intent, will make your search easier.

The following may provide some ideas on how to approach an issue:

You need to distinguish the experience of the child you once were from that of the adult you now are. It is easy to forget that you began life without any worldly awareness and that you were naive, helpless and dependent. Compared to the adult you have become your earliest state of mind gave you a very different perception of who you are. The child you once were, is still running your emotional life with its fears and insecurities.

Imagine your mother had self-confidence issues and therefore did not trust her decision and choices nor wanted to be responsible for anything challenging and confronting. Even though you would not have intellectually understood what your mother's issues were, you would automatically be exposed to the consequences of her emotional behaviour — her stress and anxiety, fear and worry and so on. Your mother's fears make it difficult for her to cope with raising you, particularly if you are her first child. You will interpret her unconscious resistance to accepting responsibility for your life, because of her fears, as unwillingness and resentment to be there for you. Consequently, you come to believe that you are the cause of the stress and anxiety or resentment and impatience. Your innate need for support and care, nurturing and unconditional love, acceptance and so on is now, in your understanding, a burden and intrusion in your mother's life, and the cause of her stress and insecurities. As a result, you do not feel unconditionally acceptable or loved because you believe that you are responsible for your mother's negative state of mind. The only response that is available to you, and the only power you have, is to deny yourself by suppressing and hiding your innate expectations and needs to be loved and taken care off. This response to what you feel becomes your way to protect her from you and your natural need and expectation for love, support, care and protection. You suppress your authentic self, your innate expectations to be unconditionally loved, wanted and accepted and to hide your innate need for attention, acknowledgement and validation. Guilt will drive you towards being self-sufficient and self-reliant and emotionally self-contained, and in the act of role-reversal, even take on the responsibility of being your mother's emotional protector.

An adult male, who is a product of this kind of family paradigm, you may unconsciously choose to take the role of being the protector and caretaker of women in your relationships. You will attract and be attracted to women who come out of their childhood feeling insecure and unconfident and who are needy and want to be taken care of, just like your mother. The guilt or over responsibility you learned to accept from her, makes you feel responsible for their insecurities.

You are convinced that you that will only be worthy of their love if you save them from everything they fear and insecurities. Your sense of guilt makes you put their needs and expectations before your own, and in the long term, this causes you feel denied. Your powerlessness to fulfil your desires and wishes is likely to create anger and resentfulness, and this can be the beginning of disenchantment in the relationship

A father who is emotionally absent and disinterested in his child will have a similar effect on its life. Whatever the justifications or reasons are for why a father was not part of his child's early life, the child will come to the conclusion that it somehow to blame. Unable to understand why the reasons for his emotional and physical absence it will believe that it is not wanted, not good enough, uninteresting, unlovable and unacceptable. It will be convinced that there must be something wrong with it because of the way its father treats it. The child will become critical of itself to explain the reasons why its father had no interest in it and ignored it.

If this was your childhood, your belief systems might read — I am not good enough (for my father), I am a burden and a nuisance (to my father), I am unlovable, unwanted, and unacceptable (to my father), I am uninteresting and stupid (in my father's eyes) and so on. Once you accept these beliefs as defining of who you are, they will determine the way you will manifest your life experiences and relationships. If negative thoughts and feelings trouble your mind and control your attitude, behaviour and choices, you have proof that you are subject to the fears held in your sense-of-self.

Only by releasing these beliefs can you be the person you were born to be. In the absence of fear driven beliefs, your perception and feelings thought and ideas will change to be representative of who you genuinely are. You will find that you will become detached from external influences that in the past would have upset you and made you feel powerless, angry, or just afraid. Your behaviour will also begin to change because without your fears your old strategic behaviours are no longer needed by you. In the absence of believing that you have to be something you that are not, your behaviour and feelings can now become spontaneous, genuine and sincere. Once your self-perception changes so will your goals and aspirations.

Without negative beliefs, there is no self-destructive intent, which was the cause for negative thoughts and feelings in the first place and so these too will wane and disappear. Your fear-motivated neediness will dissolve because there is no basis for its existence without any negative beliefs supporting it. You are no longer looking to attain from the world or others, which you believe is missing within you because the negative beliefs that created this desire are no longer present. In short, without negative beliefs at the core of your issue, there is no basis for negative perception, thoughts and feelings, or strategic behaviours. The negative intent projected by the beliefs that hold it is no longer the centre of your focus and attention because they are absent and this sets you truly free from fear. In the absence of negative beliefs, new doors will open for you, expanding your potential and your capacity to fulfil it.

Chapter 22

THE POWER OF HARMONIOUS INTENT

If you are serious about changing your life, your focus needs to be on letting go of who you are NOT, rather than trying to become what others expect or need you to be.

You will not get a permanent solution by ignoring the core reasons why you manifested your emotional issues and life problems in the first place. Once you have accepted that you are the creator of your life experiences, it does not make any sense to pin the blame on something or someone based on the observation of 'what happened', 'who said this' or 'who did that'. Without understanding the causative factors that involve you in the manifestation of your issues, you are not solving your problems.

Understanding WHO YOU ARE is the path to self-realization. Expanding the awareness of your sense-of-self, allows you to recognise the causes and come to a solution.

The part of your sense-of-self responsible for your issues does not represent your unique and authentic self. Fear holds you in a permanent state of emotional imbalance that can keep you on the edge of depression, stress and anxiety. The extent to which fear pushes you out of your centre of balance mirrors the level of emotional disharmony you have accepted in your life. When you are in a difficult or confronting situation with someone, the inner-conflict between your reasoning intellect and your fears will constantly challenge you. We collectively play out fears which we believe are issues in life or with others but do not see that we are actually emotional mirrors for one another. We create both friendships and conflict in this way. Like-minded people will be attracted to share time and space with each other, while those with strategically opposite behaviours will entice conflict.

Releasing our fears will have the effect of transforming the dynamic of the relationship we have with ourselves and that with others. While releasing your negative beliefs have changed you, the people around you are likely to have remained the same. Your new awareness has altered your view of issues and life you once shared with them. As a result, they no longer understand you, and you may feel detached from them. Sometimes that means that they no longer want to interact with you or you with them. It is only then that you may realise that the central reason why you spent time together was due to the issues you had in common. Without your fears, you can no longer relate in the way you used to.

There is also a potential that family or friends will start to change their attitude and behaviour towards you. Your changes cause the emotional dynamic between you to shift, and that can result in incredible improvements in your relationship with them.

Your greater sense of confidence, emotional stability and inner-harmony do not resonate with the fears of the past, and that shows in your new connection with others. Increased awareness and clarity of who you truly are, will replace the illusions that were created by fear, and this translates into inner-harmony and self-confidence.

The key to understanding how all of this works lies in the realisation of why and how beliefs determine our intent and provide us with the capacity to create and manifest a positive or negative reality for ourselves.

Beliefs and their intents are to our creative minds what a lens is to a spotlight, just like a lens focuses light, beliefs are an instrument of the mind that determines, focuses and shapes our intent.

The mind is the facilitator of the essence and the unique and creative forces of our spirit so that we can evolve the nature of our being by experiencing our self through what it manifests in physical reality.

The capacity of consciousness to give exclusive focus to the intent of a conviction held by the mind — a belief system — gives it the power to create and manifest its own experience of reality. Take for example light that passes through a lens which concentrates it to the point of pure brightness, as would the focus of harmonious intent. However, a distorted lens would corrupt the beam of light and clarity would be lost, just like intent contaminated by fear.

It is little more complicated with belief systems because light does not have the inherent predisposition that our consciousness has. When the sense of who we are contradicts the pre-disposed intent of our consciousness, which is to be in harmony with its essence, the outcome of its expression will always be fear based. The presence of fear in your sense-of-self will cause you to feel that your life is subject to the will and power of others and the world. This perception convinces you that others, circumstances and events control your life, but, in fact, you surrender power and authority to others through your behaviour. Now, instead of being the creator of your life experiences, you are making yourself the victim of your manifestations.

Our belief systems are a necessary construction of our mind so that we have a sense of identity, and a framework to form our intents as creative tools to manifest through action, choices and self-expression. They are a temporary or consistent concept about what something is, how it will act or behave or about a process which allows us to anticipate what outcome we will have when we interact or engage with it.

The beliefs that make up our sense-of-self and those we hold about everything in life, others and the world, should be seen as a flexible program that provides us with a level of predictability for our existence, in emotional and physical reality.

From very young, we learn what we should fear or trust, what is safe or dangerous for us concerning others, our environment and the nature of the world. Our initial experience with people, objects and food, situations or processes, can result in our trust in them because they prove themselves to be safe or support us. They can also prove to be a threat because they show themselves to be dangerous and harmful. The beliefs that cause us to trust or fear to establish themselves as a consequence of what we have learned and experienced so that we do not have to keep on testing the nature of everything we encounter in life as if it is the first time. Once we accept an experience as a safe and secure or dangerous and a threat, we create emotional stability by affirming it in the form of a belief that defines our expectations of a future confrontation with these elements. This awareness allows us to be physically and emotionally involved in the world, while maintaining personal security, without constantly having to reassess every encounter that confronts us with these choices. We cannot exist without beliefs because they give us a predictable and dependable world in which to live. By the same token, encounters that threaten our emotional and physical survival will cause us to accept fear-based beliefs that create the perception of existence in a dangerous and threatening world.

Without beliefs, our minds would be without the ability to create a meaningful life that supports the evolution of our consciousness. In the absence of a delineated intent, it cannot project or interact in concert with the energetic consciousness of others, which is necessary to manifest its life experiences. The natural and incessant force to create our life experiences is an inseparable part of our consciousness and cannot be switched off. Therefore, in the process of living life, we have no choice but to choose. Not choosing is not an option because you cannot choose not to choose, without choosing. Without exception, all of our choices contain the intentions created by our sense-of-self, and so regardless whether they are harmonious or disharmonious, they will become our life experiences. Generally, in the long term, a consciously manufactured positive intent cannot override an intent that is a product of fear. The negative intentions of a belief-system have to be understood, acknowledged and then released, to make way for positive, harmonious intentions that find their origin in unconditional love and acceptance.

Because of this truth, the only way to control what you manifest in your life is to be in control of the beliefs that define your sense-of-self because these are the source for your intent. If you believe the sky is blue and you share that fact with others, it will not have any adverse effect on you because it is only an observation. However, if you believe that blue skies make you happy or that grey skies are depressing, you have created a problem for yourself. Your happiness and mood now depend on the colour of the sky, and you have given the weather power over your feelings. You are no longer in control of your emotional state of mind, and you may even act as a victim of the weather by thinking; "Here is another grey day just to make me miserable".

You would be surprised to know how many beliefs you hold at this level that you think to be unimportant but collectively have a strong sway over your thinking and feelings. Superstition falls into this category where certain signs are believed to have the power to attract negative or positive events into our lives. Giving your power to what is outside of you will never support the expression of your truth nor bring you to live life as your authentic self. Superstition is usually a product of the desire to explain certain outcomes and events the origin of which you cannot recognise nor understand. Good and bad luck fall in a similar category. Accepting that we create and manifest our own lives individually and collectively, there cannot be any events or experiences that are accidental in the true sense of that word. It is, however, likely that there will always be circumstances and events of which we cannot understand the origin or explain as to how and why certain they happened to others or ourselves. Were we to gain insight into the characters and fears of those involved, however, the reasons and causes would likely no longer be a mystery, an accident or a product of either good or bad luck.

CREATING HARMONY FROM WITHIN

One of the most amazing qualities of our consciousness is our capacity to see beauty and grace. Exposure to something beautiful can take our breath away and bring tears to our eyes. Beauty, can present itself in just about any form and appear anywhere at any time, but when it does, we have the capacity to recognise it immediately for what it is. Our sense of beauty can vary from person to person, but there are qualities in our perception of what is beautiful that we have in common. The harmony and balance between shape, proportion and colour all play a decisive role in our perception of beauty that is physical. One of the most remarkable qualities of our consciousness is that we have an innate sense of beauty, harmony and balance. Some develop a greater awareness of beauty, balance and harmony than others but without exception, its visual, energetic or physical nature can touch everyone.

The balance and harmony that we experience as beauty exists in everything in creation as does the capacity in us to feel and experience it. When we can neither see its presence in our environment or life, it is not because it is not there, but our issues prevent us from recognising it. Just like fear distorts unconditional love by turning it into fear, its effect on us can also corrupt our innate sense of beauty, balance and harmony. We can openly express issues that generate emotions such as anger, aggression and powerlessness for example, or suppress and internalise them. Our negative feelings, thoughts and perception will compel us to seek out people, environments and even entertainment where we can experience and feel the kind of emotional energy that corresponds to our state of mind.

Being in a constant state of anger or aggression of feeling victimised, powerless, being unfairly treated or feeling inferior will cause you to be unconsciously attracted to places, people and entertainment, where you will create the very experiences you need to validate the beliefs and feelings you hold about yourself. Anything you experience, whether through friends or strangers and regardless of the environment, can be seen by you as being negative, confronting, demeaning, critical or aggressive, and can serve as a validation your negative mind-set. This kind of distorted perception can cause you to exclude yourself from others, which will be your way of 'rejecting yourself', instead of being rejected. As a result, you may choose to be alone, but more than often you will seek out those with whom you share a similar perception, to validate and justify your belief systems.

Music is a great example of this as an expression form because it can be written in an infinite number of ways. Music can be melodious and soothing or, at the other end of the scale, be aggressive and disharmonious and anything in-between. The composer and lyricist are the first in a chain of people that are involved in the production of a music score to which we may choose to listen. While the writers of a musical score and lyrics, the musicians, the singer, and the listener may never know each other; there is a strong possibility that they connect through the beliefs each holds, and the feelings and emotions they therefore share.

The act of creating music can come from a harmonious sense-of-self, or from a mind in disharmony with itself, each seeking to give a voice to the emotional joy or pain experienced. The music and lyrics will invariably come through the emotional filter created by the positive or negative beliefs each writer holds. Their feelings and perception will determine what kind of music they are attracted to and how it will be written and want it to be performed. Inner-harmony will tend towards the desire to bring harmony into the world, while inner conflict will be expressed as disharmony with the world. If you see life and the world with anger, disappointment and resentment, your emotions will show in what you create. If you perceive a world of beauty, grace and harmony, then this too will show in the end product of your creativity. The sense-of-yourself that creates your perception and feelings is always deeply involved in every act of creation and manifestation.

The music will find its place on the shelves of music shops, and if the writers are fortunate, it will be played on the radio and through other media. Whether by design or unconscious intent, those attracted to listen to your music are very likely to share similar belief systems with those who created the music. The fan clubs of some performers provide a level of evidence for this. The same goes for those who feel attracted to perform or sing the music. There is a certain congruency when music created from inner conflict and disharmony draws similarly emotionally troubled minds as an audience. This effect does not have to be absolute because we all experience life situations that can take us through a range of emotions. Just going through a period of unhappiness or disappointment can cause you to be attracted to melancholic or aggressive music. Those who are lost in their issues and suffer from a consistent negative state of mind will often be fans of music that they feel, tells the story of their anger, resentments and powerlessness. The nature of the beliefs we hold can also cause us to be attracted to other things, such as a particular fashion, a specific type of entertainment or places.

We may not be composers, musicians or lyricists but we all have the capacity to bring something special into the world through our choices and decisions. No matter what we create, whether harmonious or disharmonious, our sense-of-self is always at the source of our creations, and therefore the outcome of our creativity is also always our responsibility.

CONSCIOUS HARMONIOUS INTENT

Looking into your own emotions and beliefs concerning your family history is of primary importance in your search for the root of your issues. While letting go of your negative beliefs is one of the best ways to change your sense-of-self, there are some other things you can do to support this process. Consciously choosing not to respond to emotions that drive your negative behaviour, in tandem with releasing your negative beliefs will assist your transition. Recognition of the negative aspects of yourself may also cause you to realise the choices that cause you to manifest these negative thoughts and feelings. Remember that it is not possible for you not to choose, but you have the power to take control over your choices by releasing the fears that control your choices.

Once you release a fear-driven belief-system, it will take a little time before you have integrated the changes as a part of your sense-of-self. During the integration period, you may experience some emotional ambiguity. It is during this time that consciously selecting what you know to be positive choices will help speed up your changes. Your choices may well push you temporarily out of your comfort zone because you have chosen not to depend on your strategic behaviour, as you habitually would. Controlling your responses, reactions, and decisions at this time will actively support your transformation and will make it easier to be more authentic. However, releasing your fears will result in automatic changes in thinking, perception, feelings and behaviour.

You will progressively shift the balance from fear towards unconditional love by releasing more of your negative belief-systems, and this will move your sense-of-self towards a greater state of harmony with your essence. So, even if you have not as yet released all the causes for your issues, every time you do make a step that promotes your inner-harmony you are reinforcing your trust in what is authentic within you — the essence of your spirit. Developing aware of the causes for your issues and the intent they create will not be enough to release negative beliefs.

However, once you have let them go and you enter the process of integrating your new state, you will attain a new positive attitude that will help to bring it to completion. Old habits will begin to fade away as will the feelings that used to drive them. The old disharmonious-self connected to the issues you dealt with will become foreign and eventually absent to your mind.

UNCONSCIOUS CREATORS

We manifest every one of our life experiences — negative or positive — so effortlessly that we are not aware of doing it.

We may have learned to believe that we need an extensive education, training and skill and therefore collect degrees and diplomas, to quiet the fear that we do not know enough to be acceptable and significant.

Our distrust and doubt in the natural resources of our mind, to learn and understand, to know and remember, to analyse and comprehend, in our talents and abilities, intellect, etc., can make us avoid any form of education or learning or become obsessive to know more. Our fears may direct to professions that keep us safe from having our intellect and knowledge tested, or keep us busy acquiring more and more education, knowledge, and information. If this is our issue, we may believe that the acquisition of more education will ultimately turn us into self-confident individuals our fears stop us from being. Regardless of how much we learn, our doubt and distrust in our intelligence, logic, inspirations, creativity and any other resources of the mind, will always sabotage our best efforts. All the intellect, reasoning and logic we can muster will not overcome our fears and insecurities. The acquisition of knowledge and experience is always positive, but with it, you cannot overcome your emotional issues at their core. If you want to use what you have learned effectively, you need to deal with your issues. An axe, no matter how sharp, is only as useful as the confidence of the woodcutter wielding it, has in his skill.

The pictures and stories of beautiful and successful models, stars and their lives can become unrealistic reference points for people who suffer from low self-esteem. They might measure the state of their lives by the unrealistic media representation of the wealthy and famous. They can become convinced that to achieve the same lifestyle, happiness and success, they need to be physically and emotionally the same. In the case of women, they may compare their appearance and body shape with those who get public recognition for being beautiful and attractive to men. Men can have similar issues concerning women. Once, they accept and believe that they are not good enough, or slim and attractive enough no amount of common-sense will change their minds. Often, they were exposed to criticism and judgment by their mother or father when young concerning the value and significance of physical appearance. Once they start to relate this back to the way they see themselves, they are likely to be self-critical and then use unrealistic reference points such as the famous and wealthy to prove this point to themselves. The perception created by their negative beliefs about their face and body alters their perception to such an extent that they lose all perspective concerning their appearance and lives. According to the self-critical beliefs they hold, they will never be slim or beautiful enough. Their obsessive focus on whatever they see as a flaw and their appearance expands into critical significance in their lives. Convinced, that they will not matter, be lovable, wanted and accepted, unless they are super-slim, beautiful and desirable, they live in constant anxiety and stress. Their distorted perception of themselves can lead them to self-destructive habits resulting in anorexia and depression. Those who feel completely powerless to change themselves may eat to console themselves and create proof of what they believe by becoming overweight.

Our minds are super inventive when it comes to creating the strategies that we employ to deal with our fears. For example, we may look at the history of our choices and commitments to see what steps to eliminate because we believe they led to an issue so that we can avoid failure in the future. We can also study and examine methods, attitudes and behaviours that have led others to success to emulate their path. All of this appears on the surface to be the reasonable, sensible and a logical thing to do if you want to be successful or avoid failure. However, when we do this assuming that what and how we do something is the issue and we do not take account of the nature of the person doing it. We are so obsessed with what we should or should not do, by trying to figure out every detail of our actions and choices that we completely ignore the nature of the DOER.

We forget that each person is unique and that all those who failed or succeeded will each have their particular skills and abilities as well as issues and problems — intellectually and emotionally. Once you define your success in life by material wealth, fame or recognition, you create reference points that you have to meet to convince yourself that you are successful. It does not occur to you that the reasons and motivations for needing, wanting and amassing material wealth and power can be highly dysfunctional and destructive. You might argue that if you are wealthy, it does not matter that you are emotionally dysfunctional, but your experience would say otherwise. You do not realise what kind of your life circumstances you create; you will always see and experience it through the beliefs that make up your sense-of-self. What is the worth of all of your material success or fame, if your experience of life is marked by depression, guilt or powerlessness and so on?

When we work for others, we are expected to have trust in the value systems and standards of our employer. Their ideas of what matters and what does not may be so skewed towards profit making that they ignore basic human values and standards, to achieve their goals. If our intrinsic values are in contradiction with those of our work place, we may feel emotionally challenged by the expectations we have to meet. The demand that we compromise the fundamental intent of our consciousness can affect our performance, commitment and engagement.

Our fear that we cannot survive without our job may persuade us to dismiss our values and standards to incorporate theirs, be accepted by the company. Our idea of success and achievements has to become the same as that of the company regardless of the values and standards they go by if we are to be part of their system and culture. We may gradually become an extension of the system we work under and substitute their biased concepts of what matters in the world for the trust in the innate standards and values, integrity and principles of our being — our authentic nature. By never questioning the origin for what we think and feel concerning what others expect of us, we can become blind to the reasons for what we do and why we live. We will then unknowingly sabotage our trust in the value systems inherent in our creative and authentic self.

The truth is that we are incredibly prolific creators from the day we are born. Whatever intent we hold in our sense-of-self will become our experience of reality, whether consciously chosen or not. How much more powerful do you think you need to be? When we get lost on the path created by fear, we need to accept that we have not yet learned how to use the resources our consciousness is blessed with effectively.

Synopsis: We experience negative events in our life for which we have no explanation, unaware that the process that manifests it is within us. In resentment and fear of our undesirable emotional experiences, we cannot imagine that we could be at the origin of their creation. Our indoctrination into strategic behaviour is at the core of our emotional blindness. We are convinced that our thoughts, feelings, perceptions, reactions and responses represent who we are and that we to be strategic in our self-expression to overcome our emotional issues — fears — in life. We define our identity by our feeling, behaviour, and who believe we are — negative and positive. Others think they know us by the way we express ourselves and do not realise when we are strategic. In the absence of trust in our innate capacities and resources, and with only our strategies to depend on, we are under the illusion that we are unlovable and unacceptable, unwanted and powerless, cannot be trusted or trust in ourselves. Our perception makes the quality of our life and its success or failure reliant on the effectiveness of our strategies.

With the best will and using all of our conscious efforts we still do not find it easy to manifest the lifestyle and relationships we want. Instead of addressing the nature of our sense-of-self, we find it difficult to break our habit to resort to 'doing' to solve our life issues.

We fall into a pattern of asking ourselves the same old question:

WHAT do I have to DO to solve my problems, to have a better relationship, to be successful, to be significant, to be heard, to be accepted, etc.

While instead, we should be asking:

WHO do I have to BE to BE without my problems, to stop choosing disastrous relationships, to stop failing, to stop feeling worthless, to no longer be ignored, etc.?

As long as you do not recognise or understand that the nature of 'who you are' is responsible for your issues, then working on your sense-of-self will seem like an impractical and improbable way to solve your problems in relationships and life.

The logical reasoning part of your mind is drawn to address the tangible aspects of an emotional issue and use tactics, strategies and information to solve the problem. This method will inevitably involve assessing the behaviour and responses of others, the analysis of every aspect of an event to try and understand why something turned out badly, or wrong. Without realising we get lost in all of the superficial features of the issue and then try to resolve it by figuring out who did what and how and so on. You do not realise that you are in the process of changing what is outside of you to resolve an issue while the source is within you. Taking this approach is not wrong in the strict sense of the word, but if it is the only thing you do, nevertheless extremely limiting if you want a permanent solution. Our tendency to label our emotional and intuitive self as unpredictable and unstable reinforces our excessive trust in logic and reasoning. Our strategic, logical approach can deceive us into believing that our solutions are permanent, because they may function well in a particular instance. Consequently, we cannot see our involvement as creators of this experience because we have done nothing to understand the fundamental cause — ourselves. Our consciousness has the capacity of intellect, logic and reasoning as well as intuition, imagination and inspiration because each serves a meaningful purpose.

You will only achieve a genuine transformation of the self by changing of you — the 'doer' — instead of what you did — by transforming the thinker instead of the thought.

Confronting issues, especially personal ones, requires a change in your perception and awareness of what is an illusion and what an is not. Deeply ingrained habits and beliefs that exist in our consciousness need to make space for liberated and spontaneous thoughts, feelings and reasoning that respect and are congruent our core values. We need to have a different relationship with our feelings by having a stronger awareness of their connection to the essence of our spirit — unconditional love, acceptance and trust.

Consider this:

What and how we feel do not necessarily define us.

We are not the victims of our feelings or the environment unless we choose to be.

We are the originators of all our emotions, perception, feelings, thoughts and behaviour.

Our consciousness creates the sensation of being aware and alive through its encounter with the life experiences it manifests through the choices it makes.

Realising the truth in these statements can help us to accept our essence — unconditional love and so on — as the reference point by which we judge the quality of our choices and behaviour. Once we do, our physical and emotional life experience will make much more sense to us. Then, our negative feelings will no longer control our decisions and choices, because we will begin to see the actual reasons we create our lives. This new concept of who we are to ourselves, others and the world will allow us to recognise and address our emotional issues at their core. In turn, this will free us to change who we believe we are and consequently alter the nature of all of our relationships. The absence of fear changes our sense-of-self and with it the nature of our intent, which will open up opportunities to manifest the newly found potential of our consciousness.

By releasing your negative beliefs and fears of being present as your authentic self, you will expand the expression of your creative self, supported by your conviction that you are unconditionally lovable, acceptable and trustworthy. The renewed trust in being your authentic self will gradually facilitate its unique nature taking a greater place in the expression of your consciousness. The acceptance of your innate standards and values, integrity and principles will help to affirm new and positive beliefs and increase your self-confidence. You will find that you will only be comfortable in accepting the externally defined values and standards of others, as long as they are in congruence will those that are innate in you. Your rediscovered sense of being will change your relationships in every part of your life. Life experiences you will manifest, will be representative of your unique nature and provide you with greater satisfaction that will translate into happiness, and profound learning experiences. The characteristics unique to your authentic self will be energetically in harmony with the values of the essence of your spirit-consciousness.

As your fears diminish, your positive qualities will grow in stature and create and manifest a positive reality just as effortlessly as you created your negative life experiences. Your positive intent will shape your perception and influence your choices and decisions to create the outcome intended by your positive beliefs.

EVOLVING YOUR CONSCIOUSNESS

What does it mean for your consciousness to develop? Is it not already all it can be as soon as it is aware of being or is it perhaps a blank space upon which your childhood and society write an indelible program which you are destined to live out?

Consciousness has no limits other than those it applies to itself by the perception it holds of its being. We cannot even imagine what it would be like to exist without limits because we do not fully understand the restrictions we put on ourselves. For now, we cannot imagine an existence without fears and conditions and therefore live a restricted life. The limiting beliefs we share contracts our perception of what our consciousness is capable. Our general approach to resolving emotional issues bears this out. When we suffer from psychological issues the best we can hope for to address them is advice on what to do, how to act, think and feel, or use coping mechanisms, strategies or psychotropic drugs. None of these solutions shows a profound understanding of the nature and capacity of human consciousness.

Evolving your consciousness requires changes that represent an expansion of its previous state of being through the release of perceived limitations and restrictions on the expression of its self. You will only truly know what the effect this will have on your mind, once you start releasing your fears. Intellectual learning may seem like the obvious way for consciousness to become more than what it is, but that is only partly true. Knowledge and skill are important contributors to our survival in life, at work and in relationships but our emotions easily overrule the common-sense, which acquired knowledge supposed to provide. Neither do they give us with adequate, mental and emotional tools to completely understand and release our issues. Depending on what you have learned, your knowledge can, at times, stand in the way of personal change. The principles used to resolve mechanical or business problems do not work with emotionally biased issues. In fact, having a high IQ, academic achievements or logical reasoning provide no assurance against suffering from psychological problems.

THE CREATOR WITHIN

Consciousness has the innate capacity to create and manifest, but that does not mean that whatever you want will just appear when you want it. It would be like putting a gun in the hands of a child. Just like an infant we need to learn to become responsible creators. Manifesting our reality experience has the characteristic of also generating emotional sensations — our feelings — that reflect their positive or negative nature for us. If we were aware, we would recognise that our emotions tell us about us — the creator — and not just about what we manifested.

To manifest on levels currently beyond our imagination, we have to develop an understanding of our consciousness and the rules or laws that apply to its function and self-expression. That is a big ask when even now most people do not even realise that they are the creators of the reality they currently experience. The life journey each of us is on has the intention to lead to the same destination — to become conscious and responsible creators. Right now, we are like children in the sandbox of the play-school of the cosmos learning how we affect and manifest the nature of reality. We do not understand nor are we prepared to take responsibility for the consequences of our choices — individually and collectively. Know that all of us get there in a time frame that is right for us. There is infinite time for all of us to achieve this level of being but if you make this your conscious intent, the process of living your life will become a learning experience like no other. Learning to live in the absence of fear and to be in control of your being by existing in a state of unconditional love and acceptance, here and now, is a significant part of our education as a spirit-consciousness.

Our learning in physical reality falls broadly into two categories: The first two things we learn in life are what we have to do and who we have to be to get endorsement and approval. What we have to do is made clear by our parents through the way they communicate and impose their expectations and rules. Learning who we should be to be acceptable is usually the obscure part of our childhood experience, and usually involves compliance with the fears, insecurities, values and standards of our parents.

We should be learning to discover and embrace our authentic self and be shown how to live in harmony with our essence — unconditional love, acceptance and trust of self. Instead, by being exposed to the fears and insecurities of parents and society, we experience the rejection of our authentic self by those we depend on for our survival. We discover that we need to become what they expect us to be so that they can check their fears and insecurities. Their distrust in us becomes our distrust in ourselves. With our emotional toolbox defined by these experiences, we try to create and manifest our lives. Who we come to believe we are, as a result, will determine the life we will ultimately live.

The growth of our consciousness can only truly begin if we release the adverse effect our family experiences had on us. Once our sense-of-self no longer relates to the unwanted aspects of our family history, we will start to accept who we truly are. Releasing the fear-based limitations of our society are yet another level of change that will facilitate a return to our true nature and emotional healing on a grand scale when shared by others. Only then can we say that we have embraced a new sense of being.

You may have noticed that when fear is in control, the outcome of a choice or decision is usually not what we would have wanted it to be. Creatively manifesting a desire, concept or idea will not be a constructive act if exercised in total disregard of the consequences for a single or collective consciousness. Every expression of an individual consciousness affects all others, and for the outcome to be positive, it needs to be a gesture in harmony with others. This state of consciousness can only occur when fear is absent and if the core of our spiritual essence — unconditional love acceptance and trust — unites everyone. When this is not the case, it creates ripples of distortion which touch every consciousness adversely, and therefore reaches much further and deeper in our minds than you might imagine. Wanting to create selfishly to satisfy once needs and expectations, when they are a product of fears and insecurities, creates a raft of issues for everyone directly or indirectly associated with it. Those who share similar or complementary negative beliefs will try either try to capitalise on the opportunities the outcome this creates or become its collateral victims. In living life, however, no-one escapes the consequences of what fear will bring about, and in time all will be confronted with the emotional or physical consequences.

CONFRONTING CHANGE

Change is essential for a freely choosing creative and unique consciousness. Without change, we cannot evolve through exposure to new experiences, information and processes. Change is a big challenge for those with fear because there appears to be no certainty whether the outcome it creates will make them feel good, happy or satisfied or manifest more pain, more issues and problems. Avoiding change can become a series skilful strategic behaviours tied up in excuses and justifications. For those who fear change, the prospect can be terrifying because of their fear of not knowing how the consequences will impact them. For example: how it will affect their identity, how others will judge them whether they can cope, should the outcome be disappointing, or the fear that their strategic behaviours will be ineffective and therefore feel powerless.

Those who suffer from fear of change, and the anxiety and stress that often accompanies it, will already be aware of most of these issues. The question is, how can they transcend the fear of change so that they can enter a process of transformation? What might surprise you is that the fear of change is a negative belief system just like any other of your fears. Releasing the fear of change is the same as dealing with the belief that you are unlovable, unwanted or unacceptable and so on.

Releasing your fear of change is a great way to take the first step towards becoming authentic and living in your power.

Here is a representation of a belief system that you may hold that causes confronting change to be difficult for you:

- I have to live in fear of unpredictable, sudden, unexpected, unplanned, unchosen changes —
- For fear of not being able to survive the consequences — for fear of being overwhelmed and becoming powerless — for fear of losing control over my life — for fear it will cause me pain and make me suffer — for fear it will cause me embarrassment and shame — for fear it will make me helpless and vulnerable — for fear that it will cause me more pain and suffering

- It will cause me to be — rejected, dismissed, excluded, unwanted, unacceptable, undesirable, insignificant, judged, criticised and so on.
- And so, because of that — I have to avoid change, reject and dismiss change, invalidate change, ignore change —
- I have no choice — because if I don't — I will become powerless and have no control over my life and relationships — I will be vulnerable and helpless — unlovable and unacceptable — insignificant and worthless, — rejected and excluded, — criticised and judged — ridiculed and shamed and so on —
- Because it is always my fault, – I am always to blame – I am the guilty one, and I feel powerless to change it.

Note: You cannot make statements of this kind that will hurt you because your sub-conscious mind will not take in anything does not apply to you. If you are not sure, whether this is the case, repeat it anyway. However, you can add anything you believe to be true or delete any parts of this if not applicable to you.

The complexity and length may surprise you, but every element that relates to you needs to be owned by you to be able to release it. Fear of change is usually passed on by one or both parents. Their emotional responses to anything new or different would display their fear of change and painted it as a confrontation to be avoided at all cost. Its expression is not necessarily explicit. Sometimes, the cause of anxiety, stress, worry and avoidance behaviour, associated with change, reveal themselves if you question the reasons why they stay in the same house, in the same area, or in the same job. It can be the consistent sameness of their diet or habits and repetitive patterns of behaviour. Fear of change usually goes hand in hand with the fear of decision-making, initiating new actions and choices, or exposure to risk. The intensity of the fear of change differs from person to person, as do the reasons for it. To ascertain what your fears are and how they became a part of you, it may help to consider everything presented here.

Realistically, evolving your consciousness to higher levels of awareness and mental and emotional capability is a lifetime, if not an eternal, journey of the spirit. The importance of this exceeds anything else you may want to succeed in or achieve in your life. Dependent on the nature of your intent anything you achieve will contribute to the growth of your spirit and consciousness. It comes down to your approach to living your life — self-responsible and without fear, or in disharmony and controlled by fear.

Since your spirit-consciousness already has the innate intent to evolve in all areas of its potential being, it makes sense to live life with this intention. Our consciousness will always develop even if it chooses to exist and function controlled by fear. The outcomes that fear creates in our lives makes our experience of it unbearable, unhappy and painful should be our warning that we are functioning from a distorted sense-of-self. Sooner or later we begin to realise that we can only stop our pain and suffering if we do something to change our sense-of-self. So far, our general response to the distortions and imbalances in our own life and those in the world, have been addressed in an almost time honoured way: through strategies or laws and rules. Looking at the world as it is right now, it is clear that it is not working on any level of our civilisation. At best, we are constantly propping up processes, systems and laws to stop everything sliding from under us. We do much the same in our private lives by the use of strategic behaviours to deal with our issues. Living with the awareness that we are the creators of our life circumstances alters our whole approach to the way we live. Accepting full responsibility for our choices and their consequences modify our relationship with our self, others and the world. By sharing this intent and the responsibility that comes with it with others of like mind, we can bring about a new and very different world. What would it be like to exist in a world, where a substantial portion of the population lived with a shared intent that naturally seeks to create harmonious connections?

Self-change is a step-by-step process. Expecting that all life's issues will suddenly disappear after a couple of sessions, will only lead to disappointment. However, it is realistic to expect that every time you let go of a negative belief system, you make a conclusive change within yourself. A persistent and consistent self-responsible approach to self-change will always bring positive results. Your changes will reveal themselves in the way you feel, in how you behave and will change your perception and how the world and others respond to you.

Your very first goal should be to release the negative issues taken on in your childhood, which is a part of your life right now. Releasing these will transform you substantially and alter how you feel and see yourself, others and your experience of life. Secondly, to let go of potentially restrictive beliefs that are a product of cultural or religious influences. The third level would be existential, but it is unlikely you will be ready for this until you have made substantial transitions in the first two.

The incessant drive to evolve spiritually, mentally and emotionally is an indivisible part of your consciousness. The natural intent to expand our knowledge and awareness are the driving forces behind our curiosity, desire for experimentation, exploration and learning. The all serve to create and manifest our life experiences, as a part of our natural propensity to fulfil the unique potential that exists in every one of us. Using all of your faculties: talents, abilities, creativity, inspirations, intellect, fantasy, imagination and choices and so on, to explore and try something new or challenge the unknown, are natural processes for us. They are the psychological tools we were born with to create and manifest our life experiences which on deeper analyses reveal the characteristics of our sense-of-self. Our consciousness seeks constant stimulation in its quest to know itself and evolve, through the act of creating new experiences for itself. You could say that physical reality is a testing ground for consciousness. The inherent limitations of the environment and the existence of other expressions of consciousness are the challenges to its creative potential and capacity for spiritual growth. In this environment, every act of creation is immediately mirrored back as an experience which is defining of who we believe we are.

Without fear to hold you back, you will attempt challenges you would have previously shied away from, and initiate ideas and concepts you would in the past have dismissed. Your first efforts to create and manifest new concepts and ideas may not immediately bring the results you thought they would because you are always in the process of learning and expanding your consciousness. If your new ideas are a radical departure from convention, they can generate a new set of challenges for your mind, and for those exposed to them. If that were the case in the past, a negative response might have made you critical of yourself and cause you to give up. However now, with a new perception of who you are, you feel confident to step back and examine the result without judgment and criticism, as the self-responsible creator which you are. You will undertake the exploration of outcomes with curiosity and interest and not with self-condemnation that would reflect fear-based expectations. Everything will become a learning experience and an opportunity for personal growth. Once you are well past the fear and insecurity of taking responsibility for your problems and the fears that cause them to be a part of your life, you will want to know what you need to change within yourself to achieve your goals and aspirations.

Your perception will have altered so dramatically that it will seem as if you have entered a different world with different people, while in reality, it is you and not the world that has changed. Letting go of your fears alters the intent of your being, and thereby opens the path towards achieving inner and outer harmony, and this will form the basis from which you will create and manifest your new life. The new dynamic between you and others will transform your experience of them and vice versa. Until now, this way of being may have been foreign to you, and yet it is the path towards clear realisation and enlightenment of your spirit, and to be empowered and authentic in life.

Chapter 23

THE VOICE OF YOUR AUTHENTIC SELF

Others may see your dedication to self-development as an act of selfishness, but you should not allow this criticism to create feelings of guilt in you. Their response comes mostly from the belief that we need to support each other in our pain and suffering, and the expectation that you should put others before yourself. In their eyes, you may seem self-indulgent for only caring about your feelings, issues and problems, and not about theirs or those of others. This judgment frequently comes from passive-aggressive individuals who see themselves as victims. They are people who, because of their belief in their victimhood, feel entitled to be aggressive to get support, help and sympathy. They often hold the view that nobody suffers more than they have, and therefore do not allow their issues and problems to be overlooked or ignored. They may point to the pain and suffering of other but only do so to justify their own. Their belief in their powerlessness, fears and insecurities have become a dominating part of who they believe themselves to be. Their victimhood causes them to develop behaviour with which control their relationships. They will attract friends whose guilt issues validate their own. Depending on the manner in which they acquired their fears and insecurities, they can be pleasers or selfish and demanding. The dynamic in this type of relationship feeds the general notion that we are victims of our environment and others. To one degree or another, they expect others to take responsibility for their issues and problems and often expect to be put them first. Should they be held accountable for their fears and insecurities, they will feel attacked, criticised and judged. If you were the one to do so, you would be judged as not being on their side, and not be their friend for very long.

When we manifest issues that make us feel that we are victims of others and life, our tendency is to expect others or the world around us to change as a solution for the emotional distortions we feel. We disregard our innate capacity as creators, and the reject the responsibility that it carries, by primarily seeking resolution for our emotional imbalance outside of us, by expecting others or the world to change. If the person feels offended by what you say, they will an all likelihood demand that you apologise, regardless of the fact that you have no idea why they feel that way. Their assumption is that others are responsible for how they feel. For example, if you were to say the same thing to someone else, and they may have accepted it for what it is. The offended individual is not taking responsibility for the fears or insecurities that already are a part of their sense-of-self, and which makes them sensitive to being offended about certain matters or subjects. The reality is that no one can know what life issues or fears anyone walks around with and therefore others cannot be responsible for what you feel.

As a result of our desire to manifest, every act of self-expression has the potential to cause feelings that contradict our natural propensity to exist in a state of inner-balance and harmony. Once we give in to the negative feelings created by this, we do not realise that we allow our intent to be dominated by fear.

The truth is that were we to give our propensity for balance, harmony and inner peace absolute priority; we would be on the path of becoming conscious and responsible creators. This state of mind can will us the empowerment to deal with our fears.

Our innate inclination to create and manifest would continue to propel us to challenge the capacity and capability of our being — spiritually, mentally, emotionally, intellectually and physically — to evolve the potential of who and what we are, towards the fulfilment of who we can potentially be.

Our innate desire to grow and expand our sense of being in response to new challenges will always cause us to experience outcomes, which will at times, not match our expectations or intentions.

In that way, every act of creative manifestation — positive or negative, good or bad — can become a new learning experience and an opportunity to move the perceived limits of our potential being to a new level.

This process may appear to contradict our continued quest to exist in balance and harmony with our essence because there is no permanent outcome. The deeper purpose is to prompt us to realise both our fears and the limits they cause us to perceive, as well as the ever-increasing potential of the unique characteristics of our authentic-self. The evolution of our spirit-consciousness is infinite.

As we evolve by transcending our perceived fears, limits or insecurities, we expand the present potential of our consciousness, towards a higher state of being. There are no real limits on what our consciousness can be.

We can only be sure that the path we follow is in congruence with the nature of the essence of our spirit by continuously comparing it to the outcome of our acts of creation and manifestation because ultimately it should parallel the essence of All Consciousness.

We will experience a state of true bliss when our manifestations are in harmonious resonance with our essence and that of All Consciousness.

Realising this for yourself requires you to become aware and introspective of the present nature of your sense-of-self, to know what you need to change. Self-transformation demands you put effort, attention and commitment into your process of change. Superficially it may appear to others, that you are completely self-involved, but nothing is further from the truth. Your search for answers involves others with those you had and maybe still have relationships. They will not necessarily understand that your transformation will not only have a positive impact on you but will also benefit the relationships you have with everyone else in your life. Where in the past you played out issues resulting in conflict, in the future this will no longer be the case. Once you have released the fears at the source of your behaviour, you will automatically stop engaging others in that way. You will no longer be attracted and attract those whose issues that mirror your own. The absence of these fears and their strategies will change the dynamic and may cause those with whom you used to be in conflict, lose interest in you.

True change — changing who you are — is of immediate and profound benefit to everyone with whom you come in touch. First of all, there will be a shift in the energetic state of your being which then alters the nature of your presence and the unspoken dynamic with others. The difference in the emotional charge others experience from you results in changes in the dynamic in your relationships. A transformed sense-of-self will find expression through your behaviour, posture, attitude, and the way you speak. The manner in which your mind and body communicate your every emotion and intention is felt and understood on subconscious levels by others. A higher state of inner-harmony makes a positive contribution to all who come in contact with it but most of all to you.

Those who are dependent on the expression of your issues to be able to play out their fears and insecurities may judge your desire to become empowered, secure and confident as an act judgement and selfishness. Your inner-transformation causes them to see and experience you differently which can be challenging for some. Their interpretation of the new dynamic confronts them with their own emotional issues because you no longer accommodate them. Until you start to work on yourself, it is unlikely that you are aware that your circle of friends are people very much like yourself, and therefore a match for your issues. Your changes will trigger or show up their strategic behaviours and insecurities, which can result in a mutual review of these friendships. Friends who unconsciously rely on you to facilitate the expression of their issues so that they can feel good, safe or justified will feel most confronted by your changes, but this cannot be your responsibility. Once the fears you held that made this possible are not present in you, their behaviour will no longer make you respond in the same way. The truth is that the time has come for them to become introspective and take responsibility for their behaviour, feelings, attitude and intent. All you can do is to support them to overcome their issues, but this is something they must ultimately want to do for themselves. In the end, their negative feelings, thoughts, perceptions, actions and responses, in short, their problems, can only be their responsibility. You can never allow the issues or fears of others to deter your personal growth. It will not serve you, and it will only support them in remaining the way they are.

THE RIGHT TO BE AUTHENTIC

Expressing the belief that you are the creator of your own life experiences can invoke the idea in others that you consider yourself to be a superior, or godlike. They might ridicule you for being under the illusion that you can create something out of nothing. Religious minded individuals might even be offended by the idea, because to them it may seem as if you are blaspheming by saying that you are appropriating power that can only belong to God. Their response is predictable because they come from the belief that they are powerlessness and subject to a greater force. Having chosen to give the responsibility for their lives to an external force of their creation, the idea that they are responsible for all of their life experiences, good or bad, is very confronting. Once you see yourself as being powerless, it is inconceivable that you are the creator of your own experience of reality. Consequently, you are unlikely to accept that you are responsible for everything you manifested.

When pain, suffering and disappointment has been a part of most of your life, the concept of being the originator of your own life appears to be a lie if not ridiculous. The truth of how you are complicit in your own negative life experiences is not always easy to recognise and accept. Once you believe that you are a victim of life, you leave yourself with no way out of your emotional state of helplessness and powerlessness. Choosing to be a powerless victim will potentially condemn you to a repetition of past and present pain and suffering into the future. It is the very reason why understanding your role in the process of manifesting your life is the most significant insight you can attain. Only then can you appreciate the nature and potential of your consciousness in respect to the reality in which you live your existence. What matters is that you learn to understand how and why you create and manifest your individual and our collective reality within the realm of the present capacity of your consciousness. We need to remind ourselves that every unique gift we were born with is a part of the Source from which we originate.

As a manifestation of Universal Consciousness, you can never be more than the source that manifested you, which means that every quality that is a part of it, resides as an unevolved or evolving characteristic within us. Human consciousness is naturally endowed with all the capacities it requires to exist, survive and grow spiritually, mentally, emotionally and physically. These qualities also contain intent and purpose that translates into the drive to express, create, manifest and experience, which together is the process that we call life.

However, that does not mean that you are not responsible for creating your own life. Quite the opposite, human consciousness has been provided with all the resources and capacities to do just that. We can only evolve our consciousness if we take emotional responsibility for the reality we experience. Our mental and emotional faculties and resources are an intrinsic part of us for this very reason. Our life experiences — negative or positive — are our teachers that allow us to accomplish spiritual, mental and emotional growth. We need to learn how to live our own lives to the fullness of our potential while still in harmony with the spiritual essence we share with others. The individual contribution we make to our evolution will then also be a contribution to the harmonious expansion of collective of human consciousness and that of the world. Our learning always begins with us as individuals first and then as a collective consciousness second. When the first changes the other automatically follows.

Earth is home to an incredible variety of life forms from microbes to whales and birds and anything in between, including humans. Unique diversity exists within the same species of life, plants, insects and microscopic lifeforms. Even though it may not occur to us, but there is not a grain of sand on any beach in the whole world completely identical to another, and even every droplet of water on our planet would vary in some way from another. We cannot always recognise the unique differences in everything that exists, but that does not mean it is not so. Our senses are relatively easy to fool, and the sameness and physical consistency that we believe we see in our world is an illusion and hides the unique state of everything in reality. The point is that being unique and different is normal, and being completely identical is more than likely incredibly rare.

The problem we have with acknowledging the individuality or unique nature of others arises from our own belief that our unique and different self is unacceptable and not wanted. When our authentic-self does not match the expectations our parents, we become convinced that the failure lies with us for not being who we are supposed to be. The inner-conflict this creates results in the suppression of much of our authentic being. A child has no choice but to adopt beliefs and behaviours that conform to the parent's expectations. We are not aware that their rejection of our authentic-self makes us also dismiss it, to avoid rejection or abandonment. The belief that we should be someone other than we are and the fear of being our unique self can cause us to reject unique and different qualities in others. If we cannot be different from who we are expected to be, why should they? As a consequence, when we feel confronted with the unique nature of others. We may find that we judge and reject their individuality in the same way our unique self-was treated by our parents. Without realising we may have become part of a generational cycle of suppression and discrimination that is negative for us, as well as others.

The unique nature of our spirit is the one thing that is common to all of us and instead of creating separation through judgement, it should bind us together because each of us is an intrinsic part of Universal Consciousness. It has become a fundamental challenge for each human being — to exist in the absence of fear and to be free to express the capacity and potential of their unique and authentic being. Not just out of fear of being our authentic self but also because of other fear-based beliefs we have taken on in childhood and maturity.

Unconditional acceptance of who you truly are will allow you to accept the true and individual nature of others without fear. You are free to be your authentic self without having to deny others, with the understanding that it is the same for you as it is for others. You will be the determining factor in the creation of your life and take control over your existence once you take ownership of who and what you are. You are meant to be different from everyone else in the world, so celebrate and be proud of the individual nature of your consciousness and its potential, and give it free and unlimited expression.

And while you are at it, help others to learn to celebrate theirs.

BEING AUTHENTIC

The fears that caused us to reject our authentic self in the first place, block us from being unconditional in our expression later in life. We get so hooked on the strategic behaviours that are a product of our fear driven self, that we unwittingly create chaos through the voice of our negative beliefs. Now and then there is a moment in most people's lives where everything seems to fall magically and gracefully into place, and they get a glimpse of what it is like to live life without fear. These times may be momentary, but it is a taste of being the person you know you were always meant to be. We need to record these highlights in our memory because these become new emotional reference points for who we can potentially be as an individual. Our innate yearning to live life in harmony with our essence will always direct us to discover our true nature.

The idea of becoming your authentic self often raises new fears.

If I do not know who my authentic self is:

- How will I know that the person I will become is who I am meant to be?
- Will I like who I am becoming and will others like me?
- Will the person I become be nice or nasty?
- Will the person I become be weak or strong?
- Will others still know who I am?

The answer is that your authentic-self is an intrinsic part of your consciousness and spirit and cannot be lost, disappear, or taken away.

Only you can dismiss your authentic self. You already do this subconsciously, by giving in to the expectations of what others want and expect you to be. The fears and their associated strategic behaviours and negative feelings that you have accepted as a substitute for your unique, authentic self, also serve to suppress it.

Your authentic-self has become foreign to you because you have never felt free to give it expression. All you can remember is being who you believe you are right now even if that does not represent your true nature. The fundamental elements that make up who you are in principle lawyers good and positive. How you feel as your authentic-self is what ultimately matters. Who would not want to feel self-confident, empowered, self-assured, lovable, acceptable, trustworthy and wanted? Those who have unresolved issues of their own may not always feel comfortable with someone like that because they feel challenged by such a presence.

Engaging the process of change by peeling away each layer of fear, will ultimately leave you with the core of your being — your authentic self and its innate potential. There is no need to worry about the nature of your authentic-self because it will be positive in nature and intent. Your original character emerges out of the essence of your spirit and therefore can never be unlovable or unacceptable, bad or inferior. Instead, in its purest form, it exists in the vibration of unconditional love, acceptance and trust, which corresponds to the state of consciousness we all innately seek within ourselves.

Even though you may believe that you have never given your authentic-self free expression, there will be instances where your fears and strategic behaviours fell away. These occurrences where fear was absent allowed aspects of your original self to appear and find expression. You create the opportunity for these events when you do not feel under emotional pressure by your surroundings, fears and insecurities. These small glimpses of inner and outer harmony represent significant examples of the capacity of the authentic nature of your being and potential. In the future, they can serve as inspirational reference points on your journey to release your fears and become who you are truly meant to be.

ESCAPE FROM ILLUSIONS

We all aspire to practice our passions and desires to earn the income we need to exist. In the absence of passions and interests, we often struggle to know what kind of work we want to do. The prospect of a life without direction and a sense of purpose are not motivating or inspiring. For many, not ever knowing their passion feels frustrating and disempowering and can underpin a lifelong sense of dissatisfaction. In the absence of a passionate desire or a dream to fulfil, we often feel there no other choice but to find a job that makes us enough money to survive, and perhaps buy entertainment to occupy our time.

Without a particular focus or direction in life, we may let family tradition and the issues that come with them make the choices for us. It is not unusual for parents who never had the option to pursue their interests when they were children, to dismiss the idea of doing work that is fascinating and compelling for its own sake. The option may not even occur to them, and they will not realise that this attitude can alienate their offspring from their innate potential, talents and abilities. Other criteria concerning status and financial expectations can override what they consider to be folly. A child will usually dismiss its interests and attractions, once its parents convince it that they are justified their invalidation of what it wants and put forward their ideas of what it should be or do. Once they become an adult, they will dismiss their attractions and desires without knowing why, and at the same time feel unable to find anything that stimulates or excites them.

The unconscious and automatic dismissal of their passions and attractions can cause them to pass up opportunities they might have otherwise considered. Many find themselves following in their parent's footsteps often mimicking their career choices as part of a desire to please them and be accepted and validated. By conforming to their parent's expectations, values and standards they may sacrifice the potential of discovering their passions and desires, talents and abilities. Often, they finish up studying for degrees they will never use, or do work that is unfulfilling. The sense of feeling without purpose or direction can lead to an existence of dissatisfaction and an incessant search for something different in life.

When parents show a consistent lack of interest in the needs and expectations of their children, they may feel motivated to follow a career for the power and influence or fame and recognition. The absence of attention and involvement will cause a child to feel both powerless and insignificant. These feelings can cause it to be attracted to acting, public speaking, being an entertainer, becoming a manager, politician or any position where it can experience recognition, adulation, fame, popularity, being the centre of attention, control and power. Their beliefs in their insignificance, powerlessness and being without control determine their choice of career.

If for example, you have been ignored and forgotten and feel that you are of no consequence, the fear of being insignificant, worthless and powerless may drive you to find a position in life that gives you control and makes you the centre of attention. These fears can cause you strive to become an actor or a performer, or perhaps a public figure in the media. Finding a place in the public eye will fulfil your need to find significance by the recognition of others to convince yourself that you are special. You do not see that your need to create this response in others makes you dependent on their recognition and validation. You have effectively given them control over your sense of power, worth and significance. Once you have chosen this strategy, your fear of being powerless, worthless and insignificant will always be with you.

As it waxes and wanes throughout your career, it can drive you to take risks that can overextend your capacity to be in control. Any failure, no matter how small, will intensify your fears and can cause you to become more desperate to maintain or rekindle your success. Constant fear of losing public recognition and adulation will make it easier for you to justify compromising yourself, or to try and find something that will give you reprieve from your anxiety and stress. The only way to get out of this is to resolve these fear-based beliefs at the core. Given that you have the desire and talent to meet the expectations of your career, it will be more likely that you become and stay successful, without negative beliefs controlling your choices and decisions.

Compared to those who are passionate about their work, there are more who have chosen their career to survive because of family influences or because of particular emotional issues they hold. We need to be aware that the emotional issues at the core of each of these choices are in actuality illusions.

You can confuse your search for your passions and fascinations by following needs that portray themselves as intense interests but are a product of negative beliefs. Unknowingly committing yourself to a fear-driven interest can cause you to spend your life chasing a goal that often stays out of reach, or of which the outcome is difficult to maintain, or keeps you failing. The need to achieve often relates to the feeling of having to prove something about yourself to others — to be in control, be successful or to be wealthy and so on. Your real motivation for following this desire is your fear of the consequences should you fail — such as being powerless, being judged to be a failure, inferior, embarrassment, shame, being poor and so on.

The fear of failure and losing control, embarrassment and shame can turn the need to succeed into an obsession. The consequences generated by our negative beliefs give them negative emotional characteristics that make fear, anxiety and stress the dominating forces that propel our behaviour. Fear can convert ambition into a ruthless motivation to succeed at the sacrifice of principles and values. This kind of response has become easily justifiable in present working environments created in society because the importance of the bottom line often outweighs any other considerations. It could be said, that we are expected to be ruthless in business and but have to live by our morals and humanity in our private lives and community. This contradiction can result in inner-conflict when it becomes the central focus in the way we live life, work, do business and conduct our relationships, and our general interaction with the world. How we are expected to be with others, partner, family and children, is not congruent with the attitude and behaviour that we are supposed to show at work. Our commitment to success and recognition can become a justification for making decisions that disregard the effect they have on others so that we will achieve our aim. Superficially it may appear as if we are passionate about our goals, but in actuality, we are trying to fulfil a fear driven need to avoid being and being seen as powerless, weak, failures and poor.

That is not to say that you might not have the ability, talent, desire or interest to be a businessman, an actor, a singer, a leader or a speaker. But, if your innate talents and abilities have become bound up in fears and insecurities, they will distort the manner in which you express them. Your behaviour will become strategic because you will imagine all kinds of negative consequences, should you fail.

As long as your negative beliefs are the central reason for what you want to do in life, the potential outcomes you believe they hold will control you. It may surprise you that the nature of your goals and expectations will often change once you release your fears. Characteristically, when fear is the motivation for your aspirations, the destination will always be more important than the journey. The emphasis of your effort and attention will be on achieving the ultimate state of security, wealth, recognition, power and so on. The step-by-step process of getting there does nothing but frustrate. You cannot wait to get to your goal because in your mind that is the only thing that matters, which makes you resent having to work for every step of your journey.

Your resentment of the process works against you because you cannot commit yourself to the attention to detail each step requires. The chances are that your lack of commitment to each part of your journey to success will add up to failure and stop you from reaching your goal. Each time you fail to apply yourself, the potential for failure will get higher. It should not be surprising that people with this this way of thinking are unlikely to succeed. Rather than savouring the experience that each incremental triumph provides, avoidance of the work it takes to get there will stop them from reaching the pinnacle of their aspirations. Uncovering the deeper reasons for why you want something so badly allows you to discover your fears, and is a good start to get your priorities right. Releasing the original issues at their core may give you access to the full capability of your talents and abilities, and allow you to realise your true passions.

When the journey becomes more important than the goal, interesting things begin to happen in our minds. Every time we are successful in achieving each incremental step, the solutions and learning experiences we expose ourselves to have the power to transform us. These inner-changes will influence our perception and expectations, how we perceive our goals and aspirations, and alter what we ultimately want the end of our journey to be.

LOVE WITHOUT FEAR

Being authentic goes hand in hand with being truthful to yourself in your emotions and the expression of your feelings. You can only achieve emotional sincerity in the absence of fear, self-judgment and guilt and this applies in particular to relationships. In the process of change, you need to acknowledge all of your feelings, good or bad, positive or negative, without judgment. Self-criticism will, first of all, diminish the relationship you have with yourself, and then that with others. Your self-criticism is proof you do not accept who you are. You seek to create evidence by trying to be who you think you need to be, to get the approval and endorsement from others. Your fear that others will see and judge you over what you believe to be your shortcomings and faults will control your responses and reactions. The result will make your behaviour strategic and therefore contrived and because of that, sincerity, truth and spontaneity will be lacking not just in your relationship with yourself, but also with others.

Your relationships with others are subject to your issues and not an expression of unconditional love, acceptance or friendship. Elements based on the fear of being unlovable and unacceptable or unwanted and not being good enough and so on, have crept into your involvement with others and have come to determine who is in your life. Even though you may be in the throes of love and attraction, your fear of rejection, being a failure or inadequate and so on, will influence the way you present yourself and communicate with your prospective partner. You may do your best to present yourself as someone you believe fits the expectations of the person you are attracted to, but in doing so, you are not really yourself. Your fear of the consequences if you were to express as you believe yourself to be, — that you will be judged to be worthless and not good enough— will keep you from having a real relationship, that is sincere and honest, spontaneous and unconditional.

You learned the strategic behaviours and responses that are freely and unconsciously used by you, long before intimate relationships of this kind were even in your imagination. They may have become more sophisticated, but at their core, they are the same as they were in childhood. You do not even realise you are acting out of second nature because your behavioural response to your fears feels normal and natural. With fear in control, your relationship lacks the foundation it needs to make it successful because your issues will rule your thoughts and feelings.

Intimate relationships are in many ways your proving ground for the state of your sense-of-self. Trust issues of any kind concerning love and intimacy, gender or acceptance, will inevitably reveal themselves once you are in a relationship. In a relationship, unconditionally love and acceptance mean to place none or at least, as few conditions as possible on your partner. Until you have dealt with your fears and insecurities concerning love, acceptance and trust, you will find this difficult. To acquire this state, you need to have as little fear as possible concerning giving, receiving love and trusting love. Releasing the fear of expressing your emotions will give you to be the freedom to be sincere, spontaneous and authentic, and will create greater freedom and self-confidence in revealing your emotional self. Your true sense of trust in love is only as strong as the love and acceptance you have for yourself, and there is no alternative to this.

You might think that by being aware that there will always be fears to be resolved and that you have to unblock all your issues before you can start a relationship but this is not true. A relationship can work well even though there may still be parts of your attraction to each other that is attached to fear. The key factor in being in a successful long-term relationship does not only depend on the absence of emotional problems. Certain issues — that cause you to feel passive-powerless or aggressive powerless — will attract abuse or make you abusive in their expression, and these must be released before you embark on a relationship. The reason for this lies in the fact that you will always attract a complementary counterpart of your issues. Once you have released the most paralysing of your issues, it is relatively emotionally safe to make yourself available again, even though your constant alertness is required.

The key quality to look for in a partner is their willingness to accept responsibility for their feelings and behaviour and who they believe themselves to be. They also need to be willing and prepared to search for the causative reasons within themselves. Emotional self-responsibility that excludes self-blame, guilt or fear of confrontation, is the lubricant that will allow you to maintain dialogue in times when issues come to the surface. Emotional self-responsibility will support individual growth and strengthen the love between you.

CONFLICTING NEEDS AND EXPECTATIONS

On the surface, the dynamics of relationships in stress and conflict appear to be very complicated. The main reason for this is not in the actual complexity of it. The habitual patterns of thinking and feeling we have developed over many generations cause us to only pay attention to what we see on the surface. Many centuries of influence have distorted our perception of our consciousness and gradually convinced us that the reality we perceive and experience has nothing to do with who we are. We become completely lost the belief that how and what we do in life is the reason for our life experiences. Hence, we also think that we can find the answers for what goes wrong in life in the same place. In this view, reality exists independent and separate from us by its own set of rules and laws. We have become convinced by the idea that external forces and influences are responsible for our undesirable life-experiences, thereby, most of the time, turning us into victims. This 'program,' which has become the basis for our perception of ourselves in life, is also the reason why relationships are often challenging and problematic. Disagreements and conflict usually result in mutual blaming and therefore find no resolution other than perhaps compromise.

When you are in the middle of a relationship conflict, and you are emotionally overwhelmed by your issues, it is hard to see what is going on. There are fundamental principles that hold true in every relationship whether they are friendships, intimate or in the work place. First of all, all relationships are a dynamic between two people, and that means that both parties are involved and contribute to what is being played out between them. In this respect when there is conflict, there are no innocent parties in a relationship.

Our innate and authentic qualities and our issues or fears, together make up the attraction we have for one another. To grow and evolve, the original self also seeks to connect with its counterpart. Our fear-based-self wants to do the same but brings us into relationships that we experience as troublesome and often conflictual. Should we not resolve our issues, our spiritual and emotional growth becomes stunted. In the act of expressing our negative self, we reveal the complexity of our psyche more clearly than when we are authentic and true to our essence.

Every conflict with others is evidence of an inner-confrontation between our authentic sense-of-self and the fears we have accepted as our substitute for our identity. If it remains unresolved, the contradiction between our negative beliefs and unconditional love and acceptance become an inner-conflict we have to live with every day. The insecurities that each partner holds will feel as if they are real and then can become influential forces in their relationship. Remember that we are at the centre of our own life experiences and do not know that we are different from who we believe we are. We can only change our selves by letting go of who we are not and manifest a new and different experience of life and relationships

Each emotional transformation is an incremental step revealing a new sense of what unconditional love, acceptance and trust represent to you. Its influence in the form of self-esteem and self-trust will gradually become stronger. Once your accumulated changes reach a point where the qualities of the authentic-self outweigh the negative part of your sense-of-self, your positive sense of being will grow exponentially. The ever-increasing presence of your unique, spontaneous and authentic self and power of your life-force will become a natural part of your self-expression. The need to create proof that you are lovable and acceptable to be validated by others will completely vanish. Your unique, authentic self, supported by your essence, will grow in stature and prominence as your fears diminish.

Your transformation also affects the nature of your conscious and subconscious intent and with it, your perception and values, standards and feelings, thoughts and behaviour. Your world cannot be other than a very different place from the one you used to know because the person you have become will be very unlike the person you once were.

Chapter 24

UNCONDITIONAL BEING

Do we have the capacity to create the life we want through our choices or are we destined to live our existence through our fears and insecurities? Is it possible to be so out of touch with the nature and capacity of our spirit-consciousness, that we are blind to the fact that we individually and collectively manifest the reality we experience as life? How have we become convinced that others and our environment determine how free we are in life? If our senses give us proof that we are conscious and alive and the reality of our surroundings, is that no evidence that our interpretation of this experience is real and valid?

Even though you may never have even thought to ask these questions up until now, it should be clear that they are extremely relevant to how your life will unfold for you. If you are to have a life that makes sense of your existence, you need to have them answered. Once you realise that it is just as possible to exist in the illusions created by your beliefs and emotions as it is to be in the reality of your spirit, you have choices of which you were not even aware. We will not realise the influence our inner-identity exercises over every aspect of life until we let go of the negative mental states responsible for this distortion in our perception.

The incredible flexibility of human consciousness and its capacity to adapt allows it to survive in even the most adverse emotional circumstances. Unfortunately, this very same flexibility and adaptive capacity can also lead to self-deception and cause you to live in illusions. Once the mind accepts psychological fears as if they are the same as a threat to your physical survival and responds identically, your consciousness is controlled by illusions. This kind of fear is very different than for instance standing on the very edge of a cliff with the potential to fall. Humanity across the world is subject to this deception which is a product of our survival mechanisms. This psychological vulnerability is not a result of one lifetime of human existence. The indoctrination of fear based ideas and beliefs is a result of countless generations subjected to an ever-increasing level of distorted perception. Initially, these may have been a result of the physical survival instinct triggered by the forces of nature. In other circumstances, because controlling forces and institutions promoted them within various cultures. Once fear gets hold of one individual, and through behaviour and attitude transfer it to others to germinate from one generation to the next. Children under the age of 10 are particularly vulnerable to taking on the fears that adults portray. On a fundamental level, this has created a not always subtle, but extremely persistent fear-based intent that has led humanity away from its natural bond with the essence of its Origin. The further we remove our consciousness from this, the more we begin to view ourselves and therefore others, as being responsible for our fears issues and negative life experiences. Consequently, we cannot help living life, with fear and suspicion. Once enmeshed by these our negative beliefs, we can see no other way, but to depend on our strategies to survive.

Fears and insecurities create a negative dynamic with others and the physical world that takes us into an ever-expanding circle of fear, of distrust and aggression, neediness and guilt. The fear-based expectations and strategies they generate then dominate our lives. The apparently logical and statistically proven official explanations for the ills society, do nothing to reveal the core reason for their existence and do little to improve the emotional well-being of humanity. Instead of providing a clear insight into the nature of our consciousness and life, the conclusions commonly go no further than noting the circumstances and the behaviour of those involved. The solutions offered by society are no more than advice on strategies, the institution of rules or laws are the only means by which to control the individuals who appear to be the source of the problems.

Knowing what is right or wrong with us can be confusing when our issues are welcomed in some environments and judged in others. We celebrate behaviours and activities that serve to build wealth, success or make money for yourself or corporations. Were we to display these in our personal life with others they have the potential to attract criticism and create conflict, thereby confusing who and how we should be in life. The inconsistency with which society judges human behaviours only serves to create confusion in people and in particular in the young.

The real 'battle' that humanity needs to win is not within the physical world but in our minds — that of unconditional love, acceptance and trust in the positive nature of our spirit-consciousness over fear. With fear increasingly becoming the dominant and controlling force in the world, humanity is pushing itself towards a crisis which appears to be one for our physical survival but is really a crisis of consciousness. The strategies and behaviour that come from fear are either justified or condemned or treated as psychological disorders. Many believe that there is no reason to question their behaviour, attitude or feelings if it matches that of the majority of the population.

Using consensus as your frame of reference for what is normal and acceptable is a grave error in judgment when you consider that everyone is subject to their fears and those of others. Statistical consensus has become our point of reference of what is normal and what is not. The analysis of numbers and averages determines our concept of normality, rather than the appreciation of the unique qualities of our consciousness and the core values to which we naturally aspire. We try to define normality by counting commonality, not taking into consideration that the overall state of human consciousness is a product of many thousands of years of progressively distorting influences. The level of misconception we live with is hard to measure because we are at present psychologically so far removed from our highest possible state of being. Without any specific reference points to apply, we cannot trust our perception to determine what that can be. Trapped in a psychological bind, we deny denied ourselves absolute clarity of the actual potential of our consciousness. Our beliefs, distorted by fear are the very reason why we cannot recognise who we have the capacity to be in the first place.

The truth is that because of fear, we all suffer from different levels of distortion in our perception of ourselves and the world. That distortion ultimately translates into pain and suffering on a personal level and collectively.

Once the mind is caught up in these often subtle but commanding negative beliefs, they control how we are in life. Extracting ourselves from their grip can then become extremely difficult because it requires us to question our perception of who we believe we are. Fundamentally, the discovery and subsequently released of our fear-based belief-systems need to lead us to be in harmony with our unique and authentic self and harmony with our essence. We are conflicted because our issues present themselves in such a logical manner, through our interactions with others, that on the surface our interpretation of the experience appears real and valid. We do not question our reality experience because fear deludes us by causing us to feel and think that without engaging in certain actions and behaviours we will not survive. Once caught up in this we do not even realise that we live our lives disconnected from the Essence of our being — unconditional love, acceptance and trust. These are the very elements that form the cord that connects us with our spiritual origins, to each other and All Consciousness.

Unaware of the innate reference points provided by our inner essence, we lack the capacity to discern inner and outer harmony and disharmony. The ability that fear has to dominate our thoughts, feelings and behaviour ensure that we no longer have the clarity to separate the illusionary self from our authentic being. Without these reference points, our consciousness becomes like a ship without a compass and rudder and will lack the direction and focus the awareness of our essence would furnish. Instead, fear readily becomes the driving force that will control our self-expression, choices and destination in life.

You may think that making superficially different choices or developing new strategic behaviours will help you to step out of this illusionary psychological framework, but that is not so. Your strategies may be temporarily successful and get you the result you hope for, but you will still be the same. Only changing your sense-of-self will produce a change in the perception of who you are.

Remember that changing the thought and not the thinker, the doing but not the doer and the strategy but not the strategist, will ultimately NOT work. By relying on this approach to life, you will always surrender control and power to others. Like everyone else, you are functioning on the illusion that by influencing or changing people and the material world, you are dealing with your issues. None of what you have done would have addressed the core reasons why a negative situation arose in your life in the first place. By not confronting the creator of these events — which is you and your negative belief systems in your sense of yourself — you set the stage to repeat your past issues in the future.

The distortions that we live with may appear subtle, but the consequences they have for our consciousness are certainly not. Every time you do not accept responsibility for your life, you disempower yourself in some way and thereby give fear validity and justification. It adds to a further separation from being in harmony with the spiritual essence of our being as is presently manifested by collective human consciousness. Instead of being in a state of personal empowerment, our state of consciousness moves us to that of victimhood, powerlessness and aggression. From being self-responsible to blaming others and feelings of guilt.

As long as we are conscious beings, we will incessantly create. We cannot ever stop manifesting our reality whether our belief systems support or contradict our essence. It is not something you can ever stop doing or even apply selectively— you have no choice in this. You cannot choose not to choose. Therefore, life, as you experience it, will always remain your responsibility.

We are clever at manufacturing justification, reasons and causes for our ills to escape responsibility for our choices but do not realise that we disempower ourselves in doing so. The mechanism by which we have come to experience life is the opposite of what we think it is — instead of others and the world doing it to us; we are doing it to ourselves.

Conscious living begins by becoming aware of your behaviour, emotional responses, thoughts and feelings. In the beginning, it is a process of continued questioning of every part of your self-expression as if you have a mini-me sitting on your shoulder, watching your every thought, feeling reaction and response. Objectively observing and questioning yourself can reveal many negative facets in your behaviour, attitude and needs.

Developing a clear understanding of any negative belief systems that run your life is an essential step in becoming conscious in life. Arriving at the determination that you have had enough of being subject to a particular issue does not make the causes disappear, but you can use it as a starting point. Similarly, the core reasons for your problems will not magically reveal themselves. The connections between a negative experience and the beliefs that created them can initially be obscure and difficult to recognise. You need to become conscious of every emotional step your mind goes through that leads to a behaviour or/and action, a choice and feeling. Developing self-awareness is the journey your consciousness needs to take to sophisticate your mind. Any detail you uncover will contribute to your understanding of your sense-of-self and empower you to change.

If you have never questioned your behaviour, feelings and nature before, you could find this extremely challenging. But, if you can accept that blaming others and the world for your emotional experience of life will never permanently change anything, you will realise that you have no other choice. You will be amazed what there is to learn about yourself and others by becoming conscious of the difference between who you believe you are and your authentic self. Patient exploration of the reasons for any behaviour and feelings associated with negative events through self-interrogation and self-reflection will bring insightful results. Persistence will always pay off as long as you apply the principles described in earlier chapters.

YOUR EVOLUTION

Media in all its forms ensures that you will always hear or read about some terrible event and experience people go through. In observation, the reasons or causes for these disasters are often difficult to explain because each one of us is the creator of their reality. Without comprehension of the individual causes and reasons why someone may be part of a horrific event, can make hard to understand and accept. As an outsider, we can therefore not explain the reasons why awful things happen to people of all ages and walks of life anywhere in our world. Violent death through war, hunger, poverty, disaster and illness are just a few scourges that can cause unimaginable suffering. The presence of all manner of pain and suffering in the world is not accidental or bad luck. Individually and as a national and international collective, we are all creative and active contributors to what happens in the world. Our personal and collective fears, distrust and greed, are the core contributors to these manifestations on our planet. Understanding the nature and capacity of humanity's collective mind and that of Universal Consciousness is still a new frontier in our journey into consciousness. At this time, there is no doubt that we create our life experience not just on a personal level but also as a collective, and that this propagates to all levels of our existence. If one can recognise that fear of all kinds is at the root of these miseries, then the absence of fear in each can transform this universally.

Our understanding of human consciousness is still limited. Science is still not sure where 'the awareness of being' resides, let alone its capacity, origin and nature. We are a long way away from understanding the way all consciousness is interconnected. The lack of an official understanding of what it is and how it functions handicaps us as individuals in developing awareness of the nature of our being and recognising what having issues is all about. Even if we had an insight into our consciousness, we would not necessarily know the emotional state of mind of that of someone else. Explaining the reasons why someone loses their life in a tragic event is difficult when you do not know the exact and intimate emotional nature of their thoughts and intent of their belief systems. Science is on a constant quest to understand the universe and beyond— including human consciousness as discoveries in quantum physics and astronomy show. What they find raises more questions about the nature of consciousness and reality than they can presently furnish answers.

It is reasonable to assume that the nature of reality and consciousness are interrelated and interdependent, even though from our perspective, physical matter and life appear very different and separate from thought and intent.

However, the concept that their dynamic relationship binds them together in a web of inter-connective consciousness is far from new.

To recognise what is real and what is not depends on our clarity of perception and so the question arises how we are to achieve that. The evidence is that our inner-identity, represented by the beliefs we hold to be true, determine our perception because it influences our interpretation of what we experience. The same process also applies to our concepts, ideas or facts as well as the physical world. We struggle with this because just like we have learned to believe that our emotional issues are caused by what is outside of us, we also are convinced that the experience we have of something is solely determined by the presence of the object and not by us. We do not realise that our memories and the beliefs that we hold as a consequence colour what we see and feel in respect to which we expose ourselves. The ultimate truth is that 'it' all begins with you. 'It' is about us living a life in harmony with the authentic nature of our being and allowing acts of creative manifestation to expand the nature of our consciousness.

We need to remind ourselves that we are aware energy clothed in flesh and that our physicality is a disposable part of our being. Life and death are nothing but transitional phases for our spirit-consciousness. Existence in material reality puts us in physical bodies to have an intense and focused creative experience of our being, by manifesting who we are in physical reality. In being physical in a material reality, we have a tangible experience of what is created by our intent — consciously or subconsciously. Our experience of reality is then a mirror of who we are. If we are open to it, this will allow us to recognise the nature of the intent within our beliefs through what we create and manifest. You will be disappointed if you make the mistake of believing that there are exceptions to this. Anytime you exclude the essence of your being — unconditional love and acceptance — from your life, your consciousness will create from fear, and this will mirror your life-experiences.

We are all on a personal journey to evolve our being but how we walk this path will always be our choice. What we experience on our quest for personal development is therefore also always our responsibility. Our relationships with others play a definitive part in our self-education. We subconsciously choose relationships that present us with emotional conflict because they provide us with the opportunity to recognise unresolved issues. Each party brings their reasons for being with each other, even though this will create the issues and potential conflict. However, the underlying and innate intent to evolve our consciousness by finding resolution within themselves is always consistent.

Growth and change in a relationship are easier if both parties can address their contribution to a negative dynamic in a framework of self-responsibility and without blame or criticism. This dynamic between one another can take a relationship to another level of intimacy and understanding.

In the spirit of the idea that 'what we teach we need to learn', we need to be aware that we all have something significant to share with others. Each of us has an innate responsibility to help and lift others to higher levels of awareness and resolution thereby supporting the fulfilment of their potential and interestingly enough, our own. Assisting the growth and expansion of another consciousness without taking control over their life choices, and without sacrificing your own, brings benefit to all consciousness. However, the influence of fear can make us selfish and therefore insensitive to this. If we do not allow ourselves to receive this gift from others, it will be because we harbour reasons for wanting to prove that we do not need any help or support or are right and perfect. Our destiny is to know how to create and manifest our existence in the absence of fear and complete awareness of consequence to our self, others and the world.

FEARLESS SELF-QUESTIONING

Even though the process of creating our reality-experience is real and tangible, the reasons and causes for we manifest can be invisible to our senses because it so is interwoven in our life experiences. We need to change who we believe we are before we can integrate a new perception into our life. Our greatest learning is in our understanding of how our consciousness affects others through the dynamic that our sense-of-self creates. As we gradually grow from within, we will see how each consciousness is intermeshed with all others to create the fabric of world consciousness that we individually and collectively experience. The concepts in this book represent an understanding of a small corner of spiritual-consciousness, the actual capacity of which is beyond our current comprehension.

Knowledge of the nature of your issues and fears and how and what it manifests in your life gives you the power to change it. You become a mindful creator when you take ownership of your issues by being self-responsible, and cease to be a victim of others and your surroundings. Your life is a product of your choices, which means: You can choose not to do anything and live your life with your issues and suffer the consequences. Or, you choose to confront, accept and release you fear-based beliefs, and thereby transform your sense-of-self. How you want to experience your life is and always will be your choice.

If you choose to change, you need to keep track of every part of your involvement in any negative experience for you to understand how it came to be a part of your life. From there on, whenever something negative has happened, you have to ask yourself how and why you played a part in it.

Always hold yourself accountable and be responsible for your part in it by asking:

- What did I say or do and why did I say or do it?
- What was the intent behind my behaviour and what was my behaviour primarily trying to achieve?
- What did I feel before, during and after the event — Was I anticipating a negative response or confrontation? Was I afraid, angry or offended, embarrassed or ashamed, powerless or in guilt and so on, and if so why?
- When was the first time I had these feelings, thoughts or behaviours? What caused them and why were they triggered now?
- What is it about the present circumstances or the people involved that create this emotional effect in me?
- Who was involved and what do you see is their part in the incident?

These are just some of the questions that you could ask yourself, but there are always more. Keeping notes is a good way of measuring your progress and perhaps mark the changes in your understanding of yourself and others.

YOUR AUTHENTIC TRUTH

You will find that the first ten years of your childhood hold the core reasons for all, if not most, of the negative beliefs you hold. All of these beliefs represent different levels fears, defined by powerlessness or helplessness. Your experience of your childhood has become your conviction of who you are. You need to work with your version of the truth regardless of what other explanations may exist. Even though others in your family including parents and siblings may have a different or even contradictory understanding of your life experiences, it is the version you accepted that counts. The only way to find answers that are meaningful and specific to your issues is by recognising how you experienced your relationship with your mother, father and siblings. It is the only 'truth' that will explain the negative beliefs you have acquired. You will see that each of your siblings and your parents has had a different experience and will, therefore, see events from their unique perspective. The effect their childhood had on them and how it formed their sense-of-self will not necessarily parallel yours. Therefore, your issues may be similar but not be necessarily identical to theirs. Each member of your family is unique from one another which is probably more visible through the differences in their behaviours.

Your understanding of the unique nature of your belief-systems — negative or positive — is essential to your process of change. In early childhood, your particular interpretation of events was the defining force that determined the nature of the belief systems accepted by you as the truth of who you are. In your quest to find a resolution for your fears, the interpretation you naïvely gave to your emotional experiences is the only truth that is relevant, regardless of what others believe.

Each family member will have their take on events through the lens created by their issues, and while they are worth listening to, you need to be aware that no one can be truly objective, including yourself. Your primary goal is to have a non-judgemental understanding of the effects the emotional paradigm of your family had on your sense-of-self. You should always consider and respect the opinions of your family members even if their view does not agree with yours. You are the only one who can validate or dismiss what you believe to be your truth. Once you conceptually understand how you came to accept your negative beliefs, you need to put these into a belief system structure to release them. The words that ultimately make up these negative beliefs must reflect the interpretation you gave it as a child. To ensure that these statements are an effective means for releasing your fears, they need to contain intent, cause, context and consequence. Try and imagine and feel what it would have been like for you to your parent's fears and insecurities. How and why they spoke to you, whether they were present or disconnected, interested or ignored you, etc., are all dynamics that will have influenced who you believe you are now. Use what you discover to get a better insight into the way you hold your beliefs about yourself.

Our unique nature ensures that the dynamic between our parents and us is different from that of our siblings, and this means that our version of events will not be the same. Being as accurate as possible is very important if you want to be sure that the negative beliefs and how they are structured represent the core of your issues. Just keep in mind that the beliefs-systems and their structure reflect that they are fear based. Once you place cause, intent, context and consequence in one negative belief, it can help you to realise other associated with it. In this way, you can unravel the emotions, feelings, thoughts and behaviours in different contexts but related to the same issue.

If for instance, you were criticised when a child, you are likely to be critical of yourself but liable to be critical of others. Your exposure to this will cause you to find fault with yourself and perhaps others. Often in hindsight, you may be angry with yourself for not being, doing or saying what you believe you should have. You are likely to feel and think that you are not good enough, inferior or inadequate and do not meet expectations. When it comes to expressing your opinions, thoughts, desires or choices, you find yourself getting anxious and fearful because you are always in anticipation of judgement and rejection. What you discover about yourself can be somewhat confronting, and may at times feel reluctant to accept that you are causing your problems. However, knowing your issues and understanding what makes them have so much power over you, puts you in control, and gives you the opportunity to change them. Just remind yourself that no matter what the source for your issues looks like, they are not representative of who you truly are — your authentic self.

In the beginning, it may not be easy to deal with what you will see as the negative 'truth' about yourself, but persistence and being honest with yourself will pay off. Habitual thinking patterns can cause you to go back to the idea that the reasons for your issues are outside of you when they are not. Your misperception would prevent you from recognising the real answers even though they may be right in front of you.

For some, it is almost impossible to find fault with their parents, even though they have all manner of issues in life and relationships. The lack of definite evidence can make self-examination more difficult because it means that the in spite of the issues you undoubtedly have, you cannot relate them back to anything in your childhood. In families where the parents are relatively passive, well intended, often non-confrontational and without extremes of expression, the issues are obscure because there are no emotional peaks to highlight them. Always remember that you were not born with a negative sense-of-self or behavioural strategies. The key is to find greater objectivity when looking at the personalities of your mother and father, and their behaviour. Also, you may subconsciously justify many of their unacceptable traits, to avoid being critical and judgemental of them.

In your search for personal truth, there can be no place for an ego mentality that needs to prove itself right or wrong, or for criticism or judgment. Neither is misplaced responsibility in the form of guilt. The resolution of your issues through the release of fear, and thereby building a new and harmonious relationship with yourself, is all that matters. Your reward is the continual growth of your spirit mind towards its original destination and thereby manifesting a rewarding life. Discard nothing of what you discover because every bit of information will eventually add up to an answer to an unresolved question. Everything you find out about yourself has significance, purpose and meaning and will ultimately lead to an explanation as to why your life the way it is.

Self-discovery can be like collecting the pieces of a puzzle that appear to have to have something to do with an issue but do not seem to fit. Sometimes it only makes sense when you get the final pieces, and every detail magically comes together to create an answer that is relevant. Trusting that every bit of knowledge is significant in your process of becoming aware, even though its significance may not be immediately apparent to you. From the beginning of your life, your mind has stored the memory of every beat of your heart and every breath you have taken, and naturally every childhood experience you have ever had. At the start of your journey into your consciousness, it may take time for the necessary information to come to your awareness, but this will become easier as your knowledge grows.

UNNATURAL BEHAVIOUR

Your behaviour is a perfect place to begin looking for clues for how you influence the creation of your world. How you behave in situations that are challenging for you is a usually a tell-tale sign of the underlying fears you hold.

Once you begin to pay attention to these feelings and associated behaviours, you will recognise that you have difficulty exercising control over your responses to certain situations and people. Your aversion or avoidance, aggression or criticism, anger or resentment in response to the behaviour or attitude of others or particular situations, actually says much more about you than it does about them.

Behaviours and attitudes that seek to prove a point or demean others, — is abrupt or aggressive, — superior, over-entitled and dismissive of others, — is excessively pleasing and accommodating, — draw attention or vies for acknowledgement and approval are all out of balance and expose the presence of issues. Behaving in a dominating and controlling fashion is not an asset but an issue because it is a product of fear. Suppressing our spontaneity to avoiding conflict, blame or guilt, because we are in fear of upsetting others is not an admirable trait but an emotional issue.

When fear controls our behaviour, there is nothing natural about the way we interact with others. Everything we do and say is likely to have an agenda of sorts. By attracting and being attracted to those who's our issues fit in with our fears we keep on recreating the relationships we had with our parents. Our behaviour parallels the way we related to our parents and causes us to continue our childhood into adulthood. This return to childhood creates an emotional familiarity that gives our actions, responses, feelings, and thoughts a sense of normality. Our behaviour and is a big part of the outer façade that we subconsciously depend on to overcome our negative beliefs or fears. We also think that because they feel so much a part of who we are that they also represent our real nature or personality. Most of the time you are not even aware that you are trying to fool yourself and others that you are someone other than who you believe you are.

Without your fears and in unconditional love acceptance and trust with yourself and others, your presence would adopt behaviours that would honestly and sincerely allow others to see who you genuinely are. You may have had moments in your life when you felt safe to be yourself and display your true self. If you have, then imagine these moments to be your enduring state of mind and self-expression. The absence of fears and insecurities creates an ease of being that will open the doors to life's experiences and sensations without placing conditions on the experience itself, and thereby limiting and distorting your involvement and participation.

GENERATIONAL TRANSFERENCE

The effect the 'emotional DNA' of your parents has on your sense-of-yourself is as significant as the physical DNA they passed on to form your body. Their fears in the form of issues and insecurities will have played a deterministic role in the formation of your sense of self. Should they have been fearful of making decisions and choices, be overprotective or controlling, critical and judgemental, distrusting or fearful, anxious or stressed and so on, it will impact your sense-of-self. Your experience of them will determine how you are in life and what you will manifest as a life experience. It is inevitable, and you should not doubt it. The question you should ask yourself is not whether your parent's issues had a negative effect on you. The real question is: In what way did their fears influence my belief of who I am?

The dynamic of relationships dictates that the behaviour of one parent will complement that of the other and this makes the effect they will have on a child inescapable. Often, because their issues are interrelated, they often share the same core fears for their behaviours. Usually, one parent will present an aggressive, controlling behavioural profile and the other passive and powerless. Together, they will create the family paradigm to which they subject their offspring. When a relationship is new, different and often opposite behaviour is often viewed as an asset rather than a problem, thereby creating the illusion that they are the perfect match. The complementary nature of their contrasting behavioural styles and attitude forms a significant part of the fascination and attraction they have for each other. For example, if one partner is controlling and dominating, and the other feels insecure and fearful. If one believes they are uninteresting and insignificant, and the other needs to be the centre of attention and charismatic, etc. Together with physical attraction, these behavioural patterns create the impression that one partner will fulfil the needs and expectation of the other, adding to the desire to get involved with each other. What they both will not see is that a significant part of their attraction for each other has its roots in fear.

NOT BECOMING YOUR PARENTS

At an early age, our consciousness absorbs all impressions that come via the senses of the mind and the body. These sensations are at first new but always referenced by the innate expectation to be unconditionally loved, wanted, accepted and trusted. When a child is required to meet conditions to receive love and be accepted, it provokes the feeling that it will be rejected or abandoned should it fail and this we call fear. Once parents establish these conditions with their child, it feels that the potential for exclusion, abandonment or rejection is ever present. The beliefs it then forms and the alternative behaviour it takes on inspired by fear, are a protective measure to avoid abandonment, rejection and exclusion. Whenever anyone acts out of fear, they do so with the intent to create conditions that secure their emotional safety. By the time adulthood is reached they will unconsciously place these same terms on others to avoid realising their fears. In doing so, they are likely to parent their children in the way their parents raised them. Unfortunately, we are all guilty of this in one way or another.

If your parents harbour fears of being emotionally present they are likely to have difficulty showing or expressing, giving and receiving love and affection, as well as other emotions by which they feel confronted. You will leave your home environment with similar fears that will turn you into an emotionally inhibited individual, or potentially excessively expressive.

Your parent's issue with the expression of love and affection will leave you to believe that you are not lovable and acceptable and this is very likely to make you needy for love and affection. Your yearning to feel love and acceptance can make you very needy of your partner or if unfulfilling, look to your children as a source for your need to be loved. Either behaviour will distort the relationship with them and creates conditions concerning your love and acceptance of them.

The need to feel loved and wanted can also result in anger because of the powerlessness you experienced by being denied by your parents. This anger may be directed at your partner when he or she does not fulfil your expectations. You can also make your children the target for your frustration because they naïvely demand from you what you never received — unconditional love and acceptance. There are many different dynamics and scenarios possible in the emotional dynamic between you and your partner and children. We need to realise that these fears and complementary behaviours do not disappear the day you become a parent. Their presence in your sense-of-yourself ensures that you will unconsciously express them in your parenting.

Parents who use aggressive or passive behaviour to control their children by always telling them what to choose, think or do, can make them become fearful of doing this independently and prevent them from developing self-confidence. By teaching their children that they cannot trust in themselves or depend on their judgment, choices and resilience, making them mentally and emotionally dependent on others. The parent's attitude usually comes from their fear of having to confront difficulties, failure, problems or aggression. Their insecurities are likely to make them overprotective, fearful and controlling of their children. Regardless of their good intentions, their offspring will adopt these fears as their own and become afraid of life, decisions and confrontation and so on, just like they are. Without having trust and confidence in their mental and emotional capacities and resources, they will constantly need validation and support from others before they do or choose anything. They will live in a constant state of powerlessness and vulnerability because being overprotected made them convinced them that they are powerless, fragile and vulnerable in an aggressive and untrustworthy world. The caring, protective nature of the parent's behaviour hides that they act out of fear and insecurity, which is a product of their sense of vulnerability and powerlessness. They create the same lack of trust in self-worth and confidence in their capacities and power that they grew up, with in their children.

In most family dynamics, to one degree or another, one parent will be the aggressive-powerless victim while the other is the passive-powerless victim. Otherwise, their personalities could not co-exist. The children will be made powerless in some way by both parents — generally through intimidating aggression by one parent and the guilt created by the other. Children subjected to this dynamic may adopt one or two behavioural scenarios. The main point to be made here is that as a product of this kind of environment, you will have to contend with negative beliefs. Many of these issues will become visible when you have children, and the demands of parenting take your role in life into an entirely new direction. There will be demands on you that you are not prepared for, and for which there is no formal training. What follows is a potential scenario for you to ponder.

An aggressively controlling parent tends to choose and decide for the children and set the standards and values of behaviour in the family. They are also likely to be critical and judgemental of their offspring. Their attitude, reactions and responses will adversely affect the sense power and self-trust their children will develop. The parent's distrust in their choices and decisions will cause them to doubt in their thinking, reasoning and judgement. Their insecurity can result in their child becoming fearful of making choices and decisions independently and as adults, being independent. They will not develop trust in the personal power, resources and abilities with which they were born. Instead, their fear of the potential of negative consequences and failure will make them try and avoid any situation where they are expected to make critical decisions or confront a situation where failure is a risk. Entering a cycle of avoidance and indecisiveness will result in constant procrastination. In the belief that they cannot trust themselves to know the right decision to make, they become dependent on others for support and advice.

Alternatively, a child's intense fear of making bad decisions can trigger the need to prove and convince others that it can make its own choices. This act of rebellion will usually result in conflict and confrontation with the dominant or controlling parent, who feels challenged and criticised. However, the child will try to be in control and empowered by emulating the behavioural patterns of the dominant, controlling parent. The child assumes that being this way gives it power and control as demonstrated by the parent who is trying to control it. This need to prove they are right, know better and more does not stop when they become parents, and so the outcome for their children will be predictable.

Even though both the aggressively behaving child and the passive child have similar issues, they are judged and treated differently because of their diverging behaviours. Parents commonly see the passive child as desirable because of its tendency to comply and accommodate and the aggressive child as being problematic, obstinate and unacceptable. The parents do not realise that their child's response is a result of the way it experiences their behaviour and attitude. Children exposed to this take on a sense-of-self that makes them believe and feel that they are powerless and have no control, as well as feeling guilty for needing and wanting their innate needs and expectations met. The strategic behaviours each child employs are their way maintaining the emotional link with their parents without whom they feel they cannot exist. Feeling vulnerable and powerless, they protect themselves from rejection and abandonment by being strategic in their responses and reactions. Both of these children feel that they are victims of the emotional dynamic in their family. One believes it has to wait for permission and approval to do and have what it wants and how it should be present. The other tries to achieve the same outcome by using aggression to challenge, what it feels is rejection by the parents and try and be proactively independent. Each child will choose to emulate the attitude and behaviour of either the passive or aggressive parent for its emotional survival, depending on which it feels safest. Commonly, the dominating parent will be at loggerheads with the aggressive child and will be more attracted to be in a relationship with the compliant one. The passive child, often through its feelings of guilt, is likely to be closer to the passive parent, who is powerless and fears confrontation, criticism and blamed, all of which it will eventually inherit.

Children who grow up in this kind of environment may already be showing their strategic behaviour at school in the form of bullying, or by being the victim of it.

Potentially, the aggressive sibling may become the bully who needs to push others around to feel powerful and in control. Unconsciously, they will seek passive, powerless children to dominate to deal with their fear of being powerless. Both victims and aggressors are likely to come from similar psychological, emotional environments, where they are either aggressively or passively disempowered — through intimidation, aggression and control or guilt, victimhood and powerlessness. However, most intimidating and dominating personalities do not welcome confronted and held accountable. When made responsible for the actions and choices they will often default to their fundamental issues of powerlessness, and start to behave and act as if they are the victims of others, instead of the other way around.

A dysfunctional family paradigm does not necessarily have to be physically or emotionally aggressive, or abusive. Any emotional environment that is in some way consistently oppressive and controlling will have a disempowering effect on the development of a child's sense-of-itself. Parents who create guilt, use passive criticism or have a passive victim attitude, are just as much a negative emotional influence on the mind of a naïve child as parents with aggressive, controlling and intimidating behaviour. Regardless, whether subjected to aggression or the blame that creates guilt, it will always assume that somehow, it must be responsible. Any form of suppression or guilt will educate a child into learning negative strategic behaviours that will both be harmful to itself, and others.

For children, growing up with parents who are physically present but do not have the capacity to give and receive unconditional love, acceptance, trust and cannot connect emotionally, feels like being abandoned on a daily basis. This kind of emotional environment has deep-seated consequences for the emotional development of children. Children are still trying to discover who they are through the dynamic with their parents. The absence of emotional interaction leaves a child guessing whether it is lovable or not, acceptable or not, trusted and wanted or not, and so on. Parents are expected to make a child feel unconditionally lovable, wanted and acceptable through loving and affectionate behaviour and attitude that is unconditional. A child needs to have these values mirrored by its parent's behaviour and attitude to have them affirmed. When it experiences a consistent lack of validation of its innate expectations that it is unconditionally lovable and acceptable, it becomes doubtful and insecure about its worth, value and significance. In the absence of receiving the emotional signals that would endorse that it is unconditionally lovable, acceptable, wanted and trusted, it will feel that its authentic and unique self is not wanted and rejected.

Communication in such a family tends to be impersonal and only concerns itself with the generalities of physical life, such as day to day physical needs and concerns. Everyone learns to avoid any direct reference to each other's emotions, issues or personal opinions. Exposing others to emotions or feelings that confront or do not fit in with expectations, particularly in a direct personal context, is usually taboo. Directly holding one another emotionally accountable and responsible for any conflict is likely to be judged as unacceptable and will get a negative response. These subliminal rules are learned very early in life through the way the parents respond, behave and react to you in childhood in response to your spontaneous self-expression.

However, the process of living life will always manifest what we fear, and so frequently a family with these issues will often produce at least one sibling whose perception and behaviour contradicts the prevailing family paradigm. The presence of an emotionally expressive child is confronting for those who live by the unspoken rules of emotional suppression, and this can result in favouritism and conflict. The majority have learned not only to suppress their emotional expectations, such as the desire for closeness, affection, love and a host of other feelings but also in engaging with those of others. Their fear of being emotionally present and expressive, and responding to the emotional needs of others causes such parents to employ behaviours and responses designed to discourage this, if not make it wrong. Being dutiful, being physically caring such as providing, cooking or the giving of gifts, are often used as poor substitutes for an emotional exchange of love, affection, closeness, intimacy, interest and involvement with their children.

Censorship of your unique and authentic self, dismissal of your spontaneous creative potential and suppressing your thoughts, feelings and emotional truth, will have a devastating effect on every aspect of your life. To protect yourself from being responsible for upsetting or offending others, you will censor yourself by putting everything you say through an emotional filter to avoid upsetting others. Every response and reaction will be automatically strategized and kill any spontaneous expression including your emotional truth.

You are likely to choose relationships that repeat your childhood experience. You will feel an attraction for personalities that are emotionally unavailable, and find it difficult to be present and involved. They are attracted to you because you learned not to have this expectation from others and so because of that you will never emotionally confront them or make demands because you are afraid to be guilty for upsetting them. In the long term, this kind of relationship will probably not satisfy you, but your fears may keep you there for a long time.

Alternatively, you may choose a relationship where the potential for confrontation and guilt concerning emotional expression is minimal because your partner has similar issues to your own. You may not realise that a relationship like this is like an unspoken contract where each promises the other never to make any emotional demands or confront. Unfortunately, this often includes the sincere expression of love and affection. Essentially, your issues in relationships are a mirror of the family paradigm in which you grew up.

To live consciously means becoming aware of every emotional element in your life that acts as a restriction, suppress you and stops you being who you truly are. It also means becoming aware of who you truly are, your capacities, gifts and individual powers. You can only make choices with the awareness of the consequences if you recognise the nature of your limiting beliefs and the potential of your unique and authentic self. Making choices and decisions in the knowledge of consequences — positive or negative — is the way you can begin to assume control over your life. Awareness of your negative beliefs is the first step towards releasing them to transform your sense-of-self and your life. Discovering and becoming aware and accepting your authentic self and its unique nature will take you to a new life experience.

YOUR REALITY IS YOU

Your experience of reality is a representation and reflection of who you believe yourself to be — your sense-of-self — good or bad. By now you may realise that getting to know yourself in depth is a process and requires commitment and consistency.

There are four distinct levels at which we can sense our being:

- The essence of our spirit: Defined by the core values of unconditional love, acceptance and trust which together with our innate drive to express, create and manifest the nature of our being — our authentic self — creates our experience of ourselves in the reality that we call life. We actualize our experience of reality through an incessant stream of decisions and choices that we make to emotionally and physically survive and evolve. Our acts of manifestation create the sensation that is 'being conscious and alive' which allows us to recognise the nature of our sense-of-being or who we believe we are.
- Our unique and authentic self – The person we truly are and which is an intrinsic and defining part of our consciousness – represented by qualities, potentials and gifts that define the potential of our consciousness, our innate talents and abilities.

The fear driven behaviours of our parents will challenge and reject our original, naïve but spontaneous and creative being. Their invalidation of our authentic self will ultimately cause us to suppress it ourselves subconsciously.

- Our subconscious sense of who we believe we are — This part of the self is our inner-identity, made up of all previous fundamental elements with the addition of positive beliefs or fear-based beliefs with their strategic programs. Prompted by our innate desire to be loved, wanted, accepted, trusted, independent, learn, experience, sense and so on we unconsciously express all of our beliefs systems — negative or positive through our behaviour, feelings, thoughts and perception, and so on. The beliefs that define who we believe ourselves to be, whether rooted in unconditional love, acceptance and trust or the conditional beliefs that create fear rule our self-expression. When they are negative, they will manifest our fears, insecurities, our sense of powerlessness and vulnerabilities.

- Our conscious sense-of-self – the ego-self or how we consciously label who we are or want to be known –We often call this part of ourselves our personality. It can hold any belief or conviction that defines us for ourselves and who we are to others or the world in general. Some of the belief systems we hold are superficial and commonly reflect our desire of how we want to be seen by ourselves and by others. Functioning on this level, we may be aware of certain fears and insecurities that directly relate to the emotional dynamic with of others or events, but the source and therefore the fundamental reasons for these negative experiences usually escapes us. At this level of our perceived identity, we respond to feelings and emotions that reflect beliefs that are either in or out of harmony with our essence. We then experience the product of our fears through the anger and powerlessness, anxiety and stress, and pessimistic thoughts and ideas and so on. WE react by drawing on our learned strategic behaviours to emotionally and mentally survive. Our conscious self is also the place where we can experience the outcome of our positive and harmonious beliefs. This part of our consciousness also allows us to present an identity to the world through our behaviour and attitude that we believe will make us loved, acceptable, wanted, special, respected, significant, and so on, to others. Or, give us the appearance of victims by showing ourselves to others as powerless, helpless, worthless and insignificant, etc.

Out of all of the different layers of consciousness that make up your sense-of-self, the self you are most aware of and is best known to others is your conscious ego-self, which is the origin of your emotions, strategic behaviour and attitude are the emotional face you present to the world. The stories you create for the benefit of yourself in your relationships with others, allows you to hide the fears you hold, and to convince yourself that others see you in the light you want to see yourself.

The perception you have learned to accept and believe to be true becomes your default and can keep you blind to the actual reality of what your authentic-self. The distractions created by your ego-self can cause you to remain unaware of the deeper, negative intents that drive your emotions and strategic behaviours. Your vision of life and the world will on the surface appear to be logical and clear, but taking into consideration that your fears distort your perception of reality, it will not be what you think or believe it is. The concept of love, acceptance and trust that you currently hold to be true is formed exactly in this way. Although you may think that you know what love is, your understanding is likely to be highly distorted because of the fear-based beliefs you hold. The accepted idea of normality you may share with others can make it very difficult to see and recognise, that you are not functioning from unconditional love and acceptance. Unless you realise that you are the central figure in all of your life experiences, you will not recognise that you must be the problem and therefore responsible. Until then, you will probably avoid being accountable and responsible for the problems and failures in your life and relationships.

It is important to acknowledge that when you enter a relationship that you are the one choosing your partner and that you agree to date them and become intimate with them. If you want to understand why you are in a relationship that is happy or fulfilling, or why you are in one that is in conflict or abusive, you need to look at yourself first. As the constant figure in all of the relationships that you engage in by your own choice, you can only look at yourself as the responsible party. You may find that a tough concept to face up to but accepting it is the first step towards taking control. Becoming aware of your negative emotional contributions places you in a position of strength because you are the only one that has the power to change you.

Here are some examples of two types of people with issues that produce complimentary behaviours:

For example:

- A 'convincer' and liar will choose someone who is distrusting and suspicious.
- A suspicious and distrusting individual will seek someone who can be persuaded to trust them — a 'convincer'.
- A controlling dominant person will find significance and worth by choosing a needy, insecure and helpless partner.
- Someone who feels needy, fearful and powerless will seek a partner who will take control and protect them from their fears and insecurities.
- Someone who habitually blames others will choose someone who feels constant guilt to avoid being held accountable.
- A guilt-driven person who fears to be made responsible will be attracted to someone for whom they can take emotional responsibility.
- Someone who believes that they are unwanted and unlovable and have learned to give love to receive it is likely to attract a selfish partner needy for love and acceptance.

- A selfish person, incapable of giving love but is nevertheless needy for love and affection, will choose a partner who will give love and affection without expecting it.

We may believe that we know the reasons why we select our partner, but this is rarely the case. Most of the time we so caught up in the physical and emotional attraction for each other, that we do not care or even want to know why we feel this way about a particular individual. Our need to feel loved and wanted and sexual traction overrules and other consideration until it all goes wrong for us. Even then we tend to lose ourselves in the blame game and do not see our role and contribution to the outcome.

We often confuse our attachment to someone with unconditional love because we do not appreciate the conditions we place on our relationship with them or theirs with us. When issues appear, this lack of awareness becomes a problem because we cannot address the issues if we do not understand what they are. When conflict escalates, and becomes unresolvable because we do not recognise the real reasons, then going our separate ways is often the only solution. Unresolved, current issues can cause the separation process to become extremely painful and drawn out. Partners, who are unaware of their fears and insecurities and therefore cannot see how they contributed to the failure of the relationship, will often assume that they are victims of one another. Letting go of each other can then become a protracted process. Even though in conflict, the unfulfilled needs and expectations they have of one another, keep pulling them back together. By hanging on to this emotional dynamic, they still feel bound to each other, even though each persists with blaming one another. The anger they hold is a result of the powerlessness each feels because they cannot force each other act and behave in a way that fulfils their expectations of one another. In spite of being resentful of each other, for not being who and what they expect each other to be, they feel as if they cannot live with or without one another. As a result, neither can move on. Each has to find resolution independently because the real problems for these issues lie within themselves.

Your understanding of the dynamic in all of your relationships and the emotional part each play can provide clues to how your early family environment influenced your mind. The emotional patterns of behaviour that are active in your relationship will mimic those experienced in childhood. When issues appear in a relationship, there are no innocent parties. What each partner individually experiences, can only be their responsibility.

Owning your behaviour in relationships is a good starting point for self-realisation.

From the perspective of being a contributor to the issues you experience in a relationship, these may represent some of the behaviour and attitudes you may have:

- Blame: You make your partner or others responsible for the issues, fears and insecurities you feel, thereby avoiding being held accountable and confronting your shortcomings.
- Expectations: You expect your partner or others to be or provide those things for you that you feel powerless, incapable or too vulnerable and so on, to deal with yourself.

You feel entitled to expect your partner to accommodate your fears needs, wishes and desires and so on, without you having to ask or explain.

- Guilt: You suppress your needs, truth, beliefs or power to avoid blame for upsetting your partner or being a burden to them. As a result, you monitor and filter everything you express, to avoid eliciting a negative response from others for fear of attracting guilt, criticism and rejection. Whenever something goes wrong, you fear that somehow you will be seen as the guilty one.

You can never do anything right for your partner and others, and always fail them and blame yourself for your shortcomings

- Creating Guilt: You aggressively hold others or the world responsible for your negative life experiences — nothing is ever your fault. Or, by acting the victim of everything and everyone, by default others and the world are responsible for the negative emotional events in your life.
- Dominance and control: You expect your partner or others to listen to you and be obedient and subservient to your choices, ideas and expectations and to accept your determinations and expectations, as being right and justified without question. If they do not, you feel threatened in your power causing you to become aggressive for fear of losing your position of power.
- Criticism and judgment: Your partner or others disappoint you regularly and cannot do anything that is right or good enough to deserve your approval, no matter how many times you point this out to them. You must believe that you are vastly superior to them.

- Anger and aggression: You get upset whenever things are not the way you expect them to be. You feel others, deliberately oppose and contradict you to undermine your need to be in control.
- Emotionally unavailable: You find it difficult if not impossible to show what you feel for your partner and others. You expect them to "know" that you love and care for them and believe that all the things you do and buy are enough to prove this. You avoid any situation, where you may have to reveal what your real feelings. Your strategy is to withdraw and become emotionally and physically unavailable. You feel like a victim of the emotional needs of others because you never received love and attention in your childhood.

Start by asking yourself the following questions about your behaviour and that of your partner:

- Am I taking responsibility or am I holding my partner responsible for what I create in my life and how does my partner respond to this?
- Do I apply the same standards and values to myself as I do to my partner and vice versa?
- Do I complain, nag, criticise and am I judgemental, or do I feel my partner is?
- Do I feel needy, powerless, dependent and inferior in my relationship?

Or, does my partner behave that way with me?

- Do I support my partner to evolve into their best self and do they support me in the same way?

Or, are we competitive and envious of one another's achievements and success, popularity and significance?

- Can I be open and free, honest and truthful in my communication and the expression of my feelings with my partner, and can my partner be so with me?

Or, do I have to tread on eggshells whenever I want to speak my truth in fear that they will get angry, upset or cannot cope?

Or, is it the other way around?

- Am I free to fulfil my potential, passions, and desires?

Or do I put others before myself because I believe that I will only be loved if I nurture and protect others from their fears and insecurities?

- Do I expect that my partner or others focus all of their attention on me and put me before themselves?

Or, do I put others before myself to please them and be loved and accepted?

- Does my partner have to meet my expectation of what I want them to be so that I feel safe and in control?

Or, does my partner expect me to be that way for them?

- Do I expect that my partner will never emotionally confront, challenge me or hold me accountable because it would make me feel powerless or a failure?

Or, do I demand that my partner accepts my ideas, beliefs and choices as the only option?

Or, am I always compliant to the expectations and needs of my partner because I fear I cannot trust my intelligence, judgement, decisions and choices, or that they will reject me if I do not?

- Do I feel the need to point out my partner's failings and shortcomings?

Or, does my partner always criticise me and cause me to feel inadequate, hopeless and dumb?

Being truthful with yourself is paramount if you want to get the most out of questioning yourself. The basis for conscious living lies in becoming aware who you believe yourself to be, as distinct from who you authentically are. Distinguishing the illusionary part from the authentic-self is accomplished by recognising what part of who you have learned to understand you are is fear driven. Even though you may not know who your authentic self is, you will begin to realise what parts of you do not represent who you are. Not just by recognising your fears within yourself, but also to appreciate what is real and what is illusionary in others and the world. Being able to predict and anticipate the consequences of your negative or positive intent within your actions and choices, makes you aware of how you create your life experiences. Once you know how your belief systems affect your relationships, success or happiness, you have the option to alter the outcome by changing who you are. Releasing your fears allows you to begin to create and manifest your life from a place of ever-greater authenticity and inner harmony. Supported by an enhanced awareness of the nature of unconditional love, acceptance and trust, you will become conscious of your different intents and their effects in your life.

Conscious living requires you to monitor and be aware of your state of mind, emotions, thoughts and behaviour. You might imagine what you might call a 'mini-me' sitting on your shoulder as an objective observer whispering in your ear.

Your 'mini-me' might ask you why you just said something or the reason why you reacted in anger or guilt. It will question your feelings and behaviour, actions and choices, in response to every situation. This 'mini-me' will act as a more objective observer of your emotional or impulsive self by using your reasoning mind.

The conclusions extracted from your self-observations can raise the awareness of the nature of your thoughts, feelings and behaviour. You can use it as a temporary tool that allows you to become aware of the deeper motivations behind your strategies and self-expression that have led to undesirable events. The knowledge you gain can take you to realise the negative beliefs you hold, the fears that drive them and the intent they hold.

Whatever your life experiences may be at this time of your life, they will be a consequence of what you manifest from the belief systems that define who you believe yourself to be. If your life experiences are positive, then you are expressing a positive part of your sense-of-self. Should they be negative, then fear-based beliefs are controlling your self-expression. However, there is more information available to you if you are prepared to dig a bit deeper.

For instance, you are likely to feel upset and sad if you are constantly alone, and without a partner. Being alone, feeling lonely and having no-one to love and to love you, can be the very situation you fear the most in your life. You may think that now you are alone and feeling your worst fears, it proves that you will never find any one and will always be alone. You are not aware that what you are experiencing represents the exact consequence implied by the fears you hold about not being in a relationship, being alone and unloved. Holding the belief that you are unwanted, unlovable and unacceptable is the reasons you are not in a functional relationship. These issues with intimacy and relationships will cause you to behave and respond in a manner that makes you appear unavailable and not interested in being with a partner or desperate to accept any condition for a relationship as long as you are not alone.

The issues will be related to negative beliefs concerning: feeling unlovable, unwanted, unacceptable, rejection, abandonment, trust issues with your opposite gender, commitment, fear of being trapped, being powerless, losing control, low esteem, etc. In this case, you need to look for the issues and their associated fears in childhood, and analysing the dynamic with your parents.

It is the same for any other issue in your life. For instance, if you have persistent failures and little or no success, it may be obvious to you that you should try and find new strategies to create success. However, instead, you should be asking yourself instead what is going on within your mind, that causes you to manifest failure instead of success. If you consistently experience failure in your life, it is evidence that the beliefs responsible for your focus and intent in respect to this part of your life are negative and therefore responsible. Releasing these negative beliefs responsible for steering you towards failure, will automatically open up your mind to the opportunity of manifesting success.

The process of living life will invariably present all of us with negative events that are a mirror for our emotional issues. Each negative experience gives you the opportunity to discover more about the nature of your mind. Understanding your fears, can diminish your fear of unwanted outcomes, and create the opportunity for change. The path towards self-realization and transformation is littered with opportunities that present themselves as failures, disappointments and pain. Changing your perception of what you judge to be a negative experience, brings you a step closer towards the expansion and transformation of your consciousness. This change can make life a very different journey. Keeping in mind that you are the only one that can raise the bar for the person you want to be, and the life experience you want to have.

Chapter 25

LIVING UNCONDITIONAL LOVE

Although we are coming to the end of this book, we are still very much at the beginning of all there is to learn about our consciousness and the process by which we create our perception of physical reality. In many ways, this an introduction to the different elements that are involved in the process that we call life. How the expression of our consciousness creates the experience that is our life is fundamentally very different to what we have been led to believe. These new ideas challenge many closely held beliefs of who or what is responsible for what we experience as our life. It alters our understanding of why we behave the way we do, the origin of our feelings and emotions, choices and decisions and what shapes our perception and thoughts. Understanding the nature of our consciousness reveals the motivations for our conduct in relationships and more. It provides us with a new awareness of reasons for the many different ways our lives unfold for us and ultimately shows us how to gain real control over our existence by releasing our fears and insecurities. By choosing to accept responsibility for our lives, we take ownership of the fear-based beliefs that are self-defining and acknowledge that the point of power in life lies within our consciousness. The release of our negative beliefs and the resulting absence of many fears allows us to become the self-responsible creators of our own life experiences. We can only fulfil the potential with which we were born if we live life as we were meant to be. The core purpose of our journey in life is to evolve our consciousness and spiritual being while fulfilling our potential, through the many faculties with which we came into the world. We all have the capacity to achieve this by setting our minds free from our perceived restrictions represented by releasing our fears so that we embrace the positive and responsible creator living within every one of us. In doing so, unconditional love, acceptance and trust will become the core values by which we will manifest our lives.

WHEN THE AUTHENTIC-SELF IS MISSING

The first and most significant emotional event in childhood, which will shape the future of our lives, occurs when we are most vulnerable and naive. Our parents are unaware that the fears and insecurities they inherited in their childhood determine the way they will parent us. The conditions they subconsciously place on their relationship with us will eventually become our issues, fears and insecurities. They cause us to feel that our authentic and spontaneous self is unacceptable because their fears make their acceptance and love for us conditional. It does not take long for us to begin to distrust and reject and dismiss our unique and authentic self. The invalidation our unique and authentic-self and its innate spontaneous creativity also convince us that we unlovable, unacceptable and to a large extent unwanted. We gradually accept this experience as being representative of who we are — our sense-of-ourselves — and this relegates us to living our lives strategically to survive emotionally. Once these negative beliefs control our perception, feelings, thoughts and behaviours, we subconsciously settle for love, acceptance and trust that is conditional which become the source of fear.

By the time we arrive in adulthood, we know no better that fear is a consistent aspect of life. If we want to live life as the person, we were meant to be there is no other choice but to confront and resolve these issues for ourselves. Not doing so will not only have negative emotional consequences for us but also for others. Once fear is a part of our psychological being, the consequences of expressing them will manifest throughout our life. The emotional fallout our fears create will also contribute to the negative state of collective consciousness.

Rediscovering the true nature of your authentic and unique self is a journey within itself. Realising that you have unique qualities, interests, talents and abilities is a joyful experience, which builds confidence in your freedom to express yourself. The progress created by releasing your fears is incremental, but your baby steps can become big strides, creating massive changes in who you are and what you manifest in your life as a consequence. Sometimes, even after releasing many of fears, it can still feel that there are areas in your life where you are not entirely confident and secure within yourself. Your awareness shows that there are still areas where you have not completely embraced being unconditionally lovable and loved, acceptable and accepted, and therefore cannot be authentically yourself. In truth, our consciousness is by its very nature complex with many different sides to its nature. The innate capacity of your mind to evolve, grow and expand in complexity and awareness means that there will always be more emotional and mental elements to transcend. Your consciousness is an eternal work in progress, and you have more than a life time to grow and expand the nature of your being. Your fears are layered by your consciousness for you to deal with in a natural order of priority and significance that is unique to you, Trust that whatever fear you believe you need to deal with is the right and appropriate issue for you to confront. Usually, critical issues make themselves emotionally prominent in your current life experiences, because they are a priority at this time.

Sometimes after the release of certain fears with which you identify very strongly in your life, you may feel a sense of emptiness, like a void in your mind. The absence of the negative thoughts and feelings related to the issue that used to preoccupy your mind leave it empty and it can feel as if you have lost purpose and meaning in life. This sensation presents itself because you have spent so much of your mental and emotional time obsessing about these fears that in their absence, your mind is unoccupied. On the positive side, you can put the newly acquired time and space you have freed up in your mind to creative use, by exploring new possibilities in life.

Living life as our authentic-self does not always automatically bring a flood of positive experiences even though many undesirable elements will disappear from our lives. Creating a life that is exciting, constructive and fascinating demands your input and engagement and does not happen by itself. The positive nature and structure of our sense-of-self depend on the beliefs we hold to be true about ourselves and the world. Releasing a negative fear-based belief about something does not necessarily imply that one that is positive will replace it. In fact, you may not have any convictions about certain aspects of life at all and therefore lack the ability to bring them into reality. The core intent that exists in our authentic self, as an intrinsic part of our spirit-consciousness, is specific to unconditional love, acceptance, trust and being wanted, etc. We encounter these emotional states in a different guise in our daily interaction with others and life. Our thoughts and feelings may be aggressive, impatient, judgemental or those of powerlessness and vulnerability. We may feel that we want to avoid or confront, speak up or be silent, take control or give in for reasons that are fear-based or rightful entitlement supported by our belief in unconditional love and acceptance. The absence or the presence of our core values play a role in every aspect of our existence. By reintegrating them as the core values by which to live — fulfil our aspirations and potentials, conduct our relationships, do our work, engage with the environment — we will open the door to new learning and understanding.

To create and manifest a life that is positive and allows us to evolve, we all need to unconditionally accept that we are entitled and deserving to be unconditionally loved and wanted, accepted, trusted. Consequently, we must be unconditionally loving and accepting of ourselves and others. This state of mind reflects our natural aspiration to exist in harmony with the true nature of our essence. By the fact that we exist and are aware of being conscious, we are entitled to be unconditionally loved and lovable accepted and acceptable and so on. The experience of a childhood excluded from unconditional love, acceptance and trust will make the idea of unconditional love a foreign concept and therefore difficult to realise. If this is the case, you can remind yourself of the true nature of your spiritual essence by repeating and accepting the following statement:

I now know, believe and accept, and I am unconditionally convinced

that I was born, that I came into existence, awareness and consciousness

with the innate entitlement, right and deservedness

to feel and experience, receive and give, exist and live in unconditional love, unconditional acceptance and unconditional trust,

to be unconditionally loved and accepted, wanted and included, trusted and believed, considered and praised, to be heard and listened to, recognised and appreciated, acknowledged and validated, endorsed and approved of, to receive unconditional attention,

and so, because of that I am free to unconditionally express, reveal, articulate, demonstrate and give a voice to my authentic and unique self, my true nature, my spontaneous life force and truth,

my unique potentials, talents and abilities, my intellect and creativity, my emotional power and strength

this I know, this I believe, this I accept, trust and believe unconditionally.

This belief system statement will be most effective if you repeat this after you have done a session to release your negative, fear-based beliefs. You also have the option to do this independent of a session but do not use it as a substitute for releasing your fears. A belief that is harmonious with your authentic-self serves as a reminder of who you truly are and how you should think and feel about yourself and that you are entitled to live to fulfil your potential in the world. However, you need address your negative beliefs systems first and separately, to accomplish genuine change within yourself.

The potential of our spirit-consciousness to evolve and expand our awareness is immense, and so is its capacity to manifest our life through the intent of our beliefs. The nature of our subconscious intent — positive or negative — plays an influential role in what we will create our life experiences. As a result, we need to be aware of who we believe we are to understand the kind of fears we hold. We have become addicted to fear, and its influence in our life represents the greatest obstacle we need to overcome. Our indoctrination in the culture of fear convinces us that we are powerless without our strategic behaviours and this makes us behave and act either as helpless victims or controlling aggressors to emotionally and physically survive. Our fears create an adversarial mentality in us which reveals itself in the way we conduct our relationships and relate to the world in general. It shows up as anger, aggression, shame, guilt, conflict, abuse, criticism, blame, inferiority powerlessness and so on. It causes us to hold others accountable for our ills and stops us from looking at ourselves as the responsible party for our problems in life.

You do not have to wonder what that world would be like if the human race lived in the grip of fear because this is the world we live in right now. The present state of the world, many of the economic systems and institutions find their roots in all manner of fears. The fears to which we collectively contribute show up in the world as crime, conflict, violence, war and famine. We are all involved — when it comes to being responsible for manifesting the world we live in, there are no innocent bystanders because we are all a part of the process.

By leaving our illusionary fears behind, we will open doors to a different reality experience and create a different world as a consequence. To do so, we need to make unconditional love, acceptance and trust the new core value of our consciousness. When we begin to share this with others and with those who are similarly focussed and whose path parallels ours, we will have a positive effect on humanity and ultimately on the very nature of reality. We can trust that the positive intent within our sense-of-self will always find manifestation in the world. It is the nature of consciousness to give expression to the sense of own being and manifest it, regardless of whether it comes from the intent of love or fear.

AWAKE TO TRUTH

Up until now you have effortlessly and unconsciously manifested your life without necessarily being aware of how and why. Your lack of understanding has allowed you to claim ignorance of the reasons for many of situations and circumstances you have experienced. With what you have learned so far, this can no longer be the case. If you are fundamentally tired of reliving the same negative emotional experiences in your relationships or life in general, over and over again, you now know that you are the one who can and has to change to bring an end to this.

Once you have chosen to release your fears, your altered perception will allow you to recognise that every relationship you have, engages two dynamics.

The inner-dynamic — between your mind (sense-of-self) and the essence of your spirit — determines the kind of relationship you have with yourself. When the mind is in harmony with the essence of our spirit, it is the source of inner-harmony and strength. When the mind holds fears and is in contradiction with its true nature, you believe yourself to be powerlessness, unlovable, unacceptable, unwanted, a victim, inferior, etc. Your inner-perception puts you in conflict with your authentic and unique self.

The outer-dynamic reflects your interaction with others and the world and takes the form of your negative or positive feelings, perception, thoughts and behaviours. It will also define your attractions and fascinations and so on. How your outer-dynamic interacts with others depends on the nature of your inner-dynamic. Your attitude and the kind of behaviours you employ to engage others will reveal the harmonious or disharmonious nature of your sense-of-self or inner-dynamic.

Even though your inner-dynamic will be at the origin what your outer dynamic will be, you will be most aware of the experiences of life and relationships created via the outer-dynamic.

In the absence of fear, the essence of your being, your authentic and unique self and your sense-of-self will converge towards the same resonance or vibration. Your perception, behaviour and feelings will change in response to your new inner-state. Without the need protect yourself using strategies you will attract and create relationships founded on positive self-beliefs and expectations. Without you even trying, your choices and decisions, behaviour and responses, perception and thoughts, emotions and feelings will no longer be negative. Your awareness will shift to a different level allowing you to see emotional qualities in others that were previously invisible to you. The fact is that you will have changed your world by changing who you are, and in doing so, you have taken a significant step towards being who you were always meant to be.

Once in the awareness, that we are spirit-consciousness, and therefore not limited in our existence by our physical body, we also know that we are not the victims of our surroundings, of others or the universe. We can then feel safe to connect unconditionally with others and with all of consciousness.

We will be in the awareness that emotional strength and the power come from within and that we can trust in it and depend on it to support us and keep us safe.

Manifesting the world without fear, in which everyone can exist and be true to themselves, requires the contribution of each consciousness in the form of unconditional love and acceptance. Even though our potential is immense, fear will stop us from realising it.

In many ways, human consciousness is like a child, still playing in the sandbox of physical reality, limited by the illusionary fears it holds to be true, and unaware of the extent of its incredible potential and capacity.

The understanding of intent and consequence are central to our development of the awareness of the nature of our consciousness. Any belief — positive or negative — is not a just static energetic construct in our minds. The belief systems by which we live our lives are highly volatile energy pattern of consciousness, which contain very particular intents. Each system of beliefs is an emotional program resident in your consciousness that will attract and be attracted to others, whose belief system patterns are in harmony with it. Harmonious patterns of conscious and emotional energy will attract others like it, as it is the case with negative or dis-harmonious patterns. At this point, the very nature of the power generated by patterns of beliefs becomes very significant. Should they resonate out of harmony with our core essence, their vibration becomes representative of fear. If harmonious with the essence of spirit, its intent will be based on unconditional love and acceptance and therefore be positive. The resonance of a negative belief reflects fear-based emotions such as being unacceptable, guilt, and rejection, powerlessness and anger and so on. Your disharmonious state of mind causes to attract and become attracted to those whose belief systems are of a similar or complementary resonance. We are all familiar with the consequences of the intents that flows from our beliefs. They are the source of our experience of pain and suffering, conflict and disagreement, anger and aggression and so on, or for positive, happy and fulfilling experiences in life.

The core intent of the positive resonance of our spirit-consciousness is an indivisible aspect of 'All That Is'. When our sense-of-self creates from intentions that are in harmony with its essence, everything it encounters will gravitate towards it because it supports the manifestation of a positive dynamic with others and the world. All beliefs, regardless of their nature, actively transmit their intent into our universal space, and then connect and interact with those that are complementary or in harmony with it. Once they form a dynamic relationship with each other, they will create an interaction, event or experience.

THE ESSENCE OF BEING

To get a more philosophical perspective on this process, it helps to understand what role pain and suffering and all other negative feelings play. Your mind manifests negative emotions such as sadness and loss, powerlessness and anger and depression as signposts to inform you that are in an emotionally disharmonious state. The intent behind their presence is to make you aware that the beliefs that you have activated and are living by are a distortion and driven by fear. Your negative emotions are a direct warning to make you aware that you are 'out of–harmony' with who you are and that illusions control your life choices. Your emotional stress is a signal from your mind to prompt you into reassessing the nature of your sense-of-yourself so that you can address your fears and insecurities — your negative beliefs systems.

The experience of "Universal Consciousness" starts within us. We are an intrinsic part of everything that is. Fears are a part of most people's existence, but their particular origin, nature and how we experience them is very individual. Our need to survive our fears is the reason why we are collectively living much of our lives with illusion, first of all with ourselves and as a consequence with each other. The world we created with our fears is not the environment that allows us to fulfil our potentials as creative spirits.

The simplicity of being in harmony with your true nature appears to be at odds with the enormously complicated emotional and psychological issues you experience when fear is in control. We are so carried away by this river of fear flowing through us that it envelops every part of our lives. So much so, that living in the absence of it appears difficult if not impossible. In the absence of our deceptive friend, we can feel powerless and insecure. That will change, once you realise that what you believe to be true about yourself and the world is the source of everything your mind acts out, feels and experiences. Discovering that you are the source for everything that you create and manifest in your life is profoundly empowering. Your authentic-self endows you with the power and control over what you choose to accept as a truth or to reject it because it is an illusion. This awareness is the resource that allows you to achieve a state of being that finds its strength in unconditional love and acceptance.

All consciousness is innately attracted to exist in a state of unconditional love, acceptance and trust. It, therefore, gravitates to be at one with its essence and this propensity is far more persistent than fear. New and unexpected circumstances in our lives can always bring fear to the surface to alert us to an issue with which we have not dealt. No matter what it may relate to, in overcoming it, our consciousness will evolve, and in its absence, we will find the fulfilment of our being.

Once we become aware of our own negative beliefs and release them, the existence of fear in others and how it controls them will become obvious. This insight will expand your perspective of human nature and realise that you are not the only one that suffers the consequences of fear. Judging others by the way they live their lives would be like being in judgment of yourself. However, you may be able to help them understand the part they play in their issues, by asking them questions that they should be asking themselves, concerning their negative life experiences. Questions that will lead them to realise that they are active contributors to the situations or events that cause them pain and unhappiness. A new understanding of the reasons for their issues may motivate them to look at themselves for a solution. It is unfortunate that most people are only prepared to look at themselves when they can no longer bear the suffering their issues create in them. It is common that most people need to feel the painful consequences when their strategic behaviours fail them before they are prepared to look at taking responsibility for their lives.

You may find it hard to believe that the resolution of your fears can have a significant impact on the influence of unconditional love, acceptance and trust in the world yet they are the very forces by which the world will change. Working on yourself does not make you selfish, egocentric or uncaring about others because it is an essential part of self-transformation. The resolution of your fears will enable you to exist within the power and potential of your being and then you will be able to make contributions that actually matter to others and the world.

The genuine value of your life achievements
lies not only in your effect on others or the world,
but in how they changed the nature of your being.

The success of your life
is in the realisation
of the responsible creator
within.

RAE-20/08/2017-BALBAO-V02

ABOUT THE AUTHOR

Rudolf Eckhardt is from the Netherlands and has lived in Australia since 1963. His philosophy of how humans create their own experience of life and relationships rises out of more than twenty-five years of work as a therapist with many different nationalities in Australia and other parts of the world. Eckhardt developed the Core Belief Therapy.

Printed in the United States
By Bookmasters